Withdrawn from
Davidson College Library

Library of
Davidson College

Politics in Industrial Societies:
A Comparative Perspective

Politics in Industrial Societies:
A Comparative Perspective

Lawrence C. Mayer
with
John H. Burnett
both of
Texas Tech University

John Wiley & Sons
New York • Santa Barbara • London • Sydney • Toronto

Copyright © 1977, by John Wiley & Sons, Inc.

All rights reserved. Published simultaneously in Canada.

No part of this book may be reproduced by any means, nor transmitted, nor translated into a machine language without the written permission of the publisher.

Library of Congress Cataloging in Publication Data:

Mayer, Lawrence C
   The politics of industrial societies.

   Includes indexes.
   1. Comparative government.   I. Burnett, John H., joint author. II. Title.
JF51.M443   320.3   76-54694
ISBN 0-471-57986-6

Printed in the United States of America

10 9 8 7 6 5 4 3 2 1

To Arthur and Mildred Mayer, Leonard Mayer and two Maurys, past and present.

L. C. M.

To my parents and Jean, David and Margaret

J. H. B.

Preface

This books grows out of the increasing interest in the concept of postindustrial society. Because the term *postindustrial* has become something of a catchword and often implies a difference in kind rather than degree, we prefer to use the concept of a mature industrial society. We hope this will avoid the question of whether a number of the nations we discuss have crossed the threshold into the postindustrial era.

The concept of the mature industrialized world is relatively recent, and many if not most of its characteristics remain to be delineated and then explained. Throughout this book we explore the questions of whether and how the nature of these societies has altered (or is likely to alter) their respective political processes. Most previous treatments of postindustrial society discuss the concept in general terms while only considering its application to the United States alone. We, however, present a systematic comparative analysis of the effect of a mature industrial society on the political process.

In doing this, we undertake the difficult task of producing a book suitable for textbook use while analyzing and perhaps even contributing to the ideas and theories of the field. We believe that the educational process is more successful when approached from the viewpoint of discussing ideas or explanations. This approach, which incorporates only those facts relevant to explanation, will enable students to understand and to retain more than would a detailed description of specific political systems. We hope that some of the suggested patterns and generalizations will stimulate further research by other scholars.

In taking a comparative approach and in suggesting explanations, we do not confine the discussion to the traditional "major" nations (Britain, France, West Germany, and the Soviet Union) nor do we describe exhaustively any of the nations being considered. We include a number of smaller and often neglected nations (such as Italy, the Benelux nations, the Scandinavian democracies, and countries of the older Commonwealth) that possess contextual characteristics of great value in modifying and refining the kinds of explanatory generalizations that political scientists make.

We also make a contribution with respect to integrating the study of the Soviet Union into the broader field of comparative politics. One theme of the book is the question of the extent to which the authoritative political format of the Soviet Union renders it unique and, also, the extent to which imperatives of an industrial society generate common, political patterns despite variations in ideology, culture, or constitutional format.

This book is suitable both for courses focusing on Europe and for courses on general comparative politics. Because the book incorporates most of the useful information about the relevant political systems and summarizes the relevant literature, previous familiarity with either the nations being considered or the concepts or literature of comparative politics in general is not required. Moreover, courses on comparative politics profit when the concepts are introduced with reference to the substantive context of actual political systems.

We thank our colleagues in the Department of Political Science at Texas Tech who generously gave of their time and energy to read and offer suggestions on parts of the manuscript. Lee Sigelman must be singled out for the number of chapters read and the thoroughness and helpfulness of his critiques. James Clotfelter, Murray Havens, Otto Nelson of the Department of History, and Miles Simpson of the Department of Sociology each read and offered suggestions on one or more chapters. Ronald Inglehart of the University of Michigan and Larry Hill of the University of Oklahoma critiqued the entire manuscript in a most helpful and constructive manner. We are grateful to all of them. We, of course, are responsible for any flaws that remain. Wayne Anderson, editor at Wiley, has been most helpful and encouraging. It is a pleasure to work with him.

Lawrence C. Mayer
John H. Burnett

Lubbock, Texas

Contents

Chapter 1 Introduction	1
The Logic of Comparison	2
Objects of Explanation	5
Contextual Variables	10
Structural Variables	13
A Look Ahead	23
Part I The Contextual Impact on Politics	27
Introduction to Part I	27
Chapter 2 Patterns of Nation Building	29
Religion and Church in the Development of Europe	32
Feudalism	39
The Ease of National Consolidation	42
Insular versus Permeable Borders and Defense	44
Evolutionary or Discontinuous Development	48
Conclusions	62
Chapter 3 The Cultural Context of Politics	65
Attitudes Toward Authority	67
Political Values	83
Beliefs and Ideologies	84

Affect and Alienation 98
Feelings Toward Other People 103

Chapter 4   Social Stratification and Politics   108

Crosscutting versus Cumulative Cleavages 111
Mass Societies in the Industrial World 112
Segmented Societies in Europe 115
Class versus Symbolic Criteria of Cleavage 123
Equality and Social Mobility in Industrial Societies 136
Conclusions 145

Part II   Policymaking Structures and Processes   149

Introduction to Part II   149

Chapter 5   Policymaking Structures   152

Constitutions and Constitutionalism 153
Sovereignty 164
The Logic of Parliamentary Democracy 165
The Role of Representative Assemblies 172
Executive Roles 188
Conclusions 200

Chapter 6   Administrative Patterns   216

Bureaucracy as a Model of Rational Efficiency 217
The Weberian Ideal Type of Bureaucracy 222
Bureaucratic Recruitment 226
The Structure of Administration 233
Bureaucratic Values and Behavior 242

Chapter 7   Political Parties   247

Typologies of Party Systems 249
Toward a New Typology of Party Systems 261
Parties and Electoral Systems 263
Party Program, Ideology, and Base of Electoral Support 267
Party Organization and Origin 293
Conclusions 308

Contents xi

Chapter 8   Interest Groups 312

Pluralism and Polyarchy 313
The Level of Organizational Life 316
The Relationship Between Parties and Interest Groups 318
Group Tactics in Parliamentary Democracies 321
Types of Interest Groups 325
The Autonomy of Interest Groups 332
Representation of Interests in the Soviet Union 333
Conclusions: Patterns and Variations in the Policy Making Process 338

Part III   Policy Outcomes and Convergence Theory 343

Introduction to Part III 343

Chapter 9   Economic Policy and Social Welfare 345

The Triumph of the Market System in the West 346
Problems in Market Theory 350
The Growth of the Welfare State 357
Patterns of Health Care Delivery 358
Protecting the Unemployed 362
Planning 362
Keynesian Economics: Trying to Save the Market 365
Nationalization and State Socialism 366
Conclusions: The Rational Engineering of Social Welfare 369

Chapter 10   Patterns and Themes in Industrial Politics 372

The Convergence Theme 375

Index of Authors and Name 379

Subject Index 383

Chapter 1

Introduction

One of the most significant developments in comparative politics since the Second World War has been the increasing emphasis on building general propositions applicable to a variety of nations and cultures. In the past, comparative politics had often been characterized by the intensive study of and accumulation of information about particular foreign countries. Although such study is useful, the value of the information can be increased and additional knowledge can be acquired through comparative analysis. In the belief that comparison offers significant advantages for the study of politics, this book is written on a topical instead of a country-by-country basis. Rather than attempt complete treatments of particular countries, we generalize with respect to certain variables.

The subject is the politics of mature industrial societies. Data are drawn from European societies including the Soviet Union, Great Britain, the Scandinavian democracies, the Benelux nations, Italy, France, and the Federal Republic of Germany, with occasional references to the United States and to the older Commonwealth nations (Australia, New Zealand, and Canada). The objective is to delineate patterns in the decision-making structures and processes, both formal and informal, in such societies and to suggest explanations for whatever variations in such patterns we are able to discern. Thus, we also examine contextual factors that may have an impact on such decision-making structures and processes, especially the state of technology.

Following are several questions around which our analysis of industrial societies focuses. The answers to these questions constitute the themes of the book and the criteria for what kinds of data are considered relevant. Do societies with an advanced state of technology tend to produce certain common types of issues and similar processes to deal with these issues? To what extent does this occur? Do these common patterns differ from formal constitutional structures?

Although we expect to discern patterns in the politics of industrial nations, it is obvious that differences in the politics of such nations remain significant. To what extent do these differences appear to be related to differences in ideological, cultural, or physical contexts and in historical experiences? Do systems with different values arrive at different policy decisions while the decision-making processes are becoming increasingly similar through such factors as the increasing importance of the "technocrats" (skilled and trained specialists)? This last question is particularly important because the Soviet Union is one of the societies to be examined.

The plan of the book in dealing with the above questions is to divide our consideration of industrial political processes into three parts. First, we consider the impact of contextual factors—those factors external to the political system that have an impact on that system and its outputs. We feel that patterns of nation building, culture, and social structure are the most important such contextual factors; accordingly, they comprise the topics of the three chapters in Part I. Second, we consider the political systems of the respective nations under consideration and the processes by which they reach decisions and resolve issues. This includes such constitutionally designated structures as legislatures, cabinets, and bureaucracies, as well as those structures not so designated that nevertheless play a significant role in the decision-making process, such as parties and interest groups. Third, we take a brief look at some policy output. We do not attempt anything like a comprehensive review of the policies of the respective nations. Instead, we seek to suggest by example that variation in policy content is to a large extent a function of the previously discussed contextual factors and the nature of the political process.

Our hope is to explore the theme of the impact of technology-related factors in the context of a comparative treatment of European and Anglo-Saxon politics. Because the comparative approach is a major feature distinguishing this from other books about European politics, a brief explanation and justification of that approach seems in order.

The Logic of Comparison

In political science we seek to explain political phenomena. This means that we seek to say why things are the way they are or why they happen the way they do.

Introduction

We do this by generalizing. When we want to know why a particular thing occurs, we identify that particular thing as one instance of a class of things, a class that is regularly associated with another class of things. To illustrate, when we want to know why organized violence occurred in a given country, we may identify violence against a regular, legally constituted government as an example of that class of phenomena called revolutions. Next, we may be able to say that revolutions are regularly associated with another class of events or observations, such as a certain state of the economy, so that whenever we see the one class of phenomena at a given time and place, we can also expect to see the other class.

Naturally, the grouping of a number of things or events, different in some or even most respects, under a common label on the basis of some property they share involves a certain amount of interpretation. The common label imputes meaning to these events. There is an almost infinite choice of properties that may be considered significant enough to justify using them as the basis for such groupings or classification. What is there, for example, that events called revolutions have in common to distinguish them from all other events? The foregoing discussion barely suggests the importance and complexity of this process of grouping, ordering, naming, and interpreting observations. This process, generally referred to as conceptualization or the formation of concepts, is widely discussed elsewhere.[1]

Causation and Contexts

Whenever we are able to say that two concepts or classes of phenomena regularly occur together, we usually express or imply the conclusion that one causes the other. In the example given, it would be suggested that certain properties of a nation's economy cause revolutions to occur. Two important points must be remembered about such a conclusion. First, we can never prove causation. The only thing we know is that the two phenomena regularly occur together. The conclusion of causation does not necessarily follow from the facts; a certain amount of interpretation or inference is involved in moving from the facts to the conclusion.

Second, no single, definable "cause" is going to result invariably in any event as complex as a revolution. Revolutions are the result of many factors. All of the major events, behaviors, or phenomena that political scientists find worth explaining are of such complexity that they are the product of a nearly infinite number and variety of factors. The consequence of this is that any proposed explanation of

---

[1] For example, Karl Hempel, *Fundamentals of Concept Formation in Empirical Science* (Chicago: University of Chicago Press, 1952); Abraham Kaplan, *The Conduct of Inquiry* (San Francisco: Chandler Publishing Co., 1964), Chap. II; Lawrence Mayer, *Comparative Political Inquiry* (Homewood: The Dorsey Press, 1972), Chap. 1; Arthur L. Kalleberg, "The Logic of Comparison: A Methodological Note on the Comparative Study of Political Systems," *World Politics,* Vol. XIX, No. 1, October 1966, pp. 69–82.

a significant phenomenon is likely to hold true only in part of its observed applications. That is, a certain state of the economy, if indeed it has a causal impact on the outbreak of revolution, will actually result in a revolution only part of the time. A given property of a nation's economy is not a sufficient condition in and of itself to produce a revolution. This economic condition will result in revolutions only when certain other conditions are present, such as certain attitudes on the part of the people, a certain size and effectiveness of the government's coercive forces, etc. In short, an explanation of a revolution in terms of one or two variables can only hold true, "other things being equal."

The resolution of the difficulty, if there is one, is to distinguish insofar as possible those contexts in which the explanation applies from those in which it does not. The phrase *explanation applies* refers to the situation where the general statement purporting to account for the thing to be explained generates a valid prediction. The statement asserts an observed relationship between two concepts or two classes of facts. Thus, when we say that if a country has an uneven distribution of income beyond a certain magnitude (concept one), a revolution will follow (concept two), we then imply that if the economic precondition is observed, a revolution is *expected* to follow. When it does not, the logical step is to identify in what way, other than the nonrealization of the expectation, the exception is different from all the other cases in which the expectation was realized. In this way, other relevant variables could be identified and their impact on the original hypothesis assessed. A portion of the "other things being equal" clause would accordingly be specified.

Generalizing About Unique Nations and Events

The major assumption underlying our comparative approach is that it is possible to generalize across sociocultural units despite their admittedly unique properties. We assume that it is possible and useful to designate significant properties shared by various political systems. The often unstated assumption of opponents of a comparative approach is that each sociocultural unit or political system is unique. Each system is said to be a result of a unique historical heritage, geographic and demographic context, political actors (especially leaders), social and political institutions, economy, state of technology, and countless other factors that make each system unlike any other. Moreover, it is assumed that these factors that together comprise each unique national profile are so intertwined that it is impossible to analyze meaningfully any of these factors apart from the context in which they are located.

For example, some would argue that we cannot generalize about revolutions because each revolution is unique. There was, after all, only one French Revolution (of 1789). This unique series of events was the product not only of the history and culture of France but also of a particular state of technology and particular actors on the scene. The French Revolution would have been a very different phenomenon were it not for the purely coincidental presence of Robespierre, Danton, etc. Similarly, had there been no Lenin, the Russian Revolution probably would not have taken the course it did. Carried to its logical conclusion, the "great man" view of history amounts to a denial of the possibility of systematic analysis of sociopolitical events. Overlooked by this point of view is the equally plausible possibility that situations and roles create the men to fill them.

As Crane Brinton aptly demonstrated some time ago, despite their many unique properties major revolutions do have enough common properties to enable us to talk about them as a group.[2] All of them occurred, for instance, in a time of rising prosperity. Indeed, the very concept of a generalization presumes that the objects of the generalization will be in some respects unique. A generalization states the common properties among elements that are otherwise different. Without their unique aspects, the generalization would become a statement of identities. If every revolution were exactly like the French Revolution, the proper name and the generic term would be synonymous. Consider the phrase, "All French Revolutions of 1789 . . ." to realize the absurdity of this.

We have sketched the considerations that lead us to conclude that it is both possible and useful to generalize about and thereby explain political phenomena on a cross-national basis. We are not here concerned with problems of empirical conceptualization and the testability of our general statements, problems we feel serious research must ultimately consider. Instead, we intend to try to account logically for outcomes or phenomena whose essential meanings are widely comprehended on an intuitive level. The "causes" that we suggest bring about these phenomena are similarly justified on a logical rather than empirical level. The contribution of this book to theory construction in political science is to suggest relationships rather than to resolve puzzles. In short, we hope to suggest some possible causes for the important similarities and differences among industrial political systems—causes that make intuitive "sense," and causes that fit the facts insofar as we can determine them. We hope that such causal suggestions provide food for thought and, ideally, stimulate further inquiry.

Objects of Explanation

Our attempts at explanation will focus on such elusive concepts as the effectiveness of the systems under consideration, their stability, and their responsive capacity.

---

[2] Crane Brinton, *The Anatomy of Revolution* (Englewood Cliffs: Prentice-Hall, 1952).

Structure and Process
It should be noted that these proposed outcomes or objects of explanation are governmental processes rather than structures. It may be useful to distinguish structures from processes. *Structure* is a static concept; it refers to a state of affairs. *Process,* on the other hand, is a dynamic concept. It seems to imply movement from one state of affairs to another. Structures thus engage in processes. Specifically, structures refer to recurring or established patterns of behavior and interaction. Social groups, including such governmental structures as legislatures and bureaucracies, are not things. They are composed of sets of individuals. But, given the widespread overlapping membership across different groups, it is not the people who constitute the group but what they do in their roles as members of those groups that defines their behavior in a structure.

The concept of *role* refers to the contextual frame of reference that generates a pattern of expectations for behavior. Thus, if a man assumes the role of professor, he may be expected to maintain certain standards of decorum and reserve in his interaction with others—for instance, women students. The same person assuming the role of suitor toward the same female students would be expected to behave much less formally.

Structure is a term often used interchangeably with the term *institution*. When interaction among a set of roles falls into a pattern over time and the persistence of that pattern is both accepted and expected, we may say that the pattern is institutionalized. Thus, institutionalization may be thought of as a form of routinization, and patterns of interactions among roles that fall into routines become institutions.

Clearly, therefore, *structure* and *institution* are terms that refer to a broader variety of phenomena than legal, constitutional entities of government. Classes, cleavages, and stable patterns of power constitute some of the politically relevant structures of society.

In emphasizing processes rather than structures, we are making an essentially normative judgment that what governments do and how they operate is more important than the formal structures of the government. Such formal structures will be analyzed, however, with respect to the role they play in or the impact they have on the processes.

The Concept of an Industrial Society
The effectiveness of a system in this book is defined as that system's capacity to deal with issues, resolve conflicts peacefully, and manage tensions. The issues, conflicts, and tensions are generated by the unavoidable differences of interests among the components of any mature complex industrial society.

Because the focus of our book is on such societies, it may be useful to clarify the properties that distinguish them from other societies. An industrial society presumes an advanced state of technology and a resultant knowledge explosion that requires specialization and division of labor. With so much knowledge required to maintain an advanced state of technology, no one can develop the requisite degree of expertise on more than a narrowly defined set of functions. As a result, the functions or tasks of a technologically advanced society are distributed among different social roles with the occupants of each role performing only a specifically delineated set of functions. To illustrate, a society at a preindustrial state of technology might simply have leaders. An industrial society will have, by contrast, religious leaders to lead religious functions, judicial officials to carry out adjudicative tasks, political leaders to carry out political functions, etc. Moreover, there are specialists in raising or growing each type of food, making each type of clothing, protecting citizens against outlaw predators, and fighting fires and disasters. In primitive societies each citizen took care of all of these things by himself—for example, the pioneer who erected and maintained his own cabin on the American frontier.

The occupants of each role in an industrial society develop a set of interests arising out of that role, interests not necessarily compatible with those of the occupants of other roles. Thus, for example, high corporate profits do not necessarily benefit blue-collar labor, and high wages do not necessarily benefit corporate executives. Industrial societies therefore contain a variety of real or perceived interests arising out of the very complexity of such societies, interests often in conflict with one another. Such conflicts of interest generate different, contradictory, but perfectly sincere conceptions of what constitutes the national interest. Any judgment of what is in the best interest of the community or society is necessarily in part a result of the social role of the individual making such a judgment and interests arising out of that role. To put it another way, no one is looking through a microscope at society; we are all on the slide. Although he may have been partly correct, it was no surprise that it was a former head of General Motors, Charles Wilson, who said, "What's good for General Motors is good for the country." Conflicts of interest give rise to differing conceptions of wise policy, and the differences generate issues.

Governments or political systems exist in large part to resolve such issues. Political structures are therefore not deliberately created to frustrate the natural inclinations of people living in some harmonious and idyllic state of nature. We feel that governments are a necessary response to the conflicts that inevitably arise in any society.[3] It would seem to follow from the foregoing discussion of industrial societies that the role of government tends to increase as the state of technology

---

[3] This view that some form of authority is a necessary response to a basically nonharmonious set of human interests appears to be more reflective of the thought of philosopher Thomas Hobbes (*The Leviathan*), who viewed the state of nature as a "warre [sic] against all" than of the converse position of John Locke. Locke, who had great influence on American political thought, conceived of an essentially harmonious "state of nature," which logically leads those in this school of thought to support minimum government. The difference between Hobbes's position and our position is that while Hobbes regarded conflict as inherent in the nature of humans, we view it as a function of a state of advanced technology.

advances. We are suggesting here that a laissez faire orientation toward the role of government (a feeling that governmental control and regulation ought to be minimized) presumes a universal harmony of interests and is inappropriate for the realities of an industrial society.

Our concept of an industrial society supports the pluralist view of politics. Pluralists view society as composed of numerous autonomous groups, each to some extent in possession of potential political power and each with distinct interests. This view suggests that resolutions of issues emanate spontaneously from the relative power and intensity of involvement of the various interests that choose and are able to participate with respect to given problems or questions. The most effective role of governments in this process is the bestowing of authoritative legitimacy on particular resolutions. Thus, we will see that the Soviet Union is, according to the official ideology, a classless society and, because class divisions constitute the major basis of cleavage to a Marxist, a society largely without internal conflict. It will be interesting to see how this ideology and the realities of a complex, industrial society with conflicting interests are reconciled in that system.

Effectiveness, Stability, Responsiveness

Insofar as interests and issues generate demands on the system, tension or stress is created. An effective system is one with a capacity to process such issues or demands into outputs. Such outputs may be categorized into three basic forms: material gratification of demands or actual alleviation of the deprivation, symbolic gratification, and coercion or repression. To illustrate, President Nixon may have dealt with a demand by Americans to end the Vietnamese War in three ways: by ending it, by sending Henry Kissinger on symbolic missions and announcing "secret plans," or by arresting or otherwise penalizing antiwar activists.

The stability of the system refers to the minimization of unscheduled changes in the government per specified time period. Such unscheduled changes would include the resignation of the head of government (usually with the cabinet) in a parliamentary democracy due to the loss of the support of a majority of the lower house of the legislature. Parliamentary governments are expected to rule only at the sufferance of such a legislative majority. A test of support, either by direct vote or by the attempt of the government to propose and support legislation, is commonly referred to as a confidence question. The term *government*, when dealing with parliamentary democracies, refers to the prime minister and the cabinet.

An important question is the extent to which the stability of open or "democratic" systems may be explained by the same sets of factors that explain the stability of authoritarian systems. Clearly, on the surface it would appear that factors such as raw coercion play a far greater role in the latter type of system with respect to the suppression of issues and the imposition of an apparent facade of national unity. These puzzles are subject to inquiry.

The responsive capacity[4] of a system refers to the extent to which the institutionalized properties of a political system predispose it to produce authoritative decisions that satisfy the demands and perceived interests of that society. It would include material or symbolic gratification of demands as outlined above but not the third alternative of repression. On the surface, this variable might not seem to be applicable to the Eastern European and other authoritarian systems. But all systems must have some responsive capacity—for example, the emphasis on consumer goods of the current five-year plan of the Soviet Union. The difference in this variable between democratic and authoritarian systems lies in the degree and mechanisms of responsiveness. It may be, for instance, that in authoritarian systems the mechanisms and processes of responsiveness are less formal and less institutionalized.

Democratic governments vary with respect to responsive capacities. It is relevant to ask in this regard whether the composition of the government and the direction of policy output are determined or even affected by the results of elections or whether these things are determined—autonomously from electoral results—by various bargaining processes among the members of the elite. It is also relevant to inquire into the relationship between the extent to which the composition of the elite is highly representative of the distribution of opinions and interests in its society and the government's responsive capacity with respect to its policy output. That is, to the extent that we choose to maximize the standard of representativeness, we may have to sacrifice something with respect to the standard of responsiveness.

Legitimacy

Responsiveness is a factor in the establishment of legitimacy for the regime. *Legitimacy* means the extent to which a regime is accepted by the preponderant mass of the governed as having the right to rule. One political scientist, David Easton, coined the term *diffuse support* to refer to support for a regime or administration irrespective of its policy output.[5] This level of support is related to the notion of legitimacy.

The costs of satisfying all material demands in a complex society are simply too great. The costs of raw coercion may be even higher. Imagine a policeman in the back of every automobile having to compel each driver to obey traffic signals. A certain level of compliance must be relied upon in all systems regardless of governmental output.

This legitimacy is acquired in systems when the masses have a perception that

---

[4] This variable was suggested to us by Gabriel Almond and G. Bingham Powell, *Comparative Politics: A Developmental Approach* (Boston: Little Brown & Co., 1966), pp. 201-203.
[5] David Easton, *A Systems Analysis of Political Life* (New York: John Wiley & Sons, 1965), and *A Framework for Political Analysis* (Englewood Cliffs: Prentice-Hall, 1965), pp. 124-125.

in the long run the existing government or regime will serve their interests better than any foreseeable alternative. It is immaterial whether this perception is accurate; people act on the basis of what they perceive to be true instead of on the basis of some objective reality. Nevertheless, it seems clear to us that a system that did not respond to some degree, either materially or symbolically, to deeply felt demands would soon find itself without the threshold level of legitimacy or diffuse support required by all governments in order to survive.

Contextual Variables

In order to explain certain aspects of either government or governmental performance, an analysis must include any relevant variables irrespective of whether such variables are clearly and overtly political. By relevant we mean variables whose essential nature would lead one to believe that they have a significant impact on those phenomena and processes we seek to explain. Clearly, governments do not operate in social, cultural, economic, and historical vacuums. Governmental structures are situated in, and interact with, a sociocultural and economic environment or context. It is not possible to place governmental structures in a test tube and pump out the influence of such contextual factors. Thus, because variables such as social structure and belief systems are among the determinants of the properties of those political structures and processes we seek to explain, we cannot ignore them with the excuse that they belong to sociology or some other discipline. Causal relationships do not respect rigid boundaries between disciplines.

It follows from the foregoing that any attempt to explain (in the sense of "account for") the similarities and differences between nations with respect to political variables (assuming the dubious proposition that political variables are clearly separable from other kinds of variables) must include a thorough analysis of those "nonpolitical" contextual variables that have a significant impact on the "political" variables we seek to explain.

The Concept of a Political System

We frequently substitute the contemporary term *political system* for terms such as *government* or *nation-state*. *Political system,* being a more inclusive term, is more suitable for causal inferences. A system is a set of interacting elements that can be distinguished from those elements not in the system. A political system is composed of those elements that participate directly in whatever the political function is defined to be (the political function is usually something like authoritative decision making). All elements that participate in this process are included in the concept of the political system, whether or not they are part of the formal constitutional structure. For example, in the Soviet Union the Politburo of the Central

Committee of the Communist Party is the structure where actual decision making occurs, although we would not get this impression from reading the Soviet Constitution of 1936.

As systems interact with their environment, political systems can be viewed as interacting with their various contexts. Thus, many variables become relevant for analysis—any variable that has a significant impact on the political process.

The concept of a political system has an additional advantage over the more familiar concepts of nation-state or government. Insofar as the concept implies a set of interacting elements, processes and relationships are more readily conceptualized within the system framework than within the framework of the more static concepts.

Geographic and Historical Variables

Geographic and historical variables are closely related. The principal geographic variable is whether a nation has insular or permeable borders. Insular borders are physically difficult to cross or permeate, especially in an earlier state of technology when the countries under consideration were in their formative periods. Conversely, permeable borders were relatively easy to cross or permeate in an early state of technology. We suggest that the permeability of a nation's borders may be related to the extent that centrifugal forces threaten a nation's integration and internal coherence. On the other hand, insular borders would tend to increase the ability of a new nation's leadership to hold the various components of the system together and weld them into a coherent or integrated whole. Border elements may oscillate in allegiance from one center of political power to another if clear physical barriers do not place each given locality within one system or another.

The ease with which national integration is achieved—or the extent to which the centrifugal forces of a political system are controlled—is one determinant of the variable of whether a society develops along relatively open or authoritarian lines. The concept of an open society implies a tolerance of differing conceptions of right, truth, justice, and the national interest. Of more importance for our purposes, the concept implies a willingness on the part of the elite to share power and the values of that society with those other sectors of the society that develop sufficient group consciousness to claim such power and values. To oversimplify, a political system that develops with relatively secure borders is more likely to develop along relatively more open lines.

Other physical properties may be conveniently considered under the heading of geographic variables. For example, the quantity and variety of natural resources are important.

The principal historical variable is whether a nation has developed with long-term continuity along evolutionary lines. Some nations undergo a development characterized by sharp, revolutionary breaks with the past, and relatively more violence has characterized the process of nation building and political change in these nations than in those systems characterized by an evolutionary or gradual development. A history of political violence has been hypothesized to be one factor in a present propensity to solve problems in through violence. Violence as a tool apparently becomes legitimated through usage, but it is a function of a number of variables such as the responsive capacity of a regime, its effectiveness, the extent of coercion, and the state of the economy. These and other variables are discussed below.

Nations with insular borders have tended to develop along evolutionary lines, while those with permeable borders have had more sharp, revolutionary breaks with the past. While apparently unique historic events are said to have had major impacts on the way various systems have developed, it is possible to classify and generalize about most of them. This applies not only to obvious general events such as the incidents of repression, violence, or invasion, but also to certain personality types emerging in leadership roles and some of the conditions under which they tend to appear.

The Concept of Political Culture

In addition to the historical context, systems exist in a cultural context. While culture has traditionally been considered as more properly within the province of sociology, it clearly has a major impact on those political phenomena we seek to explain. Accordingly, it deserves our attention.

Political culture is a concept that has attracted increasing attention and popularity in the past decade in comparative politics. It represents an attempt to link the analysis of individuals and the analysis of whole sociopolitical systems (such as cultural units or nation-states). This linkage is sought by attributing to whole systems the properties of individuals. Those properties are essentially what we call "dispositional"—that is, the internalized mental states that predispose an individual to react in certain ways to certain stimuli. We can make the connection between the individual and system levels of analysis by attributing to systems those individual properties that are most typically or predominantly held by individuals in that system. It is recognized, of course, that no mental state will be present in all individuals in any complex system. Thus, a system may be said to have a democratic political culture (assuming that so general a concept could be defined), despite the existence of a number of authoritarian personality types in that system.

The components of a political culture include attitudes (conceptions of how things ought to be), beliefs (conceptions of how things are), customs, mores, feelings, knowledge, and general orientations toward problem solving.[6] Among the relevant attitudes are those toward authority (egalitarian, deferential, submissive, or authoritarian), toward national purpose, toward questions such as tolerance of differences and tolerance of opposition, and toward concepts of value (anything held dear, such as the work ethic in the United States that says, "you shouldn't give anyone something for nothing"). Another relevant attitude would be a sense of civic obligation (what good citizens ought to do). The meaning of these components and their application to the nations under consideration is discussed at length in Chapter 3.

Structural Variables

While the term *cultural variables* refers to the dispositional properties of individuals aggregated to the group or system level, *structural variables,* it will be recalled, refers to recurring or established patterns of behavior and interaction. Social groups are not things; they are composed of sets of individuals. But people define the groups by what they do in their roles as members of these groups. It will also be recalled that formal, legal agencies of government are just one of several types of politically relevant structures.

Social Stratification

One structural variable of paramount importance for explaining states and processes of any political system is the social stratification system. This refers to the criteria by which the individuals in a society are grouped and to the conditions for movement from one category to another.

One criterion for grouping may predominate over others. Some societies may be grouped along socioeconomic lines. In others religious affiliation may cause people to divide or group without regard to class lines. In still others, identification with the geographically defined region in which one lives may supersede religious or socioeconomic considerations.

It is a characteristic of complex industrial societies that a number of such criteria for grouping and dividing people will be present in any given society. In some systems the people grouped along one criterion (class, religion, etc.) are the same who are grouped by other criteria. This is referred to as a system of segmental cleavages, where those who are with you by one standard are with you by most other significant standards. A situation where the people who are of one

---

[6] Two extended discussions of the concept are Sidney Verba, "Comparative Political Culture," in Lucien Pye and Verba, eds., *Political Culture and Political Development* (Princeton: Princeton University Press, 1965), and Mayer, *op. cit.*, Chap. 9.

socioeconomic class, such as blue-collar laborers, are also of the same religion, live in the same geographic area, and share a basic ideological orientation would constitute an example of a segmental cleavage.

In other societies, the groupings do not coincide, and the composition of each grouping differs with each criterion. An example of this would be a situation where within one grouping—say, those who share a certain religion—some individuals belong to one socioeconomic class and some belong to another. Within each subgrouping—say, poor Protestants—some will be Easterners, some Westerners, and so forth. This type of classification system is commonly referred to as a system of crosscutting cleavages. The impact of the type of social cleavages on politics is discussed at length in Chapter 4.

The specific content of the most significant criteria of cleavage in a society is itself an important variable. The nature of the politically relevant issues that a society generates is to a large extent a function of the criteria. A system in which the primary focus of identification is socioeconomic class will tend to generate issues involving questions of allocating values (economic issues), while societies divided along cultural, religious, or ethnic lines will tend to generate ideological issues.[7] Of course, a situation where the basis of division is a "cause" will generate ideological issues as well. The recent division in the United States between proponents and opponents of the Vietnam War is a case in point. Issues of allocation or interest involve questions of who gets what or how much. Such issues are really questions of degree rather than either/or alternatives. They thus become susceptible to resolution by compromise. If employers are willing to pay $2 per hour and the workers demand $4 per hour, it may be possible for the two sides to meet halfway at $3 per hour. Ideological issues or questions of principle are framed in terms of a choice between the right and the wrong. There is no obvious middle ground between such positions, and there is no logical compromise with evil or error. Thus, it may be expected that issue resolution will be easier in societies in which the primary perceived criteria of cleavage are socioeconomic rather than cultural, ethnic, religious, regional, or causal.

The ease of social mobility is another relevant variable under the heading of social structure.[8] This refers to the presence or absence of structural channels on the one hand or structural impediments on the other hand for upward movement from one level of the stratification system to another. A free, universal system of public education may facilitate upward mobility in some societies, for instance. But to the extent that the educational opportunities available to those in the lower

---

[7] See Robert Alford, *Party and Society* (Chicago: Rand McNally, 1963), for an extended development of this argument.

[8] See Seymour Lipset and Richard Bendix, *Social Mobility in Industrial Democracies* (Berkeley: University of California Press, 1963), and David Apter, "A Comparative Method for the Study of Politics," *American Journal of Sociology,* Vol. LXIV, November 1958, pp. 221–232.

strata are not really the equivalent of the opportunities available to those in the upper strata, the educational system may operate to perpetuate the existing stratification system.

Probably more important than the actual prospects for upward mobility is the widespread perception of how readily the structures of society permit upward mobility in the stratification system. This perception and the consequent hope result in a belief that one has a stake in the system. The absence of such a belief, of course, means the absence of diffuse support for the political regime (support that does not depend on the performance or policy output of the regime). The absence of that perception of a stake in the system is called alienation. The widespread American belief in the Horatio Alger syndrome whereby anyone can rise from rags to riches by the proper effort, perseverance, and diligence has undoubtedly contributed to the high level of diffuse support for the American system on the part of American have-nots. The support of men such as Harding and Coolidge by a significant proportion of American blue-collar workers at a time when their share of the American pie was distinctly below average may be attributed to the fact that these workers shared a belief in reward to the fittest and most deserving.

The significance of the perception of the stratification system as either open or closed is in part a result of the normative consideration of whether the opportunity for such upward mobility is considered to be a necessary component of social justice. When cultural or ideological considerations have imparted a widespread belief in a "natural hierarchy" to society, whereby those who occupy the higher strata do so legitimately (because they are more "fit to rule"), consequently occupants of the lower strata *should* not aspire to occupy the upper levels. In such a system, a relatively closed stratification system need not detract from the degree of diffuse support bestowed on a system. People might be less inclined to be critical of a system for failure to provide or permit upward channels of mobility if they were less imbued with the norm of egalitarianism.

Mass and Pluralistic Societies

In our earlier discussion we concluded that any complex industrial society contains a number of distinct and sometimes conflicting interests based on the technological necessity of specialization and division of labor. But it does not necessarily follow that these distinct interests are perceived as such by the relevant actors or organized into formal groupings or associations. On one hand, it may be that the structure of a society is composed of the governing elite and relatively unorganized individuals. Such a society is commonly called a mass society. On the other hand, a society may contain a number of formalized structures grouping individuals at a level of generality or inclusiveness lower than the national government. Labor unions, interest groups, lodges, etc., would illustrate such groupings. This would be called a pluralist society. Obviously, this typology refers to *relative tendencies*; no society is totally without intermediate groups, and no society is totally without unorganized individuals. Nevertheless, some societies have a clearly more well-developed organizational structure below the level of the government than other societies.

Clearly, mass societies can support norms of extreme egalitarianism. All atomized individuals are similarly subject on the same level of impotence to the omnipotent elite. Authority becomes removed from the level of immediate consciousness.

Nevertheless, as sociologist William Kornhauser has suggested, mass societies are less supportive of democratic political structures than pluralist societies.[9] Perhaps one indication of the importance of this idea is the fact that communist and fascist systems devote tremendous effort to the creation and preservation of mass societies. Communist systems are sometimes distinguished from other authoritarian, nondemocratic types by their attention to and even insistence on public indications of participation and support of the regime. Election campaigns, slogans, pageantry, awarding titles and medals, and a variety of civil ceremonies are all intended to perform the function of political socialization while at the same time demonstrating solidarity between the elite and the citizenry.

Although the concept of totalitarianism has now been largely discarded by most scholars, its distinguishing characteristic was often described as the destruction of all groups between the regime and the individual or of the line between the state and individual personality. It was argued that the success of such a regime depended in large part on the degree to which it could mobilize these atomized, alienated individuals by means of promises of better or utopian times. In more contemporary terms, the idea involved might be described in terms of the claim of the Communist Party to be the aggregator and spokesman of the interests of the entire population.

In this context, it is significant that Kornhauser points out that mass societies are more vulnerable to "totalitarian-type" appeals, which are generally founded on mass movements and are more susceptible to mobilization by the elite. Individuals lack the sense of competence to resist the omnipotent government and hold it accountable. Groups, on the other hand, can act as a buffer or check with respect to governmental activities. Opposition to government must be organized if it is to be very effective. Thus, when General Charles DeGaulle presented plebiscites to the French people asking them to indicate approval or disapproval of his policies, the absence of well-organized alternatives meant that the choice was in

[9] William Kornhauser, *The Politics of Mass Society* (New York: The Free Press of Glencoe, 1959).

effect between DeGaulle and chaos. Under these circumstances, it was no surprise that his policies were approved.

Kornhauser also suggests that without the buffering, filtering, and aggregating role of intermediate organizations, the elite can become highly vulnerable to an unrestricted quality and quantity of demands, thereby impeding their capacity to govern effectively. This is not to imply, as Joseph Gusfield has eloquently argued,[10] that pluralist societies are some kind of guarantee against the collapse of liberal democracy. Many other variables are involved.

Given this caveat, we suggest that much remains of Kornhauser's argument that pluralist societies should be more supportive of stable, effective democracy, *other things being equal*. Survey data (such as the Almond and Verba study)[11] suggest that organizational capacity is positively related to a sense of political competence. Nie, Powell, and Pruitt[12] have demonstrated that the level of organizational life is the best single predictor of the level of political participation in a society. These and similar data support the conclusion that individuals find it easier to identify and interact with intermediate-level organizations than with remote national governments.

Democratic and Authoritarian Systems

Perhaps the most familiar structural variable in the array of political systems surveyed in this book is the distinction between democratic and authoritarian systems. The concept of democracy, partly because of its familiarity and partly because of its emotional content, is one of the most difficult concepts for political scientists to discuss. Almost every conceivable type of political system has claimed to be democratic in some respect. The leaders of the Soviet Union, a nation that most Westerners regard as the antithesis of what they intuitively feel democracy connotes, maintain that their institutional format is based on the principle of "democratic centralism." Other countries with communist systems use titles such as the German Democratic Republic and the Democratic Republic of Vietnam. Sukarno's Indonesia was referred to by the leader himself as "guided democracy." Sekou Toure of Guinea and Kwame Nkrumah of Ghana, each generally regarded by Westerners as the epitome of a dictator, also spoke of their respective systems as some form of "hyphenated democracy."

---

[10] Joseph Gusfield, "Mass Society and Extremist Politics," *American Sociological Review*, Vol. XXVII, No. 1, February 1962, pp. 19–30, for a dissenting rejoinder.

[11] Gabriel Almond and Sidney Verba, *The Civil Culture* (Princeton: Princeton University Press, 1963).

[12] Norman H. Nie, G. Bingham Powell, and Kenneth Prewitt, "Social Structure and Political Participation: Developmental Relationships," *The American Political Science Review*, Vol. LXIII, Nos. 2, 3, June, September 1969, pp. 361–378, 808–832.

There are no precise, universally accepted criteria for classifying a system as either democratic or authoritarian. (We use the term *authoritarian* as the generalized antonym for *democratic*; terms such as *tyrannical, despotic,* or *totalitarian* either have specialized or emotionally pejorative connotations.) Some scholars, often of a leftist political orientation (for instance, the British Marxist, Harold Laski[13]) have suggested that democracy connotes the maximization of material equality in a society. This is defining democracy in terms of its goals and purposes. The procedures used to accomplish these purposes are, in this conceptualization of democracy, irrelevant. By the logic of such a conceptualization, if the Soviet Union managed through (or in spite of) police-state terrorism to impose a redistribution of values in the society such that the Gini coefficient (which measures the extent to which resources are *un*equally distributed) was lower than the United States', the Soviet Union would be "more democratic" than the United States. Such a conclusion would conflict with the meaning we intend to convey by our use of the terms *democratic* and *authoritarian*.

We prefer to conceptualize these two categories of political systems in terms of procedures. *Procedures* may be distinguished from *substantive considerations* in that the latter term refers to content, in this case the content of a system's policy output, while the former term refers to the method or rules by which decisions are reached. Thus, according to our conceptualization, a system may opt for any set of policy alternatives and still retain the label of democracy providing it meets the procedural requirements for the label. A democracy may elect to adopt, for example, any set of economic institutions and policies all the way from a laissez faire or unregulated market system through a Keynesian system (governmental regulation of the supply of money via taxing, spending, and monetary policies) to either a form of state socialism (governmental ownership of *major* means of production, distribution, and exchange) or a welfare state (governmental guarantees of security, access to services, and material well-being regardless of ability to pay). Thus, the political variable, democracy or its antithesis—defined in terms of procedures rather than socioeconomic outcomes—renders either type of political system logically compatible with any type of economic system. Because the distinction between capitalistic, socialistic, and welfare-state economies (insofar as these systems are precisely distinguishable) rests on an economic dimension that is conceptually distinct from the political dimension, it is logically possible to speak of either a socialistic or a capitalistic democracy. In fact, most European democracies have opted for degrees of governmental ownership or control that few Americans would be likely to tolerate for the United States for the foreseeable future. It might also be useful to recall that the major industries in Nazi Germany were privately owned and run for profit. A procedural conception

---

[13] Harold J. Laski, "Democracy," *Encyclopedia of Social Sciences* (New York: Macmillan, 1942).

of democracy is less narrowly circumscribed in that it allows democracy to be compatible with a variety of socioeconomic systems and policies.

The procedures we have in mind are twofold: 1) the elites would be chosen in more or less regular, competitive elections; 2) in the event of disagreement among those who have authority to choose, the alternative gaining the support of a majority of those having such authority would prevail. This definition does not specify a particular political pattern; it can include both presidential and parliamentary formats, for instance. (The former is what exists in the United States. It involves separation of powers with a head of government elected independently of the legislature. The latter involves fusion of powers with a head of government who is chosen from and accountable to the legislature.) Democracy becomes a generic term and is not confined to any particular institutional pattern.

We suggest that our attribution of significance to this set of procedures is not arbitrary. These procedures can be justified logically in terms of a basic problem of politics—the control of authority. Political authority of one sort or another is found almost everywhere. Because of the interdependence and functional specialization of roles alluded to earlier, individuals have to a greater or lesser extent lost sole control of their own welfare and destinies in industrial societies (if indeed they ever had such control). Decisions must therefore be made collectively. Further, in no industrial society are the people in any sense capable of making such decisions. First, the complexity of modern problems eliminates all but a specialist from a capacity to deal with them. Second, leadership itself is a specialized role requiring special skills. Third, the masses lack the time or initiative to acquire the necessary information even to know the problems or issues facing their societies, let alone to comprehend policy alternatives. All of this reflects the thought of Robert Michels, who suggested an "iron law of oligarchy" shortly after the turn of the century.[14]

This essentially means that in any society the actual authoritative decisions for that entire society are deliberated and made by a small group of leaders who comprise a tiny fraction of the total population of that society. In short, all societies are governed by the elite. Rule by "the people" in any modern, complex society is probably impossible. The difference between those countries we call democratic and those we call authoritarian is that in the former case there is periodic competition between alternative groups of elite for the occupancy of key decision-making roles. The idea of competition should render the elite in democratic systems more formally *accountable* for the consequences of their decisions. Further, it should serve to *narrow the bounds of discretion* for the democratic elite.

The elite in any system are to some extent accountable for what they do. Even

---

[14] Robert Michels, *Political Parties*, Eden and Cedal Paul, trans. (New York: Dover Publications, 1959), especially Part Six.

in authoritarian systems there is always the possibility of significant domestic unrest, civil disobedience, and, in the most extreme cases, revolution. All governments must maintain a significant level of legitimacy and diffuse support. Rule by raw coercion is unfeasible because of its enormous inefficiency. The costs of coercion alone are simply prohibitive. Even Hitler's Nazi regime was based on widespread popular support for the man and his policies. Many Germans tried to convey the impression after the war that Hitler and his close associates were the only real Nazis and that the great masses of people went along reluctantly out of fear. But Hitler was popularly elected under one of the most wide-open electoral systems ever used after widespread public dissemination of all of his intentions.[15]

Clearly, a great deal more dissatisfaction with the performance of the incumbent elite would be required to catalyze a revolution or even direct dissent with the risk of severe punishment than would be required to result in a vote for an available alternative elite at a regularly scheduled election. This is, of course, a relative distinction. The tendency of the American electorate to reelect incumbent presidents despite some apparent misgivings about their first-term performance indicates that the democratic elite also have a margin for failure to fulfill the expectations of those to whom they are presumably accountable. Nevertheless, it is not too much to suggest that the margin enjoyed by the Soviet elite is significantly wider. This does not imply that the Soviet margin for failure or dissatisfaction is unlimited; it is just wider. Thus, periodically, the democratic elite are formally forced to justify what they have done, what they are doing, and that they are likely to do in terms of the perceived interest of the electorate. This narrows their bounds of discretion and renders them more nearly accountable for their performance.

Centralization of Power and Accountability
To the extent that we have focused on accountability as the democratic answer to the problem of authority, we have violated the basic American assumption about authority. The problem of authority is essentially this: how do we grant the power to act for the collective good—a need that arises from the fact that political conflict is present everywhere—without also granting the power to act against the public good. Power implies discretion, and discretion implies the ability to choose to act for or against the public good. Power to act cannot be separated from the capacity to use that power for undesired ends.

Americans tend to subscribe to Lord Acton's dictum, "Power corrupts . . . ."

[15] In the 1933 elections, the Nazis received 37 percent of the vote, far more than any other party. When combined with the support for the German Nationalist Party, ultraright-wing opponents of the Weimar Republic, the figure represented just over 51 percent of the popular vote and a majority of seats in the Reichstag. The Nazi support climbed to 43 percent in March 1933, but those elections could hardly be called free due to extensive Nazi intimidation of opponents.

Consequently, they deal with the problem of authority by so fragmenting it among autonomous centers that the ability to act tyrannically can only come with the unlikely spontaneous agreement among all independent semipower-wielders. (They are called semipower-wielders because each independent center of power has the power to halt action but lacks the power to bring about affirmative action.) The ability to act in response to widely perceived public need and demand suffers from the same unlikely prospect of spontaneous agreement among autonomous power-wielders. Consequently, it may be argued that a highly fragmented and decentralized power structure is inherently nonresponsive.

Accountability thus presumes a centralization of power. It is illogical to hold structures or individuals responsible for situations they lack the capacity to control. Because the American pattern of fragmentation of power is the exception rather than the rule among Western democracies, it is useful to note that far from being a necessary precondition of responsive democracy, such fragmentation of power may actually diminish a nation's responsive capacity. Periodic elections between competing groups of elite should serve to render the governing elite accountable for the results of the way it governs, providing 1) that the governing elite in fact has the power to govern; 2) that the competition for leadership is genuinely open.

The concept of an open, competitive election implies more than just the right to put up opposition candidates for office. It implies the right to mobilize and organize opposition so as to make the competition meaningful and effective. Given their monopoly on the dissemination of ideas and attitudes in the Soviet Union, if the leaders in the Kremlin suddenly allowed opposition in their elections and did not penalize people for voting for such opposition, Communist Party candidates would probably still win easily. Thus, the standard of genuinely competitive elections, in which the incumbents stand some reasonable prospect of being unseated, carries with it the corollary standards of tolerance and freedom of speech and the press—in short, civil liberties.

Competition between the elite groups does not require alternating elite groups. It is entirely conceivable that despite open competition between two or more sets of elite groups at more or less regular intervals, one group (such as a party) may retain long-term dominance. As long as this dominance is the outgrowth of a perception that the incumbents serve the system's interests better than available alternatives instead of being the result of the suppression of opposition, we suggest that the discretion of the elite is still appropriately circumscribed and democratic accountability maintained. Thus, one government or party retaining power for a long time would not violate our conception of democracy, provided that the government retained its power by winning periodic competitive elections.

Given this broad procedural definition of democracy, the term is consistent with a variety of structural or constitutional formats. But the precise pattern of these political structural arrangements is a significant variable for the outcomes we wish to explain. Clearly, it would be relevant to know, for example, whether power is concentrated or fragmented, as discussed above. Institutional arrangements such as federalism or separation of powers would appear to encourage a decentralization of power. However, such institutional arrangements may in fact be "formalistic" in any given system.[16] That is, despite their existence on paper, they are not utilized in practice—at least not in the way they were designed to be used. To illustrate, federal institutions in Australia do not reflect real or perceived differences in interests or outlooks between the states. Nor do they reflect a great deal of state autonomy from the national decision-making processes or any substantial modification of the highly disciplined, national orientation of the political parties. Separation of powers in the United States may be substantially impugned by presidents who make and carry out policy with increasing autonomy from the expressed will of Congress. In the federalism of the Soviet Union, although the union republics do reflect genuine ethnic differences, they certainly do not possess any substantial autonomy from the will of the central authorities in Moscow. It may not be too much to suggest that such institutional arrangements reflect decentralizing imperatives that emanate from sociocultural phenomena instead of suggesting that political institutions can cause such decentralization of power. It is still useful to know that if actual decision-making power is shared by a number of relatively autonomous centers of power in a given society, the society's capacity to act collectively is to that extent impeded.

Most industrial nations are organized on the principle of fusion of power rather than an attempt to establish autonomous veto groups to check and balance one another. In fact, the United States is virtually alone among the major powers in adopting a formal "separation of power" arrangement. It should be recognized, of course, that in practice the legislative, executive, and judicial functions are not clearly separated in the United States, and the three major branches of government are not clearly distinguished with respect to which of these functions they perform. The United States is characterized by its attempt to establish the autonomy of decision-making institutions sharing the various functions of governing.

Specifically, the other industrial nations have tended to adopt a parliamentary form of government. In fact, in a strictly formal sense, the Soviet institutions are parliamentary in structure if not in operation. Parliamentary government is a situation whereby the political executive or head of government (usually a prime minister and cabinet) is structurally a committee of the supreme representative institution (usually a legislature). The head of government (or policymaking

---

[16] This concept is developed in Lawrence Mayer, "Federalism and Party Behavior in Australia and Canada," *Western Political Quarterly,* Vol XXIII, No. 4, December 1970, pp. 795–807.

leadership) is composed of individuals distinct from the head of state (the symbolic and ceremonial head of the system such as the monarch in Great Britain or Sweden). In the United States, the president fulfills both roles. It is generally either explicitly specified or implicitly understood that members of the "government" (the accepted term for the prime minister and the cabinet) are also duly elected members of the legislature—generally the lower house in the event of bicameralism. In parliamentary democracies, the "government" is responsible to that house of the legislature—often, but not always, collectively so.

Responsibility means that it is understood that the government will continue to rule only at the sufferance of a majority of the appropriate house of the legislature. The withdrawal of such a mandate may be indicated by the legislature's refusal to approve any significant legislative proposal emanating from the government. It may also be indicated by a general vote of "no confidence" not tied to any particular issue.

In some countries, the government is composed of the leadership of the party that controls the legislature. In such cases, considerations of party structure limit the extent to which the legislature can operate autonomously from the government. Under such conditions, except for broad limits on the government's discretion, the only meaningful check on the government is the existence of regular competitive elections. This would entail a concentration of formal powers.

Any consideration of the relevance of political structures could not overlook the increasing political relevance of the administrative sectors. For a variety of reasons explored below in the appropriate chapter, more and more of the allocative "bread-and-butter" decisions (who gets what, where, when, and how) are made by bureaucrats. In fact, we argue that this tendency increases with the complexity (modernity) of the society. Consequently, the bureaucratization of the political system is becoming a hallmark of industrial societies.[17]

The logic of bureaucratic organization is based on a presumed separation of politics and administration—an assumption that does not fit the observable world. The suitability of bureaucratic behavior patterns for policymaking roles will therefore be explored. The extent of the bureaucratization of a system and the variety of bureaucratic organizational forms are also important structural variables.

A Look Ahead

In the chapters that follow we intend to survey the major industrial systems of Great Britain, members of its former Commonwealth, and Europe on the basis of

[17] See the position of Fred Riggs, *Administration in Developing Countries: The Theory of Prismatic Society* (Boston: Houghton Mifflin, 1964), who argues that the dominance of the bureaucratic sector is a distinguishing property of nonwestern, partially modernized political systems.

the aforementioned variables. Due to limitations of space and of the expertise of the authors, Japan will be omitted from consideration although it clearly qualifies as an industrial society. While the smaller European powers will receive proportionately less emphasis than the larger ones, they will definitely be included in our analysis. This is especially true for cases that add a context in some significant respects unique for the testing of generalizations. To illustrate, the omission of the Scandinavian democracies with their stable multiparty systems seriously weakens the attempt to relate the effect of the number of parties to political stability. Similarly, the highly developed welfare economies of these nations offer a context for the testing of propositions about economic policies not quite found elsewhere. Belgium and the Netherlands appear to refute the easy generalizations about the effect of segmental cleavages on political stability found in some earlier books about Britain, France, Germany, and Russia. Thus, we intend to consider, in addition to the four nations traditionally covered, the Scandinavian democracies, the Low Countries, Italy, Austria, Eastern Europe, and the Balkans.

We are not certain that our distinction between the politics of industrial systems and those of nonindustrial systems constitutes a conceptualization of two essentially distinct phenomena. It is quite likely that we are speaking here of a continuum whereby all nations are to some imperfect degree industrialized and where the threshold level of industrialization separating one of the dichotomized classes of system from the other is arbitrarily set. In short, it is not a question of a clear distinction between industrialized and nonindustrialized nations. It is a question of the degree to which any given nation has achieved economic industrialization and structural complexity. Thus, although readily quantifiable indicators for measuring the level of industrialization are evident (such as gross national product and per capita use of electricity), and although the differences between the politics of the most highly industrialized and the most highly primitive systems are obvious, labeling nations at the intermediate level of industrialization can be troublesome.

Despite all this, some form of categorization appears to be a prerequisite to useful analysis. We are dubious about the usefulness of the attempt to formulate universally applicable propositions about politics given the enormous variety of sociopolitical systems in the world. Consequently, some more manageable portion of the world's political systems must be defined and set aside for analysis.

We believe that the concept of an industrial system yields a group of systems with sufficient common properties to render meaningful analysis feasible. Insofar as the actual pattern of socioeconomic and political structures reflects a given state of technology, industrial systems should manifest enough convergence of such patterns to make generalization about the properties of such systems possible. This should be true despite vast differences among systems with respect to their ideology (Marxism, capitalism, social democracy, etc.).

We are not suggesting that industrial systems are alike in most respects.

Generalization does not demand identity or even great similarity. It merely demands that one or more significant properties be shared by entities that are in other respects not alike.

In the chapters that follow we attempt to accomplish two basic purposes. First, we hope to demonstrate that meaningful generalizations can be formulated across systems—generalizations that account for important differences between systems. The emphasis on generalization through comparison using a topical rather than geographic organization is still too rare among textbooks dealing with industrial political systems. The somewhat dated *Government by Constitution* by Herbert Spiro is perhaps the most admirable exception.[18] Because our emphasis is on the formulation and testing of generalizations rather than on the complete, intuitive understanding of given political systems, we feel free to consider aspects of any industrial system relevant to the generalization in question. If some facet of Belgium's stratification systems is significant, we consider its impact on whatever it is that we are trying to explain without feeling obligated to analyze exhaustively all aspects of the Belgian system. As a consequence, we consider a greater variety of systems and contexts than is often found in other works dealing with industrial societies. Such books tend to consider only Great Britain, France, the Federal Republic of Germany, and the Union of Soviet Socialist Republics.

A second purpose—if fulfilled—would also render a significant contribution to the field of comparative politics: we include the Soviet Union in an attempt to explore the extent to which some of the well-known generalizations in comparative politics apply to an authoritarian system. The last decade has brought a number of interesting developments in the study of communist systems. Two of the most significant have been the attempt to replace the concept of "totalitarian" with something more useful and the call for an integration of political science and communist area studies.

The limitations of the totalitarian framework for contemporary analysis have been widely discussed and do not require detailed treatment here. It might be useful, however, to point out some of the main arguments. Virtually all definitions of the concept have centered around ideology, a single party usually led by a single leader, a monopolistic control of societal organizations, and—perhaps most crucial—the use of terror. It has become increasingly obvious that while these categories may have described regimes such as Hitler's Germany or Stalin's Russia, they no longer apply. The role of ideology is uncertain, there is no longer a single leader in the same sense, and the monopolistic position of the party is being questioned by intellectuals and specialists such as the military, economic managers, and lawyers.

Perhaps most important is the subject of terror. Because its existence has always been felt by many to be the essence of totalitarianism, any substantial

---

[18] Herbert Spiro, *Government By Constitution* (New York: Random House, 1959).

change would affect the usefulness of the definition. There can be no doubt that there has been a drastic reduction in the Soviet Union's use of terror or, to use Allen Kassof's term, "gross irrationality" in the period since the death of Stalin.[19] Although some terror still exists, in the form of committing dissidents to psychiatric wards and other devices, the emphasis has shifted to other forms of social control. These involve for the most part the replacement of fear and coercion by material incentives, persuasion, indoctrination, and a variety of methods of social pressure. Thus, we are left with a situation in which a concept that once served a useful purpose may now be dysfunctional.

It is here that the call for an integration of communist studies and political science becomes most relevant. It is perhaps a fortunate convergence that at the very time there is need for a new concept for studying communist systems, there is an emphasis on viewing those systems in the larger context of comparative politics. One of the disadvantages of the totalitarian approach was that it tended to focus on the uniqueness of the societies involved. The new development provides an opportunity to think in terms of similarities as well as differences.

It is only in the last 10 years or so, therefore, that communist systems have been widely treated in the total context of comparative politics. While no all-encompassing framework has yet evolved from these attempts, there have been several very interesting and useful proposals concentrating on the manner in which the Soviet Union and similar regimes are related to noncommunist ones. One is the so-called developmental approach, which views the Soviet Union with an emphasis on modernization, economic growth, and other problems shared by developing nations.[20] Another focuses on the single-party aspect in relation to noncommunist nationalist regimes.[21]

Most significant for our study, however, are the approaches that suggest consideration of the Soviet Union as a mature, industrial, bureaucratic system susceptible to comparison with other systems possessing similar features.[22] At the risk of being presumptuous, we hope to make a contribution in the direction of making communist studies a more integral part of comparative politics. We hope to suggest patterns and properties shared by a number of European industrial societies and political systems including those claiming a communist ideological position.

---

[19] Allen Kassof, "The Administered Society: Totalitarianism Without Terror," *World Politics,* Vol. 16, July 1964, p. 559.

[20] For example, John H. Kautsky, *Communism and the Politics of Development* (New York: John Wiley & Sons, 1968).

[21] Robert Tucker, "Toward a Comparative Politics of Movement—Regimes," *American Political Science Review,* Vol. LV, No. 2, 1961, pp. 281–93.

[22] For example, Kassof, *op. cit.;* Alfred Meyer, "The Comparative Study of Communist Political Systems," *Slavic Review,* Vol. 20, March 1967, pp. 3–28; Alfred Meyer, "USSR, Incorporated," *Slavic Review,* Vol. 20, October 1967, pp. 369–376.

Part I

The Contextual Impact on Politics

Introduction to Part I
In this first part of the book, we are concerned with the context of politics. The political system is seen as consisting of those structures that participate in the formulation of authoritative public policies such as legislation, administrative decisions, executive orders, etc. Clearly, such policies are not formulated in a vacuum. They are affected by the social, cultural, economic, geographic, and historical contexts in which the policymaking structures are situated.

Out of such contextual factors come disagreements about public policy. Such disagreements constitute issues to be resolved by the political process discussed in Part II. Because the nature of that political process and the policies it produces are substantially affected by these contextual variables, the variables, hitherto dismissed as belonging to other disciplines, take on political relevance. Accordingly, political scientists cannot leave a consideration of the past to historians, a consideration of social structures to sociologists, and so forth. These contextual factors are an indispensable part of any reasonably complete explanation of important variations among political systems.

It must be noted that we are considering these contextual factors in order to explain political phenomena. Our focus is on the political. Our treatment of contextual factors constitutes a means to political explanation rather than an end in itself. Our objective in Chapter 2, for example, is not to write a history of Europe or to explain the "why" of any past events (for example, why did the French Revolution occur?). Our goal is to show how selected historical events and patterns can help explain contemporary variations among industrial political systems. Our focus on an explanation of the present provides a criterion of relevance for selecting some historical factors while ignoring others.

Similarly, we do not claim to present a complete description of the culture or social structure of any country. Instead, we seek to consider those aspects of sociological variables that have a significant input on variations among political systems.

The context of politics affects the political process in two kinds of ways. First, these contextual factors generate political issues, as stated above. Second, these contextual factors also generate constraints that circumscribe the options about the nature of the political process (discussed in Part II) and the kinds of policies and decisions this process produces (considered in Part III). An obvious example is the inability of the United States to opt for the kinds of welfare-state policies seen in most European nations due in large part to the cultural value of competitive individualism, the belief in the self-regulating market, and the historical experiences that produce these cultural characteristics. Related to the idea of constraints is the degree of support or lack thereof for the political process that may be found in the process's cultural and social context. Clearly, the absence of support can be an important constraint on the discretion that may be exercised by the political process.

Chapter 2

Patterns of Nation Building

As stated in Chapter 1, it is not the intention of this book to give complete historical, cultural, or institutional accounts of particular countries. It is, instead, to generalize with respect to certain variables and their importance. As implied in that chapter, many of the differences among the systems under analysis can be attributed to variations in their historical experiences. Specifically, the major explanatory variables with which we wish to deal are part of the pattern of nation building. The relevant variables include the role of religion and churches, institutionalized patterns of feudalism, evolutionary versus discontinuous development, and insular versus permeable borders.

Nation-states are not natural phenomena. They did not appear on the political scene until centuries after the fall of the Western Roman Empire. It would be difficult to conceptualize a nation-state in the modern sense without the concept of sovereignty. But the modern conceptualization of sovereignty—"supreme power over citizens and subjects, unrestrained by law"—is the major contribution of the French philosopher Jean Bodin in the sixteenth century.[1] Of course, the actual

---
[1] Quoted from George Sabine, *A History of Political Theory,* (New York: Henry Holt and Co., 1955), revised edition, p. 405.

Chronology

	BRITAIN	FRANCE	RUSSIA
862			Rurik dynasty begins
988			Christianity official religion of Kievan Rus
1066	Norman conquest		
12th century		Carpetian dynasty begins	
1215	Magna Carta		
1223–1240			Mongol invasions
1337		Beginning of Hundred Years' War	
	Development of monarchy		
1461		Louis XI	
1480			Ivan III repudiates Mongol rule
1509	Henry VIII		
1500s	Rise of mercantilism		
1553–1584			Ivan IV: first Tsar
1562–1598		Wars of Religion	
1598			End of Rurik dynasty
1613			Romanov dynasty begins
1643–1715		Louis XIV	
1649–1658	Cromwell		
1688	Glorious Revolution		
1689–1725			Peter I, the Great
1707	Union of England and Scotland		
1750–1800	Enclosure movement		
18th century		"Old Regime"	
1750	Beginning of capitalism		
1789		French Revolution	
1790	Burke's *Reflections*		
1792		First Republic	
1798	Speenhamland Law		
1801	Union of Britain and Ireland		
1804		Napoleon I: Empire	
1825			Decembrist revolt
1832	First Reform Bill		
1834	Poor Law Amendment		
1848		Revolution: Second Republic	
1852		Napoleon III: Second Empire	
1861			Emancipation of serfs
1867	Second Reform Bill		
1870		Third Republic	
1884	Extension of suffrage		
1894		Dreyfus Affair	
1900	Labour Party		
1905			Revolution
1906–1911	Social insurance		
1917			Termination of the monarchy Bolshevik revolution
1918	Parliamentary reform Universal suffrage		
1918–1920			War Communism and Civil War
1921–1928			New Economic Policy
1922			Establishment of USSR
1924			Death of Lenin
1928–1933			First Five-Year Plan
1930	Depression		
1946		Fourth Republic	
1953			Death of Stalin
1958		Fifth Republic under DeGaulle	
1964			Fall of Khrushchev

	GERMANY AND ITALY		OTHER COUNTRIES AND GENERAL DEVELOPMENTS
		476	Fall of the Roman Empire
768	Charlemagne		
962	Beginning of Holy Roman Empire		
1077	Henry IV at Canossa		
1152	Frederick I, Barbarossa		
1198–1216	Pope Innocent III		
	Height of the Papacy		
1294–1303	Pope Boniface VIII		
		1453	Fall of Constantinople
			End of Eastern Roman Empire
		1450s	Netherlands united
1517	Martin Luther's Theses		
	Beginning of Reformation	1523	Gustaf Vasa, King of Sweden
		1541	John Calvin ruler of Geneva
		1568–1648	Dutch War of Independence
1555	Peace of Augsburg	1650	Monarchial absolutism at its height
1648	Peace of Westphalia	1800s	Industrial advances in Scandinavia and Belgium
1806	End of Holy Roman Empire		Philosophy of laissez-faire
		1831	Belgian constitution
1848	Revolutions	1848	Karl Marx's *Communist Manifesto*
	Frankfurt Assembly		Constitution in Holland
1859–1870	Unification of Italy		
1866–1871	Unification of Germany		
1870	Growth of socialism		
1883–1889	Bismarck's social insurance laws	1898–1908	Growth of social welfare system in Belgium
		1896	Universal suffrage in Netherlands
		1907	Universal suffrage in Austria
1912	Universal suffrage in Italy		
1919–1933	Weimar Republic		
1922–1943	Mussolini in power in Italy		
1932–1945	Hitler in power in Germany	1936–1939	Spanish Civil War
1946	Italian Republic		
1949	Germany divided into East and West		
		1968–1970	Emergence of new party alignment in the Netherlands
			Belgian constitutional revisions into a de facto federal state

consolidation of political authority had proceeded to a considerable extent in many places centuries before the idea or theory of the nation-state had developed fully, and personal fealty was accorded various feudal lords by ever-larger groups of people. However, this allegiance tended to be personal—to the individual rather than to the role he occupied—and few of these incipient units survived problems of leadership succession. Even those that did survive and eventually evolve into nation-states hardly assumed all the properties of a nation-state much before the thirteenth to sixteenth centuries.

Bodin's conception of sovereignty meant that somewhere there must be the final or ultimate power to make and enforce authoritative rules (laws); the sovereign is accountable to no other power. Thus, for example, a secular sovereign's subjects could owe no allegiance to a higher or supposedly universal ecclesiastical authority. Consequently, the medieval papacy's claim to a "plenitude of power" in moral or theological matters, a claim most clearly associated with Innocent III (1198–1216) and Boniface VIII (1294–1303), was incompatible with the conception of sovereign nation-states that had already begun to develop. Hence, at the time that the Roman Catholic church was putting forth its claims to authority in their most vigorous and extreme form, such claims as those of Boniface VIII, were already becoming anachronistic. Papal claims to a plenitude of authority in moral matters were incompatible with secular claims of sovereignty over subjects because sovereignty is inherently a nondivisible concept. It is not possible to delineate with precision spheres of activity such as the aforementioned distinction between moral and other matters. It is difficult to imagine any significant social or political activity without moral implications. Hence, the basis for such a division of sovereignty is impossible to specify.

This absence of agreement on the location and scope of political authority that characterized medieval Europe meant in fact that there was no legitimate machinery for the resolution of conflict. The period between the fall of the Western Roman Empire and the development of the nation-state system (about a thousand years) was characterized by a power vacuum. This state of affairs was in large part responsible for the large number of wars that characterized the period.

Religion and Church in the Development of Europe

To fill the vacuum in political authority, the aspirants had to contend not only with each other but also with the institutionalized Catholic church, especially as represented by the medieval papacy. Together with the feudal institutions discussed below, the church became the major source of legitimate authority in this period. The various self-proclaimed "emperors" (Charlemagne, the Holy Roman emperors, etc.) who aspired to be heirs of the political legitimacy of the Western Roman Empire reigned but did not rule. That is, they did not possess much effective control over those who were nominally their subjects. The church, by contrast, possessed an enormous hold on its flock. It was unquestioned by the great masses in medieval Europe that the institutional church had a monopoly on the avenues to salvation and that the alternative to total submission to the mother church was eternal damnation in the fires of hell. In this climate, it is not surprising that the church was able to assume many of the secular responsibilities formally assumed by Rome.

In this climate of unquestioned belief in the church as the only avenue to salvation, the threat of excommunication—a church edict with varying degrees of punishment—was usually adequate for bringing to heel any challenger to church authority. Although his actions are sometimes interpreted as something from which he also expected to gain, the spectacle of Holy Roman Emperor Henry IV standing barefoot in the snow at Canossa for three days in 1077 to beg the forgiveness of Pope Gregory VII constitutes one of the most striking symbols of the power that the threat of excommunication permitted the papacy to wield over secular rulers.

Two important consequences for the development of modern European society ensued from the dominance of the church over medieval Europe. First, the church fostered an otherworldly orientation. That is, the most important thing for a medieval Christian was salvation—not the improvement of life on earth in terms of longevity, comfort, or pleasure. The search for knowledge about the physical world and the advancement of technology and human welfare were not matters of great concern. Thus, it may be said that by these standards Western civilization was maintained in a relatively stagnant and backward state for much longer than it otherwise might have been. As will be pointed out later, the Russian Orthodox church had a similar lack of concern for worldly matters. In Russia this often had the further effect of leaving the power of secular rulers uncontested.

Because the imperatives of scientific inquiry demand that conclusions be readjusted constantly to a state of consistency with an ever-changing and ever-expanding body of evidence, the notion of a final, complete, and absolute body of truth is incompatible with such inquiry. Given the emphasis on dogmatic conformity in medieval Christendom, it is not surprising that the zenith of the church's power and influence coincided with a low period in the political and technological development of Western civilization. The political consequences of this cultural, intellectual, economic, and technological stagnation will be considered in the following chapter on political culture.

The second major consequence of the power of the medieval papacy was that as an effective competitor for temporal power, the church was able in many cases to impede the successful establishment of effective secular institutions. This was most apparent in Italy where the pope, zealously defending the temporal power of the papacy, forbade Catholic participation in the Italian state until well into the present century.[2] The effect of the church on secular authority appeared to an extent proportional to the church's influence throughout Europe. The church had a major impact on Italy and the Germanies. The papacy effectively resisted the efforts of the Holy Roman emperors—especially Frederick I (Barbarossa) and Frederick II—to establish control over their claimed domains. This failure to consolidate the Holy Roman Empire into an effective political system left much of what is now Germany and Italy a collection of relatively autonomous feudal fiefs.

It must be emphasized that the church's influence was not the sole cause for the success or failure of nation building in any given area. Instead, it is one of several important factors whose influence must be analyzed. The most successful cases of nation building in Europe were those areas where the influence of the church was lessened by considerations of geographic distance, distinct historical events, or both. England and the Scandinavian democracies immediately come to mind.

The Protestant Reformation

The secularization of society, which seems to be one precondition for an effective and responsive political system, occurred only in areas where the temporal power of the universal church declined. However, not every area where the influence of the medieval papacy declined in fact underwent what could reasonably be called secularization. In some areas the forces of the Reformation replaced a rigid and dogmatic Catholicism with an equally rigid and dogmatic Protestantism. Calvin's Geneva and those parts of Germany affected by Luther exemplify the latter. Luther was intolerant and authoritarian, and his brand of Protestantism was perhaps as dysfunctional for the effective processing of social and political issues as Catholicism. Yet some effective challenge to the power of the medieval papacy did seem to be a necessary if not a sufficient precondition for the secularization of society. In any event, the consolidation of major nation-states and the decline of the temporal power of the medieval papacy occurred at approximately the same time. The failure of Pope Boniface VIII to coerce England ar d France in the early fourteenth century constitutes one of the major manifestations of this transformation.

The Protestant Reformation had consequences that varied with the power and legitimacy of the temporal political authority in each area. In those areas where a ruler maintained sufficient internal sovereignty (such as Gustaf Vasa in Sweden or Henry VIII in England), he could resolve the issues generated by religious differences. In areas lacking such authority, bitter religious warfare was the result.

The Eastern Church in Russia

The Russian situation was somewhat different from that of Western Europe. The religion involved was Eastern Christianity received by way of Constantinople

---

[2] His decree of *non expedit* barred Catholics from voting or holding office in Italy from its issuance in 1874 until about 1913.

rather than Rome. The Byzantine tradition produced a tendency toward submission, or at least cooperation, with respect to political authority. At the very time the grand dukes of Moscow were establishing their authority, the Russian Orthodox church became independent of Constantinople. What could have been a competitive situation became instead one of cooperation.

The fall of Constantinople to the Turks in 1453 had a major impact on Russian development. For the church it meant there was no longer a source of foreign support and assistance. It also left the Russian church as the major manifestation of Orthodox religion. The first of these elements led church leaders such as Metropolitan Alexis to choose submission to the state and cooperation with its policies. The second led secular rulers such as Ivan III to champion the cause of the church. With Constantinople defeated, Ivan saw an opportunity to make Moscow its successor, and the idea of the "Third Rome" was born. With church and state lending mutual support, Moscow would take its place in line with the Roman and Byzantine empires.

The metropolitans played a cooperative, submissive role by such actions as excommunicating princes who refused to fight the Tatars. In contrast to the Holy Roman emperor begging the pope's forgiveness, the metropolitan of Moscow led a delegation to beg Ivan the Terrible to return and rule over them. For the most part, the church concerned itself with ceremony, ritual, and the soul. It had little interest in theology or political affairs.

Over the centuries, however, the tsars used their power to reduce that of the church. Several times in the first half of the sixteenth century the Moscow grand dukes removed metropolitans. The Byzantine heritage was such that while tsar and patriarch worked cooperatively, the tsar ruled and was defender of the faith. When Patriarch Nikon challenged the primacy of Tsar Alexei, a church council in 1666 deposed him and reaffirmed the duty of church officials to obey secular authority.

This theme of obedience was repeated in what is generally considered to have been the culmination of the process of asserting secular authority over that of the church. Many of the reforms of Peter the Great were opposed by conservative Orthodox churchmen. A 20-year vacancy in the patriarchate was followed by the Church Statute of 1721. Intended by Peter to reform the church so that it might play a more positive social role, the statute abolished the patriarchate entirely and replaced it with a collegiate body, the Holy Synod, appointed by the tsar. From this point the church became a department of the state bureaucracy and lost whatever political power it had.[3]

---

[3] Michael Florinsky, *Russia, A History and an Interpretation* (New York: The Macmillan Company, 1953), p. 415.

The Degree of Secularization

The importance of religion in a given system depends on the early presence of an authority such as Gustaf Vasa or Henry VIII with sufficient legitimacy or coercive capacity to impose a resolution of the religious issue (for example, Catholicism versus Protestantism) in his domain. The Germanies epitomized the consequences of an absence of such authority. Religious wars were endemic following the Reformation. The peasant revolt in 1524, the Schmakaldic Wars settled by the Peace of Augsburg in 1555, and the Thirty Years' War ended by the Peace of Westphalia in 1648 all were in large part a function of Protestant-Catholic divisions, divisions that could not be settled by imposition by the Holy Roman emperor or the Imperial Diet. For that matter, religious strife occurred in France periodically until the slaughter and expulsion of the Huguenots (French Protestants) by a relatively strong Catholic king resolved the issue in favor of a union between church and state.

It seems reasonable to conclude that pervasive religious strife increases the importance of religion in any given political system, and the probability of such strife in turn is increased by the absence of a single, legitimate sovereign authority able to impose resolutions of issues on the domain in question. After all, religious differences do not lend themselves to resolution by compromise. They are framed by their nature in terms of dichtomized and mutually exclusive alternatives: right or wrong, true or false, good or evil. That is why the resolution of such issues must be imposed by the effective use of power, sometimes with violence.

The difference between the religious wars in Germany and the violence used by Gustaf I to impose Lutheranism in Sweden is that Gustaf possessed enough power to act decisively, but in Germany, with neither the Catholic nor the Protestant forces possessing a decisive edge in coercive capacities, the issue could not be resolved. As already indicated, the religious wars there reerupted several times. Thus, the violent elimination of politically significant religious differences can have the effect of enabling a system to resolve issues pragmatically and peacefully. We are reminded of the comment by Adolf von Thadden, the head of the ultranationalist National Democratic Party in West Germany, who was asked by a reporter, suspicious that the party was "neo-Nazi," if he was antisemitic. Thadden replied that it was unnecessary because Germany had "solved our Jewish problem."

We are suggesting that the major explanatory variable accounting for the relative secularization of the systems under consideration is the sequential variable—whether the political authority was able to consolidate its control over its claimed domain prior to the religious divisions that followed the Reformation. When a political authority possessed enough power or legitimacy to resolve that issue, however violently, one of the most potentially disruptive issues was no longer a factor in the development of that system. In terms of the process of stable development, the key is whether the issue was resolved instead of whether the resolution was "just" or peaceful. The measure of whether authority was effective becomes whether it was in fact able to impose a settlement. In the Spanish Netherlands, for example, Phillip II failed to impose Catholicism on that domain in the sixteenth century and religious strife resulted. Thus, that monarchy did not possess internal sovereignty in the Spanish Netherlands. The result was that Belgium and Luxemburg were split from the Netherlands.

The argument can be construed as circular if we are saying that effective authority imposes a resolution and the measure of whether an authority is effective is whether it does impose such a resolution. What we are suggesting, however, is that the settlement of the religious dispute by an authority that is by definition effective will diminish the political importance of religion in that society. Secularization—the diminished political importance of religious and other ideological considerations—is not the same thing as the settlement of religious differences and does not logically or necessarily follow such a settlement. We are suggesting that secularization, insofar as it can be precisely conceptualized and measured, does in fact tend to occur in those societies where issues arising out of religious differences were settled one way or another quickly after they arose.

It is argued in the following chapter on the cultural basis of politics that secularization of a society contributes to the peaceful resolution of conflict by compromise, hence leading to the development of stable and effective government. Protestantism emphasized the individual's relationship with the diety rather than institutionalized conformity with the theological dictates of the papacy. Moreover, it is arguable that it was mainly a reaction against Rome, not a movement for any body of competing religious "truth" or behavior. Thus, in many of the areas affected by the Reformation, secularization came more readily than in Catholic Europe. The Protestant brand of religion, lacking a strong institutionalized defender, did not resist secularization as vigorously. Moreover, there was less concern in much of Protestant Europe than in Catholic Europe with rooting out doctrinal heresy. Religion in such areas eventually assumed a smaller role in the daily life of the masses. The result of this secularization may be seen in present-day England and Scandinavia, where, despite formally established churches, only a small percentage of the population goes to church regularly or professes belief in strictly trinitarian doctrine.

Important exceptions to this must be noted. Martin Luther himself was one of the strongest religious zealots in history. Calvin's Geneva was a study in totalitarian thought control and imposed doctrinal conformity unmatched until Calvin's Puritan intellectual descendants imposed a similar system in America's Massachusetts Bay Colony. (It might also be noted that areas of Protestant zealotry, such as Switzerland and the Germanies, were precisely those areas where Catholic-Protestant differences erupted into the fiercest active conflagration.)

Religion and the Rise of Capitalism

A famous thesis—associated with the names of Max Weber and R. H. Tawney—argues that Protestantism contributed to the commercial revolution and the rise of capitalism.[4] Based on a conceptualization of the world as divided between the elect and the damned, the Protestant (especially the early Calvinist) saw success in open competition as an indicator of who was among the elect. The acquisition of material goods in competitive commercial endeavors thus acquired a moral sanction in contrast to the otherworldly ideal of medieval Catholicism. Moreover, Protestantism helped circumvent Catholic impediments to the commercial revolution such as the position against usury.

Clearly, the commercial revolution contributed to the subsequent explosion in technology known as the industrial revolution. Technological innovation was to a significant extent a consequence of the entrepreneurial function, the entrepreneur being the man who provided the capital for and managed his own business.[5] The entrepreneur sought to maximize a profit beyond his labor and capital investment. This required that he rise above a pure or strictly competitive economic situation, a situation where no one producer controlled enough of the market for his product to affect the price of that product by himself. In such a situation, returns tended to equal capital and labor investments in the long run. Price theory suggests that higher returns would bring less efficient producers into the field, thereby increasing supply and lowering prices to the point where returns equal investment. The entrepreneur could rise above such a "fair return" on his investment and acquire "pure" profit by breaking out of pure competition—that is, by producing a superior product or producing the same product more efficiently. Thus, he was a major factor in the creative innovation that characterized the technological development of Western Europe.

It can further be argued that the commercial revolution contributed significantly to industrialization by making available the capital necessary for such industrialization.

It should be emphasized that the Weber-Tawney religious explanation for the differential rates of industrial development remains a theory that is widely but far from universally accepted. McClelland, for instance, has suggested that the rate of economic growth is a function of a psychological variable, the pervasiveness of achievement motivation in a society.[6] He has presented an impressive body of evidence to support his proposition.

---

[4] Max Weber, *The Protestant Ethic and the Spirit of Capitalism*, 1904, Talcolt Parsons, trans. (New York: Charles Scribner, 1930); R. H. Tawney, *Religion and the Rise of Capitalism* (New York: Harcourt Brace and Company, 1937).

[5] This is a major point of Joseph Schumpeter, *Capitalism, Socialism, and Democracy* (New York: Harper & Row, 1950), especially Chap. XII.

[6] David McClelland, *The Achieving Society* (New York: The Free Press, 1967).

The Geographic Impact on the Salience of Religion

The impact of Christian religion on the social and political life of Europe appears to correlate negatively to some extent to the distance of the area in question from Rome. Even France, nominally a Catholic country, has been significantly more receptive to anticlerical appeals than the Catholic parts of the Germanies, and there is more alienation from religion in general in France than throughout the Germanies. Similarly, Catholicism in the Netherlands has been less concerned with doctrinal conformity than the Italian variety. Despite some apparent exceptions such as the strong religiosity of the Flemish subculture in Belgium, clearly a country in northwestern Europe, it is still true that religion has attained a political significance strong enough to threaten political stability or generate religious conflict only in the Germanies, Italy, and to a lesser extent France. Geographic accident may thus be one possible factor in accounting for the differences among European states with respect to their receptiveness to the forces of secularization.

Although religion may retain a significance in countries relatively far removed from Rome, the most obviously and completely secularized nations—the Scandinavian democracies, Great Britain, and the older Commonwealth countries—are those farthest removed from Rome. Thus, although distance was clearly not a sufficient precondition of secularization, it may have been necessary. The concept of distance here must also take into account physical barriers. Factors such as the English Channel, the North Sea separating the Norwegian-Swedish peninsula from the rest of Europe, and the Pyrenees Mountains between France and Spain may also have been a factor in determining how autonomous a culture was from the influence of Rome.

Feudalism

Feudalism is the name given to the temporal structures and institutions that dominated Europe between the fall of Rome and the rise of the nation-state system. Feudalism was not a single institution but a set of institutions that varied with respect to time and place. Basically, it involved a set of reciprocal rights and obligations between lord and vassal. These terms are defined below.

Feudalism evolved largely because the political vacuum and absence of law and order left property owners vulnerable to brigands and marauders. Thus, weak landowners would place themselves under the protection of a larger one, giving the more powerful individual title to the land. The original landowner (now called a vassal) retained private jurisdiction but not ownership of the land, land called a fief. The fief was a political unit of land that contained one or more productive estates called manors. A system of agricultural production grew up around these manors known as manorialism. The vassal, who was at least a knight or who occupied some higher status role in the feudal hierarchy, did not till the soil of his fief; the serfs and a few freemen outside the feudal hierarchy did this. Manorialism was a system of economic production. Feudalism was a system of political-military relationships. Because feudal relationships involved title to land, feudalism is often confused with manorialism. They should not be confused, and in fact one existed for a time without the other.

In return for the protection of the new owner of the land (the lord), the previous owner owed military service to the lord. In practice, the relationship was more complex than implied here. Other reciprocal rights and obligations were involved.

To complicate the system further, fiefs were often subleased or "subinfeudated." Landowner A might grant a fief to vassal B, who might in turn grant part of it to C. Thus, B became at once both lord and vassal, lord to C and vassal to A. A lord desiring a piece of one of his vassal's fiefdoms could conceivably become a vassal to his own vassal. These situations were not unknown, and they made for great confusion due to the conflicting loyalties and obligations involved.

The consensus of historians seems to be that feudalism provided some measure of social peace out of the anarchy and chaos that followed the collapse of the Western Roman Empire. However, armed conflict between feudal lords of various stature was almost perpetual.

Nominal kings and emperors of the period were little more than feudal lords with large feudal holdings. Sometimes kings were vassals to other kings or feudal lords. Clearly, they lacked internal sovereignty. A map of the Europe of about 1000 A.D. would show a large number of feudal holdings. Many people now say that nation-states are presently too small for efficiency and peace, and movements for European unity are given increasingly serious attention. Yet, the territory now occupied by a major nation-state, France for instance, was once composed of a large number of feudal principalities, duchies, etc., such as Normandy, Brittany, Aquitaine, Francia, Champagne, and Toulouse. A list of such principalities cannot be comprehensive or precise because the boundaries between them were very fluid. Europe was characterized by political decentralization in the extreme. The lack of uniformity in currency, law, and justice demanded political consolidation. The imperatives of the commercial revolution made unity all the more necessary.

The Enclosure Movement

The commercial drive for consolidation may be seen in the Enclosure Movement in Great Britain in which the spread of sheep-grazing drove the peasants off the land and consolidated agricultural holdings in the country.[7] Where feudalism declined rapidly and more thoroughly (in the face of such commercial considerations), the peasantry was removed as a factor. Peasants appear to be susceptible to

---

[7] See Barrington Moore, Jr., *The Social Origins of Democracy and Dictatorship* (Boston: The Beacon Press, 1966), p. 28.

mobilization for various disruptive purposes by forces of either the right or the left. They have been both a conservative and a regressive force against political and economic progress and, at other times and places, a potential revolutionary force (as in France, Russia, and China). It is noteworthy in this regard that the peasantry provided a considerable portion of the manpower in the early stages of the French Revolution, and then shortly after provided the basis for a counterrevolutionary uprising in the Vendée. Countries where the peasants remained as a strong force had a poorer record with respect to evolutionary progress toward stable democratic institutions that countries in which they disappeared from a significant role in the political process. On the Continent, a growing commercialization of agriculture did not emerge to destroy feudal structures with the speed and thoroughness with which they were destroyed in Britain.

The Enclosure Movement appears to have had a second important consequence for the character of modern Britain. It provided the aristocracy with an economic base that was independent of the monarchy. Such aristocratic independence appears to occur in those societies where political evolution takes the form of the decline of royal absolutism, not its growth. We infer that aristocratic independence contributed to the decline of royal absolutism.

Aristocratic financial independence may also be observed in Sweden and Denmark in the early sixteenth century as a consequence of the confiscation of the church lands following the Reformation there. In fact, the lure of such vast ecclesiastical holdings was probably a major incentive for the aristocracy and monarch to oppose the Roman Catholic church. Thus, while members of the French nobility became parasitic supporters of the monarchy, culminating in the lavish court of Louis XIV, the English nobles were in a position to demand increasing concessions from their monarch in return for their resources, which were badly needed by the monarch for such foreign adventures as the Hundred Years' War in the fourteenth century.

Russian Serfdom

In Russia, up to and including the sixteenth century, the peasantry was free. Then the peasants gradually became serfs, reaching their lowest levels at the very time Western feudalism was breaking down. It is generally agreed that there were two primary elements in this process of serfdom. First, the free peasants became so indebted to their landlords that they could not possibly settle their accounts and be free to leave. The result was a kind of de facto subjection to the landowner. The second element concerns the financial needs of the state. As agriculture became the chief source of tax revenue, it was in the interest of the government to promote stability by such measures as prohibiting the migration of peasants.

In its stage of fullest development, from about the middle of the seventeenth to the middle of the eighteenth centuries, serfdom meant that the peasant became a virtual slave who could be sold, sent to Siberia, or otherwise disposed of by the landlord. The basic arrangement, known as the *pomestie* system, can be described as one in which the nobility was granted land by the state as payment for civilian or military service and supported itself on that land through the work of the serfs.

How did this Russian system compare with feudalism? Some of the same elements were present. There was a hierarchy of aristocratic landowners. There were many large estates, contractual arrangements, and eventually hereditary rights and duties. But it would be difficult to say that it was feudalism. Western feudalism was a more natural development. It arose largely due to a lack of central authority, depended on the efforts of the barons, and evolved relatively naturally into the next stage.

Russian serfdom came later, ended later, did not result from a political vacuum, had a nobility that had no well-defined legal position and was not a collective participatory force, produced a situation in which serfs eventually became little more than live chattel, and was finally ended by fiat only late in the nineteenth century. In sum, it is probably accurate to say that Russia did not have a truly feudal tradition in the European sense. More importantly, the position of the nobility was more like the parasitic French than the assertive English.

The Ease of National Consolidation

The ease with which a society manages to consolidate into a relatively cohesive unit and bring under control whatever centrifugal forces threaten it seems to be positively related to its willingness to admit a wider range of interests and people to a share in the decision-making process. Ease of consolidation is defined by the extent of the time lag between the widespread development of national consciousness among the masses in a geographically defined population and the establishment of effective political authority over the members of such a perceived political unit. Thus, France's and Sweden's consolidation were not far apart (Sweden under Gustaf Vasa in about 1500, France under Louis XI in the late fifteenth century). However, Sweden's followed closely upon the widespread dissemination of the idea of a Swedish nation, but France's did not. The idea of a French nation is difficult to pinpoint, but it could be argued to exist at least as far back as the reign of Phillip Augustus (1180–1223).

In general, it can be said that where national unity was effected by the difficult subjugation of autonomous power centers within the projected national borders, the resulting government tended to be more authoritarian; there was a general unwillingness on the part of the elite to grant demands of newly conscious groups for the right to influence or participate in the national decision-making process. The governments of the newly consolidated nations of Italy and Germany in the late nineteenth century epitomized this authoritarian result. The Italian *Risorgimento*—the struggle for national unification—was essentially led by the middle class and urban intelligentsia and exhibited almost a contempt for the largely peasant masses, an attitude that fostered alienation among such excluded groups toward the nation.[8] Similarly, such failures as that of the middle-class Frankfurt Assembly in Germany in 1848 meant that the middle class was to be excluded from influence in the Germany subsequently formed under the leadership of the authoritarian Prussian aristocracy.

It is significant to note that the Frankfurt Assembly and other liberal revolutions in Europe in the 1830s and after indicate the existence of a demand on the part of groups such as the German middle class for political influence. After the French Revolution of 1789 and the subsequent Napoleonic forays to the East, liberal ideas had been pretty well diffused throughout Europe. Thus, while it may be fair to say that the process of national consolidation necessarily occurred in all countries under consideration through some form of authoritarian leadership, those nations that had to wait until after the spread of liberal ideas in the nineteenth century experienced greater frustrations in the process.

Clearly, the frustrations and consequent alienation from the nation-state or regime produced by exclusion from the political process are a function not only of this exclusion but also of the extent to which the excluded groups perceive that they are entitled to political influence. It is probably arguable that the breadth of participation in England's political process under William the Conqueror was more limited than participation in Germany under Bismarck and the emperors before the First World War. In eleventh-century England no significant groups felt they were being denied a right to political input. Thus, the early English kings were not repressing their subjects in the sense of claiming more authority than the governed were willing to accept. By the time a middle class had developed to the point of demanding political influence, the authoritarian imperatives of nation building were no longer a factor in England. Similarly, the regime of Gustaf Vasa in Sweden may be construed as quite authoritarian by most reasonable standards; however, middle class and peasant demands for political influence were not a factor in fifteenth-century Sweden. A key element in sixteenth-century Russian consolidation was the close church-state relationship mentioned earlier. Thus, the Austrian ambassador to Moscow reported in the early 1500s that "one and all agree" that the grand duke's will "is the will of God, hence what the prince does is divinely inspired."[9] He went on to say that the prince was regarded only as the fulfiller of God's purpose. In short, it is not the fact of exclusion from the political

---

[8] Raphael Zariski, *Italy, The Politics of Uneven Development* (Hinsdale, IL: The Dryden Press, 1972), pp. 22–23.
[9] Sigmund Von Herberstein, "The Vicar of Muscovy," *The Horizon History of Russia* (New York: American Heritage Publishing Co., 1970), p. 114.

process that we consider of prime importance, for it was a widespread phenomenon in nearly all countries at the time of national consolidation; instead, it is the exclusion of groups demanding inclusion.

The significant variable in this regard appears to be whether the process of national unification occurred prior to the spread of the idea that political participation or influence is a human right. Where groups are excluded that perceive a right to political influence and have developed enough consciousness as a class or interest to generate political demands or ideas, their demands tend to be formulated in more extreme or ideological terms. The extremism of such political ideas will in part be a result of the bitterness and frustration of such excluded groups. It is also a result of the absence of any necessity to moderate their demands or ideas in the light of the practical exigencies of actual application. Moreover, the influence of particular interests or groups is rarely total. In practice, the ideas and demands of any one group must be compromised with competing ideas of groups with whom power and influence are shared. Ideas and demands formulated in the abstract are distinctly more likely to be extreme and unworkable than the ideas and demands of groups sharing the practical day-to-day responsibility of seeing their decisions enacted into public policy. When these ideas are formulated in the abstract, the only standards for formulation are rational consistency or consistency with metaphysical assumptions. Without an opportunity to apply the ideas, practical standards are simply unavailable.

Thus, where political consciousness exists for a significant period of time among articulate sectors of the population prior to their admission to the political process, a heritage of arguing political ideas in ideological terms will follow. This was the case of the French intellectuals under the French *ancien regime* in the eighteenth century. It was certainly true for the German intellectuals and for spokesmen for the Italian working classes. The other orientation, pragmatism, is difficult to reconcile with extremist ideas. Pragmatism in the formulation of political ideas commonly occurs where the source of the ideas is given the responsibility of making public policy (or at least a significant share of it) shortly after the development of national consciousness. It will be argued in the next chapter that pragmatic orientation increases the probability of success in the peaceful resolution of issues.

Insular versus Permeable Borders and Defense

The ease of national consolidation is probably in turn a partial function of the permeability of a nation's borders. The most rapid and painless national unifications occurred in Great Britain, which is surrounded by water, and in Norway and Sweden, which are separated from the Continent by the North and Baltic Seas. This does not mean that the existence of natural borders guarantees the absence of centrifugal forces. Clearly, Italy and Spain, mountains in the north and water on three sides, would belie such a claim. The existence of other factors can impede national consolidation despite insular borders. The realization of Italian nationhood, for example, was impeded by the existence of the Papal States, the behavior of the popes, the imperial ambitions of the Holy Roman emperors that motivated them to overcome the barrier of the Alps, and the internal obstacles of the Apennine Mountains, which isolated many of the Italian city-states from one another.

Water may or may not be a barrier. With respect to Italy it can be pointed out that the Mediterranean was one of the most easily and frequently traveled bodies at a crucial stage of technology (as compared to the colder, rougher North Sea or English Channel). The presence of the Moors, one of the factors hindering Spanish nation building, may be taken as an indication that the Straits of Gibralter did not constitute a formidable obstacle. Russia's river system made it easier for invaders to penetrate, but it also facilitated national consolidation and internal communication. The English Channel was clearly an impediment to foreign invasion. The armies of Napoleon and Hitler were stopped at the water's edge.

Thus, the significant variable for nation building is not natural borders themselves but relative freedom from foreign invasion. The former becomes significant only to the extent that it prevents the latter. It does appear, however, that freedom from foreign invasion has not been enjoyed without natural borders. Thus, natural or insular borders may be a necessary but not a sufficient precondition for freedom from foreign invasion.

Standing Armies

One of the most significant benefits of freedom from the threat of foreign invasion is that nations are spared the necessity of maintaining a large standing army. This force can become a potential source of power autonomous from the government and a possible source of organization and resources that may be used to mobilize extraconstitutional opposition to the regime. On the other hand, existing military power can be used by the government to suppress constitutional opposition to incumbent rulers or their policies, thereby generating the feelings of frustration and alienation that are thought to be a destabilizing political force. At the very least, the capacity for such repression would diminish the responsive potential of a government. Once a large standing army exists in peacetime, it looks for things to do in the absence of defending the nation from external enemies. A peacetime army may assume the task of maintaining internal order (sometimes defined as the status quo) or of defending the interests of the class from which its leaders are drawn.

The influence of the military on German politics is well known. The conservative and authoritarian dispositions of the Prussian monarchy and military were probably mutually reinforcing. Throughout German philosophy, martial values were extolled, thus enhancing the autonomous state of the military and rendering civilian control more difficult. Georg Wilhelm Friedrich Hegel and Heinrich von Treitschke were German "intellectuals" known for their exuberant glorification of military values and who had enormous influence on the Prussian and German culture. While it may be too much to say that the Prussian culture became the German culture when Prussia "conquered" Germany, the influence of the former on the latter was certainly enormous.

Hegel perhaps had the greatest influence from several points of view: his stress on the importance and priority of martial values, his influence on an exaggerated nationalism, and his espousal of a romantic, antirationalist orientation. These, of course, are related. Hegel wrote of the "spirt of the folk" in Germany as the culmination of a progressive unfolding of the "world spirit." Hegel's attribution of a necessity to such an evolution of ideals and spirit influenced Karl Marx's use of the dialectic method to impose the idea of "scientific" necessity to his desired restructuring of political and economic institutions.

To Hegel, "the ideal is real" whereas Marx was a materialist. "Freedom" to Hegel consisted of service to the state and to the culmination of German nationalism. Hegel wrote, for instance: "The state is the divine idea as it exists on earth . . . we must therefore worship the state."[10] Because Hegel and two of the predecessors who influenced his thought, Johann Gottfried von Herder and Johann Gottlieb Fichte, defined the nation as a unit determined by natural bloodlines, the intermingling of the idea of German nationalism with theories of racism is not surprising.

Hegel extolled the glories of war in such statements as "It is in this state of war that the omnipotence of the state manifests itself."[11] The German historian Heinrich von Treitschke carried this a step further when he wrote, "war is not only a practical necessity, it is also a theoretical necessity."[12] Thus, Hegel and his philosophical allies attached an ethical value to war in of itself irrespective of what war could achieve. "War," wrote Hegel, "has the deep meaning that by it the ethical health of the nation is preserved. . . . War protects the people from the corruption which an everlasting peace would bring upon it."[13]

No attempt has been made here to give a systematic summary of the thought of these writers. We simply point out that nationalism, racism, and martial values have been extolled by the most revered names in German philosophy and history. Thus, the xenophobic nationalism, racism, and call to war of a man such as Hitler

---

[10] Quoted in Karl Popper, *The Open Society and Its Enemies* (New York: Harper Torchbooks, 1962), Vol. II, p. 31.
[11] *Ibid.*, p. 65.
[12] Quoted from William L. Shirer, *The Rise & Fall of the Third Reich* (New York: Simon & Schuster, 1960), p. 99.
[13] Popper, *op. cit.*, p. 69.

found a receptive audience in Germany, in part because such values had been bestowed with a long-standing legitimacy by the most respected German intellectuals. These values rendered German society receptive to the major role played by the military, a role rendered imperative by geographic and historical considerations, and possibly enhanced by these values.

A large standing army is also part of the French heritage. France has also suffered from the presence of permeable borders. It is located on the western end of the Great European Plain, a broad, rolling, easily traversed land extending from the Atlantic shores of France to the Ural Mountains. France is bounded on the south by the Pyrenees and the Alps and on the north by the North Sea. The French army nearly undermined the Third Republic in its prosecution of Captain Alfred Dreyfus for treason. Dreyfus, a Jewish officer in the French army, was a convenient scapegoat for the conservative, authoritarian forces of army and church. His innocence was vigorously proclaimed by liberal friends of the republic, and eventually his conviction was reversed after he had spent 12 years on Devil's Island. The issue, extending far beyond the question of the guilt or innocence of one individual, was framed in terms of the honor of the army, loyalty to France, reasons of state, and preservation of the values of the church versus broadly stated principles of individual rights and justice. Thus, the case's significance went far beyond what the facts would appear to warrant, and the case threatened to tear French society apart. The role of the French army in the downfall of the Fourth Republic is discussed in a later chapter.

Much of the foregoing discussion can be illustrated by the example of Russia, whose borders are very permeable. According to one often-mentioned figure, there were 133 foreign invasions of Russia from 1228–1462.[14] Through much of its history, the country was in conflict with such powers as Sweden, Poland-Lithuania, and the Tatars. Later it encountered Napoleon and then Germany. By far the most serious invasion was that of the Tatars; it lasted 200 years, took Russia out of the European orbit, and made cultural development almost impossible.

As mentioned earlier, one implication of such a situation is the development of a large standing army. The Russian example dates from the effort to drive out the Tatars in the fifteenth century, and its major influence was through the role played by the officer corps and the palace guard in palace revolutions. These revolts occurred on a number of occasions, but were most significant at times of crisis such as the period in the eighteenth century (1725–1762) after the death of Peter. The Decembrist uprising in 1825 (influenced in part by the ideas of the French Revolution) was probably the last true example of such a revolt by the palace guards. Military men did not become active as major political figures, but tended to work behind the scenes.

Another aspect of permeable borders is more political in nature. With real or

[14] Florinsky, *op. cit.*, p. 79.

potential enemies on all sides and no protective barriers, there is a strong natural inclination to think in terms of security. In view of the recent history of the presidency and the military in the United States, it should not be difficult to understand the result. This constantly perceived military danger can easily constitute a justification for a strong ruler with the capacity to act quickly and decisively. In the United States questions of defense and security strengthen the power of the executive; in Russia they helped to create and sustain the authoritarian position of the absolute ruler. Under these circumstances it is easy to understand a national instinct toward unified power.

The internal role of standing armies is also mentioned above, especially with regard to their use in the maintenance of order and the status quo. Because they are expensive to maintain, these forces can result in popular opposition to the burden of their expenses. The point, of course, is that the army can be used to collect the very taxes that sustain it, while at the same time putting down opposition to government policies.

The discussion has so far focused on the dangers of foreign invasion posed by a lack of geographic barriers. The other side of the coin is that the same absence of obstacles also facilitates expansion and internal migration. The same geography that caused Russia to be invaded also made possible the creation of a state that now covers approximately one-sixth of the earth's land surface.

In summary, those societies that suffer the experience of being invaded or conquered with relative frequency often tend to react by placing a high value on military strength. In other words, susceptibility to external attack enhances martial values. It almost amounts to another version of the challenge-response thesis used most notably by historian Arnold Toynbee.[15] This could be seen after Napoleon overran Europe, and it can be seen today in newly independent nations emerging from colonial domination.

Evolutionary or Discontinuous Development

Only a few of the nations under consideration can point to a lengthy evolutionary or incremental development free from sharp breaks with the immediate past. A precise definition of an evolutionary (as opposed to a revolutionary or discontinuous) heritage presents a problem for methodological purists. Implicitly, the distinction involves the question of duration—how long must development proceed without a discontinuous break with the past? The mandates of logic cannot provide an answer to such a question.

To illustrate, England is commonly thought of as the epitome of evolutionary

---

[15] Arnold Toynbee, *A Study of History,* two volumes, abridged by D. C. Somervell (New York: Oxford University Press, 1946).

rather than revolutionary development, but English history was marked by two major revolutions—one amounting to a virtual civil war. The civil war was responsible for installing the Cromwellian republican "Interlude," and the revolution of 1688, the "Glorious Revolution," is famous as a "bloodless" coup. Moreover, it must not be assumed that English history is notably free from the use of violence to achieve political objectives. There has been more than one instance of regicide. Charles I lost his head over the cause of royal absolutism, and Edward II suffered a most painful and undignified demise at the hands of rivals to the throne. The War of the Roses between the feudal baronies of York and Lancaster constituted another widespread internecine conflict. Thus, the simplistic proposition that a heritage of political violence is a major cause of a modern propensity to violence as a means of resolving political issues is of dubious value. Certainly, if we are to regard England as an example of evolutionary development, we cannot make the mistake of equating evolutionary development with the absence of political violence.

In what sense may we consider England's development as evolutionary rather than revolutionary? The Cromwellian "Interlude," as it is often called, was just that—an interlude. It was a mere 11-year break in a pattern of development of an increasingly circumscribed monarchy without a basic change in the locus of sovereignty that may be traced back to William the Conqueror in the eleventh century. A "republic" is probably as out of context with the British culture as a monarchy would be with the culture of the United States. The "Glorious" or "Bloodless" Revolution of 1688 may be easily interpreted as a return to constitutional or limited monarchy from the pretensions of royal absolutism of James I. These ideals of royal absolutism could probably be characterized as always out of place in the English context but were clearly in decline by the time of Magna Carta and were certainly atavistic in seventeenth-century England. Therefore, we can discern a pattern of continuity with the past, an evolution toward constitutional monarchy dating back perhaps to William the Conqueror, perhaps to Henry II, but at least to Magna Carta in the thirteenth century.

The evolution of British decision-making machinery may be seen as a series of practical, ad hoc (in the sense of being nonprincipled) responses to given needs and problems as they arose. Royal consultation with the nobility, regularized about the time of the Hundred Years' War, was based on royal needs for funds to finance that adventure and on the independent financial base of the nobility. The nobles were summoned to Whitehall for a "speaking" (in French, *parlement*— hence, the origin of the term *parliament*). Commoners were included as a consequence of their financial success during the commercial and industrial revolutions. With needed resources, these groups were able to bargain for concessions against the monarch; hence, power in England went "out of court." This term refers to the process of actual power being exercised increasingly by agencies and structures apart from the monarchy in the name of the monarch, or more specifically in the name of the crown. In England, sovereignty or ultimate legal power resides not in the people but in the legal abstraction known as the crown. Originally, the monarch exercised most of the crown power, but gradually the power came to be exercised increasingly by others. Crown power, incidentally, is not delegated or limited to any specific list as is the power of the United States government. It is a residual repository of power.

The "going out of court" of crown power in the process of monarchal bargaining with independent sources of wealth should be seen in relation to the French situation, where the monarchy was able to maintain a virtual monopoly on significant sources of the nation's wealth. In fact, the British aristocracy stood out with respect to its early financial independence (as did the Swedish aristocracy) compared to the other countries under consideration. Subsequently, the early success of the industrial and commercial revolutions rendered the middle classes of these countries financially independent earlier than in much of the rest of Europe. Certainly, this has to be one element in the fact that royal absolutism was never a major factor in the overall historical development of England and Sweden.

The ad hoc development of British institutions may be seen in the development of the office of prime minister. Beginning with George I, the Hanoverian kings were culturally and psychologically German, and the first Hanoverian occupants of the British throne had little interest in England. George I, in fact, spoke little or no English. Therefore, he chose to reign, not rule, and accordingly designated the first lord of the treasury to get on with the mundane business of governing in his name. To this day, the English prime minister is first lord of the treasury (although now a commoner) and the treasury is presided over by the chancellor of the exchequer.

The evolution of executive authority may be conceptualized as a series of concentric circles. The body collectively making decisions would become recognized as the place to be if one desired political influence. Consequently, that body would inexorably grow in response to pressures for ever-wider inclusion. Ultimately, it would attain a size too unwieldy for its decision-making role, and that function would be assumed by an inner circle within the former large body. Eventually, the role of this inner circle would become institutionalized through practice. Thus, decision making passed from the old Anglo-Saxon Great Council or *Witan,* to a Small Council, to those within the Small Council who were "privy" to the ear of the ruler or the Privy Council. When the Privy Council grew too unwieldly, power was exercised by five lords within it: Clifford, Ashley, Buckingham, Arlington and Lauderdale—hence, the origin of the term *cabal* from the first letters of these names. When this de facto decision-making group (which never became formally autonomous) grew unwieldy, a few insiders began meeting in the king's private chambers or cabinet to make policy choices.

At present, pressures for inclusion of party faithful have resulted in cabinets regularly over 25 members, too large for the function of collective policymaking. Consequently, this function is actually performed by a few inside members: the prime minister, the foreign secretary, the home secretary, the chancellor of exchecquer, the lord privy seal, and the lord president of the council. This inner circle of the cabinet has not yet been institutionalized as a group nor has its membership been precisely specified. But we can expect such institutionalization if we assume past patterns will continue under comparable conditions.

The Scandinavian context is also characterized by an evolutionary heritage. Sweden as an independent political system dates back to Gustaf Vasa, who freed Sweden from Denmark in 1523 (a sense of Swedish consciousness probably antedates this). The first Riksdag, Sweden's major representative and now legislative body, was convened in 1435 partly in opposition to Danish rule. This body has varied through the years in representativeness, autonomy from the monarch, and influence on the political process. But the structural basis of limited monarchy, constitutional government, and eventual political democracy has a long-established existence. Moreover, it is probable that the legitimacy of the Riksdag was enhanced by the fact that it was the initial structural manifestation of Swedish nationalism. Thus, despite five major constitutional settlements in the meantime, a gradual evolution of the basic structures of the Swedish system can be traced back to the sixteenth century.

The freeing of Sweden from Denmark mentioned above implies correctly that the Danes have a national consciousness that can be identified at a much earlier period. Actually, references to the Danish people go far back to antiquity, as in the old English narrative poem of *Beowolf,* although such early history is impossible to separate from mythology. It was possible to talk about Danish kings by the eighth century. We might argue as to whether the consecutive history of Denmark should be traced all the way back to the reign of Gorm the Old in the tenth century, but almost certainly it can be traced back to the Valdemars in the twelfth century. The unseating of Christian II by the Danish nobility in 1522 was more of a reaction to Christian's support of Danish commercial classes against the Danish landowners than a challenge to the legitimacy of the monarchy.

Danish history presents an interesting parallel to British history in that the need for funds to conduct a war led to an increase in the power and influence of a representative assembly in both cases. It will be recalled that this was the case in England during the Hundred Years' War. In Denmark, the need to wage war against Sweden (which was asserting its claim to national independence) led to the calling of the first representative assembly in Denmark in the fifteenth century. By the sixteenth century this body, now called the Riksraad, exercised considerable influence, and some said that in fact it governed while the king who replaced Christian II merely reigned. Clearly, limited monarchy has a long, continuous history in Denmark.

French society has a continuity, as already suggested, going back to Louis XI.

But sharp, discontinuous changes in the political format have characterized the French political system since the French Revolution of 1789. It would be difficult to overestimate the persisting political impact of that cataclysmic event on French society. The revolution involved far more than a change in political format. It was a major social upheaval. The nobility who initiated the offensive against the monarchy proved unable to control the revolutionary potential of the intellectual, urban radicals and the peasantry. Ultimately, poor artisans and peasants, fearful of the increasingly radical tide of the revolution, engineered counterrevolutionary uprisings. This fear was a consequence of the totality with which the radical currents of the revolution threatened to destroy the structures and institutions of French society. Thus, the radical phases of the revolution that followed the murder of Louis XVI aimed at a reconstruction of the entire French social fabric. To illustrate, the name given to the urban radicals, *sans-culottes,* refers to an absence of the knee breeches of the royal elite in favor of long pants. Even dress was to be changed. The radicals even attempted to offer a new calendar with renamed months. Every symbol and vestige of the old society was marked for destruction. Apparently, the radicals were limited in this aim by the peasantry on whose support they relied and whose goals were more specific economic gains.

This total break with the past generated the systematic statement of classic conservatism by Edmund Burke. In his book, *Reflections on the Revolution in France,* Burke used the phrase "the collective wisdom of the ages" to argue that civilization was built cumulatively over thousands of years. Therefore, he reasoned, it is presumptuous for any generation to think that it can start from scratch and replace a civilization with something better in that one generation. Thus, classic conservatism as it has pervaded the Continent emphasizes continuity with the past. It does not oppose evolutionary change. Instead, it suggests adaptation of existing institutions to changing circumstances. It is noteworthy that Burke supported both the American Revolution (against his own government) and the initial phases of the French Revolution. Burke appears to have been alienated by dogmatic and ideological claims to unchallenged and arbitrary power whether emanating from the masses in populistic uprising or from aspirants to monarchal rule by divine right. To Burke, politics implied a pragmatic bargaining among differing interests.

In this, the classic or "Burkean" conservatives differ from the American "right," whose adherents appear to manifest a yearning for a romanticized and partly mythical past that would lack any continuity with the actual recent past. To the extent that the American right advocates a sharp, discontinuous break with ongoing affairs, it could be characterized as radical rather than conservative according to the European orientation. All of this may help explain why European conservatives have been able to adapt to such post Second World War developments as the welfare state and strong doses of "democratic socialism" much more readily than their American counterparts. In the European context, the classic right appears to be distinctly less ideological than the left.

The destruction of the institutional fabric of French society meant that the question of the political format was thrown open fairly late in the game. No other structural format has been able to acquire sufficient legitimacy to impose resolutions of the divisive substantive issues that were already appearing on the scene. In the course of the French Revolution in 1789, the Catholic church sided with royalty and aristocratic privilege. Subsequently and until the Fifth Republic, practicing Catholicism was regarded as incompatible with support for a republican regime. (*Republican* in that context meant support for a regime of virtual legislative omnipotence, as will be explained below.) This development had the consequence of effectively barring practicing Catholics from the government in a country that is overwhelmingly (at least nominally) Catholic, and placing the government and the church in a position of mutual opposition. Moreover, loyalty to the Catholic religion meant support for alternatives to the existing republican format. Irreconcilable religious differences came to be discussed in constitutional terms, thereby increasing the intensity of conflict. For most of the Third and Fourth Republics, the failure to govern by the French center—the Catholic-based Popular Republican Movement and the nineteenth-century liberal "Radical Socialists"—can be traced to this pro- versus anticlerical division.

France has undergone several institutional changes. It is not necessary to describe their particulars here, but their extent is obvious from the fact that we are now talking about the fifth Republic. France has fluctuated between periods of legislative omnipotence and periods of authoritarian populism. The latter, often called Bonapartism after its initial manifestation in France, exercises an autocratic rule based on a claimed mandate from "the people" to further ideals of "liberty, equality, and fraternity." The idea of an almost metaphysical groundswell of public opinion giving mandate to a ruling elite apart from a regular set of procedures for competitive elections has been influential in France ever since the publication of the works of Jean Jacques Rousseau.

Rousseau's major political work, *The Social Contract*, was written during the period of prolific, repressed, and therefore doctrinaire intellectual activity in the last years of the *ancien regime*. A key concept in this work is "le volonté general"—the general will, a will that is not majoritarian, not dependent on unanimity, and not determined by any specific set of procedures that bestows legitimacy on a political elite. There are clearly some revolutionary implications in the idea that the political legitimacy of an elite is contingent on its fulfillment of its end of the contract—namely, adherence to the commands of the general will. Still, there are authoritarian implications in this as well. Modern fascism is clearly based on widespread popular support derived from mobilized, atomized individuals. Hitler's popular election in Germany (he did, after all, receive a clear plurality of almost 40 percent of the vote in Weimar's last election in March 1933) and the mobilized masses demonstrating enthusiastic support at Nazi rallies attest to this. The strong relationship between populism and authoritarian, monistic politics has been noted increasingly by students of political extremism.[16]

The term *populism* refers here to a class of political movements that share the following properties: a claim to speak for the unarticulated demands and feelings of the masses (or, in Nazi terminology, the *volk*), a claimed faith in the superior "common-sense" wisdom of the masses (a claim that frequently degenerates into antiintellectualism and that elicits perceptions of moral superiority), a claim or perception that the interests of the masses are being opposed by a conspiratorial elite, and an appeal to those who seek simple solutions for complex problems and yearn for a largely mythologized, simpler past. Thus, populism often involves, at least in part, a rebellion against the technological imperatives of modernity. The term *populism* appears to have originated with the American Populist Party, which claimed in the 1890s to represent agrarian interests against Eastern commercial interests and monopolistic industry. It is interesting to note that such movements, from the American Populists to the Third Reich, shared a strong strain of antisemitism, perhaps in part because the Jews epitomized the commercial elite that the agrarian populist despised and feared.

Monism was coined by Seymour Lipset to mean antipluralism—the idea that only one conception of the national interest is legitimate.[17] Pluralism, on the other hand, implies that there are inevitable differences in interests and that these competing claims are all legitimate. In a pluralistic context, the various interests bargain with one another, while a monistic attitude regards competing claims and interests as illegitimate and tends to seek their elimination. Thus, a populist leader, insofar as be believes that he speaks the pure, true sentiments of the people, quite logically must conclude that opposition is for selfish and parochial interests and therefore against the people.

The essential point to note about this kind of mass base is that it involves a call for support for a given elite and its policies instead of a call for a choice between organized, available alternatives. In essence, the role of the masses in this kind of political movement is to ratify a fait accompli.

Populism in this sense becomes a description of Bonapartism. In France today it is manifested in Gaullism (President Georges Pompidou's administration could also have been thought of as Gaullist). DeGaulle's technique was to call for plebiscites on his policies—calls for approval without providing (or permitting) realistic, available alternatives. DeGaulle would promise to resign if defeated, presenting the French electorate with a choice of DeGaulle or chaos.

[16] For example, Seymour Lipset and Earl Raab, *The Politics of Unreason, Right Wing Extremism in America* (New York: Harper & Row, 1970).

[17] *Ibid.*, pp. 12–17.

This view of political responsibility views the government as being responsible to the masses as atomized individuals. Rousseau and his philosophical followers viewed an organizational level between the individual and government as distortions of the "general will." This cult of the individual is a heritage of both the degrading abuse of authority under the *ancien regime* and the spirit of Rousseau's philosophy. It has become manifested in an antipathy to direct or face-to-face authority relationships that has endured to the present day.

According to the way we conceptualized an industrial society in Chapter 1, organizational development is a prerequisite for political and economic effectiveness. In the political realm, the individual lacks the resources to challenge omnipotent government. Economically, a modern society requires the concentration of its capital for the efficiency of mass production. Thus, the French cult of individualism stemming from Rousseau and the revolution that followed accounts in part for the French lag in the level of industrialization and difficulties in establishing effective democracy.

Similarly, the French concern for freedom from abuse of political powers—also a heritage of revolutionary rhetoric—has led to a suspicion of executive authority. Thus, even when liberal elements of French society have been able to control the political system, they have established political formats heavily weighted toward legislative domination of the political executive. These suspicions, stemming from the heritage of the revolution, were reinforced by continuing aspirations of the French right for a monarchical restoration. Abuse of the power to dissolve the legislature by the monarchist-oriented second president of the Third Republic, Field Marshal MacMahon, resulted in the institutionalization of a prohibition against the use of that power. The executive was thus deprived of a counterweight to the power of the legislature to vote a cabinet out of office. This contributed to cabinet instability, as will be explained in a later chapter.

Some suggest that a heritage of violence tends to legitimate violence as a tool for the resolution of political issues. Conversely, a heritage of resolving issues by peaceful means tends to undercut the legitimacy of attaining political goals by either revolutionary or coercive means. Clearly, France has a long heritage of political violence and revolutionary activity.

The frequent recourse to violence, coercion, or revolution to resolve political grievances in France may be in small part a function of the fact that success in such undertakings is physically more feasible. First, French society and government are highly centralized and concentrated in Paris, especially since the "reforms" of Napoleon. Thus, revolutionary forces do not have to spread their limited resources against numerous, widely scattered power centers. With success in Paris, success in the provinces should follow. Second, the narrowness of Parisian streets before Napoleon III eased the task of setting up an effective barricade against an army. Since the army could not bring its superior weaponry and firepower to bear under such restrictive conditions, a few sticks of old furniture were frequently a defensible barrier. In any event, the frequency of unscheduled and often coerced changes in government and the irreconcilable philosophical strains that emanated from the profound revolutionary upheaval of 1789–1794 resulted in a lack of widespread legitimacy for any set of institutions.

The longest-lasting regime, the Third Republic, was born out of defeat in the Franco-Prussian War in the late nineteenth century. As its first president, Louis Adolphe Thiers, put it, it was the "regime that divides us the least." A majority or near majority of the members of the lower house of the legislature, the Chamber of Deputies, was monarchist. It appears that the only significant barrier to the monarchists' desire to replace the republic with a monarchal restoration was their division between two competing claimants to the throne, the Bourbons and their Orleanists cousins. This so-called temporary regime survived the First World War and lasted until France was overrun by Germany in 1940.

The Fourth Republic, born out of the rubble of the Second World War, was not considered legitimate by a significant portion of its subjects and of the occupants of the Assembly. The cultural and structural properties of French society that made resolving issues difficult in both the Third and Fourth Republics will be discussed below in the appropriate chapters. Clearly, the failure to resolve the basic incompatibility between the Bonapartist and Assembly traditions emanating from the French Revolution detracted from whatever legitimacy the regime otherwise might have attained. The final demise of the Fourth Republic grew out of the failure to resolve the Algerian problem—a revolt for independence in the last major French colonial possession in which large numbers of Europeans had resided for generations. The threatened colonials and the army refused to accept the absence of effective action against the Algerian insurgents and were a major force in the 1958 collapse of the Fourth Republic. Ironically, by disposing of Algeria anyhow, DeGaulle betrayed the expectations of the army and the colonials who supported his return. The history of the Fifth Republic to date appears to offer the best prospect for stable government in France since the Revolution.

The Low Countries have a mixed history with respect to continuity. The Netherlands split off from the Spanish Netherlands in the 1570s and has been an independent nation almost ever since. The exceptions were a brief period of occupations by the Napoleonic armies and an even briefer reunion with Belgium under the aegis of the Netherlands. Neither exception seems of sufficient duration to break the feeling of Dutch national consciousness dating back to the sixteenth century.

Belgium, on the other hand, did not achieve status as an independent nation until the nineteenth century and lags behind other European countries in the formation of a national consciousness. But here is where our neat, tidy theory begins to break down—that long, uninterrupted national consciousness leads to high legitimacy for the regime and political format, which in turn leads to political stability and successful processing of issues. Belgium is not known for either cabinet instability or frequent changes in regime or constitutional format. (We will see in the next chapter that the stability of Belgium also violates the expectations we derive from standard generalizations about the impact of cultural and social variables.)

Belgium has not been particularly successful in the resolution of issues. There is increasing evidence that the two cultural-linguistic subcultures, the French-speaking Walloons and the Flemish-speaking Flemish, are finding the resolution of the differences between them increasingly difficult. In 1971, after a year of hard bargaining, a principle of cultural autonomy was established for each of the subcultures. Each subculture is governed by a "cultural council" empowered to issue decrees on matters "considered the *exclusive* province of each cultural community" (italics added). It is difficult to reconcile such language with the principle of national sovereignty inasmuch as the exclusive power over anything in the hands of a subsystem is incompatible with the concept of final, supreme, or ultimate power in the hands of the general system. It may not be too much to suggest that insofar as nation building is related to the establishment and maintenance of internal sovereignty, Belgium is no longer a nation in that sense.

It should be noted, however, that no one has actually opposed the principle of cultural autonomy for these groups. Thus, subcultural autonomy may be a resolution of a large number of otherwise irreconcilable differences, a resolution that does not generate divisive political issues. This may be compared to the American South, where the autonomy of that region was resisted by the forces of union, resulting in the American Civil War.

Religious strife has never been a major factor in Belgium. Even the relatively secularized Walloons are at least nominally Catholic and do not vigorously oppose strong public support of clerical education. Thus, their Liberal and Socialist Parties simply accepted the Catholic position on this potentially divisive issue and thereby removed it from the political arena.

We seem to be left with the proposition that a lack of evolutionary development and continuity with an extended past will weaken the legitimacy of a regime and render it more susceptible to instability given the presence of divisive issues. The variable of divisive issues is one of those "other things being equal" qualifiers that are never equal, qualifiers to the relationship between historical continuity on one hand and political stability and success on the other.

Germany has suffered from frequent regime changes (new constitutions in 1871, 1919, 1949), and its experience with democratic institutions may be argued to be more limited than with an authoritarian format. It has already been suggested that the German philosophical heritage manifests a distinct authoritarian strain. Further, the fact that the authoritarian Prussian kingdom was a major source of the German political culture gives that type of political format a longer heritage than the German nation-state itself. Thus, not only did the liberal, democratic format of the Weimar Republic lack an acquired legitimacy of its own, but it might be argued that it also had to contend with a competing legitimacy for an authoritarian format, a legitimacy whose roots far outdated those of the Weimar state.

Since the fall of Hitler's Third Reich in 1945, Germany has been partitioned into two separate states: the German Democratic Republic (East Germany) (DDR) and the Federal Republic of Germany (GDR). This division was imposed by the allied powers due to competing interests in the Cold War and out of fear of a possible recurrence of the German military excursions of the twentieth century. The Democratic Republic was initially administered by the Soviet Union, while what is now the Federal Republic was administered by Britain, France, and the United States. Berlin, located in the heart of the Soviet-administered zone, was similarly partitioned into four zones, a partition that evolved into a bifurcated allied and communist division. The allied "island" of West Berlin in the heart of the Soviet-controlled Democratic Republic has raised numerous problems of allied access through East German territory to West Berlin. It thus seems that the Cold War has ensured the long-term partition of Germany. Nevertheless, the idea of a unified German state has persisted among the Germans. The constitution of the West German state is called a basic law rather than a constitution because the latter term connotes a permanent sovereign status for the political unit it covers. With the passage of time the imperatives of reality have meant that eventual reunification of Germany has shifted from a serious hope to an idea to which most Germans pay only lip service.

Meanwhile, the legitimacy of the Bonn republic must be increasing with the passage of time. Its survival during its early years was probably due in large part to the substantive success of its domestic economic policies and the restoration of German national status on the international scene. In other words, it is likely that whatever loyalty and pride the typical West Germans felt for their system was attached to the results of its policies rather than to its political format. Data from a research study of the United States, Britain, West Germany, Italy, and Mexico support this conclusion.[18] The survey, taken in 1959, reveals that only seven percent of the Germans named governmental or political institutions when asked, "Generally speaking, what things about this country are you most proud of?" Contrast this figure with 85 percent for the United States and 46 percent for the United Kingdom. Even in Mexico, 30 percent of the respondents expressed pride in their governmental institutions. Yet 33 percent of the Germans, a figure that exceeds any of the other four nations, expressed pride in their economic system.[19]

---

[18] Gabriel Almond and Sidney Verba, *The Civic Culture* (Boston: Little Brown and Co., 1965).
[19] *Ibid.*, pp. 64–65.

The capacity of such a system to survive a crisis is lower than a system with what David Easton has called diffuse support;[20] that is, support for the political format rather than for its specific output. The legitimacy of the Bonn government has been to a large extent contingent upon its success. A long enough period of substantive success can generate the level of diffuse support and legitimacy for a political format that it requires to weather substantive adversity. This is probably the basis for whatever optimism is justifiable about the long-term prospects of the Bonn republic.

Although accounts of the history of Russia generally begin with *Kievan Rus* in the ninth century, the process of national consolidation did not begin until about 600 years later in the area of Moscow. In between were the period of Kiev's glory and downfall and 200 years of Tatar rule, which isolated Russia from Europe at a time that included developments such as the Renaissance.

A number of factors converged in the fifteenth century to set in motion the process of national unification. They included the defeat of the Tatars, the fall of Constantinople to the Turks in 1453, the emergence of the powerful grand duchy of Moscow, and the position of the Orthodox church.

The cooperative relationship of church and secular leaders has already been discussed, but its importance justifies a brief mention. The Byzantine origins of the Russian Orthodox church tended to make it cooperative and even submissive to begin with. The fall of Constantinople left the church with no source of outside support and little alternative but to support the state. This was facilitated by the fact that Moscow saw itself as the logical successor to the Byzantine Empire. The resulting concept of Moscow as the "Third Rome" made possible a mutual-interest arrangement in which the princes of Muscovy became the defenders of Orthodoxy, and church leaders supported the claims to divine authority of a state that glorified the church as a new Rome. The early princes were thus accepted by the people as ruling by the will of God and entitled to obedience.

During the period of Tatar domination, the Muscovite princes had submitted to the humiliation of receiving from the khans their *yarlyk* or permission to rule. But because the Tatar presence was not as great in the forest belt (Moscow) as it was on the steppes to the south, as long as Moscow's princes collected the taxes and paid tribute to the Tatars they were given some autonomy. The result was that Moscow eventually gained supremacy over other nearby princes, sometimes with the aid of the khans. When the rule of the Golden Horde finally came to an end, symbolized by the refusal of Ivan III in 1480 to pay tribute to the Tatars, the grand duchy of Moscow became the nucleus of the new Russian state.

Perhaps it is not too surprising that the Russian pattern of development was one of monarchal absolutism. The fundamentally submissive attitude of the church

---

[20] David Easton, *A Framework for Political Analysis* (Englewood Cliffs: Prentice Hall, 1965) pp. 124–125.

eliminated that potential rival. The otherwordly orientation of the Eastern church, combined with the period of Tatar rule, deprived Russia of the Renaissance, the Reformation, and the attitudes and institutions to which these movements contributed in the West. Finally, there is the question of whether the constant warfare with neighbors required (or at the very least justified) authoritarian power.

This pattern of the development of autocracy and absolutism was relatively continuous from 1450 until about the beginning of the present century. This does not mean, of course, that the process was always steady, even, and without struggles. It will be remembered that the secular rulers had their conflicts with religious leaders such as Patriarch Nikon. Many of the other elements of European development were also present, but they came in a different sequence and were weaker and short-lived. Businessmen did not develop the attitudes of a merchant class. At times the nobility asserted itself as a force, but it was always reduced to dependence on the tsar. In the case of both merchants and nobility, the tendency was to look to the ruler for favors and privileges rather than to develop an attitude of individual enterprise. In several instances a kind of popular assembly (*zemsky sobor*) was called, but representative assemblies and traditions never really developed. Industrialization was late in coming, and the serfs were not even emancipated legally until 1861, so there was no significant middle class.

There were interludes such as the "Time of Troubles," which was a 15-year period (1598–1613) of internal and external factional struggles during the time between the end of one dynasty and the beginning of another. It ended with the calling of a *zemsky sobor* (assembly of the land) composed of representatives of various classes of society. The assembly's choice of Michael Romanov as tsar established a 300-year dynasty that ended only with the 1917 revolution. This period of interlude left very few traces on the political and social landscape of the country.[21]

The period from 1906–1917 represents another interlude. Although the revolution of 1905 failed, it did result in a number of reforms. No one would describe the period as democratic, but there were hopeful signs. A *Duma,* or parliament, was convened in 1906, political party activity was permitted, criticism of the government was tolerated, and the status of the peasants was improved. It is futile to speculate on what might have been. The outbreak of war in 1914 created an entirely new situation, a consequence of which was the first 1917 revolution. The government collapsed from corruption, inefficiency, internal disturbances, and military defeat.

It has been debated just how much the Bolshevik revolution and regime constituted a radical break with the past. While there is no doubt that there are dif-

---

[21] Florinsky, *op. cit.*, p. 246.

ferences, most conspicuously the ideology, it might be suggested that there are also many similarities. If writers such as Milovan Djilas are right, one major result of the revolution was the creation of a "new class," whose chief concern was preserving its positions of privilege and power through authoritarian means.[22]

The suggestion, then, is that from the grand dukes of Moscow around 1450 until perhaps the present, absolutism has been the continuing principle of the Russian political pattern. Thus, an authoritarian format has acquired great legitimacy. Important economic or social changes have resulted in almost every case, including the present, from the decrees of rulers rather than evolutionary processes. It has been pointed out that one of the marked differences between Russian development and that of most of Europe was the absence in the former of a prolonged struggle between the monarch and the social elite such as barons and merchants.[23] The struggle (which did not exist in Russia except for periods such as the second half of the eighteenth century—called the "golden age of the nobility")[24] produced various outcomes. In England and Holland the social elite eventually prevailed, but in Prussia it was the monarch who did so. As mentioned earlier, although the French monarchy was overthrown in 1789, the conflict continues between republicanism and Bonapartism.

Russian history has not been without conflict and violence. It is marked by assassinations, murders, pretenders, palace revolts, and revolutions. But, as Seton-Watson puts it, they were all concerned with the issue of which individual should be the autocrat.[25] In other words, the question was not whether or how power should be divided but who should exercise that power.

The members of the "older" British Commonwealth—the dominions of Australia, Canada, and New Zealand—are also major industrialized powers, although they are not geographically contiguous to the European powers we have so far discussed. On first glance, they do not seem to enjoy an inordinately long evolutionary past. Australia's consolidation as a nation-state dates back only to the turn of the twentieth century. Canada's confederation dates back only slightly farther, to 1867. New Zealand achieved self-governing status in 1907. Thus, these dominions are formally among the newest of the nation-states we are considering, but they are by and large stable and successful. (This judgment may be qualified somewhat in the case of Canada, as will be shown below.)

The length of formal national status is deceptive in these cases, however. In the first place, Australia and New Zealand had established their political format decades before actual national consolidation and independence. In Australia, the

---

[22] Milovan Diljas, *The New Class* (New York: Praeger, 1957).
[23] Hugh Seton-Watson, *The Russian Empire 1801–1917* (London: Oxford University Press, 1967), p. 10.
[24] Florinsky, *op. cit.*, p. 569.
[25] Seton-Watson, *op. cit.*, p. 11.

state of New South Wales was operating a system of parliamentary democracy early in the nineteenth century. That state served as something of a mother culture from which the culture of the other states emanated. New Zealand also established parliamentary institutions by the midnineteenth century. More importantly, in none of these countries was the basic political format (a modified version of British cabinet government with federalism in two of the cases) ever in serious dispute. These countries inherited the acquired legitimacy of the British institutions much as a businessman can sometimes buy a residue of accumulated good will with a business he acquires. In that sense, the heritage of the older Commonwealth is as old as that of Great Britain itself.

In the case of Canada, however, the confederation may realistically be characterized as an alliance between two autonomous cultural linguistic systems, one of which views the other as its conqueror: the French Canadian, Catholic subculture that is essentially French speaking and all other Canadians. The latter group speaks English and is mostly Protestant. The alliance was principally motivated by a desire to resist the perceived threat of a northward push of United States "manifest destiny" beginning at about the time of the War of 1812, not by any desire to assimilate with one another. Each subculture has retained feelings of cultural superiority to the other, and each subculture retains a different sense of the past. Although the Anglo (meaning here non-French) Canadians identify with the British heritage and the symbols relevant to that heritage, the French have widely regarded their political and cultural heritage to lie in prerevolutionary France. Consequently, the British format and its supporting behavior patterns can be expected to enjoy less legitimacy among the French than among their non-French counterparts. The French Canadian separatist movement of the late 1960s may be taken as an indication of that proposition.

Conclusion

We have suggested that a number of variables in a nation's past may have a significant impact on the present state of its political system. However, it is possible to find some exceptions to nearly every relationship suggested. This is due primarily to the fact that such relationships hold true "other things being equal." Other things rarely are. Despite the fact that knowledge of any given historical variable does not enable us to predict the present state of a political system with certainty, such knowledge can increase our predictive power substantially beyond a wild guess. The problem, of course, is that the historical factors we have discussed constitute only a few of the nearly infinite number of factors that affect the present state of political systems. It is impossible to consider all relevant factors; the human mind simply could not comprehend such a quantity and variety of factors. We intend, however, to consider many of the major ones in the chapters that follow.

Patterns of Nation Building

The effort to formulate causal propositions about the present state of political systems in such a way as to derive substantial predictive power has another complication. Inasmuch as the enormous macro-level variables we seek to explain are the result of so many factors, it is rarely possible to state the necessary and sufficient preconditions for them. We have listed a number of factors that either are or come close to being necessary preconditions for such things as political stability, political success, or responsive capacity. That means that outcomes could not occur without those prerequisites. But the presence of the prerequisites may not in itself be sufficient to bring about the outcomes in question. That is, the outcomes may still fail to materialize despite the presence of the prerequisites because additional prerequisites are needed.

In the course of examining our survey of the historical development of the industrial nation-states in question, we have found it reasonable to infer a number of partial causal relationships. That is, we conclude that we have isolated some fraction of the factors that contribute to bringing about those properties of nation-states for which we wish to account. One proposition at a high level of generality that appears to be supported by the data examined is that the stability of a political system is to a large extent a function of the legitimacy of its political format and of the procedures for choosing decision makers and for reaching decisions. This legitimacy, in turn, is a function of several historical variables. Perhaps chief among these is the length of time such formats and procedures (institutions) have been dominant in a system without abrupt, discontinuous, revolutionary change. It does not appear that the amount of change is the significant variable. Britain clearly has a very different set of institutions today than it did even two centuries ago. The crucial variable appears to be the extent to which some continuity with the past is maintained. In other words, the important variable is not the amount of change but incremental and evolutionary rather than discontinuous or revolutionary change.

The legitimacy of a system's institutions appears to be negatively affected by competing sets of institutions. Thus, in those areas where religious institutions retained sufficient importance in the minds of the masses to compete with secular authorities, the legitimacy of secular political institutions was adversely affected. The importance of such religious institutions seems to have been increased by a failure to resolve the religious issue—that is, to eliminate or avoid competition between religious groups for the allegiance of the masses and the support of the state. The fact that the resolution of that religious issue was generally done violently or coercively does not appear significant for our objects of explanation.

The stability and success of political systems seem to be partial functions of the sequential variable. That is, it is not only a case of what happens or even when it happens; the order in which things occur appears to be very important. Specifically, we have suggested that the consolidation of internal sovereignty prior to the onset of divisive substantive issues is conducive to stability and success. When procedures are legitimated first, these procedures can be more effectively utilized to resolve substantive issues. Otherwise, the partisan feelings generated by divisive substantive issues become framed in terms of the alternative procedures or political formats. The levels of partisanship from the two types of issues become cumulative as the two types of divisions reciprocally intensify one another. We have seen, for example, that the French have been prone to debate substantive issues in terms of alternative constitutional formats.

Countries have been more successful in resolving issues when the issues are not framed in terms of religious or other closed-thought systems. This suggests that political success and stability are positively related to secularization. Religion seems to assume less importance in those systems without strong competition between rival religions where the religious issue is resolved in favor of one faith or another. The religious issue has tended to be resolved where a secular authority consolidates sufficient internal sovereignty prior to the salience of such religious issues to impose a solution on them. This is, of course, another aspect of the sequential variable discussed above.

It should be stressed that the factors relating to political stability and success are not necessarily those explaining the responsive capacity (the degree of democracy) of a political system. The latter variable is also a product of an almost infinite variety of historical and other variables. The most important of these historical variables appear to be: the insularity of a nation's borders with the frequent consequences of the early establishment of internal sovereignty and a lack of a standing army; the pattern of the breakdown of feudalism and the financial independence of the aristocracy; and the secularization of a society with a resulting tolerance of opposition.

Finally, it should be noted that the effect of many of the variables discussed here on political stability, success, or responsiveness is not direct but comes instead through intervening variables. Thus, some of these historical variables have cultural consequences that in turn bring about stability, success, and democracy— or the lack thereof. This will become more apparent after the discussion of cultural variables in the following chapter.

Chapter 3

The Cultural Context

Until recent decades, the study of comparative politics was confined to constitutionally designated structures such as legislatures, prime ministers, cabinets, etc. In the decades since the second World War, students of comparative politics have turned increasing attention to phenomena that had formerly been the exclusive province of sister social sciences such as sociology and psychology. These social and cultural phenomena have come to the attention of comparative politics because constitutionally designated structures do not exist in a vacuum. The contexts in which institutions are found may be expected to have an impact on the manner in which those institutions operate. These contextual variables may be divided into structural variables and dispositional variables.

Structural variables are those that refer to recurring patterns of behavior and interaction. The nature of the stratification system—the criteria by which people are grouped in a society and the standards for admission into any given category—is one structural variable. Clearly, the agencies of government constitute political structures; however, the term is much broader than that. Structures of society (the nature of nongovernmental groups and their patterns of action and interaction) frequently have an impact on the process by which authoritative policy is made; thus, the nongovernmental structures become politically relevant. Structural variables are the properties of social groups or, at the highest level of generality, whole societies. The analysis of social groups and collectivities is called *macro-level* analysis.

Dispositional variables are the properties of individuals. The analysis of individual variables is said to be at the *micro level*. Specifically, dispositional variables refer to those internal states of individuals that predispose them to respond in certain ways to certain stimuli or experiences. Thus, dispositional concepts can be used to account for the fact that different individuals do not respond in identical ways to apparently identical stimuli.

Political culture is a unique concept in that it attempts to combine and link these macro and micro levels of analysis. The concept involves characterizing social systems on the basis of properties of individuals. Thus, we may speak of France's attitude or belief about some object. But France is not a corporeal entity—a thing; it is a mental construct. As abstractions in the world of ideas, political systems do not think; consequently, they do not have attitudes, beliefs, etc. How, then, can we speak of France's attitude, thereby applying a micro-level concept on the macro level? The answer is that when certain politically relevant, dispositional properties occur with sufficient frequency among the members of a political system that we can say those dispositions are *prevalent* or typical, we ascribe those dispositions to the system itself. This is a kind of analytical fiction. The precise frequency threshold considered necessary to say that a given disposition is typical has never been specified; presumably, it is something well above a simple majority of the population. Thus, a statement that a system has a certain disposition constitutes a statement of a strong tendency among the individual members of that system. Of course, the dispositional properties may also be ascribed to parts of whole systems. In this way we speak of subcultures—distinct cultures within a society-wide culture).

The above stipulation of the meaning of the concept of political culture refers to the culture of the mass of the population. This will be referred to as mass political culture. Data on mass political culture are difficult, expensive, and time-consuming to attain (often through the technique of cross-national survey research).[1] for obvious political reasons, survey research is not feasible in closed societies such as those of the Soviet Union and other communist-bloc nations. Thus, for reasons of convenience and practicality, an increasing field of inquiry is the political culture of the elite or leaders instead of the masses.

Studying elite political culture raises questions, however. Implicit in some propositions about the elite political culture is the assumption that the elite culture reflects the mass culture, so that one can infer mass dispositions from the elite culture. But the validity of this assumption has never been subjected to systematic

---

[1] For a thorough analysis of the techniques and problems in such an undertaking, see Frederick Frey, "Cross Cultural Survey Research in Political Science," Robert Holt and John Turner, eds., *The Methodology of Comparative Research* (New York: The Free Press, 1970), pp. 173–294.

examination. In the few cases where we have data of both the mass and elite culture, they appear to be more or less reflective of one another.[2] It seems reasonable to assume very tentatively that the elite and mass cultures affect one another reciprocally but imperfectly.

The comparability of such data may be questioned. The question of the extent to which one can infer the mass culture from the elite culture may be less important for authoritarian systems than for relatively open systems. Clearly, where the channels available for meaningful mass participation are limited, the mass dispositions are correspondingly less relevant for explaining the state of that system or its output. In other words, where the elite are not structurally accountable to and therefore responsive to the masses, it matters more how and what the elite think and less how and what the masses think. Therefore, although we lack data on the mass culture in authoritarian systems, knowledge about the elite culture may prove more useful for analyzing such systems.

Political culture is a broad concept subsuming a number of more specific dimensions. The precise content of the concept is a matter of definition and varies somewhat from author to author. There is, however, a great deal of common content among the various stipulations of the concept, and the dimensions and variables listed here are reflective of that consensus.

Specifically, we are considering the following variables: attitudes toward authority; beliefs and ideologies; the distinction between an ideological and a pragmatic orientation; feelings of trust in fellow humans; an identification with common symbols; and feelings of affect or alienation toward the political system. Two major dimensions of political culture are attitudes and beliefs. The former refers to mental orientations toward some existing object including evaluative orientations; the latter consists of conceptions of the way things are (in the mind of the beholder). The two dimensions appear to be reciprocally related. Attitudes about whether people *ought* to have an equal impact on the policymaking process are based on perceptions about whether they *are* equal in political wisdom or judgmental capacities. Beliefs are perceptions about the nature of reality. They may or may not be true. However, the perceptions themselves are significant for explaining and predicting behavior. People do not act on "objective reality." Instead, they act on what they perceive objective reality to be.

Attitudes Toward Authority

The attitude toward authority is clearly relevant. Attitudes toward authority may be conveniently classified as submissive, deferential, or egalitarian. A submissive attitude is one of unquestioning, unqualified obedience to the occupants of

---

[2] For example, compare Robert Putnam, "Studying Elite Political Culture: The Case of Ideology," *American Political Science Review,* Vol. LXV, September 1971, pp. 651–681.

authority roles. A deferential attitude, on the other hand, combines an acceptance that the occupants of authority roles ought to make decisions for the social group with the qualification that such authority figures are responsible for the consequences of their decisions. Both submissive and deferential conception of authority roles assume that leaders are generally there because they are more fit to rule.

An egalitarian attitude toward authority, on the other hand, implies a belief that people are relatively equal in their capacity to decide what is best for them and for society. It may be thought of as a "who is he to presume to tell me what to do?" attitude. The ultimate logical consequence of an egalitarian attitude toward authority would be to render those in political authority to the function of a clerk carrying out the orders of the masses. The more egalitarian a social system's attitude toward authority, the more we may expect to find the decision-making discretion of its political authorities circumscribed by the necessity of securing formal approval of the masses. Institutionally, an egalitarian attitude may be manifested, for example, in the proliferation of sources of veto power over policy decisions and such populist mechanisms as frequent elections, referendums, and plebiscities or provisions for recall of public officials.

Paradoxically, bureaucracy, commonly identified as a hierarchical, organizational format, can also be a structure reflecting egalitarian dispositions. Because bureaucratization implies rational efficiency in the application of given tasks, it implies standardization and routinization of those tasks. Routinization and standardization lead to an elaborate, comprehensive system of impersonal rules applying equally to all occupants of the hierarchy of roles. This chimerical goal of perfect rationality has the effect of removing the discretionary power of occupants of authority roles and renders subordinates and superordinates (bosses) equal under the rules.[3] Thus, instead of some individuals being perceived as subordinate to other individuals in an unequal personal relationship, all individuals are perceived as equally subsumed under the organization.

One of the major issues arising in postindustrial societies involves possible alternative interpretations of the imperatives of the concept of equality for public policy. Equality can be taken to mean equality of opportunity, implying a "meritocracy." That is, status position is assigned on the basis of achievements or qualification demonstrated in competitive conditions as opposed to ascribed statuses (family, race, etc., for instance). Today, there is increasing sentiment among elements of the dispossessed sectors of society and among intellectuals to interpret equality as meaning that everyone is entitled to approximately the same level of well-being as a matter of right irrespective of what an individual earns or

---

[3]'The most comprehensive treatment of this argument is in Michel Crozier, *The Bureaucratic Phenomenon* (Chicago: University of Chicago Press, 1964), especially Chaps. 6 and 7. See also Crozier, *The Stalled Society* (New York: The Viking Press, 1973).

achieves. This could logically imply and accompany perceptions that no person can earn the right to possess political authority over another. The political manifestations of this tend to be the kind of populism described above. This issue will be discussed at some length in Chapter 4. For now, let it be noted that egalitarian attitudes toward authority logically threaten the legitimacy of any given stratification system.

Submissive, deferential, egalitarian—each of these attitudes toward authority has been said to characterize one or more of the nations under consideration. These characterizations are, for the most part, based on either impressions or nonsystematic, largely anecdotal data, but there is widespread agreement on these judgmental characteristics.

Egalitarian Nations

The view held by many Americans that egalitarian orientation is necessary for political democracy is clearly contradicted by the fact that mass egalitarian orientations are the exception rather than the rule among industrial democracies.[4] In fact, it may be suggested that an orientation combining a "healthy dose of authoritarianism" may be more functional for stable democracy than extreme egalitarianism. The reasoning is that a deferential orientation will allow the decision-making elite the discretion they require to govern effectively. In a situation where the elite are required to satisfy the day-to-day shifts in public opinion as a precondition to maintaining their authority, the stability of the government would be threatened. No elite can consistently satisfy a majority of citizens on all decisions and still develop a coherent program for processing the issues of that society.

The clearest example of a system in which an egalitarian attitude toward authority is manifested to the extent of a rejection of face-to-face authority relationships is France.[5] This rejection of authority (or individualism) was suggested in the previous chapter to be in large part a function of a history of struggle against a variety of nearly absolute authority centers (the *ancien regime,* the Napoleons, etc.).[6] This rejection of authority at the face-to-face level has thus been associated with a republican tradition. We suggest that there is a conflicting conception of authority present in the French political culture,[7] an authoritarian tradition manifested in the political format that may be called either Bonapartism

---

[4] Thomas Dye and Harmon Zeigler, *The Irony of Democracy* (Belmont, CA: Duxbury Press, 1972), Second Ed., pp. 20–21, 132–139.

[5] Stanley Hoffman, "Paradoxes of the French Community," Hoffman, et al., *In Search of France* (New York: Harper Torchbooks, 1965), pp. 8–9, and Crozier, *The Bureaucratic Phenomenon, op. cit.,* pp. 220–221.

[6] This is the theme of Alain, *Le Citoyen Contre Les Pouviers* (Paris: Editions du Sagitaires, 1925).

[7] "Conflicting ideals of authority" is the theme of Nicholas Wahl's essay in Samuel Beer and Adam Ulam, et al., *Patterns of Government* (New York: Random House, 1962), Second Ed., pp. 275–467.

or Gaullism and an egalitarian tradition manifested in political formats characterized by weak executives dominated by strong representative assemblies—specifically the Third and Fourth Republics. Paradoxically, however, the Bonapartist or Gaullist format also reflects this egalitarianism (paradoxically, Napoleon Bonaparte himself claimed to represent the revolution with its motto of liberty, equality, and fraternity).

This political format involves a mass (atomized and undifferentiated) society in which all individuals are "equal" under the remote and centralized leader. Such leadership becomes impersonal as opposed to the face-to-face authority relations that appear when leaders of smaller associations retain the discretion inherent in a leadership role. French society is characterized throughout by great centralization of discretionary authority. The smallest details are resolved from the upper echelons of the national bureaucracy in Paris. It is said, for example, that the minister of education can look at his watch and tell what verse is being recited at a given grade level at any school in the nation. Such a situation, of course, removes the local boards of education, not to mention school principals and teachers, from the role of an authority figure. The function of the teacher becomes one of administering decisions (tests, lessons, etc.) made by a remote official in Paris. In this way, a highly centralized authority structure can satisfy the expectations of extreme egalitarianism. The French have a tendency to view the instruments of the state as *les autres* ("the others") or "them" rather than "us." Accordingly, there has been a persisting French reverence for the individual versus the state and a general unwillingness to concede the state a role in the resolution of socioeconomic issues. Thus, unwillingness to subsume individual desires to the needs of the broader whole represented by the state impedes the acceptance of compromises necessary to the resolution of issues. Some observers of the French scene suggest that the foregoing tendencies have diminished considerably in the past 20 years.[8] Yet clearly, to the extent that we accept the proposition that a system is to a large extent a product of its past, an awareness of these cultural properties is essential for an understanding of modern France, and it is not likely that such deep-seated cultural properties have disappeared entirely.

An egalitarian attitude toward authority also has been said to characterize the Norwegian culture. This is reflected in the status of women, relations between the sexes ("reciprocal respect"), and parent-child relationships. Yet Eckstein reports what may be called a "functional deference." This refers to a deference to specialized roles within well-defined roles as with the asymmetric relations between a teacher and his or her students.[9] This seems to buttress our contention that an

---

[8] For example, Lowell Noonan, *France: The Politics of Continuity and Change* (New York: Holt, Rinehart and Winston, 1970), pp. 101–102.

[9] Harry Eckstein, *Division and Cohesion in Democracy: A Study of Norway* (Princeton: Princeton University Press, 1966), pp. 155 ff.

unmitigated egalitarian attitude is the exception among stable democracies and may be dysfunctional for such systems.

Deferential Nations

The country that has been widely recognized (until very recently, at least) as one of the most successful democracies in the world, Great Britain, is characterized by what Walter Bagehot, a great nineteenth-century analyst of the British system, referred to as a "deferential" orientation with respect to the responsibility of decision makers for the consequences of their decisions.[10] A deferential orientation assumes that some people are more "fit" to rule than others. This conception of an essentially hierarchical society has been challenged to some extent by the rise of the political Labour movement and the more or less egalitarian *Weltanschauung* ("world view") in the twentieth century. But this is a qualified statement because in many respects Labour has, passively at least, accepted important aspects of a hierarchically ordered society. For example, several Labour governments since the war failed to eliminate Britain's "eleven-plus" examination.

This exam is the foundation of an educational process that, instead of acting as a leveling agent as the American educational system is supposed to do, has clearly reinforced and perpetuated the existing stratification system and has impeded rather than facilitated social mobility. The English educational system consists of primary schools (public grade schools); public schools (paradoxically, expensive private boarding schools akin to such preperatory schools in the United States as Groton); grammar schools; comprehensive schools (modern secondary schools); and the higher education of the colleges and universities. After completing the primary schools at about the age of eleven, British pupils are subjected to a battery of tests of general ability. Those who pass may enter the state-supported grammar schools for a college-preparatory curriculum, an indispensible prerequisite to higher education. Only a quarter of these taking the test usually pass. Most of those who fail are relegated to comprehensive schools or some other vocational institution. They are in fact branded for life as social inferiors.

A traditional alternative to this state-supported system is the system of private boarding schools, the public schools. These schools have been the source of a significant part of Great Britain's political elite. A substantial majority of Britain's prime ministers are graduates of a few of the most prestigious of them—Eton, Harrow, etc.—as are a majority of the entrants to Sandhurst (Britain's West Point) and nearly half of the members in all modern sessions of the House of

---

[10] Walter Bagehot, *The English Constitution* (Garden City, New York: Doubleday Dolphin Books, n.d.), pp. 286-291. Bagehot's book is regarded as a classic on the topic. It is perhaps a testimony to the stability and conservatism of the British system that Bagehot's book, first published in 1867, remains relevant today.

Commons (the lower house of the national legislature). The entrance requirements of the more prestigious of these schools render a classic preparatory education almost mandatory. Such a "prep school" education is financially (and, on an informal basis, socially) restricted to the well-to-do. Moreover, the steepness of their tuition limits attendance at the public schools to offspring of well-to-do families.[11] About four percent of the population attends these schools, despite the fact that they are widely recognized as an important if not quite essential step to social and political power and prestige. Moreover, the public schools act as effective agents in imparting these hierarchical values to their pupils.[12]

The eleven-plus exams, being open to all students regardless of income or social position, may seem at first to be a more egalitarian institution than the public schools with regard to the opportunities for social mobility afforded by each institution. It is necessary to recall, however, that the capacity to learn the verbal, logical, and related skills tested by the exam is by and large acquired, whether by nature or nurture, from one's parents before reaching school age. Consequently, the offspring of unlettered working-class families tend to enter primary school several years behind the offspring of better-educated families. While it may be possible to overcome such a disadvantage in the long run, it is unlikely that one would do so by the age of eleven. The expectation that children of professional or well-educated parents are far more likely to pass the eleven-plus exams is borne out by the available data. Therefore, the practice of recruiting the political and social elite from among the university graduates, giving preference to graduates of prestigious public schools, inhibits social mobility. The high probability that members of the political and social elite will be from well-educated and/or well-to-do families serves to perpetuate and rigidify the existing class structure.

There is increasing opposition to the system from Labour (the term is used to refer both to the trade union movement and to the party unless otherwise stated). Under the Wilson Labour government, several comprehensive schools were established to admit graduates of primary schools irrespective of their performance on the eleven-plus exams. But these schools are multiplying slowly and still serve a small minority of the population. The Labour Party has let its intention be known to abolish the exams when it is in power. It is worth noting, however, that Labour did not abolish the system under the Wilson governments of 1964–1970. As late as the 1966 general election campaign, Butler and King reported that the issue of comprehensive schools (that is, the elimination of grammar schools with their selective admission policies) received only "intermittant discussion."[13] The

---

[11] Eric Nordlinger, *Working Class Tories* (Berkeley: University of California Press, 1967), pp. 29–30.

[12] Richard Rose, *Politics in England*, (Boston: Little Brown, 1964), p. 69.

[13] D. E. Butler and Anthony King, *The British General Election of 1966* (New York: Saint Martin's Press, 1966), p. 102. The faculty of Nuffield College, Oxford, has put together a readable and informative study of each British general election since 1945.

persistence of the system in the face of several Labour governments replete with that party's egalitarian ideological views may be viewed as one indicator of the British deep-seated acceptance of the hierarchical view of society. That view implies that some (generally a very few) are intrinsically more fit to fulfill the responsibilities of the sociopolitical elite than others (usually the great majority).[14]

Even if, as now seems likely, the eleven-plus exam is finally abolished, it is not likely that the English educational system will become a leveling force in the British society. In the first place, a large percentage of Britain's governing elite (the percent depends on how broadly that elite is defined) comes from the prestigious public schools rather than the state-supported grammar schools. Only Harold Wilson among twentieth-century prime ministers was not a graduate of one of these schools. A majority of modern Tory members of Parliament have been public school graduates. Further, these public schools, while criticized, seem destined to remain for the foreseeable future. The impact of the eventual replacement of academically selective grammar schools by comprehensive schools may be mitigated by the possibility of some unofficial "tracking" (segregating students into different programs according to measured intelligence) within the comprehensive school.

All in all, an acceptance of nonegalitarianism is deep-rooted in the British culture. This acceptance by the less privileged masses of the dominant values of the hierarchical British society—the control of that society by a relatively narrow, closed elite on the assumption that this elite is somehow more "fit to rule"—is manifested in the widespread phenomenon of working-class Tories. Clearly, a substantial portion of the British Conservative (or Tory) Party support must come from the working class, despite the fact that the party has stood for the perpetuation of the existing social stratification system.[15] After all, the privileged class, the Conservatives' natural constituency, is an increasingly small minority of the British population; yet, the Conservative Party has spent much more time in power than the Labour Party since the Labour Party's inception.

This phenomenon of working-class Toryism is made possible by the fact that the party has, especially since Disraeli, avowed a concern and responsibility for the industrial masses. This concern can probably be traced to the fact that the major opposition to the Conservatives from the early nineteenth century until several decades into the twentieth century was the middle-class-based Liberal Party, whose ideological view was free-enterprise individualism—survival of the fittest. This may be contrasted with the American right, which more closely cor-

---

[14] Nordlinger, *op. cit.* (p. 30) reports a survey in which a majority of the respondents agreed that the bulk of the British population was "a near moronic mass."

[15] In fact, about half the Tory vote is working class. About a third of the working class votes Tory. R. T. McKenzie and Allan Silver, "The Working Class Tory," Richard Rose, ed. *Studies in British Politics* (New York: St. Martin's Press, 1968). p. 24.

responds to British nineteenth-century liberalism. In the absence of an aristocracy, there never really was a conservative force in the United States in the British and Continental sense of that term. When Gladstone, the great nineteenth-century Liberal Party leader and sometime prime minister, enfranchised the middle classes, it was no longer politically feasible for the Conservatives to rely on the less numerous aristocracy and upper class. Accordingly, Disreali and the Conservatives extended the franchise to the working classes. Thus, the British Conservatives opposed and tried to differentiate themselves from the Liberal Party, whose social base paralleled the segment of society that in fact comprised the American right.

In any event, the British Conservatives have expressed responsibility for the welfare of the masses. The masses, in turn, expect the Conservatives to accept that responsibility. Therein lies the crucial distinction between British deference to authority and submission to authority, such as that putatively characteristic of, for example, Germany—at least through the period of the Second World War. The British grant their decision-making elite far more discretion in the function of government, far more centralization of authority, and far more insulation from the day-to-day currents of public opinion than would be acceptable to the more egalitarian Americans or to those segments of French society that dominated the Third and Fourth Republics. However, unlike the Germans, the British tend to hold their elite responsible for the consequences of this decision making on their welfare.

One indicator of a nonegalitarian (deferential or submissive) authority orientation in a system is the pervasiveness of the use of titles. A glance at the standard listing of the members of any given Parliament in Great Britain (or, for that matter, in the older Commonwealth) will reveal that most names are followed by a comma and sets of initials. These initials represent university degrees, membership in established honorific clubs and societies (Order of the Garter, Order of the British Empire), memberships in the Privy Council, which no longer functions as a body (see Chapter 5), their status as lawyers (QC for Queen's Council), etc. Similarly, Germans in public life tend to use all available titles, such as Herr (Mr.), Doktor (if one possesses that degree), Professor, Oberst (Colonel), etc. Americans and Norwegians, on the other hand, tend to play down the use of their titles. For example, George McGovern, the 1972 Democratic candidate for the American presidency, has a Ph.D, but he did not advertise himself as Dr. McGovern. Recall for comparison that the late German Chancellor was always called Dr. Adenauer.

It should be cautioned that a de facto submissive orientation may be combined with an egalitarian ideological view. In such a case, the foregoing indicators would probably not apply. The imposition of the essentially egalitarian Marxist ideological system on a Russian society with a deep-rooted authoritarian tradition had less of an impact on the actual orientations toward authority in that society than it did on the rhetoric regarding authority emanating from that system's elite.

The Dutch are also judged to exemplify a deferential attitude toward authority, according to Arend Lijphart.[16] In justification of this conclusion, Lijphart presents a variety of survey data using the aforementioned Almond and Verba data as a comparative base. For example, when asked to name the more admired personal quality from a number of fixed alternatives, 19 percent of the Dutch selected "respectful, doesn't overstep his place." This is more than any of the other four industrial countries presented for comparison. In Britain, the figure was nine percent; in West Germany, five percent; in Italy, ten percent; and in the United States, eleven percent.[17] Twenty-two percent of the Dutch named "ambitious," possibly indicating a respect for those who succeed rather than a resentment of them.[18] The figures for Great Britain, West Germany, Italy, and the United States were eleven, twelve, eight, and twelve percent, respectively.

As in the British case, Lijphart notes that this deference is related to a willingness to allow the government to govern free from day-to-day accountability for each decision. That is, the Dutch are said to be willing to grant their elite considerable insulation from the daily currents of public opinion.[19] This attitude is suggested to stem in part from the traditional dominance of the business-oriented middle class.[20] Accordingly, government should be able to "get the job done" and should not be harrassed by excessive input. The difficulty here is the imprecision of the threshold line where input reaches an excessive magnitude. It is also difficult to delineate clearly the point at which deference becomes submission with respect to the amount of discretion allowed an elite. Our definitional distinction between the two suggests that deferential types hold the elite accountable to the electorate for the consequences of their decisions, whereas submissive types do not. This is, of course, a conceptual definition that does not permit the elimination of borderline cases. Lijphart is clearly unsure of whether the Dutch deference might be more aptly named "docility"—that is, what we call submission.[21]

A deferential attitude also may be inferred with regard to Sweden. Hancock reports an absence of the distrust of authority commonly found in egalitarian settings.[22] But he also reports a high sense of citizen competence (the capacity of individuals to influence public policy) and liberalizing authority patterns in family

---

[16] Arend Lijphart, *The Politics of Accommodation: Pluralism and Democracy in the Netherlands* (Berkeley: University of California Press, 1968), pp. 102, 144–145, and *passim*.
[17] From a table in *ibid.*, p. 146.
[18] *Ibid.*
[19] *Ibid.*, p. 132.
[20] *Ibid.*, p. 123.
[21] *Ibid.*, p. 162.
[22] M. Donald Hancock, *Sweden: The Politics of Post Industrial Change* (Hinsdale, IL: The Dryden Press, 1972), p. 44.

relationships that would be inconsistent with an authoritarian or submissive orientation.

Authoritarian Submission

The Germany prior to the Second World War is widely believed to have epitomized on a collective level what is commonly understood as an "authoritarian personality."[23] That is, a number of attitudes, beliefs, and related orientations have been shown to occur together with sufficient regularity to be characterized as a syndrome. Chief among the traits that comprise the F scale (for fascism) in the classic authoritarian personality study (Adorno, et al.)[24] are an excessive concern for power relations, a high valuation of order, a strict adherence to middle-class morality, an intolerance of deviant behavior, a tendency to favor the mystic or irrational at the expense of science, and a greater respect for toughness than for compassion. The preoccupation with power relations is manifest in a norm of unquestioned obedience to those above and unmitigated domination of those below. It is sometimes referred to as "the bicyclist's orientation—above (the waist) you bend, below you kick."

To have a significant explanatory value, it should be shown that people in authoritarian regimes score significantly higher on measures of authoritarianism than in democratic regimes. Yet, Adorno, et al., used a strictly American sample. (This shows, incidentally, that even the most egalitarian countries are not without a significant number of authoritarians.) It is suggestive but far from conclusive that a limited sample of German factory workers in the 1950s produced a mean score on the F scale higher than the highest score in the American sample.[25]

Unquestioning obedience at all levels has clearly been a widespread norm in the German culture. Some suggest that concern for order is in part a compensation for the lack of order in German political history (discussed in Chapter 2) and is related to the norm of obedience. Clearly, adherence to the former norm would satisfy the latter norm. Adherence to these norms has been reflected in levels from

---

[23] There appears to be few systematic data to justify this widespread axiom. It is based on materials such as Eric Fromm's sweeping inferences from the writings of Adolf Hitler to the "sado-masochistic character" of the German lower middle class. Fromm, *Escape From Freedom* (New York: Avon Books, 1965), especially Chap. VI, or the loose generalizations of the popular layman psychoanalyst, Eric Erickson, *Childhood and Society* (New York: W. W. Norton, 1963), Second Ed.

[24] T. W. Adorno, et al., *The Authoritarian Personality* (New York: W. W. Norton, 1969). First published in 1950, this is a classic study influencing many subsequent attempts at personality typing from measured syndromes of attitudes or traits. See F Scale at pp. 225–227. It correlates significantly with measures of antisemitism, ethnocentrism (general prejudice), and political and economic conservatism. The F-scale has been criticized as confusing general authoritarianism with right-wing fascism.

[25] T. S. Cohn and H. Carsch, "Administration of the F Scale to a Sample of Germans," *Journal of Abnormal and Social Psychology*, Vol. 49, 1954, p. 471.

family relationships (not only in parent-child relations—women's liberation would not have found prewar Germany a very receptive and hospitable environment), teacher-pupil relations, etc., to orientations toward the political institutions. Harry Eckstein points out the difficulty in shifting orientations from the unquestioned obedience taught and expected at all levels of the social structure to the concept that one ought to hold one's political superiors accountable at the level of the political system.[26] For example, this expected shift in role orientations is suggested to have induced such psychological "strain" as to have made the egalitarian institutional structure of Weimar Germany imposed on an authoritarian German society untenable.

This attitude toward authority may be somewhat less pronounced in the postwar era, especially among some of the university students. Impressions on this vary. A variety of data indirectly suggest, however, that an authoritarian orientation has not disappeared. For example, Lewis Edinger reports 1959 survey data inquiring into perceptions of the obligation of citizenship.[27] Only four percent of the Germans surveyed mentioned understanding public affairs. Comparative data from the Almond and Verba survey of five nations support that study's conclusion that Germany is characterized by a passive or subject-oriented culture.[28] This means that Germans tend not to feel that it is a citizen's role to try to influence the political process. These data seem to support the conclusion that Germans maintain a perception of a relatively rigid distinction between leader and follower roles in the political arena. In other words, most Germans would apparently still accept the proposition that it is the role of the authoritative elite to govern and the principal duty of the mass of citizens to obey. Verba reports a 1957 survey in which 25 percent of the respondents said the *most* important trait to teach youngsters was obedience.[29] (It would be interesting to have comparative data from nations such as Great Britain and the United States; we find this figure high.) What is not entirely clear is whether there is a tendency since the Second World War for this norm of obedience to become increasingly contingent on satisfactory performance (or output) of the political system. If this tendency is actually occurring, the German attitude toward authority, in our terminology, would be said to be moving from one of submission to one of deference. Karl Deutsch presented a variety of data suggesting that the affect or attachment of most Germans to the output or

---

[26] Harry Eckstein, "A Theory of Stable Democracy," printed as an appendix to his *Division of Cohesion in Democracy: A Study of Norway, op. cit.*, pp. 225–287 at 248 and 254–258.

[27] Lewis Edinger, *Politics in Germany* (Boston: Little Brown, 1968), p. 106.

[28] Gabriel Almond and Sidney Verba, *The Civic Culture* (Boston: Little Brown, 1965), p. 312 and *passim*.

[29] Sidney Verba, "Germany: The Remaking of Political Culture," in Lucian Pye and Sidney Verba, eds., *Political Culture and Political Development* (Princeton: Princeton University Press, 1965), pp. 130–170 at p. 155.

efficiency of the system, especially the so-called economic miracle (German economic resurgence after the Second World War), is more important than the attachment to the democratic political format per se.[30] He also found a disturbing amount of latent empathy for the Hitler period. Nearly half of the Germans surveyed in 1955 agreed Hitler would have been one of Germany's greatest statesmen without the war. In 1956, nearly half of the respondents thought National Socialism (Nazism) a "good idea," and 40 percent in 1951 thought Germany was best off in the 1933–1939 Hitler era.[31] Evidently, the Germans accept or approve of their political system, not because it is democratic, but because it has provided economic prosperity and national self-respect. The common-sense position that Germans accept political authority no matter what may have given way to a position that German acceptance of authority is contingent on its performance.

Verba cites a variety of data indicating a liberalization of authority relations within Germany society.[32] Again, conventional wisdom tells us that the typical German husband and father totally dominated his wife and children.[33] Some scholars, however, suggest that this characterization may be overdrawn.[34] As has been pointed out, egalitarianism is the exception rather than the rule throughout Europe, and some have questioned whether German family authority patterns are more authoritarian than those in a number of other societies. We should remember that an authoritarian orientation in the sense used by Adorno and his associates or even in the sense of a submissive orientation is not identical to a deferential orientation. Further, the existence of some measure of authoritarianism in nations that did not produce a Hitler does not disprove the conjecture that an authoritarian culture in Germany is related to that country's apparently ready acceptance of dictatorial political institutions. It is not being claimed that such authority patterns are in themselves a sufficient cause of fascism or some other police-state format, only that such authority patterns may be one of many necessary preconditions of such a political format. Even Fromm, to whom

---

[30] Karl Deutsch, "The German Federal Republic," in Roy Macridis and Robert Ward, eds., *Modern Political Systems: Europe,* (Englewood Cliffs: Prentice Hall, 1968), Second Ed. pp. 351–352.

[31] *Ibid.,* p. 324.

[32] Verba, "Germany: The Remaking of Political Culture," *op. cit.,* pp. 154–158.

[33] For example, Bertram Schaffner, *Fatherland: A Study of Authoritarianism in the German Family* (New York: Columbia University Press, 1948) and David Arbahmsen *Men, Mind and Power* (New York: Columbia University Press, 1945), pp. 27–28 and *passim.*

[34] See especially Robert Lowie, *Toward Understanding Germany* (Chicago: University of Chicago Press, 1957), Chap. XIII. Lowie's "evidence" may be characterized as selected illustrations of his point. Lowie examined "available" biographical and autobiographical accounts of German families. But there is no reason to assume that this availability sample is representative of all German families.

apparently few assertions are too sweeping, qualifies the impact of psychological factors on the rise of Nazism to this extent.[35]

In any event, the paternal dominance that once characterized the German family seems to have given way to partnership marriages. It is probable that the state-centered experience of the Nazi period had an undermining impact on the hierarchical structure of the German family. Verba also reports the rigid authoritarian atmosphere of the school system of the prewar period has been ameliorated by increasing classroom discussions. In sum, it appears reasonable to assume that Germany has been moving away from the putatively submissive attitude of the prewar period. *Deferential* may be a more accurate term to characterize present German attitude toward authority. If Eckstein's congruence theory, discussed above, is to be taken seriously, the German Federal Republic's institutional format ought to stand a far better chance for survival than did the egalitarian format of the Weimar constitution imposed upon a highly authoritarian society.

The Italian attitude toward authority must be inferred from a variety of other data. Italian respondents in the Almond and Verba[36] study, like their German counterparts, felt much less of an obligation to participate in local politics than did British or American respondents. They also felt less competent to influence the political process. This indicates that Italians are not egalitarian, but neither are they deferential. They show a comparatively low level of trust in politics and politicians and a low sense of obligation to keep informed about politics. A person who does not consider it his duty to keep informed is not likely to be concerned with the accountability of the government. Even the Germans were significantly higher in a sense of duty to keep informed if not to participate (what Almond and Verba call subject competence, as opposed to citizen competence). This may be interpreted to support our conclusion that Germany is moving from a submissive toward a deferential orientation. Italy may be the most submissive of the industrial democracies. In a sense, this accords with Edward Banfield's characterization of southern Italians, based on a year-long stay in a southern Italian village, as "amoral familists."[37] Banfield's term refers to a parochialism whereby the horizons of these Italians are limited to their extended families and a cynical and pessimistic alientation from the political sector based on an assumption of pervasive corruption. Thus, while it seems that the Italians are neither egalitarian nor

---

[35] Fromm, *op. cit.*, p. 242. He says, "Those psychological conditions were not the 'cause' of Nazism. They constituted the human base without which it could not have developed." In other words, the "sadomasochistic character" of the German lower middle class, etc., was not a sufficient precondition for the development of Nazism but it was a necessary precondition.

[36] Almond and Verba, *op. cit.*, Chaps. V, VI, VII.

[37] Edward Banfield, *The Moral Basis of a Backward Society* (New York: The Free Press, 1958), especially Chap. 5.

deferential, alienation (roughly, a rejection of the political system, a lack of a sense of belonging to it and a lack of a perception of a stake in its survival) is not quite what the idea of submission to authority connotes. Banfield does report that Italians favor a strong government that "will maintain order with a strong hand." This sense of a need for order and authority is one major property of authoritarianism as we have conceived it. Impressionistic reports of Weimar Germany also indicate an alienation from that regime and a cynicism about government. Perhaps the line between alienation and submission is a weak one in that alienation from the regime at hand can easily translate itself into approval of an authoritarian political solution to the perceived inadequacies of the regime.

Because survey research is the preferred method for ascertaining the attitudes under consideration, there is an obvious difficulty in dealing with authoritarian systems such as the Soviet Union. Unable to use direct interviews of citizens of such countries, social scientists must rely more on indirect sources.

There is one significant exception to the unavailability of surveys. Although its limitations are apparent, it is worthy of consideration as a direct indication of some aspects of personality. Two separate but related projects were undertaken to examine in some depth the attitudes of a number of *former* Soviet citizens who left the Soviet Union during or after the Second World War and chose not to return.[38] The value of these studies is that they go beyond opinions about the regime they fled and include clinical and life-history examinations of basic personality. In fact, however, the disaffection of the respondents with the Stalin regime made some of their replies quite interesting.

While the results of these surveys certainly cannot be considered definitive, they provide some useful indications concerning basic attitudes toward authority. Both studies point to a need for dependence, protection, and security. Authority figures are expected to give orders, demand obedience, be stern, institute and enforce sanctions, and use persuasion, coercion, and surveillance to ensure compliance. An authority that behaves in this manner is good and is entitled to be respected and obeyed. The only condition is that such authority be concerned and interested rather than excessive and arbitrary. In this respect, Henry Dicks observed that many of those interviewed spoke of authority in terms of a good but strict father.

How might this attitude of obedience to such "good" authority relate to the practical political situation? Early in the Khruschev period it was suggested that the leadership might gain more popular support for authoritarian (or even totali-

[38] One of the two was part of the Harvard Project on the Soviet Social System and is explained in detail in Raymond Bauer, Alex Inkeles, and Clyde Kluckhohn, *How the Soviet System Works* (Cambridge: Harvard University Press, 1956). The specific references in this chapter are to Alex Inkeles, *Social Change in Soviet Russia* (New York: Simon and Schuster, 1968). The other study, done by a British psychologist, is Henry V. Dicks, "Observations on Contemporary Russian Behavior," *Human Relations,* Vol. V, No. 2, 1952, pp. 111–175.

tarian) policies and institutions by taking care to apply such policies in a manner consistent with this characteristic of the Russian personality.[39] That is, in contrast to the Stalin practices, it would have to be less harsh and arbitrary and more interested in the people. It is interesting in this respect that one of the ways in which Allen Kassof distinguished between the Stalin and Khrushchev regimes was that the latter lacked the "gross irrationality" of the former.[40] In sum, if this assessment of the Russian attitude is accurate, it might not be unreasonable to expect substantial support for an authoritarian system armed with an ideology expressing concern for the people, relying more on socialization and persuasion than coercion, and meeting more of the material needs of the public. The Russian attitude must be considered submissive instead of deferential because there is no thought of rendering decision makers structurally accountable.

The more or less dependent and submissive attitudes indicated in these limited survey studies seem to be consistent with certain elements (some of which were discussed in the preceding chapter) of Russian social and political history. The autocratic and despotic nature of Russian rulers is well known, and many would agree with John Armstrong that on the whole Russia has probably had less experience with limited government and representative institutions than any other European country.[41] It is interesting to note in this connection one of the observations from the surveys mentioned above. Even though the individuals being interviewed had fled the Soviet Union and were opposed to the Stalin regime, they expressed little concern for the need to have formally and precisely defined rights, procedures, and limitations with respect to governmental authorities.

With very few exceptions, the experience of Russia was one of submission to long dynasties such as the House of Rurik (ninth to sixteenth centuries) and the Romanovs (1613–1917) or to foreign invaders such as the Mongols in the period from the thirteenth to fifteenth centuries. The claim of the tsars was that they were all-wise, all-powerful, and ruling by divine right. They were proud autocrats who from 1721 to 1917 bore the title of "Emperor and Autocrat of all the Russias." The position of such rulers was strengthened greatly by the stand of the Russian Orthodox church, which, consistent with its Byzantine origins, taught obedience to the state. It has even been asserted that this "Caesaropapism," a system in which the emperor was head of both church and state, created in Russia a culture distinct from that of Western Europe.[42]

In addition to the religious factor, others relative to this attitude of dependence

---

[39] Inkeles, *op. cit.*, p. 127.

[40] Allen Kassof, "The Administered Society: Totalitarianism Without Terror," *World Politics*, Vol. XVI, July 1964, p. 559.

[41] John Armstrong, *Ideology Politics and Government in the Soviet Union* (New York: Praeger Publishers, 1974), Third Ed., p. 7.

[42] *Ibid.*

and submission might include the autocratic nature of the traditional patriarchal family pattern and the lack of a politically conscious middle class or peasantry. The significance of the latter is that the relatively small number of activist reformers and dissidents could not find substantial support in these groups. A contemporary dissenter, Andrei Amalrik, speaks of the "paradox of the middle class." He is referring to a situation in which the base majority of that class is so mediocre and passive that it will not support the democratic movement emerging in the Soviet Union. Paradoxically, the middle class is the very group that needs and is capable of understanding the principles embodied in that reform attempt.[43]

To this point, we have been speaking primarily of traditional Russian history and attitudes. The present political culture of the Soviet Union is often described in terms such as *elitist* and *ideological*.[44] It is difficult to separate the two since, as stated earlier, the elite is the official interpreter of the ideology. The question of where the ideology fits in this matter of attitude toward authority is much too large to be answered here.[45] However, a few observations can be made in terms of the egalitarian-submissive classification.

Perhaps it should be pointed out initially that the ideology itself has both authoritarian and egalitarian features. The latter involves such concepts as the mass participation of the people in the political process by means of a system of councils called soviets, the eventual withering away of the state, and the creation of a classless society in which each contributes on the basis of ability and receives on the basis of need. It would appear, however, that since the ascension of the Bolsheviks to power in the Soviet Union these concepts are more a matter of theory and justification than of practice.

The authoritarian aspects of the ideology as it has developed are many, and they bring us back to the definition of ideology as a closed system. Marxism-Leninism claims scientific understanding of certain fundamental laws of social and historical development and of the institutions and processes necessary to implement those laws. The next step involves the question of the relationship of the state and the individual. The individual is called on to subordinate himself to society and the state because only by so doing can both he and society realize their full potential. This is done not to strengthen the state for its own sake, but because state and society are the means being used by the elite to work toward an eventual ideal end.

Through this kind of pseudoscientific version of authoritarian theory, the elite justify both their own existence and their right to the obedience and support of the

---

[43] Andrei Amalrik, *Will the Soviet Union Survive Until 1984?* (New York: Harper & Row, 1970), p. 21.

[44] See, for example, Frederick Barghoorn, *Politics in the USSR* (Boston: Little Brown, 1972), Second Ed., p. 20ff.

[45] A pioneering and major work addressed to this issue is Barrington Moore, *Soviet Politics—The Dilemma of Power* (Cambridge: Harvard University Press, 1950).

people. Accordingly, since the Communist Party is the source of "truth," it is given a very explicit leadership role. The statutes of the Communist Party describe it as "the highest form of sociopolitical organization" and "the leading and guiding force of Soviet society" which directs the society and imparts "an organized, planned, and scientifically based character" to its efforts. Even more significant is the famous Article 126 of the Constitution of the Soviet Union that states that the Communist Party is "the vanguard of the working people" and "the leading core of all organizations of the working people, both government and nongovernment."

Thus, Russian attitudes toward authority seem to involve such factors as an autocratic pattern of government, a submissive church that in turn taught obedience to authority, an autocratic family pattern, an apparent willingness to submit to authoritarian leaders and policies if they seemed paternalistic and not arbitrary, and an ideology that claimed the right to lead the society in the implementation of the laws of social development.

What conclusions can be drawn from the foregoing discussion of orientations toward authority? It may be that a nonconclusion is called for in that no particular conception of authority is a necessary precondition of stable democracy. It is clearly arguable in the light of the American experience that an egalitarian orientation can support stable democracy. Norway also appears to be a stable egalitarian system. Deferential attitudes are clearly present in several of the most stable democracies (Britain, the Netherlands, and perhaps the Federal Republic of Germany). In sum, it is not clear whether any dominant conception of authority is incompatible with stable democracy, perhaps not even authoritarian submission. Impressions are indefinite as to whether Germany and the Netherlands are deferential or submissive. On a logical level, it would seem that extreme authoritarianism would be incapable of supporting stable democracy; however, it is difficult to find such authoritarian systems in the industrial world today. (This conclusion could be derived from Eckstein's congruence theory.) To the extent that alienation constitutes a distinct orientation toward authority, it has been associated with unstable, ineffective, and nonresponsive politics. Italy is the only relatively clear example of this orientation today, and one case does not constitute empirical justification of a proposition. It does seem fair to say that a deferential orientation is the only one in our typology that is invariably associated with stability, effectiveness, and responsiveness in our universe of nations. Thus, based on this and other logical considerations, we very tentatively suggest that, *other things being equal,* a deferential orientation toward authority generates the highest probability for political stability, effectiveness, and responsiveness.

Political Values

Values are a critical component of a political culture in two respects: the content of dominant values and the extent to which values are shared. Clearly, a lack of widely shared basic values could adversely affect the unity and coherence of a society. For example, it has been said that the French Canadian subculture does not significantly share with the others in Canada "a great deal of concern for much less understanding of civil liberties."[46] This absence of shared values is often buttressed by a lack of shared symbols representing such values or even an entire *Weltanschauung*. The importance of the *Fleur-de-Lis* to French Canada in comparison to the importance of the Union Jack and the British monarch to non-French Canada, the importance of the French Revolution of 1789 to secular, left-oriented France (an attachment not shared by conservative French Catholics), and the importance of "The Internationale" (the emotional theme song of the Communist International) to German Social Democrats between the World Wars all exemplify a lack of shared symbols connoting a lack of shared basic values within these respective nations. Absence of widely shared basic values should be expected to exacerbate the isolation of the subculture. Clearly, events, issues, and other phenomena can assume a symbolic (or emotive) content and meaning that far exceed their "objective" significance.

One of the more significant value issues with respect to content may be conveniently simplified and dichotomized into a distinction between the individual and the system. For example, Hegelian philosophy, which was highly influential in Germany prior to the Second World War (and probably reflective of deep-seated cultural properties) held that the value of individuals was a function of their role in the state.[47] Therefore, *raison d'état* (meaning roughly the well-being of the nation can justify about anything) should take precedence over the well-being of individuals who occupy the state. An understanding of this widely shared value should contribute to an understanding of prewar German politics. Note that here we are talking about the content of a value rather than its pervasiveness.

On the other hand, the value of the individual is widespread in Anglo-American culture. Thus, one can think of polar contrasts between the assumption that the state or system exists to serve the individuals who comprise it and the assumption that individuals exist to serve the state. This latter position often becomes confused with an assumption that the welfare of individuals is in the long run identical to the welfare of the system. This position also tends to reflect the ontological position that the state (or system) is an organic entity possessing a reality above and beyond the individuals that comprise it.

Beliefs and Ideologies

Beliefs frequently occur in a systemic relationship to one another such that the knowledge of one belief in an individual or group of individuals would provide a

---

[46] A. M. Lower, F. R. Scot, et al., *Evolving Canadian Federalism* (Durham: Duke University Press, 1950), p. 44.

[47] See Chapter 2 of this book for a more extended discussion of Hegel.

basis for inferring or predicting the content of other beliefs in the same individual or individuals. Some scholars refer to any belief system (a set of more or less logically related beliefs) as an ideology. In this sense, every individual and every nation possesses ideologies. Ideology is also used in a more narrow sense to refer to belief systems that are closed and comprehensive. A closed belief system is one that is not responsive to new facts generated external to it. It cannot be changed by new data.[48] A comprehensive belief system is one that generates the answer to all questions about the nature of humans, the cosmos, and human history.

Well-known examples of ideologies in the Western world are classic Marxism and orthodox Catholicism. Because they are not responsive to external data, changes in both thought systems can come only from pronouncements by authoritative sources of correct or official interpretation. For example, the official position for Roman Catholics has come from the Vatican. Of course, not all ideologies can claim one unified and official interpretation. For a number of years after the Russian Revolution, Moscow was the center for pronouncements on the ideology known as Marxism-Leninism. Since the early 1960s, however, the term *polycentrism* has been used to convey the idea that there are now a number of ideological centers of communism. Other ideologies may also have competing sources, and some (such as classic liberalism) may have no accepted source of truth. The point remains that a closed thought system, by definition, can only be changed internally by some authoritative source rather than by autonomously defined facts.

Clearly, every person and every culture adheres to principles to some extent. Individuals and systems do differ, however, in the extent to which they use such a closed, comprehensive belief system (hereafter simply called an ideology) as a criterion for what they perceive, how they interpret what they perceive, and the policy choices they make. Ideologies are simply more salient in some political systems than in others. An ideology can be used as a perceptual screen, causing adherents of the ideology not to perceive anything inconsistent with the ideology. Alternatively, the ideology can cause a reinterpretation of data to bring them into consistency with the ideology. Psychological theories of "cognitive dissonance" or "congruence" posit that individuals seek consistency in their perceptions, mental orientations, and dispositions.[49] Thus, individuals can be expected to bring their perceptions and attitudes into line with preexisting ideologies. To the extent that

---

[48] See Leon Festinger, W. H. Riecken, and S. Schacter, *When Prophecy Fails* (Minneapolis: University of Minnesota Press, 1956). This is a study of a group whose reason for being involved a prediction of the end of the world on a certain date. The rationalizations of the true believers' closed-mindedness are discussed.

[49] Probably the most widely cited statement of this is Leon Festinger, *A Theory of Cognitive Dissonance* (Stanford: Stanford University Press, 1953). This presentation is not methodologically rigorous, however. Compare Kenneth Eckardt and Gerry Hendershot, "Dissonance, Congruence and the Perception of Public Opinion," *American Journal of Sociology*, Vol. 73, No. 2, September 1967, pp. 226–234, and Robert B. Zajonc, "Balance, Congruity and Dissonance," *Public Opinion Quarterly*, Vol. 24, No. 2, Summer 1960, pp. 280–296.

one can ascribe the properties of individuals to systems, cultures can be expected to do the same.

The consequences of an ideological orientation are dysfunctional for the criteria of political success discussed in Chapter 1. An ideological orientation would distract a system from processing or responding to the "real" issues—that is, specific demands and dissatisfactions actually existing in the society and the actual conditions that cause them. An ideologically oriented system may concern itself with processing issues generated by the ideology rather than issues generated by current socioeconomic realities, or the ideology will affect the perception of these realities. A discussion of the relative merits of orthodox Marxism, Maoism, or social democracy (Bernstein's "revisionism") in place of such "pragmatic" issues as unemployment, inflation, etc., would illustrate such a distraction.

An ideology can also be dysfunctional by perpetuating issues generated by past problems. For example, the anticlerical aspects of French socialism stem from the Catholic church's position in support of the antirevolutionary forces at the time of the revolution of 1789. It may be argued that much of the rigid anticlericalism in Western European politics is based on a perception of the political role of the church that no longer pertains. Yet, to the extent that such atavistic issues are perpetrated, they cumulate with other issues, thereby heightening the intensity of political conflict. Another dysfunctional aspect of an ideological orientation lies in its closed nature. Policy choices, perceptions, and interpretations filtered through a closed belief system will by definition be less responsive to changes in the environment (the economic and social setting in which a political system operates). As mentioned in the preceding chapter, a widely accepted and plausible proposition holds that one necessary condition of political success is the capacity of a system to adapt to inevitable changes in that system's environment.[50]

A third dysfunctional aspect of ideologism for a responsive capacity of government is that ideologies in the sense used here tend to be conceived as bodies of final absolute truth rather than as statements of one's own interests or even as perceptions of the national interest. In a nonauthoritarian political setting, issues are resolved by compromise—meeting the opposition partway. There is, however, no logical middle ground between competing sets of absolute truths. Moreover, it is not logical to compromise with evil, falsehood, or error—only with different interests. Thus, the ideologically oriented logically reject the opposition as not legitimate because they view the opposition as proposing error or evil rather than a different set of interests or a different perspective. This might logically be expected to result in greater intensity in the level of partisanship. To put it more colloquially, ideologism should logically be expected to encourage a more intense dislike of the opposition. This would render compromise more difficult.[51]

---

[50] This is expounded most cogently by "systems theorists" such as David Easton. See his *A System Analysis of Political Life* (New York: John Wiley & Sons, 1965).

The direct opposite of an ideological orientation is a pragmatic orientation. An orientation will be characterized as pragmatic to the extent that an ideology is not used as a perceptual screen or as a criterion for interpretations or policy choices. Thus, political choices are judged by the pragmatist in terms of their observable consequences instead of in terms of their consistency with principles or a belief system.

Dichtomizing between ideologism and pragmatism is, of course, an oversimplification. These clearly constitute polar ends of a continuum, and actual systems are neither ideological nor pragmatic, but are combinations of ideological and pragmatic orientations. To the extent that its decisions are based on ideological principles, we say that a system's decision-making style is one of ideologism. Pure ideologism would constitute a condition of being totally oblivious to reality; obviously, no system could survive that for long. Pure pragmatism would involve a total absence of principle. The inconsistency and lack of predictability of such a position would render it untenable. Thus, this discussion is not intended to be a rejection of principle in policymaking. Obviously, some consistency and coherence in policymaking are widely regarded as desirable. Thus, both ideology and pragmatism are dysfunctional in their pure form.

Further complicating the dichotomy between ideology and pragmatism would be a situation in which policy choices are made largely on pragmatic grounds but justified in terms of widely accepted ideology. The Soviet Union may be coming around to this position.

The reasons why nations differ in the degree to which an ideological or pragmatic orientation predominates are primarily historical. When a group that has acquired consciousness as a group is excluded from participation in the political process, that group will tend to frame its demands in ideological terms.[52] These groups, lacking power, cannot be responsible for the consequences of their positions, and they are under no compulsion to moderate their positions in the face of competing demands and practical realities. (Responsibility implies the capacity to make choices and to be held to account for the consequences of such choices.) We will see in the chapter on parties, for example, that socialist and social democratic parties almost invariably play down their Marxist rhetoric and take on a distinctly bourgeois orientation when faced with the responsibility of governing their respective nations. The Social Democratic Party of the Federal Republic of Germany and the Australian Labour Party constitute classic examples of this doctrinal move

---

[52] This discussion of ideologism and pragmatism is indebted to the formulation and discussion of these variables in Herbert Spiro, *Government by Constitution* (New York: Random House, 1959), pp. 180–181, 188–189, and Chap. 14.

---

[51] Putnam, *op. cit.* (p. 672) finds that the conventional expectation that ideologues are more intolerant than pragmatic types is false. Putnam's findings, of course, depend on the validity of his "Ideological Style Index," the instrument he uses to identify ideologues.

toward the center under the pressure of the exigencies of governing a nation in crisis periods.

Ideologies, being by nature abstract simplifications of reality, do not offer workable solutions to actual complex problems. Being pure and absolutist, ideologies are not very useful in reconciling the competing claims and interests that must be accounted for in the actual process of governing. While some evidence exists that parties in a position of responsibility succumb to the pressure to be less ideological, we cannot assume that all such parties will behave pragmatically. The question of the extent to which a given government makes policy emphasizing an ideological orientation would be an open question subject to inquiry.

Patterns of Ideologism or Pragmatism

Conventional wisdom and logical reasons (discussed above) tell us that a pragmatic orientation is supportive of political values of stability, effectiveness, and responsiveness, while an ideological orientation is dysfunctional for them. That conventional wisdom appears to have been derived from analyses of the "major" industrial democracies. The United States, Great Britain, and the Scandinavian democracies—accepted paragons of those political virtues—are, as we will show, also generally characterized by a pragmatic orientation. Germany, Italy, and France combine a history of political difficulties with an identification of ideologism. It remains to be seen if this axiomatic relationship between political virtues and a pragmatic culture applies equally well to the smaller democracies.

The British culture is known for its pragmatism. James Cristoph suggests that the British manifest an "ideology of pragmatism."[53] In other words, the British concern is with the consequences of institutions or actions rather than their consistency with some principle. Cristoph suggests that the British, very conscious and proud of this trait, have raised it to the level of a national cult. This trait can be seen in the evolutionary development of British institutions discussed in the preceding chapter. It will be recalled that the development of the institution of the prime minister was generated in response to a specific need, the need to govern the country when the first Hanoverian monarchs were uninterested in assuming that responsibility. A subsequent chapter will elaborate on how the structure of the British decision-making process is permeated with processes whose justifications lie not in any discernible logic or principle, but solely in the perception that thus far they have worked.

One notable manifestation of the British pragmatic orientation is the English common law system. The Scottish system differs from the English in that the Scots

[53] James Cristoph, "Consensus and Cleavage in British Political Ideology," *American Political Science Review*, Vol. LIX, No. 3, September 1965, p. 631.

combine some elements of civil law orientation with some elements of common law. It is well to keep in mind throughout this book that Scotland and Wales are in a number of respects culturally distinct from England, although the three areas combine with Northern Ireland to form one political sovereignty—the United Kingdom. The other great legal system, which prevails on the European Continent, is civil (or Roman) in which rules are formulated in advance of disputes supposedly according to such criteria as justice and logical consistency. The resolution of specific disputes must be in accord with the codified rules and the principles they embody. In common law, on the other hand, principles have been derived more or less inductively from the resolution of specific and actual disputes.[54] Thus, the outcomes of previous cases (called precedents) take on legal significance. Subsequent cases are supposed to be decided by delineating the deciding principle or turning point in the previous cases and following it. The initial decisions are supposed to be decided on the basis of the customs of the community. The pragmatic nature of the common law system can best be understood by a superficial glance at its evolutionary development.

In the days of the first Plantagenet ruler Henry II, who ruled in the second half of the twelfth century, the island known today as Great Britain had still not completed the transition from a collection of feudal principalities to a sovereign nation. Henry's task was therefore to curb baronial autonomy and extend the legitimacy of his sovereignty—a state of affairs known in English jurisprudence as "the king's peace." Henry attempted to do this by replacing the "multitude of manorial courts where local magistrates dispensed justice whose custom and character varied with the customs and temper of the neighborhood" with "a system of royal courts which would administer a law *common* to all England . . ."[55] (italics supplied)—hence the term *common law*. The strategy of extending the legitimate jurisdiction of the crown (an analytic concept refering to the locus of British sovereignty) without directly confronting the stronghold of local customs was to have the king's magistrates resolve disputes by the criteria of the local custom. These decisions—whether logical, just, or true—were clearly the most viable or enforceable. Given the numerous disputes that arose under the complex reciprocal rights and obligations of feudalism, the services of the king's magistrates as neutral arbitrators were welcomed by the participants of such disputes. Th norm of deciding in accordance with local customs enhanced the legitimacy of royal adjudication and gave the magistrates a criterion for decisions beyond their personal concep-

---

[54] Benjamin Cardozo, *The Nature of the Judicial Process* (New Haven: Yale University Press, 1921), p. 23. Cardozo's book is a classic exposition on the spirit of the common law. The great Supreme Court justice and common law scholar Oliver Wendell Holmes characterized the process in these oft-quoted words: ". . . the life of the law has not been logic; it has been experience" (quoted from *ibid.*, p. 33). Compare this quote to Disraeli's characterization of the British political process in note 57.
[55] Winston Churchill, *The Birth of Britain* (New York: Dodd Mead, 1956), p. 216.

tions of justice. Henry's resurrection of the jury system further enhanced the local legitimacy of the common law. The role of precedent was a device that served two very pragmatic purposes: administrative convenience and consistency. Precedent, however, is not to be considered as rigid. The principles thus derived are only applicable to the extent that the context of the disputes remains similar to the context of the relevant preceding disputes.

The spirit of the common law embodies a recognition that its generalizations inductively derived can apply only approximately to particular cases. There remains considerable discretion in deciding which, if any, precedents apply to a particular set of circumstances. In this way, the common law remains flexible and adaptable. Common law embodies a recognition that rules of law can only reflect and legitimate existing norms and patterns of behavior; rules of law cannot mold behavior.

Common law procedures are further more reflective of a pragmatic orientation than Roman law procedures. Disputes in common law are resolved by adversary jurisprudence. That is, the parties to the dispute, through their chosen representatives (their lawyers), are each responsible for presenting their respective cases in the best possible light. The judge, acting as a neutral arbitrator, adds nothing to either case, raising no neglected or potential points of law and no questions regarding the evidence. In contrast, the judge in a Continental or Roman (civil) law system conducts the inquiry seeking truth and justice.[56] Thus, the emphasis in common law proceedings is on the most workable resolution of dispute, while Roman law proceedings are designed more to discover the "truth" and to impose certain standards of justice.

Thus, as Disraeli said, "Britain is ruled not by logic but by Parliament."[57] Cristoph raises some questions as to whether it can continue to be assumed that pragmatism is still the unqualified formula for political success. Cristoph suggests that pragmatism "has shrunk to cautious, narrow tinkering" that "has unfitted the country for the tasks of survival in a rapidly changing world."[58] Pragmatism carried to its logical conclusion would preclude consideration of long-term values or values not subject to compromise. A totally pragmatic system would lack fundamental properties since anything could be compromised away. Further pragmatism, insofar as it connotes the antithesis of principle, leads to a lack of coherence, consistency, and hence predictability.[59] Despite Cristoph's characterization of Britain's pragmatism, it does not appear that pragmatism has been car-

---

[56] Of course, judges and lawyers in Anglo-American jurisdictions do not always live up to these common law imperatives. The active role of Judge Sirica in America's Watergate inquiry is a case in point.
[57] Quoted in Cristoph, *op. cit.*, p. 637.
[58] *Ibid.*, pp. 640 and 641.
[59] Spiro, *op. cit.* p. 189.

ried that far. A subsequent chapter will suggest, for example, that British political parties manifest a much more coherent base of principles than American parties.

Pragmatism also appears to be a distinguishing property of Swedish politics. Hancock notes an emphasis on compromise.[60] Spiro's impression is that "Sweden is the least ideological" of the five Continental systems he examined.[61] While one must not conclude the absence of deeply felt principle in Sweden, such principles are not so strong as to preclude mutual toleration. Thus, the conservative coalition has not opposed the idea of the welfare state. If pragmatic orientation implies a general psychological property, it should imply a low salience of any type of ideology—political, religious, or otherwise. In this sense a nonideological culture becomes conceptually equivalent to a secular culture. The low rate of regular (weekly) church attendance in both Britain and Sweden (less than five percent) indicates a secular culture in those countries.[62]

Given the strong political implications of Catholic social doctrine and the consequent tradition of that church's active role in secular politics, Catholic nations should almost by definition not be expected to be secularized. Superficially, one might expect a relationship between Roman Catholicism and an ideological orientation toward politics. Indeed, one highly respected political sociologist, Seymour Lipset, went so far as to suggest that democratic instability and Roman Catholicism may be causally linked.[63] The assumption underlying his logic is the putative Catholic claim that the church has an exclusive monopoly on truth. Such a view would be incompatible with an acceptance of the legitimacy of competing points of view. This would intensify the level of conflict and preclude the compromises necessary for the peaceful resolution of issues. If Catholicism were dysfunctional for democracy, this would be of momentous significance due to the pervasiveness of the church in Western Europe.

The argument appears to break down empirically, however. The Republic of Ireland, clearly Catholic, appears to be a model of stability. The Netherlands and Austria have manifested both cabinet and constitutional stability since the Second

---

[60] Hancock, *op. cit.,* p. 63. It should be noted that to infer a pragmatic orientation from a willingness to compromise means that one cannot use the pragmatism to explain the willingness to compromise. To do so would constitute a tautological or circular argument. Unfortunately, we are working with derived or secondary data and must make the best of what is available.

[61] Spiro, *op. cit.,* p. 202.

[62] See Gabriel Almond and G. Binsham Powell, *Comparative Politics: A Developmental Approach* (Boston: Little Brown, 1966), pp. 57–58, for a discussion of a secular political culture as a property of a developed political system. To Almond and Powell, pragmatism is one component of the broader concept of secularization.

[63] Seymour Lipset, *Political Man* (New York: Doubleday Anchor Books, 1963), p. 73n. Lipset, a master at hypothesis-saving qualifications, does not explicitly argue causation. But yet if causation is not inferred, Lipset's suggested "linkage" is without meaning.

World War. Belgium has been held as exemplifying cabinet stability. However, the increasing irreconcilability of differences between the Belgian subcultures has recently led to an alteration in the constitutional format of that nation, granting considerable autonomy to each of the subcultures. Switzerland has a sizable Catholic population, as does the Federal Republic of Germany, yet those nations have been stable (at least since the Second World War in the German case). All in all, the proposition that Catholicism is incompatible with stable democracy is belied by the evidence.

Lipset's proposition was based on the characterization of Catholicism as a basically closed, dogmatic, and hence intolerant ideology. But it is questionable whether Catholicism makes a stronger claim for a monopoly on truth than many other religions. None of the religions appear to be monolithic in this regard. On one hand, the Italian Catholic political leaders appear to be highly intolerant of the non-Catholic left. Almond and Verba data indicated that about half of the Italian Christian Democratic respondents would actively be displeased by a child of theirs marrying a upporter of the left opposition,[64] as opposed to 12 percent of the British Conservatives opposing marriage with a Labourite and 19 percent of German Christian Democratics opposing marriage with a member of the Social Democrats (SPD). Kogan reports adamant opposition on the part of Italian Christian Democratic Party leaders to overtures for cooperative behavior from the Italian Communist Party.[65] On the other hand, Dutch Catholics appear to be considerably less dogmatic and more accepting of democratic values. Germany's Christian Democratic Party has manifested increasing efforts to attract non-Catholic votes.

In general, it appears that the pervasiveness of a strong conservative religious faith can exacerbate an existing tendency in a culture toward ideologism and intolerance. However, any given religion is clearly not a sufficient or necessary condition for such ideologism and intolerance. The extent to which religious doctrine can exacerbate the intensity of conflict may also be a function of the rigidity and intolerance of the opposing or secular belief system. The Belgian and Dutch liberals accepted the major Catholic demand with respect to state aid to church schools, thus removing that potentially divisive issue from the political arena. In contrast, the French republican forces have been dogmatically anticlerical since the church supported the old regime at the time of the revolution. Therefore, the intensification of political conflict is more likely to result from the presence of competing rigid ideologies than from the presence of a single ideology that is not strongly opposed. In Belgium, the Netherlands, and Canada, the relatively

---

[64] Almond and Verba, *op. cit.*, pp. 98–100.
[65] Norman Kogan, "Italian Communism, The Working Class and Organized Catholicism," *Journal of Politics*, Vol. 28, No. 3, August 1966, pp. 531–555.

secular, liberal sectors of those cultures have abandoned or avoided any attempt to impose their secularism on the Catholic sectors. Orthodox Catholicism pitted against a dogmatic Marxism and doctrinaire liberalism results in unresolvable issues in Third and Fourth Republic France. Not even the juxtaposition of Marxism and Catholicism necessarily generates rigidly ideological conflict, as the case of Austria indicates. In that country, there are two subcultures (or *lager*)—Catholic and Socialist. Steifbold reports that Austrian election campaigns are characterized by considerable ideological rhetoric as the professional partisans of the parties representing the respective *lager* become more influential. After the election, however, the necessary level of cooperation needed to sustain a "grand coalition" between the dominant parties has been possible because ideology has not been very salient for either the top elite or the masses.[66] Thus, in one campaign the Austrian People's Party used a degree of antisemitic rhetoric because the Socialist Party was led by a man of Jewish heritage. After the election, the People's Party was still able to coalesce with the Socialist Party's leader.

Stable democracy can apparently exist despite ideologically based subcultures if the top elites remain pragmatic enough to sustain intersubculture bargaining. This is what Arend Lijphart and Martin Heisler call the "consociational model."[67] In these systems, according to Heisler, the ideologically (or sometimes economically) based subsystems are "coopted" by the top elite.[68] The elite, requiring the support of these subsystems, may carry out election campaigns in terms of their respective ideologies. They resolve issues, however, by bargaining among themselves, not by ideology.

Putnam interviewed members of the British and Italian elite and offers another explanation of stability in an apparently ideological setting. He found there was no significant correlation between his measure of an ideological political style and his measure of partisanship. In other words, contrary to the logically based impressions of Lipset and others, ideologists are not significantly more likely to be intolerant of opposition than pragmatists.[69] Of course, his conclusions are a function of his conceptualizations. Putnam used a broad definition of the term characterizing responses as ideological to the extent that they reflect a tendency to generalize rather than particularize, to utilize deductive thinking, and to refer to

---

[66] Rodney Stiefbold, "Segmented Pluralism and Consociational Democracy in Austria: Problems of Political Stability and Change," in Martin Heisler, ed., *Politics in Europe* (New York: David McKay, 1974), pp. 117–177. Compare Samuel Barnes, "Ideology and the Organization of Conflict: On the Relationship Between Political Thought and Behavior," *Journal of Politics*, Vol. 28, No. 3, August 1966, pp. 513–530, who suggests that ideology is sustained by organizational support and is not a salient part of the disposition of the masses.

[67] Lijphart, *op. cit.*, and Martin O. Heisler and Robert Kuavick, "Patterns of European Politics: The European Polity Model," in Heisler, *op. cit.*, pp. 27–89, especially pp. 43–48.

[68] Heisler and Kuavick, *op. cit.*, p. 48 ff.

[69] Putnam, *op. cit.*, pp. 671–672.

named ideologies or future utopias. In other words, Putnam used the concept of ideological style to refer to a tendency to analyze political issues in the framework of principles. For reasons already discussed, we employ a more restricted definition of the term—a closed, comprehensive thought system. A closed system will be related to intolerance by definition. Thus, Dutch Catholicism certainly is principled and ideological in Putnam's sense, but it appears to be an adaptive variety and thus not closed or ideological as we have used that term. Tolerance of the respective subcultures is a widely shared impression of the Dutch political culture.

Ideological intolerance of a variety of interests or positions appears to have adversely affected stability in France during the Third and Fourth Republics. The rigid anticlericalism of French liberalism (in the nineteenth-century sense of the term and manifested in the Radical Party) combined with the salience of Catholic social doctrine for the Popular Republican Movement (MRP, the French Party of Christian Catholic Democracy) prevented the French center from governing. Further, Frank Wilson reports a persistence of ideologism among French left-wing parties.[70] This retention of the revolutionary symbols of the past has had the consequence of rendering the left an ineffective challenger to the hegemony of the Gaullists since 1958. It has made the left out of step with the bulk of the French voters (who are not revolutionary) and has impeded their coherence and unity. Programs to these particular parties function as expressions providing some form of psychic satisfaction to their members rather than as serious plans of action for the near future. The Gaullist pursuit of the restoration of French national grandeur may also be interpreted to indicate a commitment to atavistic goals out of step with current realities and problems. The ideological character of debate in the Chamber of Deputies during the Fourth Republic was so out of touch with the problems and issues actually plaguing France that the Chamber came to be called "the house without windows." Clearly, discussion of the relative merits of Marxism versus social democracy was not calculated to resolve issues arising out of a war in Algeria and rampant inflation.

Germany, by contrast, appears to have been afflicted in the past by a high degree of ideology, but, in the judgment of some observers, has done an about-face and become thoroughly disenchanted with ideologies in the postwar era. Spiro, writing in 1959, reported that Germany provides "the classic example of ideologism caused by exclusion from politics."[71] History records the repression of even moderate reform by the Prussian aristocracy in the nineteenth century. It may be recalled that nineteenth-century Germany produced perhaps the epitome and certainly the most influential of antisystem ideologists, Karl Marx. The rigid

---

[70] Frank Wilson, "The Persistence of Ideologism on the French Democratic Left," in Gary Byrne and Kenneth Pederson, eds., *Politics in Western European Democracies: Patterns and Problems* (New York: John Wiley & Sons, 1971), pp. 217–232.

[71] Spiro, *op. cit.*, p. 197.

fragmentation of politics during the Weimar period and the embracing of another ideology, National Socialism, is too well known to dwell upon here.

The disastrous outcome of the Second World War for the Germans and their espousal of Nazism seems to have resulted in a disenchantment with such ideological fervor. The data show that nearly half the Germans will accept either a democratic or authoritarian political format as long as it performs effectively—clearly, a pragmatic orientation. We will see that the German Social Democratic Party, originally a Marxist party and emotionally committed to the idea of the Socialist International even after the war, did a dramatic about-face in 1959 in an effort to attract middle-class support and accepted the social utility of free enterprise and the profit motive. These are but two of the scattered indications of an emerging German pragmatic orientation that may be contributing to the postwar stability of the system.

The End of Ideology?

The position of Seymour Lipset[72] and Daniel Bell[73] gained a certain measure of notoriety among sociologists and political scientists in the 1950s. They proclaimed the "end of ideology" as a salient factor in the politics of Western industrial nations, a claim sharply disputed by some scholars, notably Joseph LaPalombara.[74] If ideology is no longer a force in the politics of industrial societies as claimed, much of the foregoing discussion of the impact of an ideological orientation loses its power to explain current variations in the politics of those nations.

As with Putnam's thesis, it appears that the critical point of disagreement among scholars lies with their respective definitions of the concept of ideology. Lipset apparently viewed ideology as a term referring to the great thought systems generated by controversies surrounding the problems and social dislocations of industrialization, the role of institutionalized religion in the secular state, and the distribution of political authority (in our terminology, the question of political format or the nature of constitutional arrangements). Lipset asserted that the first of these problems has been solved,[75] and he strongly implied that a compromise had been reached on the other great issues. Similarly, Bell restricted ideology to an "all-inclusive system of comprehensive reality."[76] In other words, rather than a statement of principle derived from interests (for instance, the business ideology), Bell restricted the term to *Weltanschauungen*. This oft-used and imprecisely translated German term refers approximately to a total thought system from

---

[72] Seymour Lipset, "The End of Ideology," postscript to *Political Man, op. cit.*, pp. 439–456.

[73] Daniel Bell, *The End of Ideology* (New York: The Free Press, 1962).

[74] Joseph LaPalombara, "The Decline of Ideology: A Dissent and Interpretation," *American Political Science Review*, Vol. LX, No. 1, March 1966, pp. 5–16.

[75] Lipset, "The End of Ideology," *op. cit.*, p. 442 ff.

[76] Bell, *op. cit.*, p. 400.

which answers to all social questions can be logically derived. For both men, total ideologies referred therefore to the classic thought systems such as Marxism, Catholicism, perhaps Manchester Liberalism, etc. By implication, they spoke of ideologies that manifest the properties of the great thought systems including that of a closed system.

Accordingly, one of the dynamic processes of the postindustrial order, the spread of education and the acceptance of "the ideology of 'scientism'",[77] is not logically compatible with such closed thought systems. Scientific inquiry implies openness in the sense that scientific conclusions must be kept in harmony with an ever-changing body of evidence. Thus, Lipset found that these great "isms" lose their appeal with the spread of science and education.[78] It can be argued that the great "isms" to which Lipset and Bell restricted the meaning of the term *ideology* were essentially issues arising out of the process of industrialization and modernization. As such, these issues were more the properties of the industrial than the postindustrial age.

A property of postindustrial societies, according to its leading prophets, is the growing predominance of technocrats. The knowledge explosion resulting from the advanced state of technology has led to demand for greater skill levels, and hence more education, to fit into the structure of postindustrial societies. Further, the knowledge explosion has created a need for increased specialization and division of labor, which in turn means increased bureaucratization of society. Bureaucracy is, as we shall see in the chapter devoted to that phenomenon, essentially a rationalized form of orientation. Rationalization here means relating ends to means with maximum efficiency. Rationalization involves the pragmatic task of working out the most efficient procedures of attaining predetermined goals and subjecting these procedures to routinization. Technology and its consequence, bureaucratization, seem therefore to work against ideologism as an orientation. An end of ideology, as conceptualized by Lipset and Bell, would thus appear to be an exception as Europe moves from the industrial to the postindustrial age.

As suggested above, the objection to the thesis of the end of ideology, usually associated with LaPalombara, rests on a broader definition of ideology. LaPalombara conceptualized ideology as "a set of values that are more of less coherent" and seek "to link given patterns of action to the achievement or maintenance of a future or existing state of affairs."[79] In other words, it necessarily follows from his definition that ideology becomes nearly indistinguishable among Italian parties,

---

[77] See Bell, *The Coming of Post Industrial Society* (New York: Basic Books, 1973), pp. 18–20, Chap. 3, and *passim*, for a discussion of the primacy of scientific and technical knowledge in such societies.

[78] Seymour Lipset, "The Changing Class Structure and Contemporary European Politics," reprinted in M. Dogan and R. Rose, eds. *European Politics: A Reader* (Boston: Little Brown, 1971), pp. 147–148.

[79] LaPalombara, *op. cit.*, p. 7.

especially the Italian Communist Party. The finding of Kogan[80] that the leaders of the Italian Communist Party (PCI) have gone out of their way to accommodate the Italian Christian Democrats leaves one with the impression that the PCI can be called ideological only in the loosest sense of that term.

It will be shown in the chapter on parties that this phenomenon of abandoning dogmatic and utopian principles in favor of programs designed to attract the widest possible electoral support is with a few exceptions a widespread trend in the postindustrial world.

A possible exception to this trend may be found in the Soviet Union. As mentioned earlier, the ideology-pragmatism question is primarily one of the degree to which one or the other is dominant in such matters as perceptions and policy decisions. Because the leaders of the Soviet Union have always claimed to be following an ideological course, it is only natural that extensive study and attention have been devoted to attempts to determine if it really is.

It is generally agreed that ideology in the Soviet Union performs the usual functions such as communication and legitimization. Every system involves a vocabulary, concepts, and a frame of reference through which individuals can relate to others and to their environment. Every regime must also have some grounds on which to base its claim of legitimacy and to govern and be obeyed. It was noted above that in the pragmatic British system (we might also add the United States to a lesser extent) institutions tend to evolve over a period of time in response to specific needs and eventually gain acceptance. In the more ideological Soviet framework, on the other hand, "legitimacy is a prerequisite to existence" and can be gained or lost very quickly.[81]

There is much discussion and disagreement as to whether communist doctrine serves as the driving, motivating force of the system or as a public relations technique to give theoretical justification to policies arrived at for pragmatic reasons. We can find support for both positions and for a number in between. Khrushchev's successors have been called pragmatic men who are committed only to national greatness and orderly procedures.[82] It has also been suggested that although the leadership is often ambivalent and embarrassed about the ideology, it is the very group (rather than the masses) for which ideology is important and meaningful.[83]

Perhaps most relevant to the purpose of this book are two discussions of the

---

[80] Kogan, *op. cit.*
[81] Zbigniew Brzezinski and Samuel Huntington, *Political Power USA/USSR* (New York: Viking Press, 1964), p. 46.
[82] Richard Lowenthal, "The Soviet Union in the Post-Revolutionary Era: An Overview," in Alexander Dallin and Thomas Larson, *Soviet Politics Since Khrushchev* (Englewood Cliffs: Prentice-Hall, 1968), p. 1.
[83] Alfred Meyer, "The Functions of Ideology in the Soviet Political System: A Speculative Essay Designed to Provoke Discussion," *Soviet Studies*, Vol. XVII, January 1966, p. 284.

adaptation of ideology to deal with the internal and external problems and circumstances of the industrial or postindustrial period. In the first, Barrington Moore addressed the implications of the Soviet experience for the nature of modern industrial society.[84] One of the tentative conclusions he reached was that there are certain aspects of such societies that cannot be eliminated without risking destruction of the system and that therefore must be accommodated. Several of these aspects apparently conflict with the egalitarian thrust of the Soviet iedology. The indispensable aspects of an industrial society postulated by Moore include: a system of organized social inequality, the use of some form of competitive stimulus, and adherence to the existing pattern of international politics. If an ideology differs from these requirements, the theory must be revised.

Brzezinski and Huntington discussed a number of factors threatening ideology, including the development of bureaucracy and technology mentioned above as part of the "end of ideology" debate.[85] Defining *end* as a situation in which the Soviet elite would become like its Western (pragmatic) counterparts, they did not see such a result as likely. They explained the decline in the importance of ideology in the West in relation to class conflict and industrialization. Because ideologies were related to class conflict in the early stages of industrialization or the other issues that no longer pertain, the eventual easing of conflict in a more affluent era led to a decline in ideology as political parties sought to deal with current issues.

Ideology in the Soviet Union, on the other hand, is said to be based on the supremacy of the Communist Party and reinforced by Soviet nationalism. The novel aspect of the Soviet experience, to Brzezinski and Huntington, is that ideology has become institutionalized in a ruling elite whose organizational interest thus breathes new vitality into the ideology.[86] Although doctrinal content will change, the elite will adopt new and more sophisticated techniques of social control to reinforce the claims of the ideology. The thesis, then, is that an ideology can influence the content of decisions as well as being used as a legitimating device or instrument of social control long after the problems that generated the ideology have disappeared. The ideology is embodied in the party bureaucracy. The bureaucrats acquire a vested interest in the perpetuation of the ideology.

Affect and Alienation

Feelings are also a component of political culture. A crucial feeling is the degree of a sense of belonging to the system, of accepting the system as "ours" rather than "theirs." This feeling is generally accompanied by pride in the system, especially

---

[84] Moore, *op. cit.*, p. 405 ff.
[85] Brzezinski and Huntington, *op. cit.*, pp. 68–69.
[86] *Ibid.*

in the constitutional format. Those feelings are called affect. The converse or antonym of affect is called alienation. Political alienation thus refers to the feeling that one does not have a personal stake in the survival or welfare of the system. The system becomes a hostile "them" rather than "us." Clearly, a certain amount of system affect is a necessary condition for any system's legitimacy.

A related feeling is one of trust in one's government, which is both a partial cause and one consequence of political affect.

Trust in fellow human beings is related to trust in government and to that basic acceptance of differences that seems to be a precondition of an open society. Trust in fellow people is manifested in such things as an assumption that those who disagree on sociopolitical matters may still have the best interests of the political system at heart.

Trust in people and government may be a prerequisite to a deferential attitude toward authority—the willingness to grant the political elite the discretion on day-to-day decisions necessary to govern. Egalitarianism—manifested in an insistence that governmental decisions be hedged in elaborate mechanism of veto power by the nonelite—implies a distrust of government. It may be best summarized as a belief in Lord Acton's dictum that "power corrupts and absolute power corrupts absolutely."

David Easton has added to the conventional wisdom of the discipline the proposition that nations require a threshold level of "diffuse support" from their constituents in order to persist.[87] By diffuse, he means nonspecific support, support for the system in general rather than for its specific policies, successes, or failures. In other words, he means what we have called system affect. The logic underlying this position is based on the assumption that no political system can consistently satisfy the perceived needs and demands of most of its constituents. All nations must endure crises (depressions, etc.). The costs of trying to satisfy most specific demands or of repressing opposition to a regime by force is prohibitively high. Systems appear to require that their constituents feel a sense of belonging to the system, a sense of a personal stake in the survival and well-being of the system, irrespective of the performance of the system with respect to the perceived interests of those constituents.

The Almond and Verba survey addressed this variable with a question. "Speaking generally, what are the things about this country you are most proud of?"[88] Ten alternative choices were provided, and respondents were allowed to choose more than one. There was a variation in percentages of respondents who expressed pride in some aspect of the political system among the United States,

---

[87] David Easton, *A Framework for Political Analysis* (Englewood Cliffs: Prentice-Hall, 1965), pp. 124–125.
[88] Almond and Verba, *op. cit.*, p. 64.

Great Britain, West Germany, Italy, and Mexico. In the two most "successful" of the five democracies, 85 and 46 percent of respondents, respectively, named governmental and political institutions as objects of pride as compared to 7 and 3 percent in Germany and Italy, respectively. The principal object of German pride appeared to be the success of their economic system. To the extent that this is true, we can be less optimistic regarding the capacity of the German system to survive genuine crises. Less than 10 percent of the Italians named any political objects, either institutions or policies, supporting our early assessment of Italy as manifesting pervasive alienation. We may distinguish between the active alienation found among the Italians and a more passive form of alienation among the Germans. While the former refers to a positive rejection of the system, the latter refers to a lack of commitment for or against the system. The Catholic church's ban on participation in the Italian state until 1919 (the doctrine of *non expedit*), the nearly half of Italian voters who voted for a restoration of the monarchy instead of the republic in 1946, and the largest communist vote in Western Europe are among the circumstantial evidence often presented to justify assertions of Italian alienation.

According to Karl Deutsch's estimates, the typical West German does not dislike or reject the democratic values embodied in the Bonn constitution. Neither does the typical West German prefer a democratic format no matter what. Instead, the typical West German, according to Deutsch, identifies the Bonn republic with positively valued outputs such as the so-called economic miracle—the precipitous phoenixlike resurgence of that area's economy from the ashes of the Second World War to the position of the predominant economic power in Europe. Deutsch estimates the "all-weather" support of democracy in West Germany at around 25 percent of the population.[89] In other words, around half the German electorate neither is committed to nor actively dislikes any particular political format; the people will accept any format that produces the desired results of economic prosperity and national self-respect. In such a cultural climate, sharp substantive reverses such as an economic depression could bode ill for the future of political democracy. On the more optimistic side, however, the longer the regime survives due to its substantive successes, the greater the probability that the democratic format will acquire legitimacy for its own sake. Legitimacy, it will be recalled, often emanates from the long-term existence of the structure in question. There is some evidence that democracy as a value in and of itself is in fact on the increase in West Germany.[90]

As in Germany, the French have also been prone to discuss substantive issues in

[89] Deutsch, *op. cit.*, pp. 352–353. See also Verba, "The Remaking of Political Culture," *op. cit.*, p. 146.

[90] For example, Verba, "The Remaking of Political Culture," *op. cit., p. 139*. *"The proportion saying democracy was the best form of government increased from 57 percent in 1953 to 74 percent in 1960."*

constitutional terms—that is, to propose that the solution to political and economic problems lies in adopting a new constitution. This readiness to change the political format indicates a low level of diffuse support for that format. In such a situation, few political principles are perceived as fundamental or inviolable. The perceptual attachment of the French is to France as a civilization or society. The attachment of the French to particular political formats appears to be much weaker.

The expectation that deep subcultural cleavages would result in Belgium in a lack of diffuse support for the political format is supported by the fundamental constitutional revision of 1971 in which the two subcultures acquired virtual autonomy over any matters they judged salient to their cultural interests. If the term *sovereignty* is taken to mean final power to make and enforce law, sovereignty appears to have passed from the national government to the subcultural elite.

Constitutional change is not a simple term. We should distinguish between changes that alter the fundamental relationships between the parts of the system and those that do not. For example, the 1974 debate over executive privilege raised by President Nixon in the United States, bringing into question the whole pattern of relationship between Congress and the president, raised far more fundamental constitutional issues than did the proposed amendment dealing with women's rights. What we consider to be the critical variable in the question of diffuse support is the absence of any significantly influential bloc of opinion that brings the fundamental constitutional structure into question.

Thus, despite the fact that major written portions of the Swedish constitution were added less than a century ago, we can still conclude an absence of any challenge to the fundamental constitutional structure in Sweden for centuries and therefore a high level of diffuse support for the political format. While the monarchy is not venerated as a symbol of authority as in Britain, it does not appear to generate any deep controversy. Proposals for its abolition come from the Social Democrats who have not acted on it despite having the power to do so. The political format is not brought into question, and the large majority of Swedes, including supporters of the anti-Social Democratic bloc, have not questioned the basic assumptions of the nation's welfare-state policies. Thus, some observers of Swedish politics, noting the unusual degree of substantive as well as fundamental policy consensus, have concluded that Swedish politics, lacking real issues, are dull.[91] There are, however, some recently increasing signs of dissent on the fringes of the political spectrum. Nevertheless, this opposition seems to focus on the assumptions of welfare-state policies rather than on the structure of the system.

Lijphart reports the absence of any serious challenge to the Dutch political

---

[91] Spiro, *op. cit.*, pp. 53–54. Hancock, *op. cit.*, p. 81.

format even among the Dutch Catholics, although the struggle for Dutch nationhood was to a large extent associated with the Calvinist bloc.[92] (It will be recalled that Dutch independence was acquired after a struggle from Catholic Spain.) Lijphart further reports an increasing acceptance of the House of Orange (the Dutch royal family) as a national symbol by other blocs despite the historic ties between royalty and the Calvinists. Apparently several major controversies regarding activities of the royal family (for instance, Princess Irene's conversion to Catholicism, Princess Beatrix's marriage to a former Nazi soldier) have not seriously diminished the popularity of the monarchy itself. The status of the monarchy is symbolic of a consensus on the rules of the game: the resolution of issues by bargaining and compromise among members of the Dutch elite, or what Lijphart called the "spirit of accommodation." This consensus transcends the subcultural loyalties (discussed in the next chapter).

We have been talking about a feeling of attachment to and support for the regime or political format irrespective of that regime's policy output or success in the resolution of issues. This support should logically reduce the pressure on the political system to fulfill expectations and to satisfy needs. A lack of diffuse suppose should be (and appears in fact to be) related to both cabinet and constitutional instability. The two forms of instability may be related in that a readiness to bring down cabinets on insignificant justification is not calculated to maximize the viability of the system itself. Thus, cabinet instability may itself be an indication that the survival of the constitutional format is an overriding value.

A more specific feeling of attachment is the expectation that the output of the government will do justice to the people's perceived interests. In this regard, the Almond and Verba study gathered data about the expectation of equal treatment by the bureaucracy or police. The Americans and the British scored high (over 80 percent expecting equal treatment), the Germans somewhat lower (65 percent) and the Italians the lowest (53 percent).[93] This variable may be taken as an indication of faith in the performance of the system. It indicates an expectation that people's interests will be well served by the system. It may reasonably be expected that a populace with such expectations will be less readily alienated from the system by perceptions of unsatisfactory performance. While the specific questions referred to above were not administered in France, the widespread impression of fear and distrust of authority lead us to suspect that the French people would have a lower expectation of fair treatment than those in the United States, Britain, or Germany. Banfield's study of a village in southern Italy gives the impression of an almost universal assumption of lack of principle by all politicians. Banfield reports that Italians expect politicians to have one salient

[92] Lijphart, *op. cit.*, p. 80.
[93] Almond and Verba, *op. cit.*, pp. 73–75.

motivation: to enrich themselves at taxpayers' expense. The term he gave to the Italian culture is "amoral familism."[94] The overall figure for Italy reported by Almond and Verba does not appear to be as low as one would expect after reading Banfield's impressions of the southern Italian village. This difference probably reflects the substantial cultural differences between northern and southern Italy. The various properties we have described for the Italian political culture—alienation, amoral familism, etc.—apply more clearly and emphatically to the less developed and agricultural south than to the more urbanized and industrialized north. This distinction must be kept in mind whenever references to Italian society are made.

Feelings Toward Other People

The term *amoral familism* that Banfield applied to the Italian culture has only been explained with reference to the amoral part. The *familism* component of the term refers to an inability on the part of the typical Italian family to transcend the nuclear family in its orientation toward the world. The amoral and familial concepts are, of course, related. They refer to a "belief that no one will further the interest of the group or community unless it is to his private advantage...."[95] The implication is that the typical Italian is only able to identify with and support the interests of the family as opposed to the society at large and that he imparts the same value priorities and motivations to everyone else. Furthermore, Banfield implies that Italians possess these properties to a significantly greater degree than members of other Western societies. Thus, Italians are felt to be characterized by an intense distrust of the motivations of other people. Banfield's characterizations have come under criticism with regard to their simplistic labeling and the inferences drawn from an unsystematic study of one southern village to all of Italy. The basic characterizations of Banfield, however, seem in the main to be confirmed by LaPalombara and Zariski, who possess established reputations as students of Italy as a whole.[96]

A presumed lack of good will on the part of other people can translate into an absence of trust in the opposition to have the interest of the country at heart. In these situations, political competition becomes transformed into struggles between the good and patriotic on one hand and untrustworthy venality on the other. In the presence of these feelings, it would be difficult to reach the necessary compromises to resolve issues arising out of differing conceptions of the national

[94] Banfield, *op. cit.*
[95] *Ibid.*, pp. 83–84.
[96] Joseph Lapalombara, "Italy: Fragmentation, Isolation and Alienation," in Pye and Verba, *op. cit.*, pp. 282–329, and Raphael Zariski, *Italy: The Politics of Uneven Development* (Hinsdale, IL: The Dryden Press, 1972).

interest. It is not likely that competing groups of elite will view the possibility of their own defeat with sufficient equanimity to value the rules of the political game more than they value the triumph of their own political values. The parallel with the American Watergate scandals of 1973–1974 is obvious. When former Attorney General John Mitchell, in his testimony before the Senate Ervin Committee on July 10, 1973, said in effect that the reelection of Richard Nixon was more important than following the rules of the game he was accused of violating, he was voicing exactly the feeling we are trying to explain. The Watergate affair is of such momentous significance because it reveals in high places in the United States lack of tolerance for the possible success of political opposition. This is one of the most important cultural properties that is said to make stable democracy improbable or unworkable in Italy and other countries. This variable is called, using Almond and Verba's terminology, "the intensity of partisanship." The term refers to the acceptance, or lack thereof, of the legitimacy of opposition and different conceptions of wise policy and the national interest.

There is a danger of circular reasoning in this kind of analysis. The conclusion that the Italians have a higher intensity of partisanship is used partially to account for their relative lack of political stability and success. It is useful to question whether the conclusion that the Italians possess a significantly higher intensity of partisanship is arrived at partly because of the political problems the partisanship is supposed to explain. Otherwise put, we know Italy has certain political problems, and we logically conclude that a certain lack of tolerance can cause these problems. We therefore assume that the Italians must be less tolerant. To the extent that the conclusion about cultural properties is based on impressions instead of on hard data, this danger becomes more real.

Fortunately, in the case of Italy some hard data are available on this point. Almond and Verba posed a hypothetical question regarding the attitude of the respondent toward the marriage of a son or daughter across party lines. The Italians, it will be recalled, expressed displeasure about such a marriage more emphatically and to a greater extent than did the British, Germans, and the Americans. The most intense displeasure was displayed by churchgoing Italian supporters of the Catholic-based Christian Democrats toward the marriage of a son or daughter into the militantly anticlerical communist or, to a slightly lesser extent, the left-wing socialists (PSI).[97] Almond and Verba explain these differences in terms of the closer connection between politics and religion in Italy and Germany than in Britain and the United States.[98] This would seem to support our earlier suggestions about the negative impact of the salience of religion on political success. LaPalombara's perceptions of the Italian culture support these inferences.

[97] Almond and Verba, *op. cit.*, pp. 98–100.
[98] *Ibid.*, pp. 100–101.

The Cultural Context 105

He finds that, "Italian Catholics view society as laying in an almost hopeless state of damnation, owing to a denial of Christ and his teaching which . . . can be traced to the Protestant heresy. Liberalism, Socialism and Communism are direct emanations of this heresy. . . ."[99] Thus, an application of Milton Rokeach's dogmatism scale[100] reveals Italian Catholics to be much more distrustful of others and rigid in their partisanship than others, including communists.

In another set of data on the issue of intensity of partisanship presented by Almond and Verba, perceptions of a set of stipulated positive and negative qualities of members of opposition parties were elicited from respondents. In other words, respondents were asked to give impressionistic judgments as to whether adherents to different parties possess certain qualities. Among the qualities characterized as positive were "intelligent," "interested in humanity," etc. Among those characterized as negative were "selfish," "ignorant," "facist," "imperialist," etc. To the extent that fewer positive and more negative qualities are attributed to members of the opposition, politics in the country were inferred to be more polarized, and the intensity of partisanship was inferred to be higher. Polarization refers to a sharper delineation and greater gap between left and right on the political spectrum.

These data shown Italian respondents to be considerably more polarized than British, American, or West German respondents. The percentages of Italian respondents characterizing political opponents with positive qualities are considerably smaller than the percentages reported for the other three nations.[101]

These data about Italy may be contrasted with frequent characterizations of Scandinavian politics as "dull," as noted previously. *Dull* in this sense implies an absence of momentous issues at stake. Politics is incremental in style, meaning only relatively small changes in the status quo are at stake. Basic changes in the policy structure are excluded from the political arena. This style seems also to characterize the Federal Republic of Germany, the Netherlands, and—most emphatically—Great Britain. Certain cultural defense issues of momentous significance have been creeping back into Belgian politics in the past few years contributing to the recent constitutional alteration of that system into what seems to be two separate sovereignties.

It may be that only such dull politics are viable within the context of a democratic format. Only when no issues of fundamental importance are present for a significant period of time will democratic procedures prevail over the substantive issues.

Spiro has provocatively suggested that procedural consensus is more critical

---

[99] LaPalombara, "Italy: Fragmentation, Isolation, Alienation," *op. cit.*, p. 294.
[100] Milton Rokeach, *The Open and Closed Mind* (New York: Basic Books, 1960), pp. 83–86.
[101] Almond and Verba, *op. cit.*, pp. 89–91.

than substantive consensus. The logic of his position is that once the procedures have become legitimatized, they can be utilized as a means of resolving substantive issues. We find this logic compelling within limits. However, when substantive dissent reaches a threshold level of intensity, the dissent can cause the breakdown of procedural consensus. In short, there are limits to the kinds and intensity of issues that can be processed by democratic procedures.

Conclusions

To the student who is used to defining the scope of political science in a narrow sense to the formal, legitimate structures of government—executives, legislatures, judiciaries, and bureaucracies—it may seem that we have devoted an excessive amount of space to prevalent dispositions and topics that should concern students of social psychology or sociology instead of students of politics. We do not consider political structures to be independent variables. Instead, we consider them to be reflections of the cultural properties existing in a given society.

We suggest, for example, that the fragmentation of the party system (a relatively large number of parties with no one party close to being dominant) is a reflection of cultural fragmentation. Cultural fragmentation reflects an ideological style and a high intensity of partisanship that works to impede the compromises necessary to resolve differing conceptions of the national interests and wise policy (issues). An ideological style contributes to a high intensity of partisanship. A fragmented party system is also in part a reflection of an attitude toward authority that precludes the granting of relatively large amounts of discretion to any single, coherent elite. In short, a fragmented party system may be viewed as a structural means of assuring that no single elite has the power to govern, reflecting an egalitarian fear of authority. Therefore, to explain the fragmentation of the party system in terms of proportional representation (a generic name given to a number of electoral systems, as explained in Chapter 6) is to explain an outcome in terms of another aspect of that same outcome. It has been persuasively demonstrated that the various forms of proportional representation facilitate the formal representation of each shade of opinion in a society. This begs two questions: why a plurality system encouraging different shades of opinion to aggregate or coalesce was not adopted and why different shades of opinion were able to maintain their distinctiveness and autonomy from each other. The answers to these two questions, it seems to us, lie in the cultural differences we have just delineated. Proportional representation is thus seen as another aspect or means of attaining the *structural* fragmentation rather than a cause of it. The cause we seek is more plausibly *cultural* fragmentation.

The Cultural Context

Of course, cultural properties are not independent variables either. The explanation of a number of the cultural differences we have found significant were found in our survey of the historical patterns in Chapter 2.

Through the numerous suggestions we have made regarding the causal impact of the various cultural properties, we feel we have persuasively demonstrated that cultural differences among the countries under consideration do exist and that these differences in culture can be related to differences in structures.

Structure is a concept that refers to recurring patterns of action and interaction. Structure thus includes both the formal structures of government and the structures of society. This latter variable, focusing largely on the stratification system and behavior patterns, is the topic of the next chapter.

Chapter 4

Social Stratification and Politics

In this chapter, we move from a consideration of what goes on in people's minds to how they behave and interact with each other. Sometimes the behavior and interaction of people form relatively stable and persisting patterns, which sociologists call *structures*. In a loose sense, the term *institution* could be used synonymously with *structure*. But we feel that the term *institution* connotes that the structure has become a norm or expectation. Thus, all institutions are structures, but all structures are not institutions.

Institutions or structures may or may not be constituted in formal organizations. Congress, parliaments, and trade unions all constitute structures that are also formal organizations (they have, for example, precisely explicated rules of procedure, elected officers, etc.). Some formally organized structures, such as legislatures, courts, bureaucratic offices, and presidencies or other political executives, constitute agencies of government prescribed by a constitution or law. Other structures, such as interest groups, professional societies, or occupational associations, are not legally designated participants in the determining and carrying out of public policy. As such they are not governmental agencies. Yet, whether intentionally or not, organized structures do have an impact on the policymaking process; consequently, they are of interest to the political scientist.

Some social structures are not formally organized. The criteria according to which the people of any society are grouped and divided, the criteria by which some groups are considered higher than others, and the criteria for the movement of individuals from one group to another constitute a social structure, called a *stratification system*.

There are several possible criteria for the grouping of individuals, the movement of individuals from one group to another, and the interaction of such groups—in other words, several possible bases for a stratification system. Perhaps the most obvious of these is the socioeconomic class. Other possibilities include ethnicity, religion, cultural linguistic groups, geographically defined residence, etc. These criteria are often defined with a certain degree of imprecision so that it is unclear what label to affix to any individual. (For instance, what is the line between middle class and working class? Is a Catholic only a full-blooded, church-going practitioner of that faith or is it a secular person whose parents happen to be Catholic?)

The stratification system may or may not be accurately represented in the decision-making process through the party system or other means. This important question will be considered in a later chapter.

The notion of class as a basis for the stratification system is ambiguous and variously used. One basis for the class grouping lies in the nature of industrial (and postindustrial) society.

As technology expands in such a society, no one can possess all the knowledge needed to perform all of the tasks required by society. We do not, as in pioneer societies, build our own cabin, slaughter our own game, make our own clothes from skins, carry a weapon for our own defense, etc. Instead, in industrial societies we tend to perform one increasingly complex function in the productive, economic order and depend on others to acquire the skills needed to perform other functions. This is called specialization and division of labor or *functional specificity*.

The service or productive function an individual performs in the economic order (bricklayer, lawyer, teacher, mechanic, etc.) defines the person's economic *role*—that is, the pattern of expectations arising out of that individual's place in the economic order. People have more than one role, however. A person may be a welder in the productive or economic role and a Catholic in the religious role. At the same time the person may perform the functions and fill the role of parent, citizen of a region or nation, athlete, etc.

People thus fill different roles (economic, religious, etc.). Different interests arise out of these roles, often generating conflicting claims on public policy. Thus, functional specificity as an inexorable consequence of an industrial society generates political *issues*. Politics and government are not only affected by the stratification system; they are made inevitable by it.[1]

The fact that people perform a number of social roles at the same time begs the question of which of these roles tends to predominate over the others in the consciousness of the people of a given society. This is what we mean by saying certain roles are more *salient* than others. The salience of some roles over others seems to be a function of the values of that society.

In some societies, for example, higher value is placed on the religious order than the productive or economic order. In such a society, religious roles will be more salient than productive roles and a person's self-identification as, for example, a Catholic will tend to predominate over self-identification as a member of the working class. In other societies, productive roles will be more highly valued and the above order of salience will be reversed.[2]

To render our analysis more complex, the values and the relative salience of roles—and, hence of criteria of stratification—are not uniform in any complex society. Thus, some French workers will be workers first and Catholics second, while for other French workers the order is reversed.

We will see that the difficulty working-class movements have had in mobilizing the support of Roman Catholic workers is a familiar phenomenon throughout Western Europe (excluding, of course, the non-Catholic Scandinavian nations). When religion becomes salient in the consciousness of a Catholic worker, this identification supersedes that individual's identification with fellow workers. The worker may even feel a greater kinship to Catholic employers than to non-Catholic workers. The point is that the policymaking process is affected by those characteristics of individuals that are perceptually salient for them regardless of the "objective" characteristics they may possess. Thus, insofar as the policymaking process is concerned, it is not a question of how many working-class people there are by some objective criteria but instead how many people so identify themselves in preference to possible competing criteria of self-identification.

We have seen above how differences in productive or economic roles are an inevitable consequence of a relatively advanced state of technology. The term *socioeconomic class* refers, though in an imprecise way, to groupings of these roles in the economic order (including nonproductive roles in that order such as Veblen's "leisure class"). Thus, the blue-collar industrial workers may be said to constitute one socioeconomic class, bureaucratic managers another, and financiers and investors still another. Alternatively, groups such as skilled workers and

---

[1] Frank Parkin, *Class Inequality and the Social Order* (New York: Praeger Publishers, 1971). Parkin suggests that a consensual society is only possible when dominant groups have been successful in imposing their values on subordinate groups (p. 84).

[2] Bernard Barber, *Social Stratification* (New York: Harcourt Brace and World, 1957), Chap. 1.

bureaucratic managers may be grouped under a broader heading such as lower middle class. The precise grouping to be employed is an arbitrary decision.

It follows that some form of class structure in an "objective" sense is a consequence of the state of technology in any industrial society. Societies differ in the extent to which people are more conscious of their class than of other criteria of stratification and in the extent to which people will act according to their class interests. A socioeconomic class system may be said to exist in any industrial society; however, when the salience of that class system in the consciousness of the typical citizen is superseded by other competing criteria of identification, the class structure will not have a significant impact on the political process.

A nation will have class-based politics—that is, parties and demands will be based on class-related identifications and interests—when other criteria of stratification have not acquired much political importance in the minds of the typical citizen. Thus, "class consciousness" will emerge in the absence of other salient criteria of stratification. We believe that the probability that class will be the most salient criterion of stratification increases with the extent of inequality in that society.

Crosscutting versus Cumulative Cleavage

In complex societies the tendency is for more than one criterion of stratification to have salience at a given time and place. In the presence of several coexisting salient criteria of stratification, the relationship of cleavages may take one of two basic forms: cleavages may be overlapping or they may be cumulative.

A society is characterized as having overlapping cleavages when those who are grouped together on one criterion (say, socioeconomic class) are not necessarily grouped together on another criterion (say, religion). Thus, in such a situation, some poor people will be Catholic and others will be Protestant. Similarly, some Catholics will be rich and others will be poor. A system of overlapping cleavages will normally involve a number of criteria of stratification rather than our simplified two-criteria illustration.

A system may be characterized as having cumulative cleavages when people are grouped together on other criteria. Thus, there is an absence of overlap between the divisions of society whereby given individuals will be allied with individuals on one criterion and other individuals on other criteria. Cumulative cleavages result in the nearly complete separation of the divisions of society from each other. In such a situation there is little informal interaction between the individuals in one grouping or segment in society. This kind of society is sometimes called a segmented society.

We will see that the Dutch and Belgian societies are divided into nonoverlapping segments but there is overlapping of groupings within the segments. Within the religious segments there are many socioeconomic strata, and within the liberal and socialist segments there are a variety of religious affiliations. Thus, although the segments are separated, they are not mutually reinforcing in the sense we want the term *cumulative cleavages* to connote.

The most obvious illustration of cumulative cleavage is the case of Northern Ireland in recent years. There the poor—those who perceive themselves as oppressed—are almost uniformly Catholic, while nearly all of the middle class and well-to-do are Protestant. The poor Catholics tend to reside together in defined locations, while Protestants reside elsewhere. This, together with the parochial-school preference of Catholics, has the consequence that members of the two groups by and large attend schools with their own kind. The result of all of this is that a Catholic in Northern Ireland has a high probability of going through life without any meaningful relationship with a Protestant of that nation and vice versa.

The theoretical significance of the distinction is the expectation that crosscutting cleavages will result in a lower intensity of partisanship. Intense hostility toward those with whom a person disagrees on given issues requires that one view opponents as without redeeming positive qualities. To the extent that a person perceives someone as having some positive qualities, it becomes that much more difficult to hate him intensely. Further, when a person perceives opponents as having positive qualities, he is more likely to suspect there may be some merit in his position and be prone to compromise differences with him. The perception of one's opponents as without redeeming positive qualities is an exercise in stereotyping. Such stereotyping of people, being a distortion of the true complex nature of people, can only be engaged in with respect to people one does not know very well. A person is less likely to engage in stereotyping people who are known. One gets to know people by interacting with them, and one interacts them when grouped with them by one or more criteria. The meaning of cumulative cleavages is that society is divided into mutually exclusive camps with an absence of overlap. By definition, therefore, a system of cumulative cleavages entails the isolation of the several subcultures of a society. This would encourage viewing one's opponents as pejorative stereotypes without redeeming positive qualities and the positions of one's opponents as without merit. This would reduce if not preclude the possibilities of compromise.

Mass Societies in the Industrial World

The theory of mass society raises the question of whether a cleavage structure exists to a significant extent at all in the perception of the members of a society. It will be recalled from the introduction that the concept of mass society entails a division of society into a small elite and a large, undifferentiated mass of atomized individuals. The critical variable is whether individuals are grouped in a set of formalized structures that remain autonomous from the structures of government such as interest groups, religious and social institutions, etc.

Theorists of mass society suggest that atomized individuals are more susceptible to be mobilized by leaders in an authoritarian format.[3] This absence of organized attachments is said to encourage a feeling of alienation. The absence of a set of secondary associations means that there are few loyalties competing with loyalty to the government. Alienated people, easily mobilized, are perfect subjects for totalitarian regimes, which are, after all, mobilization systems. Secondary associations can serve as a check on such totalitarian encroachments. They can serve as a buffer, as it were, between omnipotent government and the relatively impotent individual. As suggested in the introduction, totalitarian movements are invariably based on a mass ideology (for instance, "spirit of the folk" in Nazi Germany).

Of the systems under consideration, the Soviet Union is the best example of a mass society in which secondary groups are not autonomous. As was pointed out in an earlier chapter, the Communist Party claims for itself a leading and guiding position in Soviet society. This doctrine of the central, vanguard role is acknowledged in Article 126 of the constitution, which declares the party to be the leading core of all organizations, both government and nongovernment. Needless to say, such provisions make opposition and the presentation of alternative policies very difficult.

One result of this arrangement can be seen in the form of elections, in which the voter in the Soviet Union is offered a single slate of candidates. The election is preceded by campaigning on the part of these unopposed candidates. The typical election speech contains a detailed account of the accomplishments of the current regime and concludes with an appeal for the continuation of such leadership. In effect, the voter is being asked for a vote of confidence. On election day the choice is limited to voting yes or no on the unopposed list of candidates on the ballot. The option of voting for another candidate is not included.

As is indicated by the constitutional provision referred to above, even the Soviet Union contains a number of nongovernmental secondary groups. All systems contain such groups as youth, trade union, professional, and other organizations. As suggested above, the question is that of their relationship to governmental authorities. In a system such as that of the Soviet Union, particularly with reference to the Stalin era, the term *transmission belts* has been used to describe their status. These groups are seen not as autonomous with their own identity and constituency, but rather as a mechanism to facilitate mobilization of the masses through transmission of the ideology and policies of the elite. Of course, as Milton Lodge has suggested, it is always possible that such "transmission belts" might

---

[3] William Kornhouser, *The Politics of Mass Society* (New York: The Free Press of Glencoe, 1954).

develop a sense of identity and group consciousness and evolve into a more autonomous, interest-aggregating role.[4]

The groups in the Soviet Union are similar to the Catholic groups in those Western nations with a large Catholic population. In such nations the church, through the formation of subsidiary groups, attempts to integrate all phases of an individual's life under its own aegis. Thus, in such nations there are Catholic youth associations, trade unions, women's associations, athletic organizations, etc. Similarly, Soviet groupings are designed to bring the various nonpolitical aspects of day-to-day life under governmental control. Like the Catholic groups, Soviet ones function more as mobilization structures than as representatives of autonomous interests. They mobilize individuals for the purposes of the state and the party.

The closest thing to a mass society among the industrial democracies is probably found in France. As previously suggested, the 1789 revolution left an enduring egalitarian heritage and a strong fascination with Rousseau's theory. In *The Social Contract,* Rousseau suggested that a true democracy consisted of the leadership of the system scrupulously following the "general will." This somewhat metaphysical concept was distinguished from both majoritarianism and unanimity. The concept was never precisely defined, however, and thus is susceptible to being used in terms of anything from the Nazi "spirit of the folk" to DeGaulle's plebiscites (see below).

In any event, secondary groupings and representative assemblies as intermediaries between the masses and the political executive are said to be distortions of the "general will." Hence, Rousseau's type of egalitarianism becomes an argument for an unchecked executive. The propensity on DeGaulle's part to resolve issues by plebiscites in the Fifth French Republic reflects this orientation. A plebiscite consists of asking voters to approve a policy proposal offered by the elite. This may be contrasted with a referendum in which the voters are given policy alternatives from which to choose. The lack of organized viable opposition in terms of alternative policies and, more importantly, an alternative elite means that rejection of a policy becomes coterminous with rejection of the government. Moreover, behavioral research has shown that opposition to government or policies is rarely spontaneous.[5] Public opinion tends to support whatever the head of government advocates. Opposition must be mobilized by groups and elite from autonomous sources of potential opposition. Thus, if a free election were held in

---

[4] Milton Lodge, *Soviet Elite Attitudes Since Stalin* (Columbus, Ohio: Charles E. Merrill Publishing Co., 1969), pp. 99-100.

[5] For example, Paul Lazarsfeld, Bernard Berekson and Hazel Gaudet, *The People's Choice* (New York: Columbia University Press, 1968), Third Ed., p. 151 ff. and *passim*. See also Hadley Cantril, *The Psychology of Social Movements* (New York: John Wiley & Sons, 1963), Chap. 4, for the assertion that lynch mobs are usually organized by leaders and are rarely if ever spontaneous.

the Soviet Union now, the Communist Party would still probably win handily due to the lack of structured opinion leadership mobilizing antigovernment demands.

In France, and to a slightly lesser extent in West Germany, organized interest groups have never been accepted as quite legitimate. They have therefore tended to adjust to more covert tactics than in Great Britain and Scandinavia. The lack of a well-developed set of secondary associations in prewar Germany rendered that society more susceptible to the propaganda barrage of the Nazis than a pluralistic society would have. It is not that Germany lacked secondary associations; the associations were extensions of the state, not autonomous from it, and as such they could not serve the function of being competing loyalties that could limit the state's capacity for social mobilization.

As in the Soviet Union, the associations served to integrate the various aspects of individual lives to loyalty to the omnipotent state. State-sponsored youth groups, women's clubs, and even an attempt at state-sponsored religion aided in discouraging the establishment of groups whose focus would be toward autonomy from the state. The relatively hegemonic control of the Gaullists in France from 1958 until the election of Giscard d'Estaing in 1974 was most likely helped along by the weakness of alternative objects of mass loyalties.

Segmented Societies in Europe

There are two types of societies in which secondary groupings are well developed and autonomous of the government: cumulative and overlapping cleavage structures. The latter is often called a pluralistic system. In such a system, because each group commands only a part of the loyalty of its membership and because it must compete with other groups on any given issue, no group will attain all that it wants. Pluralistic societies, therefore, are thought of as encouraging compromise and exercising a moderating influence on "pure" ideologies.

It is dangerous, however, to assume the converse of the above—that a cumulative cleavage structure will cause unyielding ideological dogmatism. A cumulative cleavage will *permit* an ideological orientation in a society already disposed to such an orientation. That is not the same thing as *causing* ideologism or preventing compromise.

Despite the compelling logic of pluralist theory, segmented societies are quite common among the stable democracies of Europe. Of course, labeling any given society's cleavage structure as segmented or overlapping involves a judgment as to matter of degree. Nevertheless, there seems to be widespread agreement that a number of societies are clearly more segmented than others. Thus, it makes sense as a matter of convenience to speak of the former group as segmented societies as if the variable were a matter of kind rather than simply of degree.

Some of those segmented societies are composed of several nonoverlapping segments, while others are bipolarized into two such groups. The Netherlands and Norway exemplify the former, while the latter group consists of Austria, Belgium, Switzerland, and Northern Ireland.

The case of Belgium is less clear cut than the others. Martin Heisler argues that there are three cultural linguistic segments in that country: the Flemish, the Walloons, and the Bruxellois.[6] The last group is by Heisler's own admission francophone (pro-French) and thus Walloon in orientation and denied the structural autonomy granted the other two by the new constitution of 1970. In other words, the Bruxellois do not seem to comprise a distinct subculture.

Outside the classification, Canada may be characterized as being a system of overlapping cleavages together with the existence of one subculture that maintains a high degree of autonomy from the rest of the nation. Thus, there is little overlap and interaction between French-Canadian Canada and the rest of the society; yet, non-French Canada is characterized by an essentially pluralist cleavage structure.

Italy is also difficult to classify in that there are some characteristics of a pluralist cleavage system on one hand and some characteristics of subcultural isolation on the other. Italy possesses some attributes of an overlapping cleavage structure in that the correlation between political party support and socioeconomic class, while significant, is highly imperfect. Further, there have been increasing instances of cooperation or attempted cooperation between the liberals (roughly in the classic nineteenth-century sense of that term) and Catholic subcultures and even between the Catholic and Marxist subcultures. The record of the attempts of the Italian communist to cooperate with and win the support of Italian Catholics is startling to those familiar with the historic antipathy of those two philosophies.[7] Yet, the members of the Catholic subculture in particular appear to interact little with the members of the Italian population who are not, strictly speaking, practicing Catholics. The pervasiveness of Catholic education here as elsewhere contributes to the isolation of Italian Catholics. Further, the church tends to place a moral imperative for its followers on support of the Christian Democratic Party, generating a high association between self-identification as a practicing Catholic and as a Christian Democrat. Political cooperation between the Catholics and liberals has probably been enhanced by the fact that the liberal tradition in Italy never acquired the rigid anticlerical orientation that it did in France. However, the data on partisanship cited in the previous chapter indicate that the Marxists' desire for cooperation with the Catholics is far from fully reciprocated.

It will be recalled that the moderating impact of pluralism stems from the defin-

---

[6] Martin O. Heisler, "Institutionalizing Societal Cleavages in a Cooptive Polity: The Growing Importance of the Output Side in Belgium," *Politics in Europe*, Martin Heisler, ed. (New York: David McKay, 1974), p. 181.

[7] Norman Kogan, "Italian Communism, the Working Class and Organized Catholicism," *Journal of Politics*, Vol. 28, August 1960, pp. 531–555.

ing characteristic of pluralist associations—that they command only part of the loyalty of their members. In Italy, there may be said to be an objective cross-cutting cleavage structure in that a number of blue-collar workers are also practicing Catholics. For practicing Italian Catholics, however, other potentially competing loyalties such as socioeconomic class tend not to be salient. The religious affiliation tends to be predominant and comprehensive. Thus, in the Italian Catholic subculture, pluralism as a *process* rather than as an objective structure does not operate as a moderating influence.

Belgium seems to epitomize a bifurcated, segmented stratification system. There are, as suggested above, two basic subcultures: the Flemish and the Walloons. The terms referring to the aggregated culture or to the geographic areas where these cultures predominate are Flanders and Wallonia, respectively. The Flemish language is closely related to Dutch and German. The Flemish tend, in relation to the Walloons, to be more rural, to be more religious, to maintain a closer identification with the Catholic church, and to be less economically well off and less well educated. The Walloons are French in language and in cultural orientation. They tend to be urban dwellers, secular, economically better off than the Flemish, and more highly educated.[8] The fact that the Walloons feel themselves to be more "civilized" (culturally superior) than the Flemish has exacerbated the level of hostility between the two subcultures. The Flemish do not, of course, accept the label of cultural inferiority, especially in view of their interpretation of their greater religiosity as more godly or more true than the orientation of the secular and hence "godless" Walloons. Not only do the cleavages cumulate with regard to the aforementioned variables, they are also geographically defined. It is possible to draw a relatively precise cultural-linguistic boundary across a map of Belgium, thus adding to the isolation of one subculture from the other.[9]

The capital of Belgium, Brussels, is officially a bilingual area by the constitutional reforms of 1970. The city has historically been dominated by the more urban Walloons, however. It has been somewhat difficult for the Flemish to accept their capital city as under the aegis of the alien Walloon culture—hence, the attempt of the constitution to designate the *Bruxellois* as a third distinct subculture between the other two. This appears, however, to be a legal fiction for two reasons: the francophone Walloons still dominate the area and the *Bruxellois* have neither the legal nor the administrative autonomy granted the other two subcultures.

Belgium is a classic case of mutually reinforcing criteria of cleavage. This is also true of Northern Ireland, where the well-to-do are mostly Protestant, live in the same geographic area, identify with the British connection with its attendant

---

[8] Val Lorwin, "Belgium: Religion, Class and Language in National Politics," *Political Oppositions in Western Democracies,* Robert Dahl, ed. (New Haven: Yale University Press, 1966), pp. 158–159.
[9] See the map in Heisler, *op. cit.,* p. 189.

symbols, and generally support the same political party. The subcultures in Northern Ireland have been engaged in what at this writing appears to be an unresolvable struggle over a range of issues and characterized by serious political violence. The differences on religious grounds and the absence of crosscultural interaction on a personal level are thought to exacerbate the bitterness felt by the Catholics on the issue of their perceived economic deprivations. What may have been an economic issue subject to resolution by compromise has become framed in terms of religious truth, patriotism, justice, and other such noncompromisable issues. It is easy to point at Northern Ireland for justification of the conventional wisdom that segmental cleavages exacerbate the intensity of sociopolitical conflict. By thus making issues more difficult to resolve peacefully, segmental cleavages in this view are suggested to contribute to instability as they clearly have in Northern Ireland. This is in accord with what we have shown can be logically expected of the impact of segmented cleavages.

Consociational Democracy

The cumulation or segmentation of cleavages has equally clearly not brought about either instability or violence in Norway, the Netherlands, Austria, Canada, and Belgium. The question is thus under what conditions systems can function (process issues and maintain stable political structures) despite segmental cleavages. One of the common explanations of how such segmented systems can operate successfully is the suggestion that pragmatic bargaining occurs among the very top elite of each cleavage in contrast to the expressive partisan rhetoric among lower-level elite and, in some interpretations, among the masses. This is what Lijphart, writing about the Netherlands, has called the "consociational" model.[10] This term has been adopted and used by Martin Heisler and the contributors to his book in reference to Austria, Belgium, and Norway. The term may now be part of our accepted lexicon. Heisler also uses the term *European polity model* to include the meaning of Lijphart's model plus some additional characteristics, especially that of cooptation of interests and demands.[11]

In this model, the structure of demands is not aggregated by the appropriate integrative institutions: the educational or other socializing agencies, parties, and groups. However, this failure to perform an integrative or aggregative function on the input side does not have a corresponding disruptive effect on the output side—that is, policymaking and issue resolution. The leaders of the segments of these

---

[10] See Arend Lijphart, *The Politics of Accommodation: Pluralism and Democracy in the Netherlands* (Berkeley: University of California Press, 1968) for the fullest discussion of the process. The term is actually used in his "Consociational Democracy," *World Politics,* Vol. XXI, No. 2, January 1969, pp. 207–225.

[11] Heisler, "The European Polity Model," Heisler, *op. cit.,* Chap. 2, especially pp. 47–48.

societies consult with each other on a regular basis in contrast with the other occupants of each segment who have little contact with members of the other segments. Moreover, these elite share the values of postindustrial societies involving a decline in the salience of those devisive, traditional ideologies that intensify the rhetorical conflict among the other spokesmen of their respective segments.

Thus, society in Austria is divided into two mutually antagonistic subcultures or *lager*—the more conservative Catholic subculture and the secularized socialist subculture. The gulf between these subcultures remains psychologically salient. Each subculture is represented by its political party. These parties institutionalize the expressive, ideological, and highly partisan rhetoric between the subcultures, and this rhetoric still characterizes Austrian election campaigns. But despite the bitter antagonistic rhetoric, the parties representing these two subcultures or *lager* managed to form and maintain a "Grand Coalition" after each election from the end of the Second World War until 1966. The government and opposition pattern that has since existed appears stable. It seems remarkable that the losers accept their loss, given the "virulent," ideological, and "extremist" nature of the campaigns. Stefbold attributes this to several factors in Austria.[12] First, he suggests that there exists a basically nonideological pattern of accommodation among top elite. Second, he suggests that the masses exhibit a relatively lower *intensity* of politicization—therefore of partisanship; the intense ideological partisanship of the campaigns is said to emanate from the middle-level party elite. Third, he suggests that the partial fragmentation of political authority resulting from Austrian federalism reduces the perception of an all-or-nothing stake in the outcome of the elections.[13] We suggest that this tendency would be buttressed by the proportional representation of the two *lager* in the Austrian bureaucracy (the so-called *propoz* system). In other words, if it is true, as we believe, that a characteristic of industrial systems is that an increasingly large portion of the authoritative allocation of values (the bread-and-butter decisions of who gets what, when, and how) occurs in the bureaucratic rather than the political sector, the question of who controls the political sector would not be a matter of great pitch and moment.

Federalism may have a similarly mediating influence on the potentially disruptive effect of the isolation of the French Canadian Catholic subculture on Canadian political stability. In a federal system, issues are presumably processed on two relatively autonomous levels, national and state or provincial. As long as there are multiple alternative structures for resolving perceived needs and issues, a person's stake in controlling the national structure is probably diminished. (Could the Confederacy's acceptance of the outcome of the American Civil War be understood on the basis of being able to maintain the lifestyle of the Southerners within

---

[12] Rodney Stiefbold, "Segmented Pluralism and Consociational Democracy in Austria: Problems of Political Stability and Change," in Heisler, *op. cit.*, Chap. 4, especially p. 128, 147–152.
[13] *Ibid.*, p. 173.

their own states?) British-style cabinet government as practiced in Canada requires cohesive political parties. On the other hand, the existence of the French Canadian subculture generates pressure on individual legislators to represent their parochial constituencies. Thus, we have a conflict between the centralizing imperatives of an autonomous subculture with parochial concerns. Logically, we might expect the particular demands of the French Canadian subculture to have a disruptive effect on the cohesion of Canadian parties. Stephen Muller has suggested that this problem is avoided by granting the provincial governments (especially Québec and New Brunswick, which contain most of the French Canadians) considerable autonomy to cope with matters of French Canadian cultural defense.[14] The national government is thus able largely to avoid many irreconcilable issues separating French Canadian Catholics and non-French Protestant Canadians who identify with the British Commonwealth connection.

For example, in Québec (where slightly over 80 percent of the population is French Canadian and almost 90 percent is Catholic) the resolution of the issue of public support for parochial schools was very different than in the other provinces in which the Catholics and especially the French Canadian Catholics comprised a distinct minority of the population. Thus, it was not necessary to construct a national policy on this issue of great symbolic and emotional content. The principle suggested by the Canadian experience seems to be as follows: to the extent that each segmented subculture is governed by relatively autonomous structures, the need for interbloc cooperation and issue resolution is diminished. This, in essence, seems to be the Belgian solution since their constitutional reform discussed above. This avoidance of the resolution of difficult issues between subcultures by means of subcultural autonomy is feasible only when the subcultures or cumulatively reinforcing segments are geographically defined. It has already been shown that this is the case in Belgium and in Canada. That is, it is possible to pinpoint the geographic location of each segment or subculture on a map as opposed to having the various segments relatively evenly distributed throughout the nation. The French Canadians by and large live in Québec and western New Brunswick. The Flemish live in the northern portion of Belgium (the area known as Flanders), while Wallonia, the location of most of the Walloons, is the southern portion of Belgium.

To the extent that subcultural segments cannot be geographically pinpointed, bargaining and cooperation between groups of elite becomes necessary as subcultural governmental autonomy becomes less feasible. Because the very concept of a segmented society implies that the segments or subcultures are socially isolated from each other, bargaining and compromise become difficult. Bargain-

---

[14] Steven Muller, "Federalism and the Party System in Canada," *American Federalism in Perspective*, Aaron Wildavsky, ed. (Boston: Little Brown, 1967), pp. 144-162.

ing, after all, implies contact and mutual acceptance among the bargainers. The consociational model suggests that such contact and mutual acceptance occurs only at the level of the top elite. This, however, is thought to be sufficient for peaceful issue resolution despite the isolation of the masses of each subcultural bloc from the other blocs.

Thus, unless each subculture is more or less coterminous with political boundaries and possesses its own elite, autonomy of the subcultures is not feasible. Subcultural autonomy demands some sort of structural decentralization of political power such as federalism.

The Netherlands has been thought to epitomize this model of political stability despite the existence of at least four distinct subculture segments: the Protestant subculture, the liberal (nonsocialist, secular) subculture, the Catholic subculture, and the socialist subculture. The four groups may be labeled as subcultures or blocs in the sense that various organizations of Dutch society are subsumed under the aegis of their respective subculture with little or no *inter*bloc overlap in membership. Instead, *intra*bloc overlap is the norm whereby individuals belong to several organizations within their respective blocs. Thus, rather than have socialist, Protestant, and Catholic blue-collar workers belonging to the same labor union, there is a Catholic union, a socialist union, and a Protestant union. Moreover, leaders of one organization within a bloc are likely to hold positions of influence and authority in other organization within the same bloc. Each bloc seems to be run as a kind of interlocking directorate. The continuing autonomy of the blocs from one another is indicated by the low rate of interbloc marriage. This is the basis of an inferred low rate of social contact between members of different blocs.

Lijphart suggests that overarching cooperation among the top elite and a basically pragmatic orientation by those elite explain the capacity of the system to remain stable despite the autonomy of the subcultural segments.[15] Clearly, this is the most plausible accounting for the resolutions of issues of cultural defense (those questions of principle and interest that differentiate the blocs of subcultures from each other). Other issues are resolved by a system of "within-bloc pluralism." There is, as we have already pointed out, considerable overlap in the membership of the organizations within each bloc. As Lijphart points out, "the basic cleavages in Dutch society—religion and class—go across each other at an almost perfectly straight angle. The Catholic and Calvinist blocs are true cross sections of the Dutch people, resembling the class composition of the population as a whole...."[16] Clearly, the mutual isolation of the Dutch subcultural blocs is not what we mean by cumulative, mutually reinforcing cleavages. Class and religious

---

[15] Lijphart, *op. cit.*, pp. 112, 139.
[16] *Ibid.*, p. 205.

lines of cleavage are not congruent with one another. The reconciliation of class-related differences within the religious parties should lessen the intensity of conflict in the Netherlands while religious differences in Northern Ireland reinforce socioeconomic differences and exacerbate the tensions produced by class-related issues. In the latter system, it will be recalled, the less well-off are overwhelmingly Catholic, and the Protestants overwhelmingly perceive themselves as constituting the "haves." The Netherlands are considered a segmented society only because their blocs are isolated. However, that does not necessarily mean that the criteria of stratification are mutually reinforcing. Similarly, the cleavages may be segmented, as in the case of Norway, without being cumulative or mutually reinforcing. The Netherlands therefore cannot be categorized as a system of cumulative cleavages along with Northern Ireland. Accordingly, we would expect Northern Ireland to experience more difficulty in peacefully resolving issues than the Netherlands, an expectation that is clearly borne out by events.

Lijphart further suggests that the extent of the subcultural isolation may be a positive factor in keeping political tensions low. He suggests that tensions arise from interaction between the blocs instead of from their mutual isolation.[17] He omits what seems to us to be another major variable affecting the degree of tension generated by a segmented social structure—the expectation of solving problems at the national level. The Catholic and Protestant subcultures of Switzerland have peacefully coexisted for a great length of time, as have the subcultures in the Netherlands and Austria. Thus, it seems that the violations to pluralist theory—namely, that societies with segmented cleavages remain stable contrary to expectations—occur in the smaller democracies. These systems clearly play a smaller role in the international arena. Due to a more circumscribed variety of resources, the complexity of the economies of these systems may alleviate the level and intensity of demands on the national political process in the domestic sphere as well. A lack of social integration would be of less significance if the expectations for the society as a system were diminished. In short, we are tentatively suggesting that the requisites of stable democracy may be less demanding in the lesser systems than in the major powers. To the extent that these smaller democracies have fewer and less intense issues to resolve, they can persist with social and political structures decidedly less efficient for processing issues than those required by major powers.

Eckstein finds Norway exemplifying segmental cleavages while maintaining stability. He considers a segmented society one in which "political divisions follow very closely . . . lines of objective social differentiation."[18] As in the Netherlands, Norwegian political parties represent many socioeconomic divisions. Yet, here again it is highly questionable whether this society possesses cumulative cleavages

[17] *Ibid.*, pp. 201–202.
[18] Harry Eckstein, *Division and Cohesion in Democracy: A Study of Norway* (Princeton: Princeton University Press, 1966), p. 34.

in the sense we find them in Northern Ireland. The lines of religious cleavage do not closely coincide with socioeconomic class cleavage. Thus, the constituency of the Christian Party cuts across class lines, while the constituency of the Labor Party aggregates across urban-rural cleavage lines.[19] Eckstein suggests that Norwegian cleavages are relatively intensely perceived. The fact that some criteria of stratification partially reinforce certain other criteria would generate this situation. The agrarian forces, for example, are strongest in the south and west of Norway, cumulating the geographic variable with the urban-rural split, but although the appeal of orthodox Protestantism may be stronger in the rural areas, the Christian Party instead of the Agrarian Party seems to have coopted that appeal. Thus, the Norwegian stratification system produces intensively felt cleavages. Few demands are made on the national decision-making process to necessitate reconciliation of these various social segments.

Class versus Symbolic Criteria of Cleavage

It was suggested above that socioeconomic class as a criterion for lines of cleavage may be viewed as a residual category that becomes salient when other possible criteria, such as religion, culture, ethnicity, etc., for some reason are not salient in a system. Socioeconomic class may be differentiated from other criteria of stratification on another basis. Other criteria imply perceived dichotomies such as truth or falseness, right or wrong, good or evil, "us" or "them." With such dichotomies, there is no logical middle ground as the basis for possible compromises—for meeting claims halfway. Socioeconomic class, on the other hand, is a criterion based on objective, measurable considerations—material well-being. (Money, after all, can be counted.) Issues generated by class differences are differences of interest, and compromise positions can be found. If the workers demand four pounds per hour and the employers offer two, the parties may settle on three without one party coercing the other into a position of total submission.

There seems to exist in the United States a popularly held notion—perhaps out of a concern for the threat of Marxism—that class differences are a divisive curse from which Americans are blessedly free. But, far from this notion, we suggest after Robert Alford that class differences are the easiest to resolve by democratic procedures, bargaining, and compromise.[20] Moreover, we suggest that class cleavages have been universally pervasive in industrial societies unless supplanted in salience by differences that are more difficult to resolve—ethnic, religious, ideological, cultural, etc. The question is not whether socioeconomic cleavages have existed in given societies, but whether additional cleavages have become politically salient.

[19] *Ibid.*, p. 53.
[20] Robert Alford, *Party and Society* (Chicago: Rand McNally, 1963), p. 339.

We have looked at the question of whether socioeconomic cleavage will be as universally pervasive in the emerging postindustrial world as it has been in industrial societies. Because this world is now only emerging, an exercise in "futurology" would be a very tenuous exploration, not a description of current, known structures and processes. However, among the recognized theorists of the postindustrial world, certain emerging properties of that world are widely recognized.

Given a definition of ideology in the narrow, conventional sense of a closed, comprehensive, logically related system of ideas, most postindustrial theorists agree that the world they are concerned with will be characterized by a decline in ideologism.[21]

The concept of postindustrial society entails an advanced state of technology based on a knowledge explosion. The properties of the society require management by specialization and division of labor. These organizational characteristics are hallmarks of the organizational form called bureaucracy. The bureaucratization of society supplants ideological or principled criteria for policy choices with the criterion of rational efficiency. We discussed both the rationalization of mature industrial societies and "the end of ideology" in these such societies in Chapter 3. The rationalization of mature industrial societies entails a decline in the salience of those symbols (culture, religion, ideology, etc.) that supplant the politics of interests.

Thus, what Alford has to say about the advantages of class-based politics has broader implications than the nineteenth-century conception of working class versus middle class or bourgeoisie. The specialization of mature, industrial societies renders class structure far more complex than that. Alford's thesis applies to the politics of interests as opposed to the politics of symbols. Interests arise out of functionally defined roles. Insofar as the structural basis of postindustrial societies involves bureaucratization, interests should take on an increasing salience, and the decline of ideology (in the sense used in the preceding chapter) would be a logically expected phenomenon.

It may therefore be that the critical variable for political stability is not so much whether symbolic criteria provide some stratification in the sense of patterns of interaction and objects of identification. Instead, the critical variable is the character of the significant political issues that the national political process is

---

[21] Daniel Bell is emerging as perhaps the most widely recognized theorist of the postindustrial world. See his *The Coming of Post-Industrial Society* (New York: Basic Books, 1973), pp. 28, 32, 348–355, & *passim*. Bell does not mention ideologism as such in this book but rather focuses on the spread of such phenomena as the spread of "theoretical knowledge" or the "technocratic mind view." The decline of ideology is clearly entailed by these developments, however, because "theoretical knowledge" is by definition "open" and "nonintuitive," Compare Bell's earlier *The Decline of Ideology* (New York: The Free Press, 1962), pp. 393–405.

called upon to resolve. As already pointed out, symbolic criteria of cleavage do not necessarily generate symbolically based issues in the national political process, especially when, as in the Netherlands, interest-based criteria of cleavage are present alongside the symbolic criteria.

The principal issue arising out of the symbolic divisions in the Netherlands was the question of government support of parochial education.[22] This issue was resolved in the early twentieth century in favor of government support of both Catholic and Protestant education. The class- or interest-based division between the socialist subculture and the three nonsocialist subcultures has become more salient since then.

In Belgium the same basic issue—state financial support of religious education—existed between the "religious" Catholics of Flanders and the "secular" Catholics of Wallonia, and the issue was similarly resolved. But symbolic considerations have remained salient for the cleavage between these two subcultures and are in principle definable in terms of interests. That is, Walloons tend to be materially better off and have a higher socioeconomic status than Flemish. The persisting salience of symbolic considerations in Belgium has probably contributed to the necessity for subcultural autonomy instituted by the constitutional changes of 1970 referred to above. On the other hand, the early resolution of the religious issue may have contributed to the ability of the two subcultures to coexist under the same sovereignty for as long as they did.

Britain as a Class-Based Society

Great Britain appears to epitomize the predominant salience of class over other criteria of stratification. For comparative purposes, we should note that according to the University of Michigan's Survey Research Center's 1968 election study, an American sample was asked with reference to three named social classes, "Do you ever think of yourself as belonging to one of these classes?" Affirmative responses were given by 940 respondents, while 526 (slightly over one-third) responded negatively. The same question in a British sample yielded almost the identical percentage distribution—66 percent said yes.[23]

These data seem to contravene conventional wisdom, which suggests that class is more salient in Britain than in the United States. Of course, one question is far from conclusive on a matter of such complexity. It may be that while the same number in each country find class a salient criterion of self-identification, class criteria tend to be supplanted by more salient criteria in the minds of many Ameri-

---

[22] Lijphart, *op. cit.,* p. 118.
[23] *The S.S.R.C. 1968 American National Election Study* (Ann Arbor: Inter-University Consortium for Political Research, 1971), p. 111. *Study of Political Change in Great Britain,* David Butler and Donald Stokes, principal investigators, Vol., Questionnaires and Notes (Ann Arbor: Inter-University Consortium for Political Research, 1972), pp. '63:18.

cans. It is one thing to agree that there is a class component among other components in one's concept of oneself, especially when the concept of class is explicated in the question. It is quite another thing to say that the class identification is more important than other criteria of stratification such as religion, culture, etc. The suggestion of conventional wisdom appears to be that other criteria are generally not as salient as class in England.

In Britain class-based political parties channel and mobilize class awareness, a situation that does not exist in the United States. Thus, while data on the fact of class awareness do not indicate a significant difference between Britain and the United States, data on the intensity of class awareness or on the relative salience of class awareness, if such data were available, might uphold conventional wisdom.

Class may also be said to be a salient criterion for identification in France, where a slightly smaller percentage of respondents than in the United States or England said they belonged to a class (59 percent). However, a high percentage of respondents said that they felt "solidarity" with other members of their class (82 percent of the workers and 73 percent of the middle class). Further, 44 percent of the respondents thought the class struggle was still a reality.[24] While comparable figures do not exist for England and the United States, these data indicate that class identification is relatively more intense in France than in the United States. For a large portion of the French people, the potential salience of class is not overwhelmed by other criteria of stratification. Not only does class remain salient despite other criteria of stratification in France (see below), but also the level of trust between classes has been lower and the intensity of conflict between classes has been higher in France than in England.

The following indicators have been posited for the reality of class in a community:

1 Consciousness of class.
2 The styles of life are strikingly uniform within each stratum, and clear contrasts in life-style exist between strata.
3 Interaction is patterned by strata.[25]

While consciousness of class exists in both the United States and England, lifestyles and patterns of interaction are more clearly determined by social strata in England.

These life-style differences are discussed as though England were dichotomized into a working class and other classes. Actually, the definition of class and the lines of demarcation between classes are far from precise. Hiram Stout finds four identifiable classes in England: a declining aristocracy, the upper-middle or

[24] Henry Ehrman, *Politics in France* (Boston: Little Brown, 1971), Second Ed., p. 57.
[25] Roger Brown, *Social Psychology* (New York: The Free Press, 1965), p. 114.

governing class, the white-collar workers or middle to lower-middle class, and the industrial and agricultural workers.[26] It is not clear whether this second middle class identifies and interacts more with the working class or the upper class. Some members of the upper-middle or governing class—leaders of the Labour Party and the Trade Union Congress, for example—clearly identify with working-class interests, although in speech and life-style they are not working class. Empirical evidence suggests that the middle to lower middle-class vote divides between the Labour Party and the Conservative Party. Some of the more doctrinaire socialists in the left wing of the Labour Party are more likely than others to manifest a perception of England as divided into upper and middle classes on one hand ("them") and working classes on the other ("us"). Similarly, those in the public-school, "Oxbridge" tradition (discussed in the previous chapter) are also likely to perceptually dichotomize English society between "us" who are more fit to govern and "them" who are not. The middle classes complicate such a Marxist oversimplification. If the dividing line between classes were manual versus nonmanual occupations, two-thirds of the nation would be working class; but less than half of a national sample identified themselves this way.[27] Thus, the discussion of class-related life-style differences implying a dichotomy between the aristocracy and upper middle classes on one hand and the working class on the other constitutes an oversimplification for the sake of convenience.

Class-related differences in England pervade patterns of speech, dress, leisure-time activities, and even food and drink. The differences between an "Oxford" English accent, variations of which typify upper and upper-middle classes, and a Cockney accent of the working-class are apparent even to the untrained ear. The well-known musical, "My Fair Lady," adapted from George Bernard Shaw's "Pygmalion," is basically a satire on the class-related significance of English speech patterns. Actually, middle-class speech patterns are neither Oxford nor Cockney. To the untrained ear, however, middle-class speech sounds closer to the former than to the latter. Regional differences also exist in English speech—as between southeast England and the Highlands—but they are not as apparent to the untrained ear.

It is necessary to remember that we are speaking only of England, not Scotland and Wales. Class-related differences in speech and life-style are not as apparent in the latter two areas. In Scotland a basic cleavage seems to exist between "Clydeside" urban dwellers and rural dwellers. The Scottish brogue and Welsh dialect are quite distinct from all English accents.

Life-style differences in England may be discerned in matters of taste. While upper classes prefer sherry and whisky, working classes prefer warm beer. English

---

[26] Hiram Stout, *British Government* (New York: Oxford University Press, 1953), pp. 9–10.
[27] Richard Rose, *Politics in England* (Boston: Little Brown, 1964), p. 19.

pubs are in fact segregated on an informal but widely understood basis; members of the upper classes go to tables in another room. Upper-class men in London buy sedate woolen clothing in Saville Row shops; working-class people buy the mod clothing of Carnaby Street. The rugby clientele is mostly working class; the theater and opera clientele is essentially upper class.

One important indicator of class status in England is educational background. Those of the governing class (other than the hereditary aristocracy) are overwhelmingly university graduates. To a considerable extent, England is characterized by a deferential attitude conceding that the Tory leadership is more "fit to rule" than the Labourites.[28] The Tory leadership consists not just of university graduates, but mostly of graduates of the public-school, "Oxbridge" (or Sandhurst) system. Certainly, this group perceives itself as more a part of the country's rightful establishment than, say, a Labourite graduate of the University of Manchester or the London School of Economics. The socializing function of the public-school tradition and its role in perpetuating the stratification system was noted in the previous chapter.

The idea of a class-stratified society may be interpreted to entail the notion of superordinate (or dominant) and subordinate status and roles. If so, it may be said that the British hierarchical conception of society is supportive of the class basis of the English stratification system. A person would seem more likely to feel identification with either a superordinate or subordinate class to the extent that the person perceives society to be hierarchically ordered—that is, with superordinate and subordinate roles a just and natural ordering of things. An egalitarian conception of society where each individual is perceived to possess as much wisdom as anyone else in delineating the public interest should result in few people identifying with a superordinate or subordinate class. To the extent that an egalitarian attitude exists, fewer people may be expected to categorize themselves as possessing subordinate status irrespective of objective class status based on occupational criteria. Thus, it may be possible to hear of a working-class Englishperson speak of his or her "betters," implying the acceptance of a governing class. It may be somewhat more difficult to hear such acceptance of a governing class in the United States. While data show about as high a percentage of Americans as Britishers will identify themselves as working class, working-class identification in England is more likely to become politically salient than in the United States because this identification is perceived to carry subordinate status in England. The egalitarian ideological view of the British Labour Party constitutes a norm or aspiration that conflicts with a perception that things are in fact hierarchically ordered. This conflict between aspiration and reality can be a mobilizing force along class lines.

---

[28] Samuel Beer, *British Politics in the Collectivist Age* (New York: Alfred Knopf, 1965), pp. 99–101.

Class and Egalitarianism in the Soviet Union

The conflict between aspirations (ideology) and reality is an appropriate framework for consideration of the Soviet Union. Marxist ideology depends heavily on the concept of class and envisions a future society in which class distinctions will disappear, but most observers agree that the Soviet Union in its present stage is an industrial society with a hierarchical arrangement.

The *Communist Manifesto* projected that in the course of development, production would pass into the hands of the whole nation and lead to the elimination of classes and class antagonisms. For a short time after the Russian revolution, a policy of promoting egalitarianism was in fact instituted. Through such measures as educational quotas and the end of the privileges of the old aristocracy, there was an attempt to work toward greater balance among classes. However, many of Stalin's industrial and developmental programs involved a differential reward system and thus reversed the egalitarian trend. The current official Soviet position is that class antagonisms no longer exist but that there are still two friendly classes (workers and peasants) and an intellectual stratum, all of whose interests largely coincide.

While the question of mobility will be discussed in more detail later in this chapter, several observations seem in order at this point with regard to the egalitarian aspirations of Soviet ideology. Parkin has suggested that although there is a dominant class, movement into it from a subordinate class is far easier than in capitalist societies and that there is less normative differentiation in socialist societies (that is, there is less evidence of distinctive upper-class dress, culture, etc.).[29] In terms of economics there are some indications that income inequality is less in the Soviet Union than in the United States,[30] and that the gap from top to bottom of the economic scale has been reduced in the Soviet Union with more of the population nearer the middle.[31]

No discussion of social stratification in the Soviet Union can go very far without considering the Communist Party. But the difficulty of dealing with the subject is demonstrated by the fact that one person describes it as a "new class,"[32] another discusses classes in terms of their relation to the party,[33] and a third sees the party as evidence of the classless nature of the society.[34] However, all do agree on the importance of the party.

---

[29] Parkin, *op. cit.,* pp. 155–157.

[30] Gerhard Lenski, *Power & Privilege: A Theory of Social Stratification* (New York: McGraw Hill Book Co., 1966), p. 311.

[31] Alex Inkeles, *Social Change in Soviet Russia* (Cambridge, MA: Harvard University Press, 1968), p. 138.

[32] Milovan Djilas, *The New Class* (New York: Praeger Publishers, 1957), especially Chap. 3.

[33] Lenski, *op. cit.,* p. 327.

[34] Robert Feldmesser, "Social Classes and Political Structure," Cyril E. Black (ed.), *The Transformation of Soviet Society* (Cambridge, MA: .Harvard University Press, 1967), pp. 235–252.

Using the frame of reference of the mass society, it is argued by some that the cleavage between members of the party and the rest of the population is so significant that it overshadows all other distinctions and creates a classless result. At the same time, others contend that the party is the key to what is in fact a stratified system. Lenski, for example, identifies four basic classes on the basis of their position in or with respect to the party: party functionaries, rank-and-file party members, those outside the party but not considered hostile to it, and opponents or enemies of the party.[35]

The former vice-president of Yugoslavia, Milovan Djilas, used the phrase "the new class" in his description of contemporary communism.[36] The greatest illusion of communism was, he said, that collectivization and the end of capitalist ownership would lead to a classless society. Instead, it has produced a new class, the political bureaucracy, that in many ways parallels the traditional propertied class. This new group consists of those who possess economic and other privileges because they are in control of the administrative processes and machinery of the society. Although they do not own property and cannot pass it on to their children, members of this class enjoy the material and other benefits ownership normally brings.

We have spoken of class or classlessness in the Soviet Union in terms of communist ideology and the Communist Party. It has also been suggested that the social class system seems to have unfolded more or less spontaneously in response to policies of an economic and social nature adopted by governmental authorities.[37] Regardless of intent or ideology, it appears that the processes and forces of the modern industrial state (such as division of labor, specialization, emphasis on technical knowledge) carry their own social consequences. Alex Inkeles, an advocate of this position, sees modern industrial production as providing a natural basis for social stratification and views Soviet society as one whose main outline is "remarkably" like that of advanced industrial nations.[38] Modernization may necessitate certain similar policies and structures with respect to industrial organization, education, reward mechanisms, and similar concerns.

Class Versus Nonclass Criteria of Stratification

It has already been suggested that the political salience of class is to a large extent a function of the absence of other politically salient criteria of stratification. Simplistic conventional wisdom has held that these other criteria are not politically salient in Great Britain. But regionally defined cultural considerations are clearly present there, especially in the case of Scottish and Welsh nationalism. The 1974 British elections saw a resurgence of strength of the parties representing these

---

[35] Lenski, *op. cit.*, p. 327.
[36] Djilas, *op. cit.*, p. 37ff.
[37] Inkeles, *Social Change*, p. 133.
[38] *Ibid.*

particularistic interests. It is not entirely clear, however, whether this was a manifestation of a resurgence of the political salience of Scottish and Welsh nationalism or a manifestation of the British version of the American slogan "vote NO for president"—in other words, simultaneous rejection of both major parties.[39] It seems safe to say that the conventional wisdom about the cultural homogeneity of Great Britain is overstated in ignoring such cultural differences. Part of the confusion may emanate from a common tendency to equate England with Great Britain, the latter term referring to England, Scotland, and Wales. Contributing to the fact that these geographically defined differences have been politically manageable is the fact that the Scottish and Welsh together comprise only about 15 percent of the British population.

In England, life-style differences seem to be largely pannational—that is, they are distributed relatively evenly in a geographic sense. But certain nonclass-defined cultural characteristics looming on the horizon may disturb even England's vaunted cultural homogeneity. One is the racial problem brought about by the growing immigration of "coloureds" from the Commonwealth nations. A 1974 ruling by Harold Wilson's self-consciously liberal Labour government granting amnesty to the vast numbers of nonwhites who entered England illegally provoked a widespread, vigorous adverse reaction among white English people. Enoch Powell, a Tory member of Parliament (MP), gained considerable notoriety in the early 1970s by articulating a racism that has apparently been latent in a large part of the English population.

The political salience of class is a well-established phenomenon throughout the industrial world, as indicated by the existence of one or more class-based parties in virtually all of the nations we are considering, with the major exceptions of the United States and Canada. Other exceptions in the industrialized world are those right-wing dictatorships that espoused an ideology of homogeneous nationalism such as the Papadopolous regime in Greece, Franco's Spain, or Hitler's Germany. The inclusion of Greece and Spain among industrialized nations might be questioned in some quarters.

Both the United States and Canada are characterized by politically or economically salient regionalism. The geographically defined, relatively autonomous subculture of the French Canadians was described in the previous chapter. Economic pursuits are regionally defined in Canada, detracting from the development of the kind of pannational feeling necessary for the development of class consciousness. Canada may be divided into four distinct economic regions.[40] First, there is

---

[39] Cf. Richard Mansbach, "The Scottish National Party: A Revised Political Profile," *Comparative Politics*, Vol. 5, No. 2, January 1973, pp. 185–211.

[40] Hugh Clokie, *Canadian Government and Politics* (Toronto: Longman's Green, 1944), pp. 11–12. Compare Lawrence Mayer, "Federalism and Party Behavior in Australia and Canada," *Western Political Quarterly*, Vol. XXIII, No. 4, December 1970, at p. 798. Compare also Alexander Brady, *Democracy in the Dominions* (Toronto: University of Toronto Press, 1958), Third Ed. p. 23.

the maritime region comprised of Nova Scotia, Newfoundland, Prince Edward Island, and eastern New Brunswick. Situated on the eastern seaboard on relatively infertile soil, adversely affected by Canadian tariff policies, and flanked on the west by an alien French Canadian culture, the maritime region has acquired a sense of distinctness. The Saint Lawrence Valley of Quebec, Ontario, and western New Brunswick, although not a cultural unit, can be argued to comprise a geographic and economic entity containing 80 percent of the nation's manufacturing and most of the nation's small, intensively cultivated farms. A central wasteland divides eastern Canada, containing 70 percent of the nation's population, from western Canada. To the west of this barrier lies the wheat belt of Manitoba, Saskatchewan, and Alberta. West of the Rockies lies British Columbia, where Canadian timber interests are concentrated. Each of these economic regions probably has as much interaction and sense of common interests with the corresponding economic regions directly to the south in the United States as with the rest of Canada. Thus, both cultural and economic regionalism have impeded the development of pannational class identification.

Clearly, similar forces have operated in the United States. Economically, it is possible to talk about a corn belt, a wheat belt, northeastern commercial and industrial centers, etc. To some extent, the old Confederacy was a distinct cultural unit. Consequently, the United States, like Canada, has not had the kind of relatively cohesive labor movement as a political force that characterizes most other industrial nations.

Australia, another older Commonwealth nation, has a strong, cohesive labor movement rendered possible by a basically class-stratified society. The range of economic, ethnic, religious, or other nonclass diversities occurs mostly within each of its states rather than between them. In other words, diversities are relatively evenly distributed among Australia's states and are not geographically defined. In that sense, Australia can be called a relatively homogeneous society. Moreover, symbolic diversities rarely acquire in Australia sufficient social and political salience to supersede class identification.

The pattern throughout most of Western Europe is one of class-based social movements and political parties interacting with other criteria of stratification. Thus, while a trade union party or a democratic socialist party may be found in most such systems, religious identification can acquire sufficient political salience to generate a political party with similar frequency. Catholicism is perhaps the most widespread politically salient religious identification in Europe. Calvinism also takes on political salience in the Netherlands. Catholicism but not Calvinism finds direct representation in the Swiss party system. Scandinavia's Lutheranism, England's Anglicanism, and Scotland's Presbyterianism lack significant political salience in these highly secularized nations. Where religion is politically salient, identification with that religion tends to supplant any class consciousness. Thus, in France, Austria, Italy, West Germany, Belgium, the Netherlands, and

Luxemburg, practicing Catholics are generally resistant to the mobilizing efforts of trade union or socialist movements. The trade union movements in these countries tend to be divided between a "regular" confederation of unions (often with a Marxist elite) and Catholic unions. The latter are usually more concerned with mobilizing the workers for the purposes of the church than with representing the interests of the workers vis-a-vis other sectors of the economy. Similarly, as we will see in a later chapter, major religious parties exist in most Western European nations to compete with class-based parties for the allegiance of religious workers. This phenomenon is not limited to Catholic workers. In the Netherlands, orthodox Protestant workers are similarly lost to the socialist movement.

It has been shown earlier that class-related cleavages (for instance, a labor movement) exist alongside other salient cleavages (urban-rural) in Scandinavia, despite the generally low salience of religious cleavages in Sweden and Denmark, especially. In fact, in only three political systems (among those considered in this volume) are class-related cleavages generally not forced to compete with other salient cleavages for the loyalty of individuals: England, Sweden, and Australia. The urban-rural cleavage is less salient in Sweden than in Denmark or Norway, as indicated by the fact that the Agrarian Party changed its name (and hence its appeal) to the Centre Party. Even in Australia, the Catholicism of a large percentage of the members of the Australian Council of Trade Unions (ACTU) and the Australian Workers' Union (AWU) led to a split within the Australian labor movement. There, the trade union movement normally provides the core support for the Australian Labour Party (ALP). For about a decade beginning in the late 1950s, Catholics, concerned with the alleged communist domination of the leadership of the ACTU, the AWU, and the ALP, withdrew their support from the ALP and formed and supported the Democratic Labour Party. This splinter movement kept the ALP, normally Australia's largest party, out of power during that period.[41] Again, we find the recurring conflict between the class consciousness of salaried labor often taking a Marxist flavor, on the one hand, and the Catholicism of many laborers on the other. This conflict is a function of the extent to which Catholic social doctrine finds Marxism anathema.

Sweden is very free of nonclass-related cleavages. One indicator of the salience of socioeconomic status is reported by Hugh Helco: until recently Swedish telephone directories listed surnames in strict occupational order from professional to manual worker.[42] Thus, there are no significant criteria of stratification able to compete successfully for the loyalty of working-class Swedes. Under such circumstances, the Swedish Social Democratic Party, which relies on class consciousness for its core support, has been able to aggregate either a majority or a solid plu-

---

[41] See, for instance, Frank Langdon, "The Catholic Anti-Communist Role Within Australian Labour," *Western Political Quarterly,* Vol. IX, No. 4, December 1956, pp. 884–889.

[42] Hugh Helco, *Modern Social Politics in Britain and Sweden* (New Haven: Yale University Press, 1974), p. 30.

rality of votes for an uninterrupted 40-year span. This remarkable political success, of course, is due to a complex variety of causes that will be considered in the chapter on parties.

In those nations where the labor movement is split between religious and secular workers, labor-based parties are relegated to some relatively impotent minority support. In other words, the absence of criteria of stratification to compete for the class identification of the working class may be a necessary if not a sufficient precondition for the political success of a labor-based party. The impotence of labor-based parties in the context of competing criteria of stratification, such as class and religion, may be mitigated in fragmented multiparty systems. Thus, the Social Democratic Party of Germany was an influential force in the Weimar period when a vote considerably below a majority could still result in a place in a coalition government. However, in the postwar era, under conditions of an emerging two-party alignment, the same level of support relegated that party to permanent opposition status until the early 1960s.

The purely class-based appeal that characterized the German Social Democrats right after the Second World War was doomed to failure in the Federal Republic of Germany in large part as a result of the salience of other criteria of stratification to compete with class identification. Religion has been one basis of allegiance, as indicated by the strength of the Christian Democratic Party. Regionalism has also had a long history in Germany. It should be recalled that Germany united the political subsystems of "the Germanies" relatively late in the game: consequently, the extended existence of autonomous subsystems probably gave whatever cultural or economic diversities they represented a certain legitimacy.[43] The boundaries of the present *Lander* ("states") of the Federal Republic of Germany are not precisely congruent to the boundaries of the perceived cultural or economic subsystems of the past or with the boundaries of the states of the imperial or Weimar periods. The legitimacy of such decentralizing forces of the past was sacrificed in order to dismember Prussia after the Second World War. This is somewhat ironic in view of the fact that in the Weimar period democratic majorities held on longer in Prussia than in the nation as a whole or in almost any other state. Sympathy with the mass populism and racism of Nazism appeared most early and strongly in rural and conservatively Catholic Bavaria and in Schleswig-Holstein in the north.

To the extent that many Western European nations combine the salience of socioeconomic cleavages plus symbolic cleavages, the groupings of their societies would be addressing different issues. Thus, they would be talking past one another, and the political communication necessary to reach compromises that

---

[43] Compare Arnold Brecht, *Federalism and Regionalism in Germany* (New York: Oxford University Press, 1945).

resolve issues would suffer. This situation often in fact happens in Europe by the representation of nonmanual-labor interests with symbolically defined parties. Specifically, the antilabor vote of those who oppose the claims of the working class on matters of economic interests tends to go to those parties classified under the general heading of Christian Democracy. Although these parties are defined on a religious basis, their support, appeal, and programs are usually defined in terms of opposition to the claims of the labor movement. Therefore, to the extent that the clientele of Germany's Christian Democratic Union is aggregated on the basis of economic and not religious appeal, it may be suggested that political conflict in Germany is similar to the class-based conflict of England, Sweden, and Australia.

The Christian Democratic Party of Italy tends to oppose the claims of the Italian left largely on symbolic, moral grounds, exacerbating the intensity of conflict in that system. Issues of salience to Catholic morality, such as the legitimation of divorce, take on great importance to Italian Catholics and divert attention from conflicts of economic interest.

To generalize, Europeans with perceived economic interests opposed to those of the working class do not have major parties whose raison d'être is to represent their interests. But they may be represented by religious-based, centrist parties to varying degrees.

Those parties whose intended appeal is largely to secular middle-class interests (often liberal parties with a rationale grounded in nineteenth-century, Manchester liberalism) have been in marked decline throughout the Western world. Apparently, the middle classes possess less class consciousness as such than the working classes. When the interests of the middle classes are challenged, however, they will rise to defend them although usually through the vehicle of a nonclass-based party.

Rural and agrarian forces have declined in political importance in the industrialized world, although this process has occurred at different times and with different rates in the various systems. Urbanization occurred much later in Scandinavia, for example, than in Britain. At present, however, it would be difficult to name any industrial nation in which agrarian interests constitute a major, autonomous political force. This is nearly true by the definition of industrial society.

The most important nonclass consideration in the Soviet Union is nationality. Russians constitute just over half of the population with the other half divided among a relatively large number of diverse groups. The 15 Union Republics (states) are organized along ethnic lines, with the minorities located in relatively compact groups around the edges of the dominant Russian group, which occupies the central landmass. For the most part this is a cumulative rather than a cross-cutting pattern. That is, these geographically organized ethnic groups often have their own distinct national history, literature, language, and religion, reinforcing each other within a given nationality.

It is difficult to evaluate the salience of the nationality factor and the extent to which it influences social and political questions. The Harvard Project, in questioning Soviet refugees, included an extensive study of the Ukrainians, who are the second largest group in the Soviet Union. Although nationality differences were present, the overall conclusion drawn was that a Ukrainian's reactions were determined "first and foremost" by the facts of Soviet citizenship and occupation or social class, with nationality being a very distant secondary consideration.[44]

Although the Ukrainian findings are based on empirical data, it is difficult to generalize from them because cultural factors such as religion, language, and to an extent history are more similar between that group and Russians than between Russians and other groups. There is such great diversity among the various nationalities that one can only speculate as to results with other groups. For example, the Turkic, Islamic minorities of the Central Asian portion of the country have few ties of language, history, or religion with the dominant group. Similar questions can be raised about the groups occupying such areas as Georgia, Armenia, and the Baltic States. The tentative conclusion seems to be, however, that in relation to socioeconomic class the effect of nationality is limited and latent.

Equality and Social Mobility in Industrial Societies

Equality is a concept that has often been associated with the very idea of democracy. By claiming to promote more effectively social and economic equality, authoritarian nations such as the Soviet Union have claimed to be more truly "democratic" than those Western nations we usually characterize as democracies. Much of the confusion stems from the ambiguity in the meaning of equality.

The classic liberal concept of equality implies equality before the law, where there are no legally designated differences in status, reward, or privilege without regard to performance. Specifically, it originated as a middle-class concept that entailed opposition to aristocratic privilege, promotion of individual liberties against perceived governmental oppression, and promotion of the rules that the same legal standards are applicable to all males. In its more advanced manifestations, liberal equality entailed such political goals as extension of the suffrage. Equality in this sense is not concerned with differences in opportunity that are the result of differences in the distribution of social and economic resources.

The opportunity in question is the opportunity for *social mobility*. Social mobility implies the capacity to change socioeconomic status. Although the term usually encompasses both upward and downward mobility, we are primarily interested in opportunities for upward mobility. The most recent redefinition of

---

[44] Alex Inkeles, *The Soviet Citizen* (Cambridge, MA: Harvard University Press, 1959), p. 369.

the concept of equality by such "new left" spokesmen as John Rawls[45] entails the standard that government must do more than passively avoid inhibiting such capacity for upward mobility. Rawls and his followers would assign government the responsibility to create this capacity actively.

Therefore, because legal equality often does not lead to genuine equality of opportunity, because social and economic deprivations, as well as governmentally imposed legal deprivations, can impede the realization of human potential, and because differences in the distribution of social and economic resources are correlated with differences in political influence, the idea of equality has acquired these newer meanings and entailments. The threads of this newer conception of equality may be traced back to the nineteenth-century socialists, especially to the rising influence of Marxism. This concept of equality entails the use of governmental compulsion to redistribute social and economic resources in order to reduce the differential between the rich and the poor. It is suggested or implied by this definition of equality that social justice requires that social values be assigned on the basis of need instead of being "earned" by meeting some criterion of performance.

Accordingly, social policy is increasingly directed toward a more "egalitarian" distribution of social values. While formerly such benefits as adequate nutrition, medical care, and clean dwellings were considered things to be "earned," Western societies are increasingly coming to regard these benefits as human "rights" that society must provide. Social policies directed toward egalitarian distribution culminate in the concept of the welfare state, the subject of a later chapter.[46]

The specialization and division of labor characteristic of industrial societies constitutes a principal source of social and economic inequality.[47] Certain functions require more preparation and skill to perform or are more valuable to society, and these roles are more highly rewarded. Moreover, in a capitalist society, resources are acquired by the investment of resources. It is the nature of the system that capital begets capital. Thus, a person without socioeconomic resources is denied the means of improving socioeconomic status. Consequently, in an unregulated economy, socioeconomic inequality tends to increase.[48] Given the specialization and division of labor in industrial society, a certain amount of socioeconomic inequality appears to be inevitable. This appears to be true despite the fact that Great Britain and the Scandinavian democracies have gone considerably further than the United States in developing social policies that

---

[45] John Rawls, *A Theory of Justice* (Cambridge, MA: Harvard University Press, 1971). Rawls argues that a social order is just only to the extent that socioeconomic equality exists. For Rawls, inequalities that are the result of differential capabilities are as unjust as legally engineered equality because differential capabilities are undeserved.

[46] Helco, *op. cit.* constitutes the most detailed attempt to trace the development of such policies in particular social and historical contexts.

[47] Parkin, *op. cit.*, p. 18.

[48] Lenski, *op. cit.*, p. 341.

provide guarantees of certain levels of such things as nutrition, housing, income maintenance in the event of unemployment, and medical care as matter of right irrespective of the performance or productive capacities of the individual in question. Despite the growth of these policies, definite socioeconomic inequalities remain in those societies known as welfare states. The experience of nations such as Britain and Sweden suggests that while it is definitely possible to eliminate the extremes of wealth and abject poverty, there will always be a significant gap with regard to material well-being between those who are successful in a society and those who are not. Only the former will possess the amenities of life usually regarded as luxuries.

Merit Versus Ascription to Promote Equality

One of the major issues that will characterize mature industrial societies is the conflict over whether rewards and values ought to be distributed according to conventional criteria of performance or whether they ought to be *reassigned* on a more egalitarian basis. The former position constituted the principal rationalization for the eighteenth- and nineteenth-century attacks on the feudal and aristocratic order. Achievement orientation was characterized by the sociologist Talcott Parsons as a hallmark of modernity.[49]

The redistribution of socioeconomic resources by social policy constitutes "ascription" (or assignment) of these values, irrespective of performance. Thus, in a sense, the assignment of such values is a return to a premodern orientation. But the criteria for assignment have changed.

The defense of achievement orientation depends on the validity of the standards of performance. For instance, do IQ scores or scholastic grades measure what they purport to measure, or do they simply indicate the acquisition of the values of middle-class culture? This question is very much at issue in industrial societies. An answer is that achievement standards tend to perpetuate and even increase existing inequalities.

Given the impossibility of perfect equality due to the complexity of industrial societies, the question is raised as to what is a fair distribution of assets.[50] The intractability of the equality issue lies in the fact that there is no obvious right or wrong. Instead, it appears that conflicting rights are involved. Values in a society—such as positions in the upper strata, positions in medical school classes, on college faculties, in trade union jobs—tend to be finite. Thus, the assignment of values to subordinate groups to redress previous discrimination will displace some of those who already occupy such roles. The displaced occupiers of the roles may

---

[49] Talcott Parsons and Edward Shils, eds., *Toward A General Theory of Action* (New York: Harper Torchbooks, 1951), pp. 82-83.

[50] Irving Kristol, "About Equality," *Commentary,* Vol. 54, No. 5, November 1972, p. 41.

not be those guilty of past discrimination against subordinate groups. Members of dominant strata may have gotten their positions by succeeding at the rules of the game at that time; hence, the *assignment* of subordinate groups to valued positions may entail changing the rules after the game. But, it is difficult to justify a failure to redress previous systematic and pervasive discrimination.

The foregoing is meant to suggest that as a result of the imperatives of technology entailing the knowledge explosion, specialization, and the role of the expert, socioeconomic inequality is to some degree inherent in mature industrial systems despite the egalitarian ideal of the welfare-state policies increasingly apparent in some countries of Europe and the older Commonwealth. On the other hand, Lenski, in a standard work on stratification, discerns a trend toward the reduction of inequalities. Lenski finds that in nations where the welfare state is most thoroughly developed, political power and socioeconomic privilege are increasingly separated (in different hands).[51] However, this trend goes just so far; there appears to be a point beyond which inequality cannot be reduced.

For example, the previous chapter attempted to show that the English educational system acts as a force to perpetuate the socioeconomic status of given families. Offspring of upper-middle-class professional university-educated parents have been far more likely to acquire a university education than offspring of noncollege-educated or working-class parents. The financial burden of securing a place in the prep-school, public-school, "Oxbridge" tradition (for example, Sunnyvale Prep to Eaton to Oxford, Cambridge, or Sandhurst) has effectively filtered out offspring of working-class families. The eleven-plus exam system performs the same function in the state-supported institutions. Thus, as Lenski says, "the family is the single most important element in counteracting the egalitarian tendency inherent in modern educational system."[52] We suggest that to the extent that the acquisition of the skills and culture of the dominant stratum is a criterion for educational success, educational systems will impede social mobility as much as they foster it. These educational systems certainly act to perpetuate the dominant culture by acting as a filtration and selection mechanism. That is, Western educational systems select for positions of power and influence those who acquire the skills and values of the dominant culture.

The French educational system similarly acts as a selective institution emphasizing a system of competive examinations. The examinations generally test for the skills of verbal and symbolic manipulation acquired in a classic education, skills monopolized by upper-middle and upper class families. Thus, although the examination system can be rationalized as promoting the egalitarian values so important in the French culture (anyone can have the status or role who passes the exam, regardless of birth), in actuality the system impedes social mobility.

[51] Lenski, *op. cit.*, pp. 325–327.
[52] *Ibid.*, p. 391.

This is illustrated by the following figures cited by Henry Ehrman: 86 percent of bourgeois offspring remains in secondary school for the entire six-year term, as opposed to 55 percent of those from the lower-middle class, 35 percent of the farmers, and only 21 percent of the workers.[53] Ehrman further points out that all of the children in secondary school must have already demonstrated academic talent to enter; therefore, this is further evidence that the structure and procedures of the system are particularly suited to the skills transmitted by the bourgeois culture.

The percentage of college-age people who are actually full-time students is considerably smaller in all other industrial societies than the United States. While in France egalitarianism entails the right to take the examinations or attend the school and to be judged by the same standards as everyone else, in the United States egalitarianism is coming more and more to entail the right to possess the credentials the educational systems have to offer. Outside of the United States, the educational systems have performed more of a selective function. However, the percentage of those who are in fact full-time students among college-age people seems generally on the rise.

Therefore, equality in the sense of an even distribution of resources can be approached but far from achieved in the industrial societies. The opportunity for social mobility rather than an equal distribution of resources may be taken as an indicator of the openness of a society, and the rates of social mobility may be taken as a quantitative indicator of equality of opportunity. It is therefore useful to inquire into the variation in the rates of social mobility in industrial societies.

It will be recalled that mobility may be in either an upward or downward direction. A standard study of the topic of social mobility[54] defines the process in terms of movement from manual to nonmanual occupations (upward mobility) or vice versa (downward mobility). The study is talking about intergenerational mobility in that its data compare the occupations of fathers and their sons.

The major finding is that there is little significant variation in the rates of total mobility among seven nations under consideration: the United States, Sweden, Germany, Japan, France, Switzerland, and the Soviet Union.[55] Similarly, there is little variation in the rates of mobility when measured by status criteria. Greater variation may be discerned with respect to either upward or downward mobility. No pattern in this variation is apparent, however. We are reduced to explaining this variation in terms of the proper names of nations. This is, of course, a nonexplanation. To say that there is more upward mobility in Switzerland because of the unique configuration of things that comprise Switzerland means

---

[53] Ehrman, *op. cit.*, p. 69.
[54] Reinhard Bendix and Seymour Lipset, *Social Mobility in Industrial Societies* (Berkeley: University of California Press, 1959), p. 14.
[55] *Ibid.*, pp. 25–26.

that the "explanation" is not reproducible (there will never be another Switzerland) and hence generates no predictive capacity (it cannot logically be extended to other cases).[56]

Total mobility (upward plus downward mobility) is correlated with the rate of industrial expansion.[57] This may be expected from the nature of the industrializing process. By definition, the industrializing process involved, through specialization and division of labor, a progressive increase in the number and variety of roles to fill and, through the knowledge explosion and the imperatives of modern technology, a progressive increase in the percentage of roles that are nonmanual. (Daniel Bell suggests that one of the hallmarks of the postindustrial society was a marked increase in the proportionate size of the tertiary or service sector of the economy.)[58] Although service jobs are not necessarily nonmanual, a relatively high percentage of them are. Bell notes a significant rise in the educational and skill level of the labor force;[59] consequently, industrial and more emphatically postindustrial societies may be characterized by an increase in opportunities for social mobility in the form of more higher-status and nonmanual roles. The opportunities thus created by the expansion of more high-status roles lead to a rise in upward mobility in the expanding or industrializing economy.

The fact that industrial society is in fact a performance-oriented or "meritocratic" society (valued roles allocated on the basis of merit) means that status roles are not guaranteed regardless of one's parentage if one cannot meet all the performance standards. Thus, industrial societies also have a greater downward mobility than preindustrial societies. Accordingly, both upward and downward mobility are greater in industrial societies than preindustrial societies.

Social Mobility and Stability

Social mobility is thought to be a significant force for the maintenance of stability.[60] To the extent that social mobility is based on performance standards, social mobility tends to elevate the most talented members of the lower strata to the higher strata. The lower strata are thus deprived of their potential leadership and their capacity to oppose the upper strata. Furthermore, to the extent that some members of the lower strata are elevated to the upper strata, many more members of the lower strata perceive the opportunity is there for their own

---

[56] See the excellent discussion of the status of proper names in cross-cultural research in Adam Przeworski and Henry Teune, *The Logic of Comparative Social Inquiry* (New York: John Wiley and Sons, 1970), pp. 26–30, 57 & 75.
[57] Ralf Dahrendorf, *Class and Class Conflict in Industrial Societies* (Stanford, CA: Stanford University Press, 1959), p. 58 and Bendix and Lipset, *op. cit.*, p. 27.
[58] Bell, *The Coming of Post Industrial Society, op. cit.*, pp. 126–127.
[59] *Ibid.*, pp. 143 ff.
[60] Dahrendorf, *op. cit.*, pp. 57–61. Parkin, *op. cit.*, p. 49.

upward mobility. Members of the lower strata are able to regard the system as legitimate and their individual deprivation as a result of their individual inadequacy rather than as a fault of the system. This is, of course, a function of the extent that the criteria for mobility are perceived to be performance standards. The longstanding belief of many Americans in the "Horatio Alger myth"—that hard work is sufficient to rise "from rags to riches"—may be one of the foremost examples of such a legitimating belief system. The aforementioned acceptance of English lower strata that the English elite is composed of "their betters"—individuals who deserve their positions because of personal qualities and skills—is a similar belief. In short, the belief that people "get what they deserve" serves to legitimate a system based on inequality. This belief in turn is encouraged by social mobility.

Even downward mobility can further this legitimacy. Parkin reports that downward mobile members of the middle class are more likely to believe in middle-class values than members of the lower classes.[61] These middle-class values and beliefs include the idea of "survival of the fittest" or success to the most deserving. This belief is commonly referred to as social Darwinism—the application of Charles Darwin's principles of evolutionary theory to social mobility.

Performance or meritocratic principles never completely predominate. These principles threaten some members of dominant strata who do not wish to be required to earn their privileged position constantly. Partly because dominant strata have some control over the rules of society, meritocratic or performance principles are always mitigated by institutions that operate to perpetuate the existing stratification system.

Mobility in a Closed Society

The preceding observations on mobility are very interesting when considered with respect to the Soviet Union which is often thought of as a "closed" system. There are strong indications that for the most part the generalizations concerning social mobility apply to Soviet society and that it may be no more closed in this respect than other industrial societies.

According to one study, the rate of upward mobility for the Soviet Union was in the same range (actually slightly higher) as that of the United States, France, and Germany in terms of white-collar employees whose fathers were either workers or farmers.[62] In fact, consider these statements: "mobility opportunities in Eastern Europe are more favorable than those in the West";[63] "more than in most European societies, the career is open to talent";[64] "the present rate of social

---

[61] Parkin, *op. cit.*, p. 53.
[62] Inkeles, *The Soviet Citizen*, p. 83.
[63] Parkin, *op. cit.*, p. 165.
[64] L. G. Churchward, *The Soviet Intelligentsia* (London: Routledge and Kegan Paul, 1973), p. 11.

mobility probably equals that in the United States and possibly surpasses it."[65] Djilas in his discussion of the elite "new class" states repeatedly that it is not a closed and exclusive group in terms of access.[66] On the contrary, it is constantly changing and replenishing itself by including as some of its most steadfast members former sons of the working class.

These opportunities seem to be reflected somewhat in the mobility aspirations of youths in Soviet society, who appear to be much like those of other industrial countries. As indicated by responses from both the United States and the Soviet Union, people of lower status tend to have lower goals.[67] In the opinion of at least one student of Soviet society, the image of the Soviet Union as the land of opportunity has become more salient and more widely accepted by Soviet youth.[68]

The reasons usually given to explain mobility in the Soviet Union are consistent with those already mentioned with respect to industrial nations in general and include such factors as the systems of education, the impact of economic expansion, and the need for individuals with specialized technical knowledge.

While party membership is still essential to success in the Soviet Union, there are indications that membership is obtained without too much difficulty by those who possess talents and knowledge desired by the elite. In industrial societies, these talents increasingly involve higher, specialized education. Although no one would deny that the children of the elite are disproportionately represented in higher educational institutions, or that *blat* (influence or "pull") exists, there is good reason to believe that many if not most places are occupied by those who have earned them on the basis of merit through a competitive process.

If one can acquire this higher education, which is in large part specialized and technically oriented, there are strong indications that it will open the way to upward movement. Although the subject of elite recruitment will be dealt with in detail in the next chapter, one development in particular is relevant at this point. Several fairly recent studies have examined the process of recruitment into the higher levels of the bureaucracy (*apparat*) of the Communist Party of the Soviet Union (CPSU) at both the national and regional levels.[69] A major point of agreement is the fact that there has been an increase of individuals with spe-

---

[65] Inkeles, *Social Change*, p. 174.
[66] Djilas, *op. cit.*, pp. 42, 61.
[67] Inkeles, *The Soviet Citizen*, pp. 87–92.
[68] H. Kent Geiger, *The Family in Soviet Russia* (Cambridge, MA: Harvard University Press, 1968), p. 169.
[69] For the Central Committee of the CPSU see Michael P. Gehlen, "The Soviet Apparatchiki," R. Barry Farrell (ed.), *Political Leadership in Eastern Europe and the Soviet Union* (Chicago: Aldine Publishing Co., 1970), pp. 140–156. A regional study is Robert E. Blackwell Jr., "The Soviet Political Elite—Alternative Recruitment Policies at the Obkom Level," *Comparative Politics*, Vol. 6, No. 1, October 1973, pp. 99–121.

cialized, functional technical education and experience and a corresponding decline in professional politicians with the more general or ideological background held by those who enter through such organizations as *Komsomol* (the youth organization). Research on career patterns in the communist systems of Eastern Europe indicates that this increased emphasis on technical attributes is also a consistent development in those countries.[70]

Given the degree of mobility apparently present in this "closed" system, it is perhaps natural to wonder whether it will continue. While no clear answer is possible, there has been speculation along at least two lines. First, there is the level of economic expansion. Much of the openness of the Soviet system can be traced back to the need to rebuild the economy and the work force after such devastating events as a civil war, two world wars and the purges of the Stalin period. This rebuilding, coupled with the emphasis on economic growth and expansion common to all industrial nations, resulted in a high degree of social mobility. If growth slows and fewer jobs are created, it is possible that the system might become more inbred and closed.

Second, there is increased emphasis on technical attributes. Here we must remember the claim of the ruling elite to be the vanguard and guiding force of the society. The implications of these two factors include the fact that the elite must continue to bring into its rank promising young technicians, planners, and others. The alternative, which would appear to be unacceptable, would be to risk the creation of a distinct and competing group composed of many of the most highly trained and qualified members of society.

In his study of the Soviet *apparatchiki*, Gehlen concludes that all the evidence suggests just such a conscious effort on the part of the CPSU to bring these individuals into the party.[71] If successful, this policy would improve the capabilities of the party in its attempt to control the productive processes of the country and perform its vanguard role, while at the same time inhibiting the growth of competition or opposition with the technical competence to mount a real challenge. Finally, by preempting potential opposition and continuing to provide opportunities for upward movement, the elite may perform the stabilizing and legitimizing functions already mentioned with regard to social systems in general.

The foregoing arguments have been advanced here and elsewhere suggesting that social mobility is expected to be supportive of political stability. However, there is much more variation in the stability of industrial nations than in the rates of social mobility. Recall the evidence suggesting that upward mobility is high in all industrial nations. Therefore, we cannot "explain" the stability of any country by its high rate of social mobility. It is difficult to find a truly "closed" society

---

[70] Carl Beck, "Career Characteristics of East European Leadership," Farrell, *op. cit.*, pp. 157–194.
[71] Gehlen, *op. cit.*, pp. 149.

Social Stratification and Politics

among the industrial nations in the sense of possessing insurmountable barriers to upward mobility with which to test the proposition that such societies should generate destabilizing tensions. It may be that some amount of upward social mobility is a necessary if not a sufficient precondition for a stable political order. However, because this social mobility may even be found in authoritarian systems, we cannot put that proposition to an empirical test.

Conclusions

All industrial societies are divided along some criteria. These different groupings generate demands of claims on public policy arising out of their shared orientation. These different demands result in issues.

Stability in a democratic society is a function of that society's capacity to process its issues. The processing of issues in such a society is accomplished by bargaining and compromise. The capacity to bargain and compromise is enhanced by formulating demands in terms of measurable interests instead of in terms of abstract symbols. Demands formulated in terms of interests arise out of a socioeconomic criterion of stratification. Symbolic demands are based on such criteria of stratification as culture, religion, ethnicity, etc. These issues are more difficult to resolve.

We have seen that symbol-based cleavages do not necessarily adversely affect stability. The shared orientations of groupings may not be translated into demands on the national decision-making process. Furthermore, the apparent isolation of cleavages from each other in a society does not by any means preclude communication, bargaining, and issue resolution at the elite level. The consociational model of Lijphart constitutes a suggestion that this in fact is what had been occurring in the Netherlands until about 1970. Stiefbold has suggested that this has applied to Austria as well. Heisler suggests that this process also occurred in Belgium. This top elite cooperation is apparently rendered possible by combinations of two factors, combinations that vary from country to country. The first factor is less ideologism and partisan feeling among the top elite than the lower-level elite. Second, instead of trying to resolve the issues that arise out of the most fundamental divisions between relatively isolated subcultures, the top elite often allow the respective subcultures considerable autonomy with respect to the policies most important to them. In this way, each subculture retains control of those policies that may have an effect on its cultural integrity. This is most clearly the case in Belgium since the constitutional revision of 1970. It may be seen, to a large extent, in Canada in a less formalized way. The issues that divide the French Canadian Catholic subculture from the rest of Canada are rarely expressed through the major national parties. Instead, a provincial-based party that cannot hope to govern, *Le Parti Ralliement des Creditiste,* emerged for a time to speak for those French Canadian demands that the Liberal Party could not articulate and still maintain its image as a national party. Moreover, most culturally salient policies are simply handled by the provincial instead of the national elite. Consequently, when cumulative or mutually isolated subcultures are geographically defined, some form of federalism or confederation may remove the stress of incompatible demands from the national decision-making process.

Unless the boundaries of the political subunits (variously called *states, provinces, lander,* or *cantons*) are congruent with perceived cultural or economic differences, federalism's major reason for being seems to be absent. Federal institutions have a much more divisive impact on the national decision-making process and political subunits have more autonomy in Canada where such boundaries are more or less coterminous with cultural, ethnic, religious, or economic distinctions than in Australia where they are not.[72] Similarly, federalism has a more divisive effect and subunits are more autonomous from the central government in Switzerland than in the Federal Republic of Germany or Austria for the same reasons.

The issues that parochial subcultures tend to hold most sacred tend to revolve around the maintenance of their cultural distinctiveness, to resist assimilation in the larger culture. These issues are accordingly referred to as issues of "cultural defense." The process by which a culture is disseminated to a population, including transmitting cultural properties from one generation to the next, is called *socialization*. The primary agents of this socialization process in industrial societies are families and schools. The family structure appears to remain by and large safe from significant governmental manipulation throughout the industrial world. It is the socializing influence of the school systems that parochial subcultures, concerned with cultural defense, tend to fear most. For example, in nations with large Catholic subcultures, the issue most potentially salient for Catholics was public financial support of religious schools. By quick acceptance of the Catholic position in the Netherlands and Belgium, and by strong provincial autonomy in the administration of education in Canada, prolonged divisive conflict over this issue was avoided.

We may conclude that although a pluralistic society based on crosscutting cleavages should in theory be more supportive of the stable democracy than other types of stratification systems, it is clearly not a necessary precondition of stable democracy. This fact is one more exception to the longstanding fallacy of regarding the characteristics of the British and/or American political systems as necessary preconditions of stable democracy.

The ideological view of the modern world has much to say on the issue of equality. The classic liberal conception of equality is concerned with legal equality and the drive toward performance standards for the acquisition of socioeconomic status and values. New-left and Marxian principles entail the equalization of the

---

[72] Mayer, *op. cit.*

distribution of values by authoritative assignment or ascription if necessary. Thus, some societies are more prone to accept inequality than others depending on their ideological basis. Western societies whose ideological foundations involve free-market principles and the ideas of social Darwinism or "survival of the fittest" are prone to regard poverty and social failure as natural and inevitable. The idea of socialism, whether of the democratic or the Soviet variety, and the idea of the welfare state that is gaining increasing acceptance in Britain and Scandinavia are both rooted in the assumption that poverty is both eradicable and intolerable.

While the extremes of wealth and poverty have by and large been eliminated in Britain, Scandinavia, and the Soviet Union, socioeconomic inequality remains a fact of life throughout the industrialized world. This fact stems from the process of industrialization itself, which entails a certain amount of inevitable inequality. Thus, a certain measure of socioeconomic stratification is a result of the specialization and division of labor that accompanies the process of industrialization irrespective of ideological differences among nations (free market, Marxist, etc.).

Insofar as the equality issue raises the question of the ease of social mobility, the differences between the Soviet Union and the Western nations are not as significant as one might suspect. The primary institutionalized channel for upward mobility in industrial society tends to be a system of publicly financed education based on competitive performance criteria. The educational system in the Soviet Union is competitive and based on performance criteria to about as great an extent as those of Western societies. An offspring of nonelite parents can, with ability, rise up through the educational system and acquire the credentials necessary for entry into the elite. Of course, the system is not completely open in the sense that any child regardless of birth has an equal opportunity to succeed in the system. There are differences, for example, between the urban middle classes and peasants in this regard. However, it will be recalled that the educational systems and hence the opportunities for upward mobility are far from meeting this standard of complete openness in Britain, France, or other Western European societies.

The conclusion of more similarity than differences between the Western nations and the Soviet Union with regard to social mobility may be expected from a consideration of the nature of industrial society. An industrial society is by definition a technological society. A technological society is one that depends on knowledge, skill, and performance. Therefore, the imperatives of running an industrial society require performance-based criteria of social mobility. To the extent that performance standards imply an open society, all industrial societies are open societies. To the extent that the skills required by performance criteria are imparted by the family in formative preschool years, the family as an institution acts as an impediment to upward mobility. Successful families are more likely to transmit the tools of success to their offspring than unsuccessful families. Thus, to the extent that industrial societies are performance societies, in this sense all such societies, communist or not, lack complete openness and equality of opportunity for upward mobility. The performance imperatives of a technologically based industrial society entail convergence between the Soviet-bloc nations and the Western world in the area of social mobility as well as other areas.

We have dealt with the nature of social groupings in the industrial societies and the kinds of demands generated by these groupings. The representation of the interests of the groupings in and the transmission of the demands to the national decision-making process are functions normally performed in industrial societies by political parties and organized groups. These structures are examined in the following chapter.

Part II

Policymaking Structures and Processes

Introduction to Part II

Having considered contextual factors that significantly affect the political process, we consider in this part the nature of that process itself. By the political process, we mean making authoritative public policy or making authoritative decisions resolving issues about who gets how much of what. This definition is intended to exclude the administrative function—carrying out and applying policy decisions.

This process is carried out by a variety of structures. Some of those structures are constitutionally designated for the purpose of engaging in this process. We find it convenient to call them political structures. Other structures not so designated also participate in this process, however. Administrative structures participate in the political process although constitutionally designated for other purposes. Some structures intimately involved in the political process are not usually constitutionally designated, such as parties and groups.

A description of the structures does not constitute a description of the process. One must further describe the manner in which the structures participate in the act of forumulating policies, making decisions, or allocating values. But it is not possible to describe the process without describing the structures that participate in the process.

One of the major themes of Part II is that the process of authoritative policymaking to a large extent bypasses those structures explicitly designated by their respective constitutions for such policy formulation purposes. Political structures—legislatures, prime ministers or premiers, and their cabinets—are generally staffed by people trained in the law or educated in the liberal arts tradition; in other words, they are staffed by generalists. As pointed out in the introductory chapter, mature industrial societies, by their very nature, generate issues of considerable technological complexity, issues whose ramifications can only be comprehended by specialists. Because the expertise and knowledge needed to resolve such issues remain esoteric to specialists, there are strong pressures on the generalists in the political structures to depend on and even defer to the advice and arguments of these specialists. Thus, to an increasing extent, the decisions that actually become public policy are increasingly made by those specialists outside the structures constitutionally designated for policy purposes. These specialists are found in the administrative structures, where one of the defining characteristics is that of specialization and division of labor, and in organized groups formed by and designated to represent special interests.

We argue in the chapters that follow that much actual policymaking in industrial societies is done by a process of bargaining and compromise among relevant bureaucrats and representatives of the interests concerned with the issue at hand. By definition, interests that are not organized or are less well organized tend to have a distinctly diminished impact on the policymaking process.

It is possible, of course, to overstate the extent to which the policymaking process has passed from the hands of the political structures constitutionally designated for that purpose. Clearly, some important decisions are reached in such structures. We are pointing out a trend. To the extent that any significant policymaking occurs outside of the political (as distinct from the private or administrative) sectors, this constitutes a departure from a strictly legalistic and formalistic description of the policymaking process.

Furthermore, even to the extent that the process of policy formulation bypasses the political sector, political structures still have important roles to play. One such role is the legitimation of decisions that may in fact have been reached elsewhere.

Possibly the most realistic assessment of most policy decisions is that they occur neither completely within nor completely outside the political sectors. The political sector often plays a role of what might be described as mediating the bargaining process among bureaucratic interests. It must be stressed, however, that this mediating role includes a government input, and because of the legitimacy of governmental input, the government cannot be dismissed as just another group.

The explicitly political structures—those constitutionally designated for policy formulation—are considered first. We make no attempt to describe every such structure exhaustively. We discuss the diminishing role of upper houses in parliamentary democracies using the British House of Lords as an example, and readers should be able to infer a similarly diminished role for similar reasons for the other upper houses not specifically mentioned. We generalize about the processes in which political structures engage instead of discussing each constitutionally designated structure for its own sake.

It is useful to describe the political structures first because of another role they play in the policymaking process. These structures also provide the context in which the other structures function. The tactics and organization of parties and groups, the extent of the political role of the administrative sector, and even the structure of particular national bureaucracies are to some extent determined by the political format. Thus, despite the fact that the actual decisions about who gets how much of what and why are made by structures other than those we have categorized as explicitly political, the overall nature of the political process itself is in large part determined by the context provided by these political structures.

While parties are explicitly political, they are often not constitutionally designated. Accordingly, they may play a somewhat different role from constitutionally designated structures and should be discussed separately from them. The administrative sector is constitutionally designated but not for explicitly political functions. We argue that this lack of congruence between the theoretical function of public bureaucracies and what they actually do creates special problems and behavior patterns that merit separate discussion.

The nature of mature industrial societies has the effect of heightening the organizational life of society and the importance of interest groups in the political process. The activities of these groups, as much or more than any other structure, are a major factor in the actual policy-formulation process. Accordingly, this process is best described as part of the consideration of interest groups, found in Chapter 8.

Chapter 5

Policymaking Structures

In Part I we were concerned with sociocultural contexts in which political processes operate. We now turn our attention to political processes themselves, and we have at last reached the point where a traditional study of politics would ordinarily begin.

The political processes to which we refer are those that make authoritative decisions allocating values for the whole society. An examination of these processes will begin with constitutionally designated structures and process. However, even in the area of formal policymaking, constitutions are often unreliable guides to how these processes actually operate.

Several terms are used often in the ensuing discussion. Because comprehension of them is crucial, a brief review of their meaning seems in order.

We are concerned with structures—recurring patterns of interaction. Legislatures, cabinets, and bureaucracies are governmental structures. Classes are social structures.

Accountability and Responsiveness

Our concern with constitutionally designated structures centers on two major questions. First, do these structures play the role in the decision-making process for which they are constitutionally designated?

Why or why not? Second, are those structures accountable to the society they allegedly serve for the consequences of what they do? Accountability refers to a liability to be called upon to answer for or justify behavior or its consequences. It implies that those who are accountable are made to perceive that they will somehow be better off if the people to whom they are accountable are at least passively satisfied with their performance.

Accountability presumably induces a greater responsiveness on the part of the political process. These processes are *responsive* to the extent that authoritative decisions reflect the perceived needs and demands of the governed. Accountability and responsiveness are both matters of degree.

Political processes may also be judged by their adaptability. Accountability and responsiveness are classically considered as democratic values (although, as we will aruge, they are not completely inapplicable standards for analyzing the Soviet Union). Adaptability is a value for any political system, democratic or authoritarian. It refers to the capacity of a system to change in order to accommodate changes in its input (the messages received from its socioeconomic context). Changes in output may require a structural change in the system—the formulation of new or expanded processes for transforming input into authoritative policies.

These criteria are applied in this chapter in large part to constitutionally designated structures. Accordingly, a brief digression into the nature of constitutions and consitutionalism seems in order.

Constitutions and Constitutionalism

The term *constitution* is used in two quite distinct senses. Americans tend to use it in its more familiar sense to refer to a set of fundamental written laws that designate the format of government. These laws are fundamental in the sense that they override ordinary acts of the legislature. Normally, these laws are more difficult to change than ordinary legislation. Fundamental laws do have legal sanction, however. Alleged violations of the laws are dealt with through the judicial processes.

The meaning of the term *constitution* is not exhausted by this legal conception. The British political system, for example, has no such set of fundamental written laws, but scholars do speak of the English or British constitution.

Constitutions as Fundamental Principles

The term in a broader sense refers to those procedures for making decisions and choosing decision makers that are fundamental to the essential nature of the system. The term *fundamental* means that which cannot be altered without changing the essential character of the system. For example, if a British cabinet should resist the pressure to resign in the face of an unambiguous expression of no-confidence by the legislature (a procedure discussed below), the entire structure of accountability of the cabinet to society through the intermediary agency of Parliament would no longer pertain. We argue below that it is this particular structure of accountability that defines parliamentary democracy. The structure of accountability of the governors to the governed is perhaps the most fundamental set of procedures for any system.

Other procedures are alterable without altering the fundamental essence of the system. In chapter 7, it will be shown how the procedure for choosing the British Conservative Party leader has been formalized in recent years. This procedural change could hardly be argued to change the nature of the system. Sometimes, rules find their way into constitutions that are neither procedural or fundamental. The amendment to the United States Constitution concerning the prohibition of the sale and consumption of alcoholic beverages is an obvious case in point. This amendment attempted to resolve an issue that was peculiar to a particular point in time. Various nonfundamental rules may be found in the four documents that comprise the legal aspect of the Swedish constitution. The Instrument of Government lays down a number of specific rules for the operation of the legislature (Riksdag) including a list of the committees. Clearly, this topic ought to be kept flexible as events and technology create new subject areas to be dealt with by the committees. The functions and procedures of the Riksdag committees are further specified in the Riksdag Act.

We are distinguishing between what is fundamental and what pertains to the circumstances of a particular time, presuming that some things ought to be easier to change than others. The purpose in making a constitution harder to change than ordinary legislation is that the rules inherent in the character of a system ought to be harder to change than the resolution of issues that pertain to the circumstances of the moment. Presumably, the constitution would confine itself to the former class of rules while the latter type of rules would be reflected in ordinary legislation.

This concept of fundamental principles enables us to speak of a British consitution in the absence of a set of fundamental written laws for that system. The British constitution is comprised of four basic elements, only the first two of which possess legal sanction: common law, acts of Parliament, landmark documents, and convention.

Clearly, not all rules of law have constitutional significance. The answer to the question of which are accorded constitutional significance is provided by our definition of a constitution in the broad sense—those rules that lay down fundamental procedures. Acts of Parliament such as the Habeas Corpus Act, the Act of Settlement of 1701, the Statute of Westminster of 1931, and perhaps the three major reform bills leading to universal manhood suffrage would have such significance.

As stated earlier, the principal enduring significance of the system of English common law involves its imperatives for the interpretation and application of acts of Parliament. The common law in this sense may be thought of as a set of procedures—a way of resolving conflicts—that distinguishes the political culture of common law jurisdictions from civil law jurisdiction of the Continent. The important concept that property may not be taken without due process of law is a common law right as distinguished from a statutory law right.

Landmark documents having constitutional significance are those possessing great symbolic value for the fundamental structure of the system. For example, the symbolic value of the Magna Carta far exceeds the specific feudal rights that it guaranteed the English barony. The document has come to symbolize the very idea of limited government.

Many of the fundamental procedures of the British system are without legal sanction. The office of prime minister was not even mentioned in British law until after the Second World War. The fundamental rule that the cabinet functions at the sufferance of a majority of the House of Commons is based solely on the force of convention. If members of the cabinet, upon a clear loss of confidence by the House of Commons, refused to resign, their behavior would be perfectly legal but clearly unconstitutional.

The tension between the bounds of legality and the imperatives of constitutionality in this regard was interestingly illustrated in British Guiana (now Guyana) during a period of social and racial unrest in December 1964. The Marxist Prime Minister Cheddi Jagan refused to resign, although his People's Progressive Party lost its majority and the governor had asked Frobes Burnham of the Black-oriented People's National Congress to form a government. Jagan claimed election fraud and there was no legal way to force him out. The resulting constitutional crisis was finally resolved when the body that acts as Britain's supreme court, the Judicial Committee of the Privy Council (JCPC) made a ruling that enabled the governor to force Jagan out. The crisis emanated from importing the British reliance on convention into a context lacking the history and tradition to legitimate the convention and give it force. Relying on the sanction of custom works in Britain because of that system's lengthy evolutionary development (discussed in Chapter 2). Not many systems possess such a past and consequently such strength of tradition.

When rules of constitutional significance have only customary sanction but are not part of a nation's legal structure, an interesting paradox can result. It is possible for an act to be perfectly legal but unconstitutional. Jagan's situation is a case in point. For another example, the British monarch retains as much legal power as she ever had; yet, it would be unconstitutional for her to exercise it. Bills become law when the clerk says, "La reine [or le Roy] le veult" (the queen or king wills it). But for the monarch to "will" anything not passed by Parliament or to refuse to "will" that which Parliament had passed would exceed his or her constitutional role. Queen Anne was the last to refuse with the formula "La reine s'avisera" (the queen will consider it).[1] Such a crisis would probably destroy the monarchy as the failure of other monarchs to act within the bounds of their role has destroyed other monarchies.

In systems lacking a long evolutionary development, especially in systems emanating from a revolution, legitimacy must be created overnight for the new set of institutions. Only legal sanctions can impart such instant legitimacy. That is why written constitutions are the rule and unwritten ones the exception.

Thus, one of the functions of a written constitution is to legitimate the consensus of fundamentals that has already evolved in a society. It is doubtful that a constitution can create such a consensus.

Yet, even in the case of a written constitution, we can discern constitutional significance in rules beyond those in the written constitution. We all know, for example, that the presidential electors of America's electoral college are expected to vote for the candidate receiving a plurality of the popular votes in their respective states. That the outcome of the contest for the presidency reflects in some fashion the popular vote is clearly a rule of constitutional significance. But the electors are legally free to vote for whomever they please. The imperative that the popular vote determines the electoral vote for each state is a constitutional rule with customary rather than legal sanction.

Sweden possesses four legal documents that are generally recognized as comprising its formal constitution, as noted above. Several specific, substantive rules have been included in some of these documents. There is a difficulty in placing what is fundamental and enduring with what is relevant to current issues. Policy—substantive decisions regarding who gets how much of what—must be changeable or the system cannot adapt or respond to input from its context. To make the fundamental equally easy to alter would render the character of the system vulnerable to the passions of a point in time.

Despite their incorporation of numerous substantive matters, Sweden's constitutional documents are relatively hard to amend. Apparently, the substantive matters are not of such importance as to affect the flexibility of the system. Sweden's Riksdag Act of 1865 that amended the Basic Law of 1809, and the Act of Succession of 1810 engendered considerable bitter controversy. The act made the Riksdag a bicameral representative assembly instead of the former quadricameral body representing the "four estates of the realm" and set down some detailed rules

---

[1] Ivor Jennings, *The Queen's Government* (London: Penguin Books, 1954), p. 71.

about legislative order and procedure. Thus, fundamental and circumstantial rules exist in the same instrument.

The Intermingling of the Fundamental and the Circumstantial

Clearly, the "true constitution," to borrow Spiro's term to refer to that set of fundamental procedures we are discussing,[2] is rarely completely coterminous with the fundamental written law. To varying degrees, fundamental and circumstantial rules tend to be found intermingled in the same source, whether that source be a written document or the customs of a community. The capacity to make the distinction between what is fundamental and what is not is an important criterion for political stability and adaptability. This capacity is not a function of the nature of the constitution. The Americans, with a short, general, written constitution, the British, with an unwritten constitution, and the Swedes, with a longer, more substantive and detailed written document, all seem to possess that capacity. The answer to the question of why a nation is not disposed to tinker with its procedural fundamentals is not that they are formally more difficult to change than its circumstantial rules. Instead, the answer is that procedural fundamentals have acquired greater legitimacy in some systems than in others.

We raised the issue in Chapter 2 with regard to the sequential resolution of major crises: constitutional, religious, industrial, etc. We are again referring to the question of whether the basic political format (for instance, the "true constitution") has been removed from the political arena as an issue. When the question of the nature of the regime has been resolved, current issues are not framed in constitutional terms, and that system has succeeded in separating fundamental questions from circumstantial ones. In other words, the capacity to make this distinction is a function of the nation's political culture.

The most obvious example (among the nations we are considering) of a tendency to frame circumstantial and substantive issues in constitutional terms is France. The historic tensions between the left and right in France have tended to be framed in terms of support for a format of assembly government by the left and for a plebiscitarian and authoritarian format along Bonapartist or Gaullist lines by the right. Thus, the French system could not turn to a new set of leaders (DeGaulle and his followers) and a new policy direction in 1958 without adopting a new constitution (the Fifth Republic). During much of the Fourth Republic, either a majority or near majority of the National Assembly opposed the existing constitutional format. The Communist Party could normally expect somewhere in the neighborhood of a quarter of the nation's votes. The Gaullists (RPF) varied from a high of around 20 percent to less than 5 percent after DeGaulle repudiated

---

[2] Herbert Spiro, *Government by Constitution* (New York: Random House, 1959), pp. 211–213. Our discussion of constitutionalism in terms of fundamental procedures is heavily indebted to Spiro.

his own party. When monarchists and the various neofascist variations such as Poujadism are added, the republican majority disappeared. The fact that the Fourth Republic survived as long as it did can be attributed to the irreconcilable divisions among the antirepublican forces. Even much of the traditional right easily fell into support for the Vichy regime (a regime that eventually became distinctly pro-Nazi despite earlier broad support) during the Second World War.

We find less of a tendency to frame issues in constitutional terms in present-day Italy. This conclusion is possible despite the fact that in a national referendum the present constitution was adopted by a narrow margin over a monarchal alternative. In Italy no major segment of the population actively opposes the existing political format. Even the communists are defenders of the system. Thus, Italy's high communist vote is not, unlike the case of France, an indicator of a lack of diffuse support for the system.

Apparently, the intensity of support for the constitutional order in Italy is lower than in the Anglo-American democracies and West Germany, as indicated by the very low percentage of Italians who expressed pride in their governmental and political institutions. The Almond and Verba data, referred to in Chapter 3, indicate that whatever support the Italians give to their constitutional order is essentially passive.[3]

The Italian constitution is also marred by numerous substantive propositions, especially ideals of social policy. Specifics of socioeconomic policy in the constitution have not detracted from the flexibility of the system because policy ideals have simply been ignored by the policymakers.

Historically, the Germans have not been reluctant to frame issues in legal and constitutional terms. Thus, the problem of rising support for a party alleged by some to be "neo-Nazi," Thadden's National Democratic Party, was dealt with by constitutional amendment revising the electoral law. West Germany raised the minimum percentage of the national vote a party needed to win a seat in the Bundestag to five percent rather than deal with the causes of increasing support for the party.

The relative economic prosperity and political stability of West Germany since the war have resulted in a growing, though often passive, support for the constitutional format.[4]

The written constitution of the Federal Republic of Germany is officially called the Basic Law. The term *constitution* implies an acceptance of the format it sets

---

[3] Gabriel Almond and Sidney Verba, *The Civic Culture* (Boston: Little Brown, 1965), pp. 64–65.

[4] In a 1956 survey, six percent opposed the document, 29 percent actively supported it, and 65 percent either were undecided or did not know. Cited in Karl Deutsch, "The German Federal Republic," *Modern Political Systems: Europe,* Roy Macridis and Robert Ward, eds. (Englewood Cliffs: Prentice Hall, 1968), p. 387. It is, of course, the direction taken by these 65 percent or their descendents that will be critical for the viability of the constitution.

up as relatively enduring. Because German politicians in the immediate postwar period could not afford politically to disavow the goal of reunification with the GDR (East Germany), the term *constitution* was avoided. The Basic Law is understood to be the constitution, it functions as such, and nearly all Germans accept the fact that the division of Germany will persist for the foreseeable future.

In reaction to the Nazi period, the Basic Law contains a long, elaborate Bill of Rights (19 articles). This does not, of course, render the Germans any less vulnerable to abuses of such rights than citizens of those nations whose constitutions lack such a comprehensive and formal bill of rights such as Norway, Sweden, Belgium, France, and the Netherlands. Clearly, stating rights on a piece of paper does not prevent a government from abusing them. Chapter X of the Russian Constitution of 1936 that is still in force for the Soviet Union has a surprisingly enlightened bill of rights, but many of the provisions of it are blatantly ignored. For example, Article 125 guarantees the inviolability of person, home, and privacy of correspondence. Although the Soviet Union is, in theory, a federal state, its constituent republics would find it difficult to assert their constitutionally guaranteed right to secede from the system (Article 17).

The Belgian constitutional revision of 1970 was an attempt to solve a basic cultural problem through fundamental constitutional change. The problem was apparently intense, and it is impossible to estimate the degree of support for the existing format that had to be overcome to effect the change. However, since there is some association between the age of a constitution and the tendency to remove it from the political arena, it is probable that support for the new constitution will become firmly entrenched in the foreseeable future. It is possible that a precedent of fundamental constitutional change may render an attack on that system's essential political format more legitimate in the future.

Whether a political system observes rights of individuals or groups is primarily a function of whether respect for the rights is an entrenched part of that society's political culture. Thus, Article 16 of the Swedish Basic Law of 1809 that enumerates a number of what are generally considered civil liberties and is that system's closest approximation to a "bill of rights" omits such basic liberties as those found in the First Amendment of the Constitution of the United States.[5] These liberties are nevertheless quite secure. The security of rights is basically dependent on a cultural disposition to respect them. The statutory provisions that may exist to uphold rights basically depend on a cultural disposition to respect them. They depend even more on cultural support than on constitutional provisions. Bills of rights may reflect either the ideals or the intent of a society with regard to the rights, but constitutional guarantees cannot establish them in the absence of social and cultural support for them.

---

[5] M. Donald Hancock, *Sweden: The Politics of Post Industrial Change* (Hinsdale, IL: The Dryden Press, 1972), p. 230.

Functions of Constitutions: Legitimacy and Forms

A constitution can only legitimate the norms of a society insofar as it reflects them. A set of constitutionally imposed norms in conflict with the norms of the society in which it operates will not be viable. This is the essence of Eckstein's "congruence theory."[6] The norms of authority relations in the constitutional format must be "congruent" with the norms in the society. The classic case for the absence of such congruence is the Weimar Constitution, which was based on highly egalitarian authority relations imposed on a society with very deferential or even submissive attitudes toward authority. It is psychologically difficult to condition oneself always to defer to authority at home, school, work, and all other aspects of one's life and suddenly regard oneself as an equal in political wisdom to one's political authorities. Such incompatibility between perceptions of one's roles produces psychological strain. A constitution cannot create freedom or democracy. It can only reflect, explicate, and legitimate an existing cultural disposition in that direction.

The fact that a constitution such as that of the Soviet Union contains provisions that are ignored, such as those mentioned above concerning seccession and individual rights, might lead us to regard the document as irrelevant or even as a farce. Before doing so, however, we must reflect further as to what a constitution is or does. Why does even a revolutionary, authoritarian regime such as that of the Soviet Union seem to feel the necessity to place significant emphasis on a written document?

First, there is the matter of forms. It has often been suggested that authoritarian governments pay constitutionalism the highest compliment by using its forms to mask their real nature. At the same time, dissidents inside these countries often place importance on using such forms in an effort to cause changes in the real operation of the system. While it may seem a small thing to those accustomed to observance of democratic procedures, the mere establishment of formal procedures may be seen as progress when compared to the arbitrariness of the past.

Thus, while democratic provisions may be used to conceal authoritarianism, they may also make possible the introduction of the idea of accountability. As long as the forms exist, leaders can be urged to follow them or critized for not doing so. John Hazard attempts to demonstrate that examining the forms of the Soviet Union can be a very profitable method of gaining insight into the system. Speaking in terms of western democratic forms counterweighted with antidemocratic

---

[6] Harry Eckstein, "A Theory of Stable Democracy," *Division and Cohesion in Democracy* (Princeton: Princeton University Press, 1966), pp. 225–288, and Eckstein, "Authority Relations and Governmental Performance: A Theoretical Framework," *Comparative Political Studies*, Vol. 2, No. 3, October 1969, pp. 269–326.

controls, he suggests that both can contribute to our understanding.[7] The point remains, however, that forms and realities are not necessarily the same.

There is more to constitutions than forms. They do perform certain functions even in an authoritarian regime. Every system has structures, and one of the things a constitution does is describe them. It is also true that in all systems one must be able to read between the lines. That is, to the provisions of a formal organization chart or document one must add the informal understandings and procedures. Thus, the Soviet constitution details institutions such as the Supreme Soviet and the Council of Ministers, but may give an inaccurate or incomplete picture of their relationship to each other or of the directions in which power actually flows. Authority may be described as belonging to a large body such as the Supreme Soviet, which delegates it to a smaller one, when in fact power may reside in the small group that actually controls the larger and uses it to ratify decisions. Of course, such a pattern is not confined to authoritarian systems.

Nevertheless, careful reading of a constitution will reveal much of the system it is describing. Soviet leaders have promulgated new constitutions to reflect what they felt to be new conditions. The document adopted in 1918 shortly after the revolution speaks in terms of new structures and in terms of classes. Rights such as speech, press, education, and others belong to classes rather than individuals. The formation of the Soviet Union prompted another constitution, which incorporated the federal principle. Even though provisions regarding secession and nationality representation in one house of the legislature have little or no practical significance, a federal structure based on nationality does acknowledge the existence and implications of such groupings.

The present constitution, which dates from 1936, was felt by Stalin to be necessary to symbolize the end of class struggle and to demonstrate that the Soviet Union was moving in a "democratic" direction. For that reason it is a model of liberal provisions both in terms of representative institutions and the rights and duties of citizens. In the early 1960s the Soviet leadership declared that the country was embarking on a new phase of development called the full-scale construction of communism, and Khrushchev called for yet another constitution. His successors have not seemed as concerned with the subject, so the 1936 version remains in effect.

Like most constitutions, that of the Soviet Union also leaves a large gap in our understanding by not dealing with political parties. Parties have great significance in all the countries under examination, and nowhere more so than the CPSU in the Soviet Union. But the document gives the CPSU only several very brief mentions. Because major policy decisions are made within the context of the party, the

---

[7] John Hazard, *The Soviet System of Government* (Chicago: University of Chicago Press, 1968), especially pp. 10–12.

constitution is largely a description of the structures through which the decisions are legitimated and implemented. Unlike most systems, however, the CPSU has a set of statutes (rules) that describe in detail its membership, structure, and operation. If we define constitutionalism in terms of fundamental procedures, perhaps the statutes of the party should be included as part of the constitution of the Soviet Union.

Functions of Constitutions: The Transfer of Power

We have suggested that one major function of a constitution is the legitimation of cultural norms, a process that is essential for the peaceful transfer of power. The transfer of power is an inescapable problem of all political systems. Political leadership can never be perpetual; even lifetime monarchs are mortal. Peaceful transfer of power has historically been the exception rather than the rule.[8] The resolution of the divisive questions of when power will be transferred and which of several competing claimants shall be the new power wielder is made acceptable to all concerned by the legitimation of a set of rules by which these questions are resolved.

Not all constitutions have managed to legitimate a set of procedures for the transfer of power. Frequently, authoritarian systems fail to specify such a set of procedures, a failure that precipitates recurring power struggles. After all, a distinguishing characteristic of systems is that tendency to base the policymaking process on the will of the ruler or oligarchic elite rather than on the rule of law. The rule of law refers to a system in which the will of the elite is subordinate to the legitimated procedures of the society. Of course, these procedures may dictate deferring to the will of the ruler; hence, the distinction between will and the rule of law may not always be clear in practice.

The problem in transferring power stems from the fact that competition for political power seems inevitable. Democratic constitutions institutionalize this competition in the form of open elections and of provisions for a regular or emergency transfer. The twenty-fifth amendment to the United States Constitution, for example, was adopted in order to provide for transfer under a number of possible circumstances.

Not all systems have managed to legitimate a set of procedures for the orderly transfer of power. Conspicuously, authoritarian systems fail to specify such provisions, a failure that inevitably and periodically precipitates power struggles. A number of factors work against institutionalizing these procedures in the Soviet Union. First, there is the ideological influence. Marxism deals with social competition in class terms and is concerned with tranfers of power from one social

---

[8] Leslie Lipson, *The Democratic Civilization* (New York: Oxford University Press, 1964), pp. 432–433.

class to another (from aristocracy to capitalist or capitalist to worker), not from one individual to another. Furthermore, the contention that antagonistic classes no longer exist leads to a position in which transfers of power are said to be from one friendly hand to another. By institutionalizing the myth that competition does not exist, the Soviet system relegates inevitable political conflict to the realm of informal, raw, and unacknowledged power struggles.

The ideological problem is complicated by existing structures. The parallel and overlapping organization of party and state bureaucracies is one source of difficuly. Only the latter is discussed in the constitution, but experience indicates that the former is of greater importance in matters of succession. Historically, one dimension of the struggle for power has been that of the top party leader against his government counterpart. To complicate things even further, in both party and government documents supreme authority is collective and rests in a large body instead of in a particular office. Officially, the top offices in both hierarchies are elected or appointed by the Supreme Soviet or its party equivalent with no provisions for fixed terms or public elections.

All of this is to say that the formal documents of party and government do not provide for an orderly transfer of power. Succession decisions (as part of the entire policymaking process) tend to rest on the will of single or oligarchic rulers rather than on the rule of law as expressed through the written legitimated procedures of the society. Does this mean that the process is necessarily chaotic, disorderly, and unpredictable?

To use Myron Rush's terms, the question of succession remains essentially indeterminate but it is possible to identify certain determinate elements arising from the nature of the system.[9] On the basis of three instances (Lenin, Stalin, and Khrushchev), some similarities and patterns seem to emerge in what is basically a crisis situation. In fact, Rush feels that Khrushchev deliberately patterned his strategy on that used by Stalin.[10] Both were successful.

The main point, however, is that any strategy or pattern results from the experience of a series of actual crises and struggles, not from a formal, established procedure. Incumbents do attempt to influence the succession process, but it must be behind the scenes. To name a successor openly would be political suicide.[11] Thus, we sometimes speak of an apparent heir, and heir presumptive, or even a counter heir, but nothing is ever made official.

On the basis of three successions, it would appear that the best position to hold at the beginning of the process is that of General (First) Secretary of the Central

---

[9] Myron Rush, *Political Succession in the U.S.S.R.* (New York: Columbia University Press, 1965, p. xv.
[10] *Ibid.*, p. 42.
[11] For an excellent discussion of the choices and dilemmas facing the incumbent in an authoritarian system, see *Ibid.*, pp. 74–78.

Committee of the CPSU (a position not even mentioned in the Soviet constitution). Why is it the best one? Not because it is designated as successor but because Stalin, Khrushchev, and Brezhnev all began there and eventually wound up as the dominant leader. At any given time, observers of authoritarian systems such as the Soviet Union can suggest with good reasons the identity of those likely to emerge in the event of a succession crisis and struggle. Thus, although it is possible to point to certain processes or patterns, the nature of the system is such that considerations of ideology and practical politics prohibit the formalization of procedures for the transfer of power.

Sovereignty

One of the fundamental elements of a constitution is the locus of sovereignty. Sovereignty, it will be recalled, refers to the final or ultimate authority to make and enforce law. In the United States, we have a system of "popular sovereignty"—the concept that sovereignty resides in "the people" (presumably referring to the aggregate of citizens) and is delegated to the elite. From this concept is derived the notion of the social contract—the idea that the legitimate authority of the decision makers must be delegated by the governed. The idea of the social contract goes well back in the history of political philosophy. Among others, it is explicitly associated with the writings of John Locke, the nineteenth-century English philosopher whose writings so strongly influenced the American Declaration of Independence. This conception of popular sovereignty was also explicit in the writings of a number of eighteenth-century French philosophers, such as Rousseau. Popular sovereignty is a fundamental tenet of French and American constitutional theory.

Although Locke and other contract theorists such as Hobbes were Englishmen, English constitutional theory is not based on popular sovereignty. Instead, sovereignty in Britain resides in the concept of the crown. In fact, the concept of the crown is virtually synonymous with the locus of sovereignty. The crown is not simply the monarch. At one time the monarch exercised most of the powers of the crown. Through the course of British political history, nearly all of these powers have passed from the hands of the monarch to ministers acting in his or her name. The decisions of judges, acts of Parliament, etc., are made in the name of the monarch, who in turn *legally* (but not in fact) still exercises the powers of the crown. Thus, even though both houses of Parliament pass a bill proposed by the cabinet, the bill does not become law until the monarch (or a person speaking for the monarch) "wills it."

The significance of crown power is that it entails the proposition that somewhere in the government there is the capacity to respond to any public need or demand. Government under the concept of crown power does not legally have to receive an explicit or implicit delegation of power from the people in order to act.

To illustrate, the United States faced at the onset of the 1929 depression a great public outcry that the government do something. However, the Supreme Court said the federal government could not regulate the economy because of states' rights, and the states could not regulate the economy because of due process of law. The British could not understand this no-man's-land of power where no government agency could act no matter how great the public demand. Because the power of government in Britain is not contingent on a delegation from the people, the question could not arise of whether government has the legal power to do something.

It should be recognized that the locus of sovereignty, an essentially legal matter, is not the same as the question of whether a government is accountable or responsive to the electorate, an essentially political matter. The locus of sovereignty in the crown does not preclude political democracy through structural accountability of the decision makers.

The Logic of Parliamentary Democracy

With the exception of the United States, Fifth Republic France, and Sweden, the industrial democracies have all been variations on the basic parliamentary theme. While the DeGaulle constitution has retained some of the forms of parliamentary government, we argue below that the basic structure of accountability in that system is much closer to the presidential format of the United States than to the parliamentary format.

So pervasive is the parliamentary format that even the formal political structures of the Soviet Union resemble it in form. As in the case of France, the operation of these forms violates the entire spirit of the parliamentary format. This spirit can best be described in terms of its structure of accountability.

The Structure of Accountability

Accountability refers to stable, recurring patterns of interaction, procedures that provide instruments for holding those who make authoritative decisions for a society accountable to that society for the consequences of the decisions. Accountability may be structured through the instrument of the direct popular election of the political executive as in the case of the French and American presidents. (It is assumed here that the American Electoral College exercises no significant independent judgment.) By contrast, the political executive in parliamentary democracies is indirectly accountable to the electorate, at least in a formal sense. The direct accountability of political executives in parliamentary systems is to the lower house of the legislature. (Clearly, upper houses fall outside the logic of the system as the proverbial fifth wheel on a wagon. Perhaps the general decline in the power and significance of upper houses in parliamentary democracies may be partially understood in the light of this lack of an obvious role for them in the structure of accountability.)

Specifically, the tenure of the political executive in parliamentary systems is contingent on the executive retaining at least the passive support of the majority of the lower house. A loss of support may be expressed in either of two ways: the house refuses to pass a major piece of legislation initiated by the executive or the house approves of a motion of censure or no confidence. When a lack of confidence is so expressed, the executive is generally expected to resign.

There are several variations of this basic theme. In the German Federal Republic, votes of censure have to be accompanied by an agreement on an alternative government (a process known as a constructive vote of no confidence). Because it is harder for a group to agree on what they are for than on what they are against, this mechanism renders the tenure of the executive more secure. The constructive vote of no confidence is in part a reaction to the cabinet instability of the Weimar Republic.

A more basic variation is found in the Netherlands, where it is not clear that the cabinet is under any obligation, legal or otherwise, to resign in the face of a legislative defeat on any given issue. The cabinet itself may pose a confidence question, however. Gordon Weil suggests that the tenure of the cabinet is independent of the vote on a single issue, but Lijphart suggests that clear and repeated assertions of no confidence, as happened in 1866–1868, have forced cabinets to resign.[12] Lijphart calls this a "semiseparation of powers." Dutch cabinets do tend to be based on legislative majorities, thus more or less preserving the basis structure of accountability. The best conclusion appears to be that cabinet accountability to the legislature is a matter of degree. The tenure of cabinets in the Netherlands is independent of the success or failure of any single bill, but repeated manifestations of opposition to the policies of the government in the States General (both houses of the legislature) or even of the Tweed Kamer (lower house) would put intolerable pressure on the cabinet to resign.

In Sweden, the formal, constitutional requirement that the cabinet's tenure depends on the confidence of a majority of the lower house was adopted only in 1967. The absence of formal arrangements did not prevent recurrent cabinet crises in the early years of the twentieth century. When losing the support of the legislature, many cabinets resigned "voluntarily." It is unclear as to when a recurring practice becomes an expectation and informal "constitutional" requirement. The

---

[12] Arend Lijphart, *The Politics of Accommodation: Pluralism and Democracy in the Netherlands* (Berkeley: University of California Press, 1968), pp. 135–136, and Gordon Weil, *The Benelux Nations: The Politics of Small Country Democracies* (New York: Holt, Rinehart and Winston, 1970), p. 131.

requirement that the tenure or the political executive be contingent on the support of the legislature is a pragmatic and logical means of preventing or at least overcoming a condition of political stalemate resulting in political immobility. Cabinet responsibility to the legislature simply reflects the reality that governments cannot govern without the passive support of the legislature and that this responsibility sets the limits of executive discretion. Whether or not cabinets are legally or constitutionally compelled to resign in the face of a loss of the support of the legislature, the political position of cabinets in these circumstances is in fact untenable, and it makes sense for them to resign. That is why Swedish and Dutch cabinets have in fact resigned when they unambiguously lost the support of their respective legislatures, even though they were under no formal compulsion to do so.

In presidential systems the tenure of the executive is independent of the will of the legislature (for example, the presidents of the United States and Fifth Republic France). Here the executive must reach compromises with the legislature in order to govern, even though the executive's tenure is autonomous of that body. The difference is that in the presence of legislative discontent with executive programs in parliamentary systems, compromises and adjustments in those programs must be reached before the formal expression of that legislative dissatisfaction in a legislative vote or decision. In the presence of an intransigent executive or legislature, a presidential system may produce political stalemate and immobility, as has happened on several occasions in the United States. A presidential system does not produce pressures for compromise and accommodation as intense as those produced where a formal mechanism exists for the removal of an executive for political reasons. (Although the Nixon affair left the situation unclear, the American mechanism of impeachment is apparently unavailable for political reasons.)

In some cases, such as Britain, the cabinet (prime minister, heads of government departments, and several close advisors) is collectively responsible to the legislature. The entire cabinet would be expected to resign in the event of an expression of no confidence. In other cases, such as in the Fourth Republic of France and Italy, the premier on prime minister alone resigns and the cabinet may remain. The importance of this difference is that individual members of a cabinet in a situation of individual responsibility may find it advantageous to bring down a government of which they are a part. No risk to their position is involved, and there would be the possibility of elevation to a higher post—for example, prime minister in a new government.

Thus, the confidence mechanism in parliamentary systems means that the lower house of the legislatures poses a theoretical threat to the tenure of the executives. The absence of this ultimate sanction in presidential systems does not, of course, completely remove the accountability of executives to their legislatures. In its refusal to pass legislation, its power to override presidential vetoes, and its capacity to investigate executive activities, the American Congress appears capable of placing at least broad limits on the discretion of the American president.

The capacity of the French National Assembly to limit the discretion of its executive may be even more restrained. The assembly can counteract the will of a determined executive only by a vote of censure of the prime minister and his government. The conditions for such a vote of censure have been severely circumscribed. The details of executive legislative relations in the Fifth Republic are discussed below.

Mechanisms for Accountability: Questions, Confidence, and Dissolution

There is a certain logic in holding the executive accountable to a representative assembly in addition to that executive's periodic accountability to the national electorate. Accountability implies the availability of information about the activities of the structure that is being held accountable. Legislatures, in full-time sessions and given certain investigatory powers, have greater access to information than the ordinary voting public. Congressional investigations in the United States serve this function (most notably in recent years in the case of the Senate Watergate Committee headed by Senator Ervin), as does the well-known question period in the British House of Commons.

On each day except Friday in the House of Commons, the first hour is reserved for questions addressed to the ministers or other government officials responsible for the activities or policy under inquiry. Questions are submitted in writing two full days before an answer is expected; therefore, the responsible official is given an opportunity for a careful and informed reply.[13] If the member is dissatisfied with the government's defense of its activities, he will serve notice that he intends to pursue the matter at length in the daily debate on a motion to adjourn.[14] The significance of this procedure is that it provides a regularized structure whereby the government can expect to be called to account in the sense of being forced to react to informed adversary questions on its policies and, accordingly, to justify those policies in terms of some reasonable conception of the public interest.

This accounting occurs on a day-to-day basis. Thus, members of the cabinet are expected to behave as if they might at any time be called upon to justify their official activities and the intended consequences of these activities in terms of the public interest. By contrast, President Richard Nixon and his advisors apparently behaved with the expectation that their claim of "executive privilege" would protect them from the necessity of explanations to Congress. The institutionaliza-

---

[13] Eric Taylor, *The House of Commons at Work* (Baltimore: Pelican Books, 1963), p. 106.
[14] *Ibid.,* p. 108.

tion of accountability through interrogation on a day-to-day basis may effectively circumscribe the executive's perceived limits of discretion.

A similar period is set aside for questioning ministers in the West German Bundestag. In Sweden members of the Riksdag may, with permission from the chamber, submit questions to relevant cabinet ministers. These written questions are known as interpellations. A question period similar to Britain's was introduced in the Riksdag in 1964; however, interpellations continue to be used. Questions and interpellations are also provided in the Low Countries. Thus, some form of day-to-day accountability for the consequences of executive decision making through the procedure of interrogation is generally provided in parliamentary democracies.

The difficulty with this mechanism in terms of its effectiveness in enhancing accountability is that neither the legislature nor the executive may be able to cope with the expertise or the influence of the bureaucratic and interest-group sector. The increasing delegation of day-to-day "bread-and-butter" decisions to this sector in mature industrial societies because of the increasing complexity of the decisions is fully discussed in Chapters 6 and 8. The nearly perfunctory ratification of the recommendations of this extrapolitical sector into authoritative public policy threatens to render the accountability of cabinets irrelevant.

However, it would cearly be premature to regard the activities of political executives as without serious consequences. Because of their greater access to information and because of their more continuous watchdog function than the average citizen can perform, the representative assemblies may be more capable of holding a powerful executive accountable than the atomized individual voters. It seems more effective to hold an executive accountable for the consequences of his or her actions through a legislative structure than through a direct structure of accountability to the voting public.

Confidence, Stability, and Dissolution

To many Americans, the notion of a legislative capacity to remove the executive from office for dissatisfaction with performance short of the commission of felonies conjures up pictures of revolving-door governments such as experienced in the Third and Fourth French Republics and in Germany's Weimar Republic. This issue, in fact, was raised during the proposed impeachment of Nixon.

To keep this matter in proper perspective, only one British government has fallen due to a loss of its legislative majority in the twentieth century. (Moreover, this was a case of a minority government. The last instance of a majority government falling was nearly 100 years ago.) The same could be said of Canada, although more of its governments are minority cabinets. (A minority cabinet is a situation in which no single party has a legislative majority; therefore, a coalition of two or more parties is required to form a government.) Why has this confidence mechanism resulted in cabinet instability in some systems but not in others?

The institutional explanation sometimes offered is that the British cabinet or prime minister possesses the power to cause the dissolution of the legislature followed by a general election. Legally, the monarch orders the dissolution at the "request" of the prime minister. (The role and power of the monarch is considered below.) This executive power was thought to provide an effective counterweight to the legislative capacity to overthrow cabinets, thus establishing a kind of check-and-balance mechanism in executive legislative relations, a kind of reciprocal accountability. The absence of an effective power of dissolution in Fourth Republic France was held in large part to be the difference between it and Great Britain with respect to cabinet stability. (In the Fourth Republic the power of dissolution could only be invoked when the government was defeated by an absolute majority of the legislature. However, all but one of the defeats of governments in that system were by relative majorities. Thus, French assemblies were free to defeat government after government without an election to place their own tenure in jeopardy.)

As with other simplistic institutional explanations, the dissolution argument raises as many questions as it answers. Presumably, a nation can choose to establish such an institution or not. Therefore, if by instituting the power of dissolution, the French could have engineered political stability, why did they not do it?

The French had the power of dissolution in their Third Republic. However, the second president of that system, Marshall MacMahon, a monarchist, abused the power in an attempt to undermine the republic. Consequently, the use of this power became identified with opposition to the republic in the perception of those forces of the French left that dominated the republic. The extreme distrust of executive authority on the part of these forces, discussed in Chapter 3, contributed to the fact that this power was never again used in the Third Republic. Thus, the Third Republic experienced legislative dominance because the forces dominating French society wanted legislative dominance, not because of any mechanism. This is another case where a procedure that was perfectly legal might have been regarded as "unconstitutional" in the broad sense of that term.

The suggestion here is that cabinet stability in parliamentary regimes depends on a cultural disposition to defer to executive authority (to grant them fairly broad limits of discretion) and for executive authority to acknowledge its accountability to the legislature. Institutional arrangements, such as the West German constructive vote of no confidence discussed above, can, of course, render the removal of a government more difficult and less likely. The question is why such institutions were adopted. We suggest the answer is generally this cultural disposition toward deference.

The Confidence Mechanism as a Threat

Even though the confidence mechanism in Britain has been largely unused in recent decades, it is still significant in that it encourages cabinets to resolve any major differences with the House of Commons by negotiation and compromise instead of by confrontation. American presidents have at times felt free to confront Congress and blatantly disregard its strongly held sentiments because the alienation of Congress was not expected to threaten the tenure of the administration. The confidence mechanism in Britain has not been used in large part because British governments have behaved as if they knew it were there. Ironically, the ease with which it could be used helped prevent the need for its use. By contrast, President Nixon's apparent confidence that impeachment would never be used probably emboldened him in his disposition to confront Congress and perhaps ironically contributed to the instigation of impeachment proceedings. The attempt to broaden the grounds for impeachment in America's Watergate affair suggests a need in democratic systems for a procedure for the removal of an executive for reasons short of proved criminality, if the check-and-balance mechanism between the executive and legislative branches is to flourish.

Institutional arrangements notwithstanding, a check-and-balance system is most likely to flourish where the executive and legislative branches of government are disposed to negotiate and compromise with each other. It will be recalled that this is a cultural characteristic manifest in Britain. The 1922 Committee of the Tory Party, the whips of each party, the question hour, and other formal and informal structures provide regularized channels for negotiation. Votes of no confidence do not occur because the cabinet adjusts its policy proposals to the limits of legislative tolerance before legislative votes (divisions) take place. The bill voted upon generally ratifies the accommodations previously worked out informally between the government and backbenchers of its own party.

Occasionally, the majority party in the House of Commons may anticipate the dissatisfaction of its own backbenchers with government performance with a change in party and hence in government leadership. This avoids the messy business of forcing a dissolution of the house and a general election. One notable example of this was in 1940 when a large number of Conservatives voted with Labour in dissatisfaction with Prime Minister Neville Chamberlain's policy of appeasing Adolf Hitler and his ineffective conduct of the war. This dented the huge Conservative majority but not enough to bring down the government. Chamberlain, properly taking this as a warning, resigned and was replaced by another Conservative, Winston Churchill. Churchill's government was, however, a grand coalition for the duration of the war, although it was dominated by Conservatives.

The replacement of Anthony Eden by Harold Macmillan as prime minister (both Conservatives) after the hostile political reaction to the British and French invasion of Suez in 1957 may be another example of this adjustment of a party to dissatisfaction with its performance. The replacement of Willy Brandt as chancellor of the Federal Republic of Germany by another Social Democrat, Helmut Schmidt, in the wake of a scandal involving the unmasking of a top German official as an East German spy constitutes another example of such an intraparty adaptation to dissatisfaction with government performance, an adaptation encouraged by the presence of the confidence mechanism.

Something of this sort occurs in Italy. The fall of a government due to the confidence mechanism does not usually entail a major personnel realignment in the government. Instead, the government is reconstituted, often under the same prime minister, with but a few personnel changes in the cabinet. During the Fourth French Republic, the apparent cabinet instability was largely confined to the post of premier and a couple of other ministers. Beyond that, there was great personnel continuity in French cabinets from one government to the next.

Thus, government response to legislative dissatisfaction with its performance may take a variety of forms: compromise and negotiation, partial personnel changes, or confrontation. Only the latter officially results in a no-confidence statistic in an index of cabinet stability. Furthermore, votes of no confidence vary with respect to the extent to which they entail changes in government personnel or policies.

The Role of Representative Assemblies

The word *legislature* can be misleading if it is taken to imply that the national representative assembly formulates public policy. Policy in industrial societies originates with the political executive to an overwhelming extent. In the United States and Great Britain over 90 percent of all legislation originates with the executive. This is true despite the fact that the American presidency does not exercise the control over the legislative process exercised by the British cabinet.

In those countries characterized by legislative dominance of the executive (for example, the Third and Fourth French Republics, Weimar Germany, and "weak" American presidencies), the policymaking process has been characterized by immobility—an inability to reach positive decisions on concrete policy proposals.

A Check on Executive Discretion

The reasons for this executive dominance of policymaking processes are both structural and historical. The historical reasons center around traditions and customs. In nations such as Great Britain, where political institutions evolved out of authoritarian traditions, executive policymaking is firmly entrenched in the culture. The representative structure in Britain evolved out of the Anglo-Saxon baronial council, the Wittan. Barons would gather around the monarch and consult with him, a practice continued after the Norman conquest. Because of its autonomous financial base (discussed in Chapter 2), the barony could exercise a kind of veto over the monarch's policy decisions. It was never supposed that the barony had the power to initiate policy, however.

The power of the aristocracy to check the policymaking discretion of the monarch through the power of the purse became more pronounced as the monarch's need for money became greater, especially during the Hundred Years' War in the thirteenth and fourteenth centuries. The use of the power of the purse to place limits on the policymaking discretion of the executive probably remains the classic role of the representative assembly. Temporary deviations from this model have occurred in theory rather than in fact. It is doubtful that representative assemblies could have ever been characterized as policy-formulating bodies, even during the so-called golden age of Parliament, the eras of weak presidents in the United States, or periods of assembly dominance in the Third and Fourth French Republics, pre-war Austria, and Weimar Germany. The legislatures in those situations effectively immobilized executive policymaking and hence national policymaking.

With the onset of the commercial revolution, control of an increasing share of the nation's wealth passed from the hands of the aristocracy to the entrepreneurs among the commoners. Hence, the power of the purse passed increasingly to the representative assembly of commoners in Britain, the House of Commons. The call now would go out to the knights of the shires and the burghers of the boroughs for "two good men, tried and true." As their spokesmen recognized their capacity to impose conditions on granting funds to the monarch, the ability of the House of Commons to impose understood limits on executive discretion became institutionalized.

The distinction made here is between deliberation—the process of criticizing and debating alternatives of public policy—and formulation of policy alternatives.[15] Spiro draws a distinction between the deliberative function and the resolution of issues.[16] He argues that the latter is the province of the political executive. There is a difference between formulating alternatives of public policy and authoritatively imposing them on society, however. The executive in industrial societies tends to formulate alternatives, but the formulations are implicitly presented to the legislature in the form of whether this cabinet proposal shall be

---

[15] See Andrew Gamble, *The Conservative Nation* (London: Routledge and Kegan Paul, 1975), pp. 6–11, for a distinction between "the politics of power" and "the politics of support." The latter comes close to what we suggest the legislative role to be in parliamentary democracies. However, we suggest in addition that the legislative role includes a check-and-balance function.
[16] Spiro, *op. cit.,* Part IV.

adopted or not. Although legislatures are incapable of effectively formulating comprehensive policy, they are capable of compelling substantial revision of the policies formulated by the government. Surely the decision of "no, not in its present form" is a resolution of the issue.

In stable parliamentary democracies, legislatures rarely formally say no to major policy proposals of the executive, for that would bring down the government and in most cases force new elections, placing the jobs of the legislators as well as those of the executive on the line. Instead, because of this understood capacity of parliaments to withdraw "confidence" from the executive, executives generally determine the existence of strongly held objections to their policy formulations in the legislature prior to a confrontation on a formal vote and adjust their policy formulations accordingly. In this way, in those systems characterized by a disposition to bargain and compromise, the confidence mechanism serves its check-and-balance function without generating cabinet instability.

The legislature is structurally suited to use its deliberative function to check and balance the governing function of the executive because it is in the legislature that the "outs" (opposition) are accorded an input in the policymaking process. It is in the legislative deliberations that minorities get to confront the majority. Thus, excluding the variable political role of the courts (which is nowhere else as great as in the United States), the legislature is the only structure where the government is continuously confronted with another point of view. It is a forum in which nongovernmental parties can mobilize that antiincumbent support that renders democratic political systems competitive.[17]

The Representative Function

Legislatures, in addition to limiting the discretion of the executive in their check-and-balance role, may be argued to perform a representative function. Two questions arise from such a conception: who is being represented and what is entailed by the concept of representation?

The first question asks if the legislators' primary duty is to the interests of those in their constituencies who voted for them, of their constituencies as a whole, or of the poliltical system at large (that is, the nation). Edmund Burke, the British political philosopher and statesman of the late eighteenth century, in a now classic speech to the voters in his constituency at Bristol, said that when the interests of his constituents conflict with those of the nation at large, the duty of the legislator is to protect the national interests. His justification was that in the long run the interests of the parochial constituency cannot be separated from those of the nation as a whole. (After being defeated for reelection, Burke was relegated to represent-

---

[17] John Stuart Mill, *Representative Government* (New York: Library of Liberal Arts, 1883, 1958), pp. 82–83.

ing a "rotten borough"—a borough that had disappeared under the shifting coastline of the North Sea and whose MP was in effect appointed.) Burke's conception of the loyalties of the representative has had considerable impact on democratic political thought and in particular on British political thought. From it is derived the British notion of virtual representation. This concept holds that the interests of each subject are represented in Parliament irrespective of which group of voters could vote for the MP. Thus, the English could logically argue from this concept that Parliament did represent the interests of the American colonies, and the revolutionary rallying cry of "taxation without representation" made no sense to them.

Alternatively, the role of the members of a legislature could be conceptualized as that of speaking for the perceived interests and demands of their hometown constituents. Sometimes the role of American members of congress has verged on degenerating into that of errand boys for constituent complaints about the policies of the political executive or bureaucracy. Samuel Huntington perceptively argued that Congress's putative role in the national decision-making process conflicts with the fact that the body is locally elected and locally accountable.[18] The notion of representing geographic areas as such is less firmly grounded in the British tradition than it is in the United States. Nineteenth-century English theory focused on Parliament representing the configuration of interests in the society.

Both conceptions cling to what Karl Bracher has called "the fiction of partyless parliamentarianism."[19] The individual legislator, as an individual, cannot strictly represent either geographic constituencies or socioeconomic interests that transcend geographic boundaries, because the discretion of the individual legislator is increasingly circumscribed by the reality of disciplined political parties. The conflicting imperatives of party discipline and obligations to represent constituency or other interests were discussed in the preceding chapter. Suffice it to say that the reality of disciplined political parties, an increasingly pervasive phenomenon in parliamentary democracies, has rendered obsolete any democratic theory based on an assumption of independent discretion on the part of the individual legislator.

The conception of the representative as an agent for a constituency becomes inapplicable to the extent that the politics of the nation under consideration are nationalized—when the dominant focus of attention is on national, not subsystem issues. In Britain, for example, the average voters perceive of themselves as voting less for the characteristics of the local candidate than for the party's leader for prime minister. Politics is similarly nationalized in all of the nations under consideration, if compared to the United States, except for Canada, with the

[18] Samuel Huntington, "Congressional Responses to the Twentieth Century," *Congress and America's Future,* David Truman, ed. (Englewood Cliffs: Prentice Hall, 1965), pp. 5–31 at pp. 15–17.
[19] Karl Bracher, "Problems of Parliamentary Democracy in Europe," *Daedulus,* Vol. 93, No. 1, Winter 1964, pp. 179–198.

strong subsystem identification of the French Canadian Québequois, and for Belgium, with the strong subsystem identification of the Flemish and Walloons.

Upper Houses in Parliamentary Systems

In federal systems, the tendency is for the political subsystems to be at least formally represented in an upper house. American readers will be familiar with the equal representation of each state in the Senate. The West German *Lander* are not only represented in the Bundesrat of the Federal Republic (in strength roughly proportionate to their respective populations), but the respective *Land* governments appoint their Bundesrat representatives, instruct them on how to vote, and may remove them. Because the delegations of each *Land* in the Bundesrat vote as a bloc on instruction from their *Land* government, the party affiliation of the individual delegate has no impact on his or her vote. The vote is instead a function of the political complexion of the *Land* government.

Each of the Australian states is accorded 10 representatives in that nation's Senate. The Canadian Senate, while not granting equal representation to its provinces, is designed "to protect the special interests of the provinces" in granting the small provinces considerably more representation than they would have had on the strict basis of population. Moreover, "Quebec . . . was given the explicit assurance of special protection in the Senate."[20] The nine Austrian *Lander* are also represented in their Bundesrat roughly in proportion to their respective populations. Like the German situation, the delegations to the Austrian Bundesrat are chosen by their respective *Land* governments. Unlike the German situation, according to one student of Austrian politics, "the members of the Federal Council (Bundesrat) . . . see themselves more as representatives of their parties and less as representatives of the interests of their *Lander*."[21] The Swiss Cantons are afforded equal representation in their upper house, the Council of State.

As indicated by its name, the Union of Soviet Socialist Republics is also federal in form. The structure of one of the two houses of the Supreme Soviet reflects the multinational character of the country. According to the constitution, deputies to the Soviet of Nationalities are elected on the basis of so many from each Union Republic, Autonomous Republic, Autonomous Region, and National Area (a grand total of over 750). It is difficult to refer to it as an upper house because both are equal in function, or, as is sometimes suggested, in a lack of function. Because each house has approximately 750 members and meets for a week or so twice a year, it is obvious that the role of the Supreme Soviet is primarily a symbolic one

---

[20] R. MacGregor Dawson, *The Government of Canada,* Norman Ward, revisor (Toronto: University of Toronto Press, 1966), p. 304.

[21] Kurt Steiner, *Politics in Austria* (Boston: Little Brown, 1972), p. 103.

of legitimizing policy instead of making it. Thus, there is a federal arrangement in which ethnic groups are given formal representation and that in itself is significant, but it is a body with no real power. In short, the capacity of the constituent republics of the Soviet Union to act and exist is not really autonomous of the will of the leaders in the Kremlin.

With the exception of Germany and Switzerland, this representation of political subdivisions in the upper house is more of a formal than a genuine phenomenon in democratic systems as well. As already explained, the imperatives of cabinet government make party label an overriding determinant of legislative voting. This is especially true when the house under consideration can bring about the downfall of a government by the withdrawal of its support. Thus, voting in the Australian Senate is essentially by party. Party label supersedes the interests of the state. Party label is far less important in the United States Senate where no confidence mechanism is operative. It would, however, be a distortion to view American senators as mere spokesmen for their states. The Canadian Senate cannot bring about the downfall of a government by disapproving a government bill;[22] hence, the pressures for party-line voting are less than in the House of Commons.

As long as the responsibility of the government is to the lower house, upper houses in parliamentary systems appear to be structures in search of a logical role in the system. Members of the government are overwhelmingly, if not exclusively, members of the lower house. It would now be unthinkable in any of the systems under consideration for the prime minister to be selected from the upper house. Lord Curzon in 1923 was the last British member of the House of Lords to be seriously considered for the prime ministership. Although Curzon was clearly the leading Tory in terms of prestige, the post went to Stanley Baldwin of the House of Commons. Because the challenges to government policy occur in the questions and general debate in the lower house of the countries under consideration, it is desirable if not imperative for members of the government to be present to defend their policies and to supply information about them. When Patrick Gordon Walker, the designate for foreign secretary in Harold Wilson's shadow cabinet, failed to secure a seat in the House of Commons in either Wilson's victorious general election in 1964 or in a subsequent by-election in 1965, Wilson had to find a new foreign secretary. Some important cabinet positions, however, are still held by lords.

The British have devised a procedure for British aristocrats to resign their peerage in order to seek major political influence through the only route now available, the House of Commons. Sir Alec Douglas-Home is the only British

---

[22] Dawson, *op. cit.*, p. 193. However, the Bennett government of 1933 said that it would resign if the Senate failed to approve of one of its measures. *Ibid.*, p. 440.

Prime Minister who has attained that post after resigning his peerage. Lord Halisham also resigned a peerage to pursue a career in Tory politics under the curious name of Quentin Hogg with somewhat less success. A Labourite member of the House of Commons, Anthony Wedgewood Benn, in fact initiated the issue by trying to renounce his inheritance as Lord Stansgate. These cases affirm that it is now a constitutional imperative for the government to be directed by members of the House of Commons. (This does not preclude the presence of a few lords in the cabinet, as the Lord President of the (Privy) Council.)

A further factor contributing to the decline in the impact of upper houses on the national decison-making process in parliamentary democracies is their tendency toward a nonrepresentative character. The British House of Lords is, of course, the classic example. Peopled in theory by all members of the hereditary aristocracy and life peers (1062 by August 1968), in practice fewer than 300 ever show up and considerably fewer than that attend regularly.[23] Life peerages are a relatively new phenomenon (created in 1958) of a nonhereditary appointment usually given to semiretired politicians. The idea was to provide a mechanism to reduce the overwhelming Conservative majority in the House of Lords. In addition, some consideration of geographic representation is present in the custom of providing a place for "representative peers" selected by the peerages of Scotland and Ireland, respectively. The Church of England is represented by the Lords Spiritual. However, there is no attempt to make lords representative of the configuration of politically relevent interests and opinions in British society. The life tenure of the lords and their largely hereditary means of selection would preclude any such standards.

Most proposals dealing with reform of the House of Lords[24] center around proposals to make the body more representative and more responsive. These proposals seem to miss the point that second chambers are inherently superfluous or redundant in parliamentary democracies. Their redundancy would only be eliminated by making the upper house representative of the same configuration of opinions and interests as the lower house. The only logical justifications for an upper house are that it either represents something not represented in the lower house or that it is less responsive than that house. As a less responsive body, it could be argued to provide a check on the popular passions of the moment. This function becomes, by definition, politically impractical. Popular forces by definition ultimately control democratic political processes. When popular passions are intensely felt, popular majorities will be impatient with rules of the game permit-

---

[23] A study by Sidney Bailey in the *Spectator*, 20 November 1953, shows 65 peers in regular attendance (43 Tories and 22 Labourites). The average daily attendance in 1965 was 225. Cited in Sidney Bailey, *British Parliamentary Democracy* (New York: Houghton Mifflin, 1971), Third Ed., p. 34.

[24] For example, Henry Burrows, "The House of Lords—Change or Decay," *Parliamentary Affairs*, Vol. XVII, No. 4, Autumn 1964, pp. 403–417.

ting "undemocratic" or "nonrepresentative" minorities to frustrate the majority will. Accordingly, the delaying power of the House of Lords was circumscribed from two years to one year in response to the lords' refusal to pass an Act of Parliament in 1945. It is likely that if the Conservatives in the House of Lords tried to use even that power to stymie a determined Labour government, their power to do so would be removed.

Because of the prestige of the House of Lords in Britain, it is able to serve an additional function, a function upper houses in other nations do not perform to any great extent. The House of Lords can deliberate on issues at greater depth than the House of Commons is able to do or can deliberate on issues Commons has not been able to debate at all. The very fact that the House of Lords is not accountable to the day-to-day shifting currents of public opinion enables its debate to assume a character that would be politically dangerous for debate to assume in the House of Commons. Moreover, lords, not being forced to process the array of issues processed in the House of Commons, do not operate under the time constraints that beset the House of Commons. In the House of Lords is an assemblage of generally highly educated people, often independent financially, and often (in the case of life peers) with lengthy experience in public life whose major function is to debate calmly issues of significance. Such a function is of obvious political value.

The House of Lords also functions as Britain's supreme court. Here sit the Law Lords, formally called the Judicial Committee of the Privy Council (JCPC). As we have already indicated, acts of Parliament cannot be declared unconstitutional in the American sense because the English constitution is not a legal document. However, the JCPC is Britain's court of ultimate appeal in all litigation. (The JCPC also had the capacity to review litigation from the nations of the older Commonwealth until well after the Second World War.)

The Meaning of Representation

What does it mean to represent someone? One possible answer is that representatives should ascertain and follow their constituents' wishes as closely as possible on as many issues as possible. This conceptualization would relegate the representative to a role approximating that of a clerical order taker, a role not requiring much wisdom or talent on the part of the legislator. Burke's answer, by contrast, in his aforementioned speech to the voters of Bristol, was that the MP owes his constituents not only his presence but his reasoned judgment. The representative is, by this conception of his role, a full-time student of public affairs whose judgments about affairs ought to carry more weight than the uninformed judgments of the average constituents. This conception of a representative's role presumes a deferential orientation toward authority. In an egalitarian culture such as is found in France, Australia, and the United States, the people are less likely to accept the proposition that the representative is a better judge of their interests than they would be themselves. The people in these cultures tend to view the representative more as their spokesperson or agent. Accordingly, the Burkean concept appears to be more viable in the deferential cultures of Britain, Germany, the Netherlands, and, to a lesser extent, Sweden.

When we come to the concept of representation used in the Soviet Union, we are again reminded of the parallel party and government structures. Of the two notions of representation mentioned above, the first would seem to apply to the government and the other to the party.

Lenin criticized traditional parliamentary structures and adopted a new form called soviets. As first developed before the revolution they were informal groups composed of delegations of workers. The assertion was that, unlike other parliaments governed by the elite, this was a new form of democracy in which the delegates to soviets (councils) would be working people. After the 1917 revolution, the soviets came under the influence of Lenin and the Bolsheviks and their nature changed. A formal hierarchy was established from the local level to the Supreme Soviet, and membership came to be based on geographic districts instead of occupational groupings. Through it all, however, the concept was that these bodies mirrored the population and did not consist of special people.

An examination of the membership of the Supreme Soviet in recent years reveals that instead of reflecting the makeup of the society, it contains an overrepresentation of such groups as party and government employees and the intelligentsia. However, several hundred of the more than 1500 delegates are workers or collective farmers. In addition, party members comprise well over a majority of delegates, but only five percent of the total population. Another indication that people elected to serve in the Supreme Soviet are not typical is the fact that many of them have been honored previously as outstanding workers, farmers, etc. The claim that representatives are average citizens rather than an elite does draw some support from a high turnover rate; that is, well over half of the delegates in any given Supreme Soviet will not normally have served in the preceding one.

These observations about the Supreme Soviet must be followed by the reminder that it is not a policymaking body, and the discussion is therefore largely one of a theory of representation. Representation in the CPSU, where policy is made, is based more on the concept that the party acts as the people would if they were really informed.

Therefore, according to its statutes, the CPSU is the vanguard of the Soviet people and brings together the more advanced, politically conscious sectors of the society. Following the "scientific" principles and theories of Marxism-Leninism, the party leads, guides, and directs the efforts and activities of Soviet society. Perhaps it could be said that policy is made in the structure, which operates on a deferential principle, and then is ratified and legitimated by the one that claims to be more directly representative of the people.

This concept is based on Lenin's revision of Marxism to explain its introduction where Marx least expected it. The introduction of communism in Russia before it became a mature industrial society was justified by the aspect of Leninism that suggested that Marxism could be imposed from without. That way, it was not necessary to wait for revolutionary class consciousness to develop spontaneously through the impersonal forces of the development and decay of capitalism. The concept of a proletariat (blue-collar industrial labor force), of course, was difficult to fit into a feudal peasant society like Russia of 1917. This external imposition of revolutionary consciousness was to be done by the elite party as the "vanguard" of the revolution. Thus, the role of the party was to lead the people rather than to reflect their wishes.

The Structure of Representative Assemblies

We have already pointed out that bicameralism makes sense to the extent that the upper chamber represents a different constituency and plays a somewhat different role than the lower chamber. Bicameralism is most easily rationalized in terms of "representing" the political subdivisions of a federal system as is the case with Bundesrats of West Germany and Austria, the Council of States in Switzerland, the Senates of Australia, Canada, and the United States, and the Soviet of Nationalities in the Soviet Union.

Bicameral parliaments without federal justification are found in Italy, France, Britain, the Netherlands, and Belgium. The case of the Netherlands is unique in that the members of its upper house are chosen by "provincial councils." Although the parliament in the Netherlands is unitary and not federal in form, the councils are accorded direct representation in the national decision-making process. Because the councils are directly elected, the Dutch upper house is indirectly elected, giving it a different electoral base than the Tweed Kamer (lower house).

The Belgian Senate is partly chosen by provincial councils, partly directly elected, and partly chosen by other senators, thus affording that body a somewhat distinct electoral base relative to the Belgian Chamber of Deputies. The logic of having provincial councils participate in the election of an upper house assumes that the councils represent a set of perceived parochial interests distinct from the national interests. In practice, the configuration of interests and parties is very similar in both houses of both Belgium and the Netherlands.

The Italian Senate has an electoral base not significantly distinct from that of the lower house, the Chamber of Deputies. In Italy, the Senate theoretically has coequal powers with the lower house, which conflicts with the natural tendency for parliamentary systems to enhance the political significance of the lower houses at the expense of the upper houses. Most, but not all, Italian prime ministers and major cabinet ministers have been members of the chamber. However, the fact that two prime ministers and several other important ministers have been members of the upper house is unusual among parliamentary systems. It is unclear whether a no-confidence vote in the Senate alone would compel a government to resign. The strength of the upper chamber renders the relationship between Italian governments and their legislature somewhat ambiguous.

Unicameralism characterizes most other parliamentary democracies, including Sweden, Luxemburg, and Denmark, with Norway constituting an ambiguous situation. The Norwegian Storting designates a quarter of its own members to sit separately as members of another house; however, due to the careful preservation of party proportionality in the membership of the offspring group, it is unlikely to function as a check on its parent chamber. Given this, the logic of the division is hard to discern.[25] Sweden and Denmark have both adopted unicameralism since the Second World War. Clearly, two cases do not constitute a trend, but these two cases, taken in conjunction with the progressive weakening of those second chambers now in existence, is certainly consistent with their lack of a logical role in the parliamentary framework.

We have already pointed out that one of the imperatives of mature industrial societies contributing to the trend toward domination of the legislature by the executive is the information possessed by the latter and not by the former. The growth of complex, specialized knowledge as a prerequisite for comprehensive and coherent action is responded to in some legislative assemblies by functionally specific decentralization of its activities. Functionally specific committees can theoretically take advantage of the principle of specialization and division of labor in the acquisition of technological expertise. The difficulty is that to the extent that such committees acquire esoteric information or expertise not shared by the whole chamber, the committees become autonomous of the whole, thus confusing formal lines of accountability.

The United States Congress epitomizes the autonomy of functionally specific committees from their respective plenary chambers. An enormous preponderance of bills introduced into Congress die in committee. In France, especially during the Third Republic, standing committees in the Chamber of Deputies acted similar to standing committees in the U.S. Congress. In parliamentary systems with disciplined parties, however, the functionally specific committees reflect the composition of the plenary chambers and are accordingly responsive to the leadership of those chambers. Thus, functionally specific committees in Sweden, the Netherlands, and Belgium routinely pass government policy on to the plenary

---

[25] Gordon Smith, *Politics in Western Europe* (New York: Holmes and Meier Publications, 1974) p. 212.

sessions of their respective chambers by margins proportional to the political makeup of the plenary bodies. The lack of political significance of the committees, in part a function of the control of disciplined parties of the individual members, deprives those chambers of the specialized and technological competence needed to hold societies accountable in mature industrial societies.

With the exception of a few specialized standing committees such as the Committee on Public Accounts and the Select Committee on Estimates, British standing committees are not functionally specific. This practice is in keeping with the British cultural preference for the "generalist" as opposed to the technocrat. But the practice further impedes Parliament from holding the executive accountable for legislation dealing with a technologically complex world.

To the extent that work is not done in committee, the legislature in today's society is increasingly incapable of providing a check on legislative discretion. As the functions of government increase, the number of bills processed per session has also markedly increased. A single plenary body simply does not have the time to consider adequately all of the issues a modern industrial society must face. A committee system such as the one in the United States actually divides up the task of resolving issues by its ability to filter out the number of bills actually reaching the plenary chamber for consideration.

None of the committee systems in Europe today performs the filtering function to the extent that it is performed in the U.S. Congress, where 90 percent of all bills introduced die in committee. For example, Riksdag committees in Sweden are forbidden by law to pigeonhole (ignore) legislation, as is done in the American standing committees. In Italy, however, functionally specific standing committees issue final approval on three-fourths of the bills introduced into the legislature and send them directly to the president for signature. One-tenth of the membership of each house could demand plenary consideration of such bills. Thus, the Italian communists, with well over a tenth of the membership of each house, could sabotage all such legislation.[26] The wonder is that they do not do so. Certain classes of bills are required to go through plenary consideration, which is another limit on this power of committees.

Legislative committees tend to be even less representative of the distribution of perceived interests and demands of society than the legislative body as a whole. The seniority system of the American Congress is perhaps the most familiar and blatant example of this tendency, which gives disproportionate influence to rural, Southern, and conservative forces in that body. To the extent that standing committees act as filtering devices, legislative action (or, more frequently, inaction) may be seriously out of step with the perceived needs and demands of society.

In view of the almost total lack of a policymaking role for the Supreme Soviet, it

---

[26] Raphael Zariski, *Italy: The Politics of Uneven Development* (Hinsdale, IL: The Dryden Pres. 1972), p. 245.

might be natural to assume that we cannot even speak of a committee system. But an interesting development in the post-Stalin period has been indications of an increased role for standing committees in that body.[27] This process, begun under Khrushchev and continued by his successors, appears to give committees several real (if small) functions.

The most important task given to the Soviet committees would appear to be that of preliminary discussion and refinement of draft legislation and decrees, where the major content has been set by the party. Gilison suggests that committees may improve legislation through coordination of public discussion and through consultations with various affected interests in the system. He also points out that the chairmen of these standing committees are almost all high-ranking members of the CPSU. We are not saying that these bodies make policy. We are suggesting that in an increasingly complex society they may have part of the task of consulting with various interests to work out the details of general policies established by the party apparatus.

The necessity of working out details in committee is partly necessitated by the infrequency of sessions of the Supreme Soviet. Thus, even though representative assemblies do not make policies, the task of formalizing policy decisions into legislation has become so voluminous as to require the principle of division of labor.

Parliamentary Debate

It has been argued by at least one student of British politics that the parliamentary function of control of the executive entails "criticism" rather than "obstruction."[28] This distinction entails the idea that, except in extreme circumstances, the legislature ought not to prevent the executive's program from being enacted. "Control" consists of publicizing and trying to persuade the public of the weak points in the government's position. By this conception, the debate preceding a division (legislative vote) is a more significant part of Parliament's function than the vote itself.

Given the significance of the debating function, the variation in the character of debate in the nations under consideration is worth noting. The concept of debate normally entails an exchange of ideas, a situation in which a proposition is critiqued or answered with a counterproposal. This conception of debate may be distinguished from a series of more or less unrelated speeches. Speechmaking has been the rule in industrial democracies; debate has been the exception.

---

[27] See Jerome Gilison, *British and Soviet Politics* (Baltimore: The John Hopkins Press, 1972). Chapters 3 and 4 deal with the assemblies of the two nations and p. 109 ff. discusses committee structure.

[28] Bernard Crick, *The Reform of Parliament* (Garden City, NY: Doubleday Anchor Books, 1965), p. 79.

The British Parliament is frequently held up as epitomizing what debate ought to be in a legislature. Nowhere is a process of extemporaneous give and take more pronounced. The pros and cons of issues are delineated; rarely does a controversial assertion go unanswered. This may be seen in contrast to the succession of speeches found in other chambers such as in France, West Germany, or the United States—speeches often seemingly unaffected by any preceding remarks.

When debate occurs in Britain or elsewhere, it tends to take the form of criticism or defense of government-formulated policy. It should be recalled that decentralized representative assemblies are incapable of taking coherent action. The ability to take such action would require the unlikely event of a spontaneous agreement on complex policy by several hundred autonomous individuals. Thus, legislatures cannot be expected to formulate coherent policy in the absence of strong centralized leadership structures in the house. These leadership structures never exist independently of the government itself. Thus, the character of debate in the House of Commons tends to take the form of criticism or defense of specific policy proposals submitted by the government. This "structuring of debate," as Spiro calls it, lends a coherence to the proceedings.[29]

Debate in the Swedish Riksdag, although less extensive than in Britain, is similarly structured into a "proposition" and "counterproposition" upon the introduction of the annual budget. The most likely debate occurs on general policy propositions at this time. Specific "bread-and-butter" compromises are hammered out in committee hearings.

By contrast, most other Continental assemblies are characterized by a series of speeches that often ramble without really doing much to clarify the issues and without the give and take of debate. This is certainly true in the Soviet Union. Perhaps the best way to explain the style of the Supreme Soviet is to refer to the rules of the CPSU. Although the party rules apply directly only to the party, in practice the principles apply to governmental structures as well. The functions of the Party Congress, which is similar to the Supreme Soviet, are described in terms of reviewing, amending, and endorsing programs and hearing and approving reports.

The ideological emphasis in the Soviet Union on unity and lack of conflict means the virtual absence of criticism involving policy or high-level officials. Meetings are dull and often consist of very long reports. Some of the speeches may point out problems in implementing policies and may call for some change, but they are a series of reports, not discussion or debate. The role of delegates is to listen, applaud, and vote approval. In a one-party authoritarian system, this is one of the procedures often used to rally support for the regime. Votes in the Supreme Soviet are unanimous in their approval of the programs and policies presented.

---

[29] Spiro, *op. cit.*, p. 253.

In competitive party systems, by contrast, debate and criticism are essential in the process of attempting to mobilize support for or against a government's position. When debate is replaced by a series of speeches, this function is poorly served. Although fulfilling this function of debating the organization of support and opposition, debate in the British House of Commons has no effect on impending divisions, which are along party lines. The real impact of debate in Britain and similar systems is the cumulative support of or opposition to the overall performance of the government as determined at the next general election. This is, of course, the basic mechanism of accountability in a centralized cabinet system.

Gilison suggests that the contrasting styles of the British and Soviet parliaments summarize and illustrate the essential difference between the two systems. The real difference is not between a monolithic leadership operating through a unanimous Supreme Soviet and a British leadership divided into competing factions and contending for power in the House of Commons. Conflict and competing groups exist in both systems but are only open and legitimate in one of them. The assemblies differ, therefore, "in that the conflict between the illegitimate Soviet factions can play no part, while the open and legitimate conflict of British parties is the very essence of parliamentary debate."[30]

The Physical Structure of Legislative Chambers

It has been argued that the character of legislative debate is affected to some extent by the physical structure of the chamber. Specifically, the British House of Commons is organized (see Figure 1) as two sets of benches running the length of a fairly confined rectangular room such that the occupants of one set of benches directly confront the occupants of the other. The individual MPs speak directly from their benches without the benefit of a written speech, a rostrum, or amplifying equipment. To make a formal speech under such circumstances, it is argued, would seem quite out of place.

By the same token, the structure of the House of Commons is said to encourage the tight party discipline found among British parties. In order to vote for the other side, an MP has to cross the floor physically to file behind the opposition benches. The process of crossing the floor in front of the speaker, God, and everyone precludes breaking party discipline subtly and without being noticed.

By contrast, Continental parliaments tend to be structured in a semicircular fashion with members of the legislature ranged from left to right according to their professed place in the political spectrum. A rostrum is normally provided, giving encouragement to formal speechmaking. Further, a vote does not entail physical movement, so no conspicuous effort is required to break party discipline (see Figure 2).

[30] Gilison, *op. cit.*, 101.

Figure 1. The interior of the House of Commons. Note that the two sets of benches face each other. The speaker sits on the raised dias. The prime minister and the cabinet sit on the front benches to the speaker's right. The shadow cabinet sits on the front benches to the speaker's left. The three chairs in front of the dias are for the "clarks" (clerks). Note that no podium is provided; the prime minister as well as everyone else speaks from the benches with only the benefit of the microphones extending from the wall (added when the building was rebuilt during the Second World War).

Some Britishers had such faith in this physical explanation of the desirable character of debate in the House of Commons and of party cohesion that when the House was destroyed by a German bomb during the Second World War, they insisted that it be rebuilt in exactly the same way—no desks, offices, or even room for all of the members on the benches. The only concession to comfort and convenience was to permit some padding on the benches.

If a necessary explanation of the character of debate in the House of Commons or of British party discipline is sought in such physical features, the explanation will not bear scrutiny. As pointed out, neither party cohesion nor debate (as opposed to speechmaking) is strictly confined to the House of Commons. Here again, we find a vulnerable generalization derived from the limited universe of Britain, France, and West Germany. The character of legislative debate is more likely to be to a large extent a function of the political culture of the system.

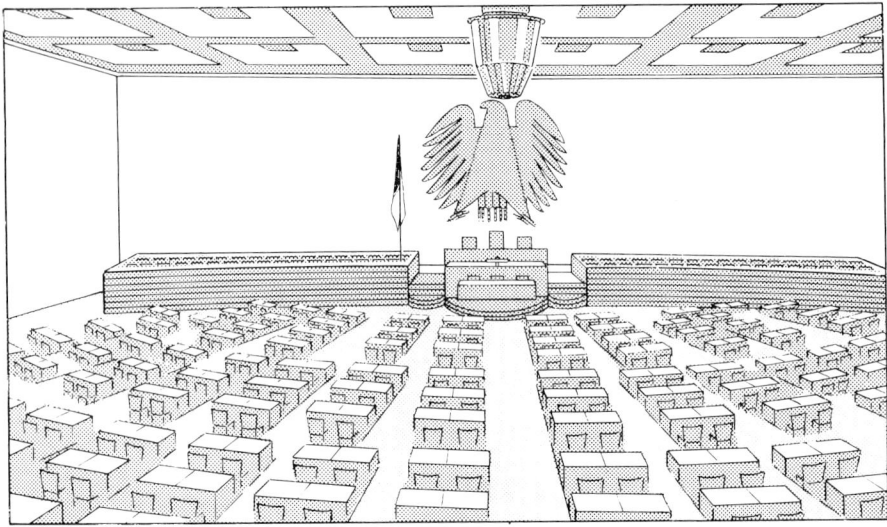

Figure 2. The interior of the Bundeshaus where the West German Bundestag meets. Note the arrangement of seats whereby government and opposition do not face each other. Note also the podium with microphones in front from which speeches are made.

Executive Roles

Parliamentary systems divide their executive functions among two distinct roles: the political role (head of government) and the symbolic role (head of state). These correspond to what Walter Bagehot, in his classic commentary on *The English Constitution*, called the "efficient" and "dignified" aspects of the constitution, respectively.[31] In the former role is concentrated the ultimate responsibility for policy formulation functions and administrative functions. The latter role concerns itself with ceremonial functions and, as the symbol of unity for the concept of the nation, integrative functions.

Presidential formats combine these two roles in one person. Thus, American presidents function both as the symbol of unity for the entire nation and, at the same time, the political and hence partisan representative of particular philosophies and interests. By effectively combining these two roles, the president can mobilize support through the role of head of state for partisan purposes.

General DeGaulle effectively did this in France. Aided and abetted by his

---

[31] Walter Bagehot, *The English Constitution* (New York: Doubleday Dolphin Books, n.d.), pp. 63–64.

enormous charisma, DeGaulle's power became institutionalized to the point where the successors of the general have had similarly great power.

The Fifth Republic has been called quasi-presidential because under the terms of the constitution the office of prime minister is at least partially accountable to the Assembly. However, the capacity of the Assembly to censure any prime minister having the support of the president of the republic is severely circumscribed by the political reality that the president could and almost certainly would immediately dissolve the Assembly. He can dissolve the Assembly up to once a year for any reason. Moreover, the prime minister is designated by the president, and thus far he has been designated according to the criterion of conformity to the views of the president. The prime minister is not required to secure the approval of the Assembly; hence, unlike "true" paraliamentary regimes, the identity of the prime minister is not a function of the views of the legislature. Prime ministers in the Fifth Republic have tended to act in the role of deputies to the president, liaisons aiding the president in keeping the Assembly in line, and potential heirs to the presidency. Prime ministers in the Fifth Republic have not established an autonomy from the president, as British prime ministers have established their autonomy from the will of the monarch. These facts, combined with the extraordinary political powers of the French president, render the word *quasi* in the term *quasi-presidential regime* without significance. The French president is as much the head of government as the American president, if not more so.

The French president may take "whatever measures are required by the circumstances" when the institutions of the republic are threatened. The determination of such an "emergency" is made by the president, and no time limit is imposed on the duration of the emergencies. This is an obvious loophole available to any potentially despotic executive who wants to exercise unrestrained power. During a state of emergency, the president rules by decree and normal political processes are suspended. (By contrast, the American experience includes the famous case of *Ex Parte Milligan* in which the Supreme Court limited the power of the president and Congress to suspend portions of the Constitution in the context of the Civil War.)

The French president, if unable to get his way in the political process, may bypass that process in other ways. He may submit certain issues directly to the electorate with a plebiscite asking the electorate to approve or disapprove of a particular resolution on an issue; a referendum implies that policy alternatives are directly presented to the voters. The French practice has been to present the electorate with one policy to approve or nothing will be done, hardly a viable alternative. Recall how plebiscitary democracy complements Rousseauean theory, as discussed in the previous chapter. While the president formally needs the concurrence of the government for the presentation of a plebiscite to the electorate, the government's lack of an independent power base renders this requirement an ineffective check on the power of the president. Like American presidents, French presidents have broad appointive power, head the armed forces, and formulate most policy. Moreover, the French president exercises major control over the agenda of the legislature. The president has the power to raise questions of constitutionality to be brought before the Constitutional Council, the court that decides these issues in France.

As in the American system, the direct election of the French president gives that official a political base of support possessed by no other institution in the system. Because no other chief of state exists to compete for the support that normally adheres to the occupier of that role in a reasonably well-integrated society, the president of the republic is capable of mobilizing much support for his partisan political purposes out of the patriotic effect that normally adheres to his concurrent role of chief of state.

Chiefs of State

Elsewhere, the role of chief of state is separated from that of head of government. In the remaining constitutional monarchies, the monarch fulfills that role. Among the nations we are considering, Belgium, Britain, Denmark, the Netherlands, Norway, and Sweden remain as constitutional monarchies. In the older Commonwealth nations of Australia, Canada, and New Zealand, a governor-general fills the role of representative of the monarch. Although the British monarch officially appoints the governors-general, the monarch routinely names the choice of the indigenous prime minister. At times, a certain amount of consultation between the monarch and the indigenous prime minister has been involved. Until 1931 in Australia and 1952 in Canada, the governors-general of these dominions were Britishers. The Canadians tolerated an alien in this symbolic and ceremonial post so long because a foreigner was not only politically neutral but was also ethnically neutral with regard to the French-Canadian–non-French Canadian cleavage discussed in Chapter 4.

The Dutch monarchy has lost much prestige in recent years due to the marital and religious activities of the royal family. The Italian monarch was deposed at the end of the Second World War as a result of his collaboration with Mussolini and fascism. Similarly, the wartime behavior of the Belgian King Leopold III resulted in his abdication in favor of his son, King Baudouin. This "royal question" reinforced the cultural question, as the Flemish and Walloons divided for and against Leopold. This politicization of the monarchy, especially when involved with the divisive cultural cleavage, did nothing to enhance the prestige of that institution.

By contrast, Britain has been fortunate in the character of the individuals that have occupied its throne in the twentieth century. Men such as wartime monarch George VI displayed genuine leadership qualities and enhanced the prestige of the monarchy. While Elizabeth II seems to lack the leadership qualities of her predecessor, she has done nothing to diminish seriously the prestige of the institution. Despite some criticism from the political left, the British monarchy probably remains the most prestigious of the world's declining number of monarchies. (It should be noted that at this writing, the marital difficulties of Princess Margaret have somewhat exacerbated this criticism. Most Britishers seem to regard the queen autonomously from her sister, however.)

The effectiveness of a monarch in fulfilling the functions of chief of state depends on the prestige of the institution and the character of the royal family. Monarchs have a certain advantage in fulfilling these functions over political leaders such as the French and American presidents. First, despite the political advantages in combining the two roles, the integrating force of the symbolic role should be enhanced when the chief of state is politically neutral. Second, the pomp that naturally accrues to royalty can add to the integrative effectiveness of this role. Pomp often seems out of place with presidents and prime ministers (as when Richard Nixon tried dressing his White House guards as characters out of a Gilbert and Sullivan operetta). Third, freed from the burdens of political leadership, the chief of state can devote more time and attention to symbolic and ceremonial duties.

Depending on the prestige and leadership qualities of the occupant of the throne, the monarch in a parliamentary system may still exercise some political influence. In the first place, the tenure of the monarch usually vastly exceeds that of any given prime minister or head of government. Consequently, a monarch may offer a longer-term perspective. Second, this perspective is not likely to be distorted by considerations of political accountability and partisan attachment. Therefore, as Bagehot once said, the monarch has three "rights—the right to be consulted, the right to encourage, the right to warn."[32] These "rights" adhere in proportion to the force of the monarch's personality, the prestige of the monarchy itself, and the weakness of the political head of government.

In the third place, the monarch officially designates the prime minister. When one disciplined party has a majority of the legislative seats or a clearly dominant plurality of the seats, the choice of the monarch is obviously limited to the head of the dominant party. This is normally the case among most of the nations we are considering, as aggregated party systems become the rule rather than the exception.

In some systems, however, elections are occasionally inconclusive. In Third and Fourth Republic France this was normally the case. It has been the case in the

[32] *Ibid.*, p. 124.

Netherlands on several occasions. When the nonlabor or nonsocialist coalitions take over in Scandinavian nations, it is not entirely clear which party dominates the coalitions. A forceful monarch, in a supposedly neutral role as arbitrator in the bargaining process among parties to form a government, may exercise some influence in that selection.

It has become apparent that not all elections provide an automatic majority (party), even in Britain. At least one minority Labour government existed in Britain in the early 1970s. The possible future influence of British monarchs in the selection of their prime ministers depends to some extent on the uncertain future success of the Liberals, Scottish and Welsh nationalists, and other minor parties. If these parties increase their electoral support, it is conceivable that they could prevent with some regularity a legislative majority being obtained by either the Labour or Conservative Parties.

Occasionally, even though it may be obvious which party dominates the legislature and therefore must control the government, it may not be obvious who is the leader of that party. This situation has occurred on several occasions in the British Conservative Party. Once was the aforementioned instance when it was unclear whether the dominant figure in the party, Lord Curzon, could assume the prime ministership despite his membership in the House of Lords. Another such occasion was when it was unclear as to whether the Earl of Home could extricate himself from Lords to run for Commons and assume party leadership in 1963. These intraparty ambiguities are now less likely, because the Tories now choose their leader by formal election. It is uncertain how much if any influence was exercised by the monarch in these deliberation with the party elite; the deliberations are never made public, only the results. The best guess is that Elizabeth II exercised very little influence, as she does not appear to be a very forceful person.

Apparently, the influence of the Dutch monarch is somewhat greater than that of the British in several ways. In the first place, the influence of the monarch in the selection of a prime minister can be greater for two related reasons: the fragmentation of the party system and the duration of cabinet crises. In the two to four months that it often takes to form a new government in the Netherlands, the monarch can exercise considerable executive influence.

In the second place, the monarch appoints a Council of State, a body of elder statesmen to "advise" the cabinet. The cabinet is not bound by this advice but apparently takes it seriously. The monarch has considerable discretion in the selection of this body.

As with the British monarch, the Dutch monarch is kept fully informed about cabinet activities. Gordon Weil suggests a cabinet willingness somehow to "modify its proposals to take the queen's view into account . . . in the Netherlands."[33]

---

[33] Weil, *op. cit.*, p. 130.

Present-day British cabinets would not manifest such concern for the views of their queen.

Presidents as Chiefs of State

In those parliamentary systems that are republics, a president occupies the role of chief of state. This role has often been filled by what may be termed an "elder statesman." That term refers to a veteran politician whose encroaching senility has rendered him so politically innocuous as to be considered nonpartisan. Lacking either the powers of a prime minister or the pomp and tradition of a monarch, the post of president of the republic generally does not carry a great deal of prestige.

As veteran politicians, some presidents (as in Italy, West Germany, or Fourth and Third Republic France) may retain a certain residue of political skill and an inclination to wield power. People such as Poincaré and Auriol in France may be cases in point. In these cases, presidents, whose tenure generally exceeds that of their prime ministers, may exercise some political impact in much the same way as monarchs. Whatever impact these heads of state possess tends to be concentrated in the selection of a government—the prime minister and the cabinet.

In the case of the Italian president, the norms of political neurtrality are not as strong as in the case of British, Scandinavian, or Low Country monarchs. The bounds of expectation (or the customary part of the constitution, broadly defined) permit the president to speak out on controversial questions, and Italian presidents have in fact done so. This would be unthinkable for one of the aforementioned monarchs. Similarly, the president of the Federal Republic of Germany is constitutionally prohibited from engaging in partisan activities. These same bounds of expectation in Italy permit the president to use his legal power of returning a piece of legislation to Parliament for reconsideration. This has been done on numerous occasions but never on a major piece of legislation. (By way of contrast, recall that it has become constitutionally unthinkable for the British monarch to say, "la reine s'avisera," rejecting a bill approved by Parliament.) The threat of this veto power of the Italian president could be a factor in the content of the legislation that is passed.

Confusion about structures in the Soviet Union probably reaches its peak with respect to executive roles. This situation arises for a number of reasons, but primarily because of the parallel, overlapping nature of state and party organizations and because of ambiguities at their top levels. The three positions to be considered are the Chairman of the Council of Ministers, the Chairman of the Presidium of the Supreme Soviet, and the General Secretary of the Central Committee of the CPSU. Once again, a distinction must be made between formal and actual roles.

According to the constitution the Supreme Soviet chooses a Presidium and a

Council of Ministers, both of which exercise what are normally considered executive functions. The Presidium, a 37-member body that acts on behalf of the Supreme Soviet, is given powers such as issuing decrees and pardons and appointing military and diplomatic officials. Its chairman is considered to be (on behalf of the entire body) the symbolic, titular head of state. The Council of Ministers, also referred to in the constitution as the government of the Soviet Union, is the highest administrative organ and is composed of various ministries and committees. Structurally, it is the equivalent of a cabinet, and its chairman is similar to the role of prime minister. There is thus a symbolic head of state and a head of the government.

The difficulty is that neither of these two governmental offices is in fact the most important executive position in terms of actual decision-making powers. It is at this point that the leader of the CPSU must be considered. Experience indicates that the two most important posts in the Soviet Union are Chairman of the Council of Ministers on the government side and General Secretary on the party side. Of the two, the latter has been clearly more important and powerful. Both Stalin and Khrushchev began as party leader and eventually assumed the post of head of government as well. After Khrushchev's removal, Leonid Brezhnev occupied the top party post and Alexei Kosygin became Chairman of the Council of Ministers (with Nikolai Podgorny in the third position as head of state).

In time it became obvious that the earlier pattern was being repeated and Brezhnev was emerging as the dominant leader, in spite of the fact that he held neither of the top government offices. Due to the overlapping and parallel nature of the state and party hierarchies, however, he does occupy a government position as a member of the Presidium of the Supreme Soviet. Similarly, the men in the two top state offices (Kosygin and Podgorny) are members of the party Politburo, which is the powerful policymaking group. Thus, the Soviet Union has a symbolic chief of state, a head of government, and a top party leader all sharing in executive functions. (see Figure 3.)

The Heads of Government

In parliamentary systems, the government consists of a prime minister and the cabinet. The role of prime minister occasionally appears under other titles: in Italy, it is officially the president of the Council of Ministers; in Fourth Republic France it was premier; in the Soviet Union it is the chairman of Council of Ministers.

The cabinet consists of the heads of the governmental administrative departments—called ministers—and several policy advisors or "generalists" without administrative responsibilities. Not all ministers are necessarily part of the cabinet. In Britain certain less significant ministers are omitted from the cabinet.

Policymaking Structures

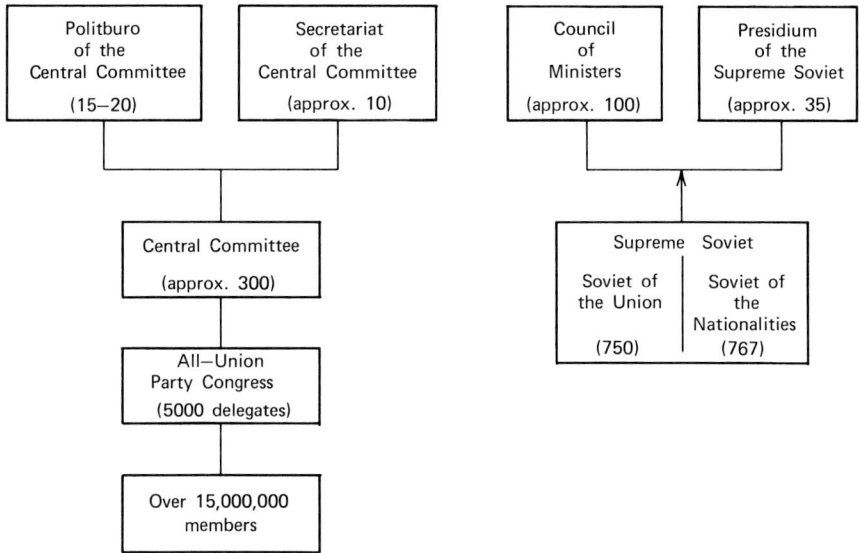

Figure 3. Top party and government organization in the Soviet Union.

The generalists are called "ministers without portfolio"—that is, ministers without a department to run. In Italy about six ministers without portfolio occupy each cabinet as a device to keep certain policy functions "from falling under the control of one of the quasi-autonomous ministries."[34] In Britain, however, this device is less frequently used. The role of cabinet generalist is usually filled by holders of "sinecure offices"—offices whose functions belong to the past. For example, the British cabinet includes a Lord President of the (Privy) Council and a Lord Privy Seal, offices still filled although the Privy Council has not functioned as a body for centuries. The Chancellor of the Duchy of Lancaster is another such sinecure office in the cabinet.

The nations under consideration differ in the extent that their cabinets function as a coherent body. In a fragmented party system such as Italy's, with coalition governments composed of several parties, the cabinet is not coherent. In Britain the cabinet appears to be quite coherent. All members of British cabinets are members of the same disciplined party and owe their place in the cabinet to the prime minister. In Italy, cabinet members are often designated by the parliamentary groups irrespective of the will of the prime minister as the price for support of the government. In Italy, Fourth Republic France, and Norway, the fall of a government requires the resignation only of the prime minister. It does not pre-

[34] Zariski, *op. cit.*, p. 234.

clude the cabinet members from retaining their posts or even moving to a higher (more prestigious or powerful) post in a new government. In Norway, however, when the Centre Party bolted the non-Labour coalition, it was politically impossible to form another non-Labour coalition. Thus, in this case, the action of the Centre Party leaders cost them their own places in the government. Generally speaking, however, cabinet stability is most likely to be adversely affected when substantial portions of the government perceive that their political interests are not necessarily threatened and in fact may be enhanced by the fall of that government. In these situations, a minister, in deciding whether to bring down a government, may perceive that the destruction of the government involves no risk to his position, while the collapse of the government may entail the possibility of his advancement—possibly to prime minister.

In Britain and the older Commonwealth nations, the cabinet is collectively responsible to the parliament. The Belgian cabinet is also in theory collectively responsible. This means that if a government should fall, the entire cabinet would be compelled to resign. In the British and Commonwealth nations, deliberations of the cabinet are secret, and only the collective result of the deliberations is officially revealed. One is not supposed to reveal publicly a minority view while remaining a member of the cabinet. Perhaps a classic illustration of this was the case of Anthony Eden, who as foreign secretary during the 1930s had to suppress very intensely felt disagreements with Prime Minister Chamberlain's policy of attempted reconciliation with Hitler. Only on resignation from the government was Eden able to make his feelings known.

In general, the principle of collective responsibility also applies to the Low Countries, although, as in Britain, a single minister within the Dutch cabinet may be forced to resign. In these nations the concept of collective responsibility does not detract from the responsibility of the individual minister for what are clearly his own serious errors of judgment.[35] The resignation of John Profumo in the celebrated Christine Keeler sex scandals in Britain was a case in point.

Cabinet responsibility works somewhat differently in the case of Italy. The entire cabinet must resign in the face of a vote of no confidence; however, most of the ministers are reappointed to the same positions in succeeding cabinets. This is in contrast to the British system, where a single party controls the entire government. Here, a transfer of power at the level of prime minister necessarily entails a total reconstitution of cabinet personnel.

Thus, in highly aggregated party systems, in which the leadership of the dominant party in effect picks the cabinet, each member of that government has a direct political interest in its survival. Except in extraordinary circumstances, to

---

[35] L. S. Amery, *Thoughts on the Constitution* (London: Oxford University Press, 1964), p. 71. Amery's book is a classic essay on the topic.

force the resignation of the prime minister would be tantamount to driving oneself out of the government. Inasmuch as a genuine impact on the official policymaking process is almost exclusively concentrated in the cabinet in these systems (recall the discussion of the decline of the individual MP above), to force the resignation of a government of which one is a part would in effect condemn oneself to the political wilderness.

Where cabinet responsibility to the legislature is quite explicit, the norm that the members of the cabinet also be members of the lower chamber is quite strong, as was pointed out above. In the Netherlands, where the structure of accountability is more ambiguous, membership in the cabinet does not require a seat in either house of the States General. Moreover, a greater percentage of cabinet members come from the upper house than would be found in the other parliamentary systems under consideration, although the prime minister is normally a member of the Tweed Kamer.

The Concentration of Formal Policymaking Processes

The assertion that the cabinet and not parliament formulates policy does not achieve realism at the expense of theory, even when the impact of those corporate forces outside the official policymaking processes, the technocracy, is discounted. The policy formulation function may be conceptualized as located at the center of a series of ever-broadening concentric circles.

The British monarch, as power began to flow "out of court" to the financially independent nobility, formulated policy in consultation with these nobles. As the number of nobles increased, the policymaking function came to focus on a group that served from within the nobility as the king's private (privy) advisors. This body was institutionalized as the Privy Council. Lowenstein says the Council reorganized under the reign of Henry VII,[36] but Elton suggests that the institutionalization of the Council took place about 1540 during the reign of Henry VIII.[37] The Royal Council of the nobility had grown rapidly under Henry VII from about 15 to 40 members. Elton suggests, consistent with the concentric circle analogy, that the Privy Council consisted of the institutionalization of the "inner ring" of the King's or Royal Council.[38]

It was soon obvious that the Privy Council had become the place to be for those who sought to influence policy. Accordingly, as pressures accumulated to appoint each and every ambitious young man in British politics to the Privy Council, that

---

[36] Karl Lowenstein, *British Cabinet Government* (London: Oxford University Press, 1967), pp. 15, 38–39.
[37] G. R. Elton, ed., *The Tudor Constitution: Documents and Commentary* (Cambridge: Cambridge University Press, 1962), p. 88. Elton's work is a standard source for Tudor historians.
[38] *Ibid.*, p. 89.

body too grew to unwieldy proportions. (The body still exists, although it actually gathers only at coronations. Appointment to the Privy Council has become a sinecure honor—a title without functions. Appointees become entitled to be addressed as The Right Honourable . . . , PC.)

At one point, five aristocrats within the Privy Council functioned as the king's actual advisors, Lords Clifford, Ashley, Buckingham, Arlington and Lauderdale. The first letters of their names gave rise to the term *cabal*. This group never became institutionalized, however, and eventually another manageable group of advisors began meeting in the king's private chambers or cabinet.

With the institutionalization of the cabinet, it plainly became the place for the politically ambitious. Accordingly, it has grown to around 25, an unwieldy number for policy formulation. At present an inner circle within the cabinet actually participates directly in policy formulation. This inner group varies somewhat but usually includes, besides the prime minister, the secretaries of state (foreign secretary and home secretary), the lord chancellor, the lord president of the council, the lord privy seal, and the chancellor of the exchequer.

Here is a clear example of the evolutionary development of British institutions out of need and experience. This fits the British common law orientation that derives its legal principles by essentially the same inductive process. This, in turn, fits the British political culture described in Chapter 3 with its pragmatic political style. As opposed to the creation of structures according to logical and principled criteria and imposing them on a society, the creation of structures by evolutionary processes is more likely to produce institutions that are, in Eckstein's term, "congruent" to the society in which they are situated and hence more viable.[39]

Thus, the actual authority to formulate formal policy (legislation) is concentrated in a relatively few hands—the inner circle of the cabinet—while actual decisions affecting who gets what, when, and how are dispersed in agencies of the administrative sector, interest groups, and the councils referred to in the preceding chapter, where the bargaining among the representatives of the public bureaucracy and organized interests has become institutionalized. This actual dispersion in the face of formal concentration is an apparently inexorable concomitant of a mature, industrial society.

The problems of industrial society are increasingly complex and numerous. The cabinet in Britain usually meets, at the discretion of the prime minister, for less than 10 hours per week. Other cabinets meet on a similarly restricted basis of once or twice per week. We should recall that most cabinet members are simultaneously head of a ministry with enormous administrative responsibilities and members of the legislature, or both. In terms of available time to allot to the task, the role of participation in the government becomes of necessity a part-time

---

[39] Eckstein, *op. cit.*

job. Clearly, this is an insufficient allotment of time for the cabinet to resolve collectively the issues of society. The increasing passage of actual decision making from the political to the administrative and organized interest sectors of the system is, as we have pointed out at length, one result of this failure of cabinets to perform their formal function of policy formulation and issue resolution.

Another adaptation to this problem has been structural and procedural adjustments within the cabinets. Increasingly, decisions are not made collectively by cabinets but are informally agreed upon in advance by the inner circle of the cabinet. Furthermore, several cabinets are increasingly delegating responsibilities to cabinet committees. One alternative to delegation would be the Swedish practice of having most routine policy matters resolved at the department level in the administrative structure before they reach the cabinet. The resolution of issues by institutionalized processes of bargaining among representatives of interests and the public bureaucracy is discussed in Chapter 8.

The Belgian adaptation to the imperatives of policy formulation by an unwieldy cabinet structure consists, in addition to cabinet committees, of a "restricted cabinet." Headed by the prime minister, this structure consists of the kind of institutionalization of the inner circle of the cabinet discussed above with respect to Great Britain. This body examines questions before they are considered by the full cabinet.[40] The cabinet committees include the Ministerial Committee on Economic and Social Coordination, which prepares "guidelines" for policies in these cases, the Ministerial Committee on Budget Management and Civil Service, and the Ministerial Committee on Scientific Policy.

The Soviet Union's experience is similar to the above. The Council of Ministers is the agency analogous to a cabinet in its responsibility for supervising the bureaucracy and allocating resources. Consisting of over 80 ministries and other agencies, it also became too large to function efficiently and experienced the evolutionary development of an inner group. This smaller group was established through usage in Stalin's regime, and then given official recognition later by a decree of the Supreme Soviet. Known as the Presidium of the Council of Ministers, with about a dozen members, it apparently coordinates and directs the work of the various ministries and state committees.

To the extent that cabinets delegate policymaking functions to committees on either a formal or an informal basis, the role of these cabinets in the policymaking process begins to resemble the role to which modern legislatures have come to be relegated. That is, plenary cabinets in actuality function to ratify, legitimate, and occasionally force the modification of policy decisions made elsewhere. Bagehot conceptualized the cabinet as a committee of parliament.[41] This "committee" has

[40] Weil, *op. cit.*
[41] Bagehot, *op. cit.*

come to assume the policymaking function that theoretically belonged to parliament. Now, in effect, committees of that committee are assuming that function. Formal policymaking becomes increasingly concentrated.

The same imperatives of a mature industrial society that have resulted in this concentration of formal decision-making power are, at the same time, creating an increasing diffusion of actual decision making. The imperatives of specialization and division of labor result in an actual autonomy of structures from each other. The process of the increasing devolution of policymaking functions to organized interests in consultation with the relevant areas of the bureaucracy, described in chapter 8, exemplifies the increasing decentralization of the actual day-to-day making of bread-and-butter decisions—decisions of allocation and priorities. Thus, the progressive centralization of formal authority has been accompanied by a decentralization of many day-to-day allocative decisions.

Conclusions

Implicit throughout this chapter is a distinction between where and how decisions are supposed to be made according to the formal institutional format (the organization chart) and where and how they are actually made. A thematic question throughout the analysis has been the structuring of the accountability of decision makers for the consequences of their decisions. That is, how and to what extent do the perceived wishes and interests of the society act to narrow the discretion of the decision makers, and what structural arrangements exist so as to narrow that discretion?

Again, we found basic similarities in formal structure among the countries considered. On the formal side one could argue, as Gilison does, that the Soviet and British systems are quite similar. Both are parliamentary and emphasize unity instead of separation of powers. The Soviet Council of Ministers, "responsible" to the legislature, is the formal counterpart of the cabinet as a committee of Parliament in Western democracies.

Looking beyond the constitutional formats, important differences between the Soviet Union and Western democracies become apparent. The most important of these differences is probably the extent to which the discretion of decision makers is limited by considerations of accountability. The mechanisms of accountability in the Soviet Union are not formally structured; consequently, the leaders in the Kremlin possess considerably more latitude than do leaders in Western nations. However, while Western leaders undoubtedly have a wider range of choices at their disposal with respect to official policy, this book raises the question of whether this range of choice is significant with respect to the actual allocation of values (who gets what). If the policy choices of the formal political leaders in both the Western and Soviet spheres have a limited impact on who actually gets how much of what, the fact that Western leaders have a wider range of choices does not matter very much. The question is whether, with the growing importance and autonomy of the interest groups and bureaucrats with their specialized knowledge (what John Kenneth Galbraith calls "the technostructure"),[42] the political sector has enough impact on the actual making of allocative decisions so that the variation in political formats is an important explanation of the decisions. Functionally speaking, for example, the representative assemblies considered play similar and relatively minor roles as policymakers. Their function seems to be more related to legitimating policies or to mobilizing support for or opposition to those policies.

It is argued in this book that the most important difference in the political formats between the Soviet Union and Western democratic nations is the existence of institutionalized and legitimate competition between organized political forces. Regardless of the depth or significance of policy choices, the competition itself is sufficient to narrow the discretion of the "democratic" elite and to compel them to adjust their decisions to accommodate many perceived public demands. To fail to make such an adjustment would be to hand one's opponents an enormous advantage.

Organized opposition to government is both more likely and more intense when there are organized forces to mobilize it. Spontaneous and widespread opposition is rare. It is one thing to be dissatisfied with incumbents; it is something else to be provided a choice between two legitimate sets of elite as potential incumbents. Each set of elite has considerable incentive to try to create public satisfaction with its promises or performance, as the case may be. The right to oppose legitimately the incumbents and to organize and mobilize this opposition may be the single most important structural arrangement distinguishing democratic from authoritarian nations.

The degree of discretion possessed by the political decision maker ranges from very little discretion in fragmented multiparty systems such as Third and Fourth Republic France and Weimar Germany to a very wide latitude of discretion in authoritarian systems such as the Soviet Union. Democratic systems with deferential cultures, such as Britain, range somewhere between these extremes. Clearly, if structured mechanisms of accountability are not present, the bounds of discretion become so wide that it is difficult to apply the term *accountability* as a distinguishing characteristic of the system. Accountability is surely present in informal ways in the Soviet Union; it is difficult to find a mature industrial society whose leaders are less accountable.

At the other extreme, if the bounds of discretion become too narrow, the deci-

---

[42] John Kenneth Galbraith, *The New Industrial State* (New York: Mentor Books, 1971), Second Ed., Chap. VI.

sion makers cannot perform the function of governing. Systems that are not governed have not been viable. The aforementioned epitomes of the absence of such discretion are all systems of the past.

It appears that presidential systems lend themselves to one or the other of the undesirable extremes between very wide bounds of discretion exceeding the expectations of democratic accountability on one hand and bounds of discretion so narrow as to render the government incapable of governing on the other hand. Accountability suffers in the latter case as well, because unless one has the power to give effect to one's choices, one cannot logically be held accountable for the consequences of those choices. In cases such as France, where the president controls the leadership and agenda of the legislature, there are no meaningful structural checks on the discretion of the president. Where the legislature is not in fact autonomous, theoretical separation of powers becomes meaningless.

If the claims of the Nixon administration to executive privilege, the unrestricted right of impoundment of funds, exemption from court order, and other manifestations of presidential autonomy had been upheld, the accountability of the American presidency would have been similarly unrestricted. Yet when, as is frequently the case, the United States Congress does function as an autonomous body, the American system is relegated to a condition of immobility or stalemate in which the power to govern (make and give effect to relatively coherent policy) nowhere exists. Paradoxically, the Nixon administration wound up in this position when it lost control or even much influence over Congress. He who claimed the most executive power wound up with the least.

We suggest that for any government to be labeled as democratic instead of authoritarian, it must have a legitimate and institutionalized check-and-balance mechanism that circumscribes the discretion of political decision makers between elections. It is further suggested that such a mechanism must not preclude the discretion inherent in the function of governing.

The checks and balances inherent in the confidence mechanism have in some cases successfully balanced these conflicting imperatives. In cases such as Britain, the older Commonwealth, Scandinavia, and the Federal Republic of Germany, the heads of government have possessed the power to govern without being given a blank check to exert their will from election to election. The discretion accorded the leaders of the Low Countries and Italy appears to be somewhat narrower but still greater than in the classic immobilized systems of great cabinet instability.

Less is expected of the governments of some nations than of others. Nations that have never played a central role in world politics or have never aspired to the status of a major or near-major power and nations whose economies are less highly industrialized and interdependent or even variegated are among those with lower expectations. These systems do not have to meet the same norms of governmental effectiveness as other mature industrialized nations with a major international role to play. Thus, for example, Switzerland violates a number of the alleged requirements of stable, effective government. We saw earlier how the culture of that nation is characterized by segmented ethnic and religious cleavages. In addition, Switzerland has a plural executive with a virtually powerless rotating presidency. In effect, Switzerland is not governed. The system persists because, given its self-conscious eschewal of an international role and a simpler, less industrialized economy, Switzerland does not have to be governed in the same way or to the same extent that the major industrial powers must be. There is less interdependence in Swiss society; therefore, less is expected of the government.

Implicit throughout this chapter is the basic question of whether the variation in constitutional formats makes for a significant difference in how decisions are actually made. We suggest that important differences exist between the Soviet Union and the Western democracies with respect to the degree of accountability for formal policymaking functions despite apparent similarities in basic constitutional format. However, we show in subsequent chapters (especially 7 and 8) that many basic allocative decisions are made outside the formal political sector. In those chapters, we detail the political role of parties and interest groups and suggest that the imperatives of the state of technology in a mature industrial nation render the roles of organized interests and of the administrative sector of paramount importance irrespective of the constitutional format. Thus, before the process can be fully understood, we examine in the next chapter the role of the administrative sector and variations in the structure and performance of public bureaucracies in the nations under consideration.

Chapter Appendix

The following are flowcharts that show policymaking structures on a country-by-country basis. Included in alphabetical order are the democratic systems discussed in the book.

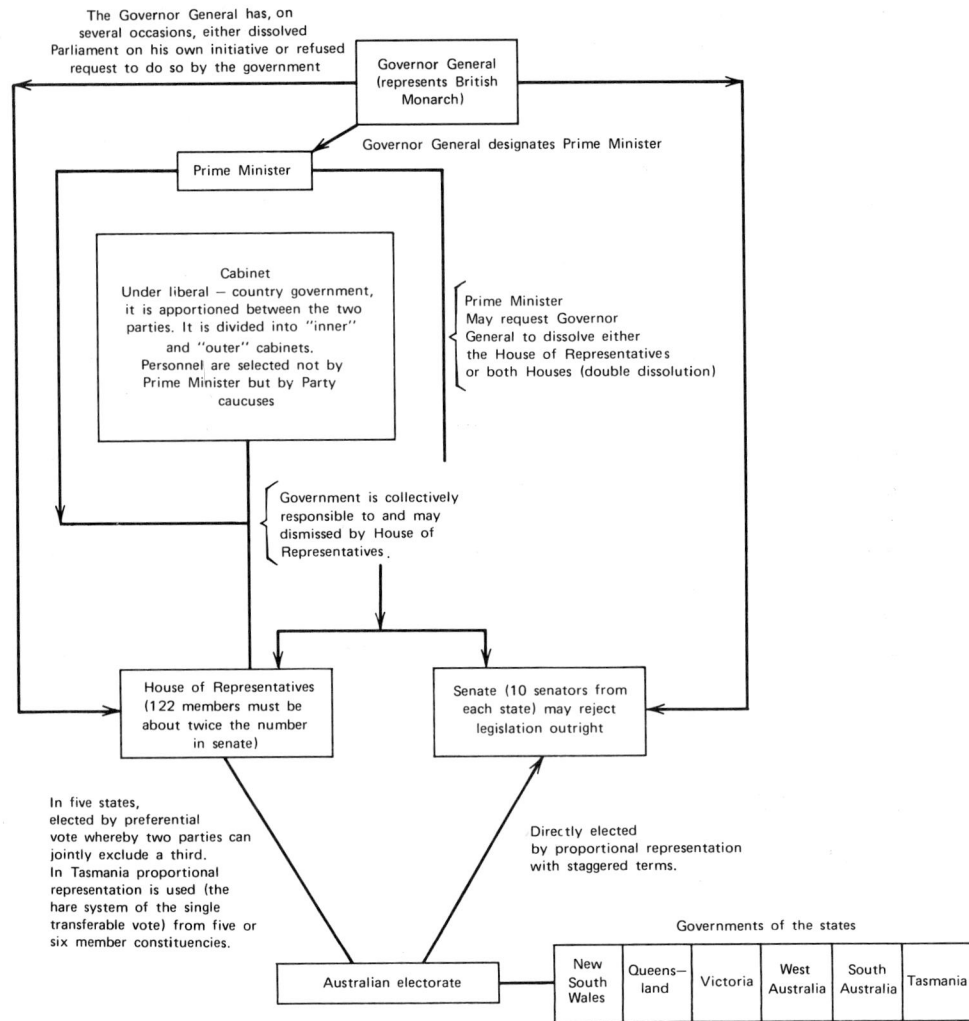

AUSTRIA

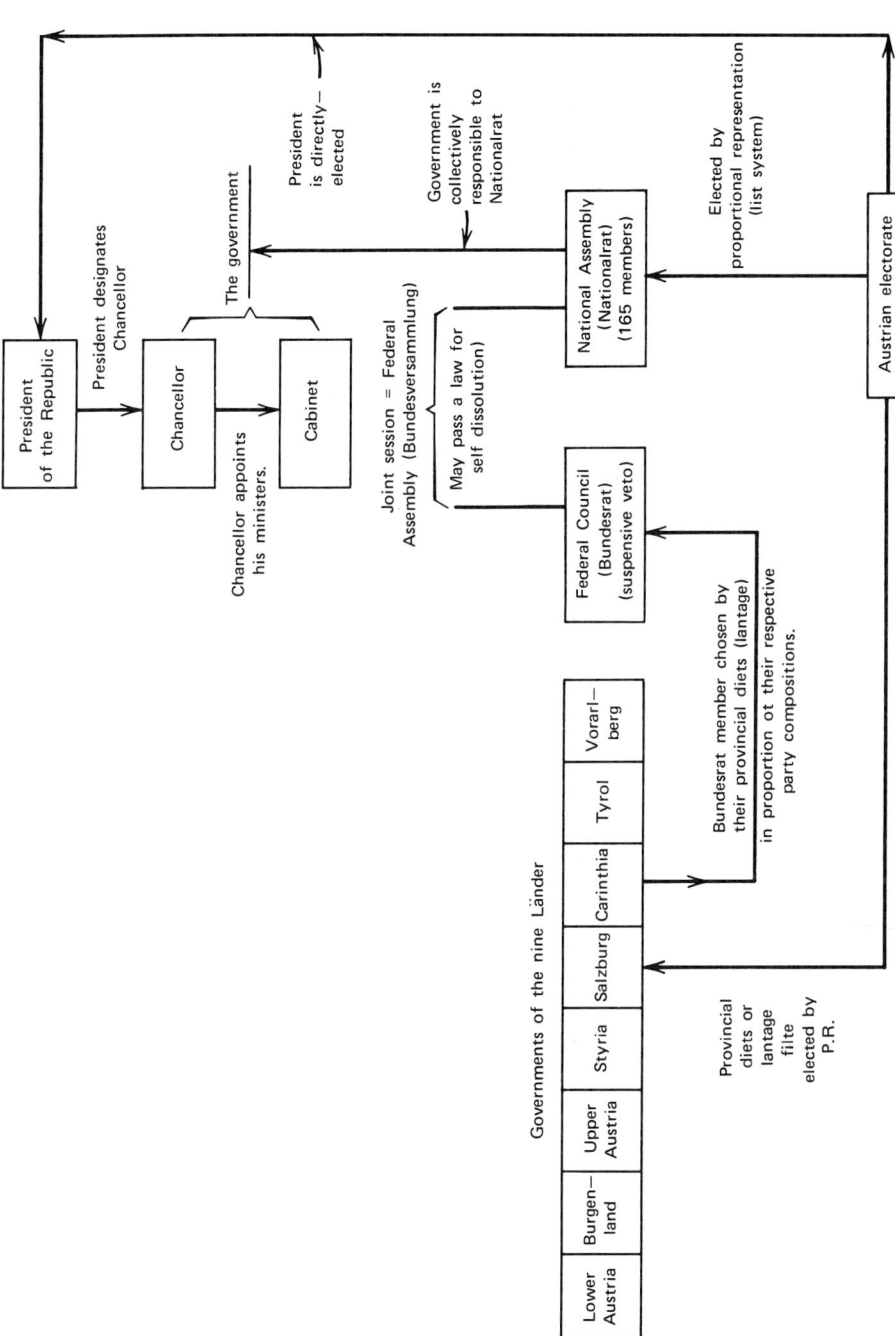

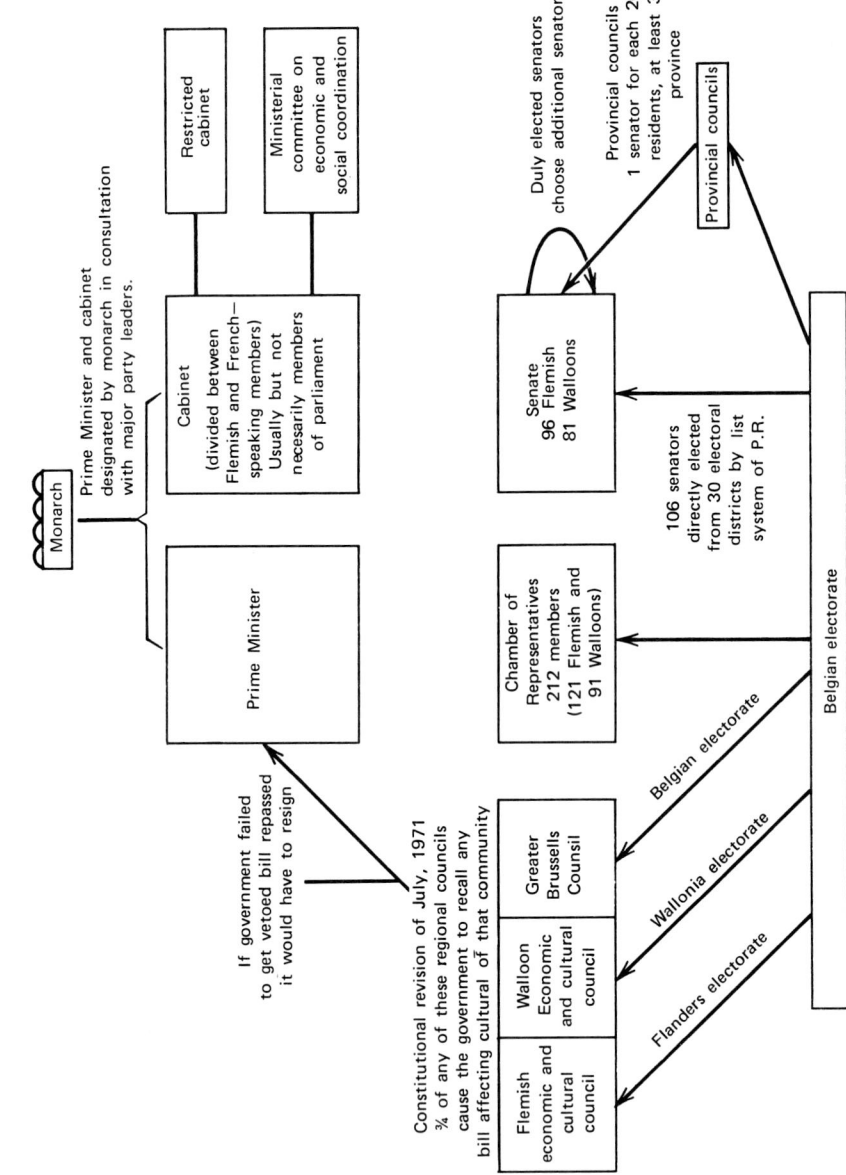

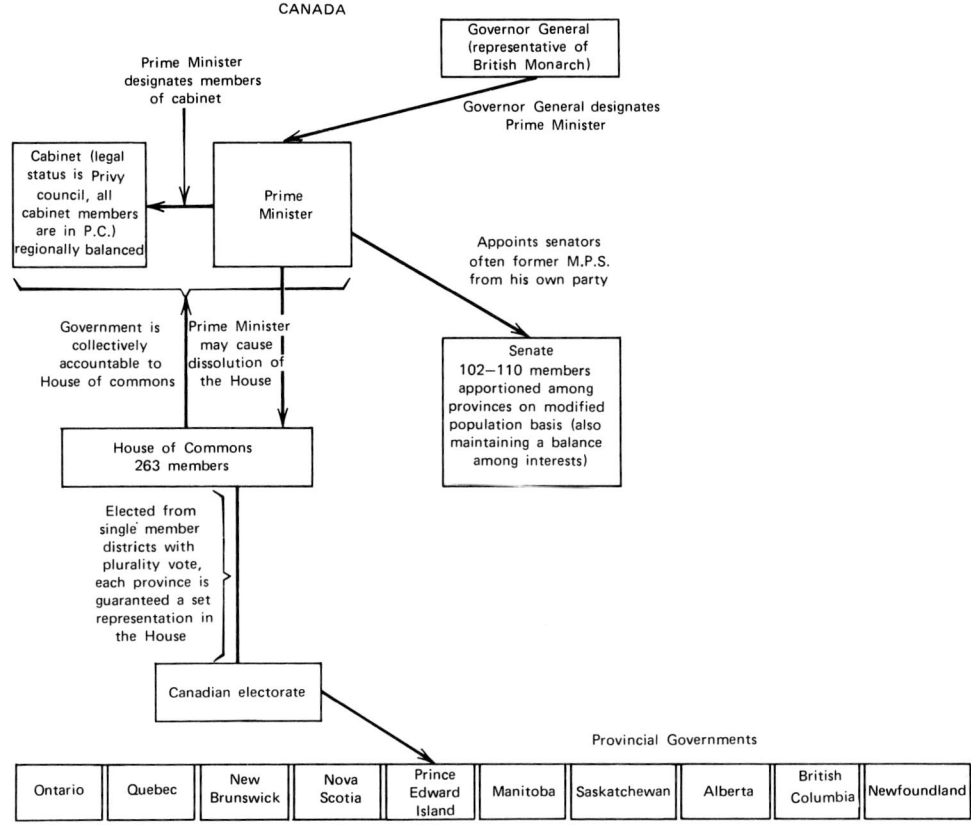

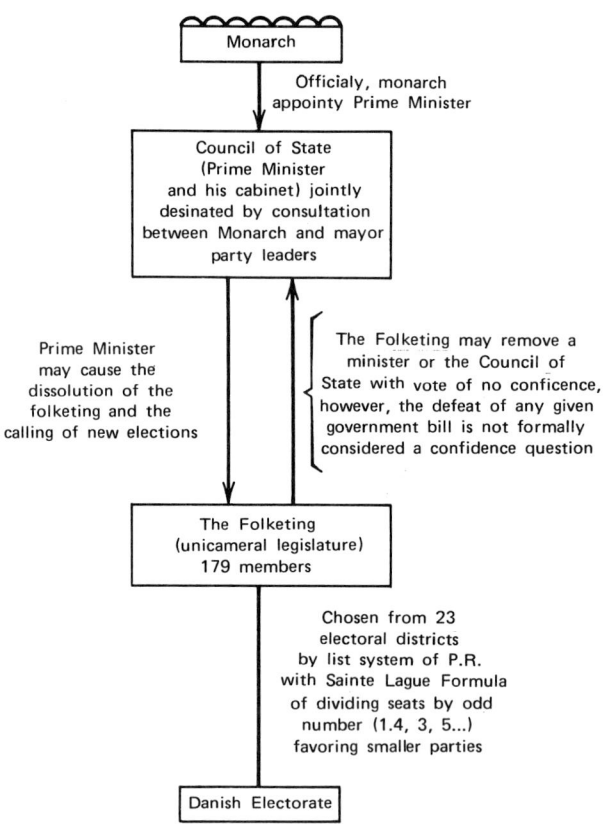

THE FIFTH FRENCH REPUBLIC

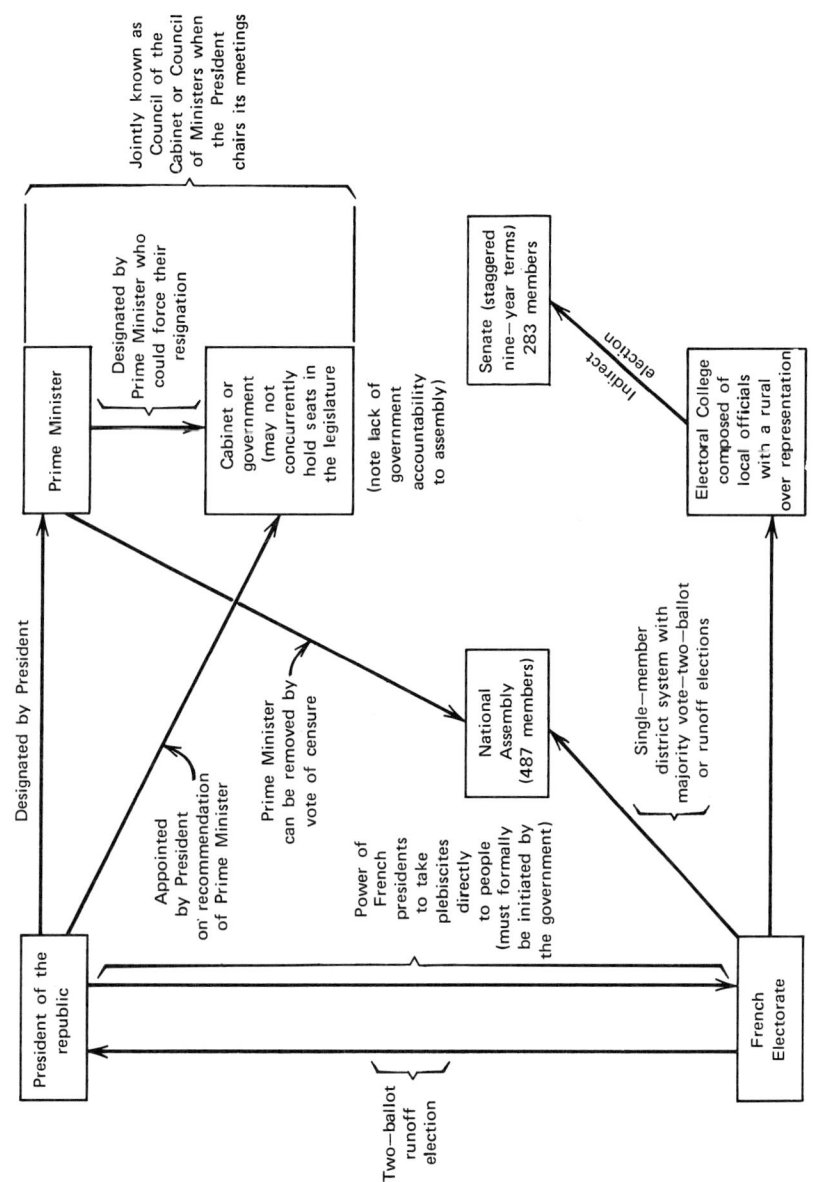

THE FEDERAL REPUBLIC OF GERMANY

President nominates the chancellor (but his choice is circumscribed by the party complexion of the Bundestag).

Chancellor

Appointed by chancellor and must resign when he does

Cabinet of Federal Ministers

Chancellor is really determined by strongest in Bundestag

President of the Republic

President elected by by Federal Assembly by majority vote (plurality after two ballots)

Bundesrat (upper house)

Jointly the two houses are called "The Federal Assembly".

Bundestag (lower house) (494 members)

247 or half deputies chosen by electorate of each land by list voting system. Numbers apportioned by land population.

Half of Bundestag (247) elected by single—member district system with plurality vote

Schleswic Holstein | Bavaria | Baden Wurtensurg | Rhineland Palatinate | Saar | Heese | North Rhine—Westphagia | Lower Saxony | Bremen | Hamburg

Government of 10 lander (states)

Members chosen by governments of their respective länder

German national electorate

GREAT BRITAIN

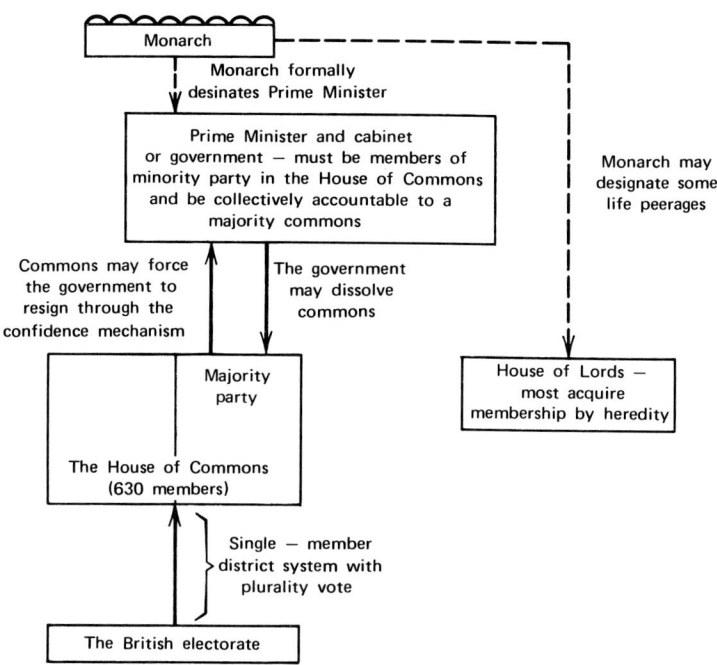

ITALY

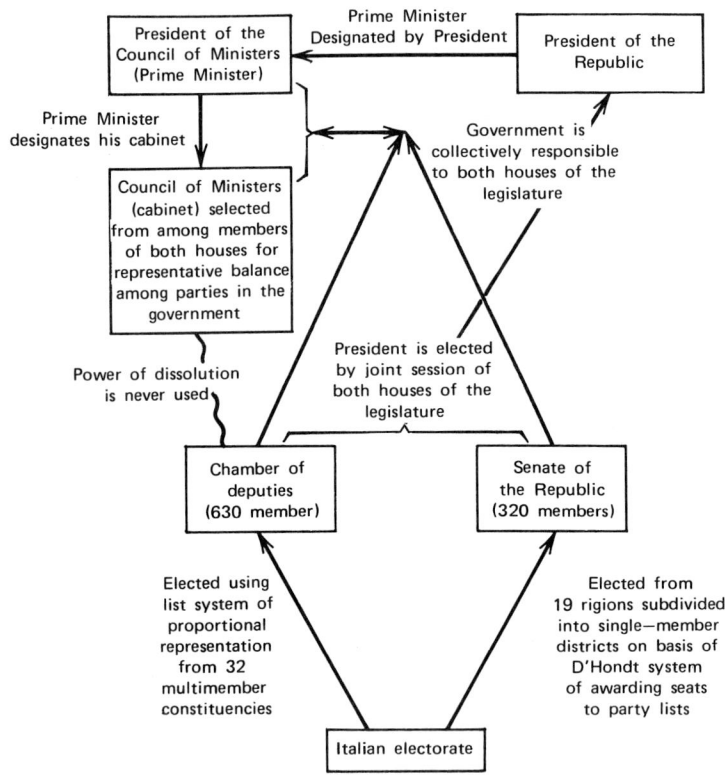

THE NETHERLANDS

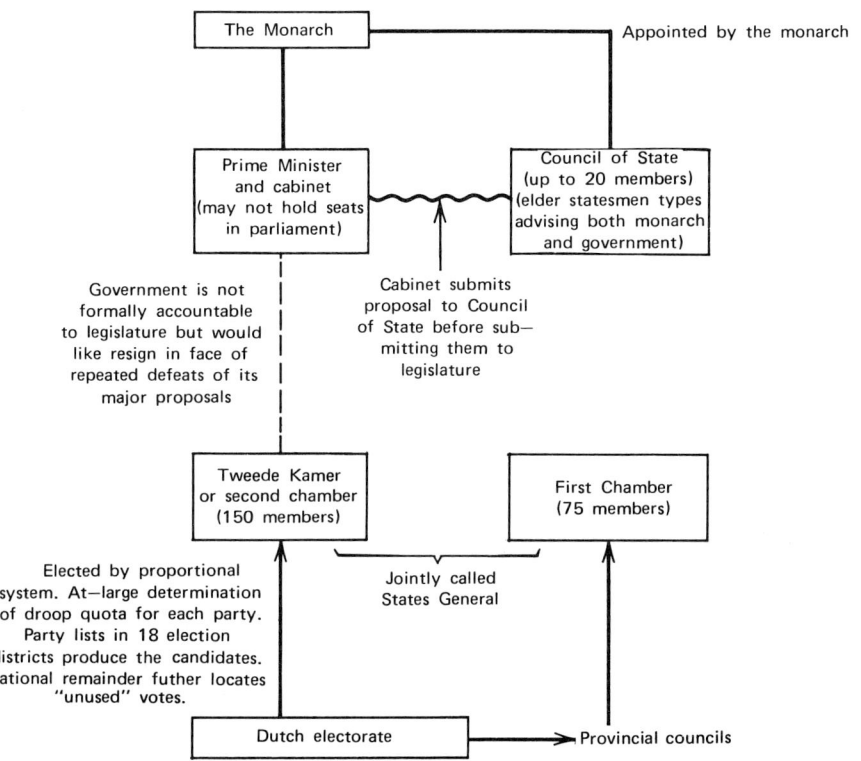

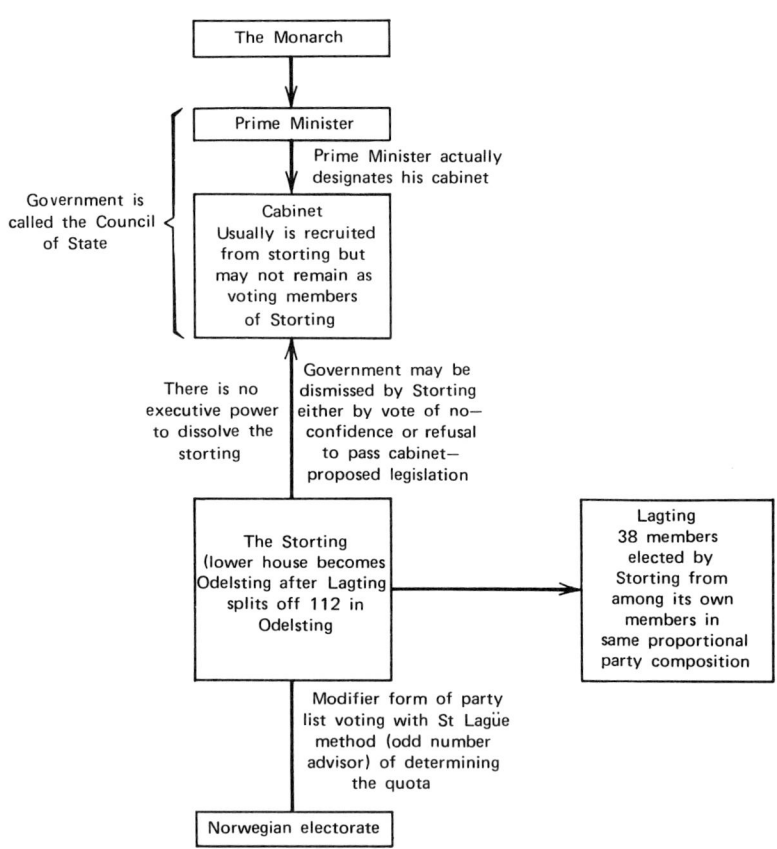

SWEDEN

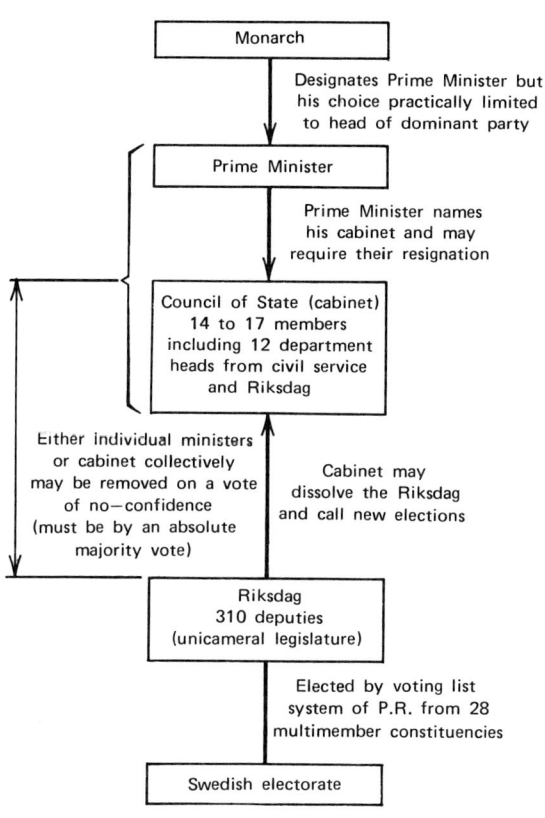

Chapter 6

Administrative Patterns

For many people, the term *bureaucracy* has acquired the pejorative connotation of monumental inefficiency. The term conjures up visions of bespectacled clerks mindlessly impairing the obviously just and reasonable solutions of problems in a sea of red tape. Fulminations against "the bureaucrats" as a stereotyped set of villains blocking "the people" from realizing their demands have had a reliable appeal in the hands of politicians with a consciously populist image. This kind of appeal has seemed particularly attractive to people who fear and resent the complex interdependence of the postindustrial era and who yearn for the simpler solutions to simpler problems of a partially apocryphal past.

It is therefore difficult for those used to ingrained pejorative stereotypes to accept the idea that bureaucracy was conceived for the purpose of optimizing rational efficiency. The term is not confined to the administrative branch of a government. Bureaucracy is an organizational form, a form that can to a greater or lesser degree characterize any large organization in or out of government. Thus, corporations and the military possess some of the characteristics of this organizational form as well as the administrative sector of governments. Joseph Schumpeter, in his classic *Capitalism, Socialism and Democracy,* suggested that ultimately it does not make much difference whether the economy is planned and the means of production controlled by the private bureaucracies that corporate enterprises have become under capitalism, or by the public (governmental) bureaucracies, as would be the case under socialism.[1]

Bureaucracy as a Model of Rational Efficiency

At the outset, it seems useful to distinguish between the terms *bureaucracy* and *administration*. *Bureaucracy*, it will be recalled, refers to a form of large organization, the characteristics of which we have not yet delineated. *Administration* refers to the process of applying policy decisions. Administration is thus conceptualized as the function of bureaucracies according to classic administrative theory.

Classic administrative theory implies that administration is distinct from politics or the formulation of public policy. Politics, in this view, has to do with choosing between alternative ends, and administration is concerned with the means of attaining those ends. The function of administration becomes one of attaining those ends by the most rationally efficient means. Rational efficiency here means the attainment of goals with a minimum expenditure of resources (such as time, energy, capital, manpower, etc.).

Classic administration theory, as stated by such advocates of "scientific management" as Frederick Taylor, posits that there is one best way to achieve any given goal.[2] Because it was presumed that there was only one way to maximize rational efficiency, the field of scientific management generated time-motion studies that attempted to delineate the one set of procedures best suited for any task or function. The effect of this orientation has been an effort to subject each role in the organization to a set of repetitive routines (routinization) that embody these standards of rational efficiency. The definition of each role in the organization by a comprehensive set of impersonal rules acts to circumscribe the discretion available to the occupant of each role. Thus, the "bureaucratic mentality" will tend to do things "by the book" and not take account of the unique circumstances of each particular case. The impersonal rules promote rationality by generalizing. Generalizing has the advantage of economy of effort (not having to decide anew each time) and of enhancing predictability.

The importance of this tendency to routinize and to circumscribe discretion in the name of rationality is that it reduces both the adaptive and responsive capacities of bureaucracies. The adaptive capacity of an organization refers to its capacity to change its output and its structure to cope with the imperatives of changed circumstances. Responsive capacity refers to the disposition of an organi-

---

[1] Joseph Schumpeter, *Capitalism, Socialism and Democracy* (New York: Harper Torchbooks, 1947), Third Ed.
[2] Frederick Taylor, *Principles of Scientific Management* (New York: Harper, 1947), pp. 36–37.

zation to produce outputs that satisfy the perceived needs and demands emanating from the social context in which it finds itself.

Adaptive and responsive capacities are desirable *political* characteristics. That is, these characteristics are desirable in setting goals or choosing between alternative courses of public policy. Administration, however, has not been conceptualized as a goal-setting activity; hence, bureaucracy was not designed to maximize desirable characteristics for goal setting. As a matter of fact, rational efficiency and adaptability are in some ways antithetical imperatives. Adaptability implies relative ease of change, but change is dysfunctional for routinization and predictability. Bureaucracy is an organizational form that was not designed to maximize responsiveness and adaptability; therefore, to criticize bureaucracy for failing to maximize these two values is to attribute to bureaucracy a function it was not intended to fill.

The Separation of Politics and Administration

The crux of the problem is that classic organization theory assumes a distinction between politics (goal setting, policy formulation, and allocative decisions) and administration (the application and enforcement of policy). Classic organization theory assumes that administrative structures do not engage in political functions. As one of America's pioneer political scientists, Woodrow Wilson, postulated, administration "is removed from the hurry and strife of politics."[3]

More modern thought has come to the conclusion that, however much these two functions may be distinguished in theory, in practice a structure engaged in administrative functions cannot avoid political functions as well.[4] That is, the administrative structures of modern government are left with a good deal of policymaking discretion in allocating the values of society.

It was in the area of development administration (administration in non-Western nations) that scholars began suggesting that bureaucracies play a preponderant role in the policymaking process. In particular, Fred Riggs's concept of "the heavy weight of bureaucratic power" suggests that bureaucracy is likely to be developed in the non-Western world before political structures.[5] Political structures (legislatures and heads of governments) constitute whatever representative and responsive structures may exist, and colonial powers had little

---

[3] Woodrow Wilson, "The Study of Administration," *Political Science Quarterly*, Vol. II, June 1887.

[4] For example, Herbert Simon, Donald Smithburg, and Victor Thompson, *Public Administration* (New York: Alfred A. Knopf, 1950).

[5] For example, Fred Riggs, *Administration in Developing Countries: The Theory of the Prismatic Society* (Boston: Houghton Mifflin, 1964), p. 222 ff. Riggs directly suggests that in a "diffracted" system, "the administration function is sharply limited by institutions" (p. 223). It is not clear from Riggs's excessive jargon whether diffracted is meant to describe existing systems in the industrial world or to constitute an "ideal type."

interest in developing these incipient instruments of self-government in their possessions. Colonial powers were more inclined to develop administrative structures to enhance their efficiency in controlling and exploiting their colonies. Hence, many newly independent nations found themselves with relatively effective public bureaucracies and weak parliamentary institutions; the Indian Civil Service was a case in point. In these nations, the administrative sectors exercised disproportionate influence on the policymaking process. The nonadaptive and routinized bureaucracies have been dysfunctional for developmental purposes; hence, non-Western societies may stagnate at the transitional stage. That is, the unilinear movement of a society from a traditional state of modernity will not be as inevitable as was heretofore assumed. A state of possessing some elements of both tradition and modernity may become relatively permanent. A strong role for public bureaucracy has been thought to be a characteristic peculiar to non-Western systems.

However, it is apparent to those who study the industrialized world that a political role for the administrative sector is not confined to the non-Western nations. The political role of public bureaucracy in the industrial world stems from two factors. First, the political (as opposed to the administrative) structures are not necessary strong in industrialized nations. We have described cases of political instability in nations such as France. In these situations, the day-to-day business of governing the country must go on despite the hopeless deadlock of representative assemblies preoccupied with recurring cabinet crises and despite even the inability of political forces to agree on the fundamental rules of the political game (precipitating constitutional crises). In these circumstances, one might expect the political role of the public bureaucracy to be even more pronounced than would be the case in a system with strongly institutionalized and stable political processes. Alfred Diamant in fact found that to be the case in France; a stable, strong, well-developed administrative sector filled the political vacuum created by the cabinet instability of Third and Fourth Republic France.[6] As Henry Ehrman suggests, the French bureaucracy has achieved "an unusual degree of autonomy because of the absence of a stable political leadership and the ineffectiveness of parliament and political parties as a voice and molder of public opinion."[7]

A second factor may operate to render the relative weight of bureaucratic power (to political power) more pronounced in the industrial world, contrary to Riggs's argument, than in the non-Western world. We suggest that the relative weight of

---

[6] Alfred Diamant, "The French Administration System: The Republic Passes but the Administration Remains," William Siffin, ed., *Toward the Comparative Study of Public Administration* (Bloomington: University of Indiana, Department of Government, 1957).
[7] Henry Ehrman, "French Bureaucracy and Organized Interests," *Administrative Science Quarterly*, Vol. 5, No. 4, March 1961, pp. 534–555 at p. 535.

bureaucratic power increases with the volume of the issues processed and the complexity of the issues raised. Bureaucracy, because it is based on the principles of specialization and division of labor and functional expertise, is well suited to process a great volume of issues and issues of technological complexity—far better suited than such relatively unspecialized structures as legislatures. Both the volume and the complexity of issues will be significantly greater in industrial societies than in non-Western ones.

The Inevitability of Bureaucracy

Each new invention creates new problems that government must address. For example, the development of commercial aviation necessitated regulation of safety and traffic patterns in the air. Obviously, no such need existed in the first decades of the twentieth century. Thus, we now have a Federal Aviation Agency and Civil Aeronautics Board where none existed in 1910. In this way, the bureaucratic pyramid widens. To return to a public bureaucracy of the size that it was prior to the First World War, society would have to lose the knowledge of how to construct such things as airplanes, automobiles, television, etc. In short, society would have to somehow undo modern technology.

Even if this were feasible, we do not see it as desirable. With all of the evils of modern technology (and there certainly are many), life was decidedly shorter, less comfortable, and less free (in terms of choices available) before the great technological revolution of the twentieth century. It seems pointless to long for an oversimplified and partially apocryphal past; technology and its inevitable concomitant bureaucracy are inseparably a part of mature, industrial societies.

For foregoing topics (the inevitability of bureaucracy and the relationship of politics and administration) are particularly significant for the Soviet Union. Although bureaucracy is inevitable and has been a prominent feature in the Soviet Union, it has always been distrusted. Many Russian literary works (Gogol's *The Inspector General* is the best known) have ridiculed and satirized bureaucrats. Communist ideology tends to support informal procedures ("popular participation") rather than formal. The term *bureaucracy* is used in the negative sense, and *apparat* is used in its place to describe structures. The concept of the withering away of the state contains the idea that when societal development reaches its highest stages, massive bureaucracies will no longer be necessary. In fact, shortly after the 1917 revolution, attempts were made to abolish or at least reduce greatly the organizational machinery inherited from the tsarist regime. These attempts were not successful, and in succeeding years the bureaucracy has continued to grow. Both capitalist and "socialist" states are characterized by organization but, as Frederic Fleron has pointed out, the continued existence of bureaucratic control and administration represents a contradiction with the basic philosophy in the latter but not in the former.[8] The fundamental differences between the two types of systems may lie less in their actual procedures than in the philosophies underlying their administrative practices.

On the second point, systems such as that of the Soviet Union are often seen as the epitome of *lack* of separation between politics and administration. The most conspicuous characteristic that comes to mind is the degree to which the CPSU is involved with the administrative hierarchy. Much has been written about the system of controls by which the party attempts to direct public administration in the Soviet Union.[9] Because of the two parallel hierarchies in the Soviet Union, in a sense it might appear that the system fits the assumptions of classic theory noted earlier. That is, the party is engaged in the political functions (goals, policy, and allocative matters), while government officials have the administrative task of implementing political decisions. But there are several problems with classical theory as applied to the Soviet Union.

First, the notion of the politically neutral public civil servant does not exist. Given the "vanguard" concept of the CPSU, it is only natural that the party should set up a system of control and supervision over the process of implementation. Barghoorn, who feels that this involvement is the greatest factor distinguishing Soviet state administration from that of the United States, sees the control as exercised through allocation of resources, personnel policies, and a system of inspection.[10]

In addition, there is the question of the distinction between politicians and bureaucrats. Over a decade ago, Brzezinski and Huntington observed that modern society is a bureaucratic society and thus needs bureaucratic leaders. Contrasting the United States and the Soviet Union, they said that the top leader in the Soviet Union is both a politician and a bureaucrat while in the United States he is usually either one or the other.[11] Then, too, there is the overlapping nature of top leadership positions in the Soviet Union. The same people occupy posts in both the party Politburo (politics) and the government Council of Ministers (administration).

Finally, as indicated in the preceding chapter, the Soviet Union has been experiencing the same developments as other industrial societies with respect to specialization. We suggested above that bureaucratic power tends to increase with the volume of issues processed. It is impossible to discuss Soviet bureaucracy

---

[8] Frederic J. Fleron, Jr., "Introduction," *Journal of Comparative Administration,* Vol. 5, No. 2, August 1973, p. 132.
[9] For example, Frederick Barghoorn, *Politics in the USSR* (Boston: Little, Brown, 1972), pp. 254–260; Jerry F. Hough, *The Soviet Prefects* (Cambridge: Harvard University Press, 1969).
[10] Barghoorn, *Ibid.*
[11] Zbigniew Brzezinski and Samuel P. Huntington, *Political Power: USA/USSR* (New York: Viking Press, 1965), p. 170.

without reference to its vast scope, size, and pervasiveness. The regime accepts responsibility for all areas of economic and social life, and as a consequence many issues are matters of public administration that in some other systems might be processed by the private sector. Due to the volume and increasing complexity of the issues, policymakers must rely more on the functional, specialized expertise of bureaucrats.

The Weberian Ideal Type of Bureaucracy

The properties that a large organization should possess in order to maximize rational efficiency were first specified by the German sociologist, Max Weber, in the early part of this century.[12] For Weber, the concept of bureaucracy was closely related to a broader view of political development and social change. Weber implicitly characterized social change as an inevitable and linear movement toward the rationalization of authority. Authority in traditional society is justified on traditional or charismatic grounds.[13] The former justification is that one obeys authority because that is what has always been done from time immemorial. The latter justification for authority lies in the personal qualities of the leader that bear no necessary relationship to performance in office. As development proceeds, authority becomes legitimated in terms of certain standards of demonstrable competence or because the authority more closely represents the perceived interests of the governed. This authority becomes legitimized on legal-rational bases. Weber's catchy label for this process was "the routinization of charisma."[14]

This routinization and rationalization of authority are essentially designed to optimize efficiency (the greatest attainment of goals with the minimum expenditure of resources). This organizational form that Weber called bureaucracy was conceptualized to bring about the rationalization of authority and the consequent efficiency in relating means to ends.

Weber specified the characteristics that a large organization should possess in order to optimize rational efficiency. He referred to this specification as an "ideal type." His ideal type of bureaucracy thus would function as a standard by which

---

[12] Weber's writings on bureaucracy appeared in *Wirtschaft* and *Gesellschaft,* published posthumously in 1921. Most of his material was probably written about two decades earlier. Selections covering his essential ideas on the subject may be found in *From Max Weber: Essays in Sociology,* edited and translated by H. H. Gerth and C. Wright Mills (New York: Oxford University Press, Galaxy Books, 1958), especially pp. 196–255.

[13] The three "pure types" of authority are discussed in Weber's *The Theory of Social and Economic Organization,* translated and edited by N. M. Henderson and Talcott Parsons (New York: The Free Press, 1964), p. 328 ff.

[14] *Ibid.,* pp. 363–373.

large organizations in the observable world could be evaluated as more or less rationalized—that is, efficient. This idea type is often used as the standard for what is called classic administrative systems—that is, existing public bureaucracies are termed classic to the extent that they resemble Weber's ideal type. It is important to bear in mind that this ideal type was derived from logic, not from observation or experience. The ideal type is not intended to describe any existing organization.

Weber's ideal type consisted of the following characteristics:

1 A comprehensive set of impersonal rules.
2 A hierarchical structure (meaning each lower office is under the supervision and control of a higher one—a chain of command).
3 Members subject to authority only with respect to their official roles.
4 Selection of candidates for office on the basis of demonstrated competence.
5 Compensation of officials by fixed salary.
6 Allocation of tasks on the basis of specialization and division of labor.[15]

These characteristics relate to the ostensible purpose of the bureaucratic ideal, the coordination of numerous individuals in common purpose such that their activities and skills complement each other. Thus, specialization and division of labor provide the organization access to a greater quantity of knowledge and variety of skills than could be possessed by an individual short of a genius. Bureaucratization permits the combination of an aggregate of mediocrities into a collective genius. The principle of hierarchy is designed to coordinate the activities of the disparate specialists into a coherent whole. The impersonalization and routinization is designed to lead to predictability.

Limitations of the Weberian Ideal

Limitations of the Weberian ideal are of two types: problems with the Weberian construct itself and problems in the applicability of the construct to actual organizations.

The major flaw in the Weberian construct is that it is internally inconsistent. The goal of coordination and coherence is supposed to be realized through the principle of hierarchy, which implies ultimate centralization of authority. Yet, the principle of specialization implies that each role possesses skills or information esoteric to itself. This entails the autonomy of each office or role from its alleged superiors. After all, one cannot control and therefore one cannot coordinate

---

[15] The precise wording of this list varies in many of the several places it appears in Weber's writings. This list is distilled and paraphrased from Parsons, ed., *op. cit.,* p. 333, and Gerth and Mills, eds., *op. cit.,* pp. 196–198.

activities one does not fully comprehend. This is what Michel Crozier, in his brilliant study of the French administrative system, calls "strata isolation."[16] The consequence of this phenomenon is that the lines of responsibility are rendered unclear, and the organization cannot function as the coherent entity it was designed to be. As Crozier perceptively suggests, the relationship between the roles of offices becomes based on considerations of power and bargaining rather than on rational efficiency. To maximize a bargaining position, the occupant of each role tries to preserve the autonomy of the functions performed. In short, to take advantage of the expertise of the specialist, it is necessary to accord him or her a degree of discretion. This kind of discretion and its concomitant uncertainty are what rationalization tries to eliminate. Thus, specialization results in decentralization and lack of responsibility, while hierarchy is designed to bring about responsibility through centralization of authority. One imperative of the Weberian ideal thus constitutes the antithetical denial of another critical imperative.

The Weberian criterion of routinization and impersonalization, designed to promote rationality, creates a problem in applying the ideal standard to actual organizations.

Rationality presumes no ambiguities in the goals of the organization. Rationality also presumes no external factors in the motivations of members of the organization. The goal of perfect rationality, treating humans as potentially efficient machines, oversimplifies the complexity of human motivation. Organizations are not closed systems. They are subject to a host of environmental stimuli.

Routinization and impersonal rules, as with any generalization, apply only imperfectly to specific situations. It is obviously more economic or efficient to make one principle to cover a variety of similar situations rather than to deal with the uniqueness of each particular case. It is also clear why a person can become frustrated with the clerk who, operating on the basis of general principles, cannot adjust to the self-evident justice of that particular case. For example, it is easier to say that 35 mph is generally the maximum safe speed on a street rather than to have the policeman decide if each driver is proceeding safely in the circumstances of that particular time and place. Such police discretion would clearly introduce an intolerable degree of unpredictability and lack of uniformity into the traffic-control process. But when a policeman, who after all is a kind of administrator, issues a citation for barely exceeding the speed limit on a deserted street at 2:00 A.M., the recipient of the citation often feels that the policeman is being unnecessarily rigid in applying the law so literally.

This illustrates a basic flaw in applying Weberian standards to actual

---

[16] Michel Crozier, *The Bureaucratic Phenomenon* (Chicago: University of Chicago Press, 1964), p. 190 ff.

bureaucracy. Policemen do in fact disregard certain technical violations of the law (such as the above case where no one's safety was endangered). Traffic laws may be enforced more rigorously on icy streets than on dry streets. Similarly, basketball referees may disregard a certain amount of body contact away from the ball, the "no harm, no foul" standard. Rules are enforced selectively in the light of the widely understood purposes of the rules. The point is that because rules, being by definition abstractions, can only apply approximately to particular cases, administrators of rules reserve to themselves considerable discretion. But classic administrative theory seeks to eliminate such discretion in the name of rationality and predictability.

Therefore, the major problem in applying Weber's construct is this: politics (choosing alternative courses of policy for the system) cannot be clearly separated from administration. Human activities do not neatly categorize. It is especially true in industrial societies that there is an increasing devolution of decision making from the political to the administrative sectors. This phenomenon is discussed below.

Another major flaw in applying Weberian idealized construct lies in the ambiguity of the standards of competence. We are not clear as to what are the criteria for a good bureaucrat. It is increasingly apparent, however, that intelligence (that is, whatever it is that standard measures of intelligence measure—generally acquired abilities to manipulate symbols) is very poorly correlated with maximum efficiency of performance of the highly routinized tasks associated with most bureaucratic roles. It is therefore questionable whether someone who scores high on the Federal Service Entrance Exam in the United States will do better at a job than someone who scores lower. As we will see below, this is carried to its logical absurdity in Continental administrative systems where, to pass the entrance exams for the highest levels of the public bureaucracy, one must have been one of the brightest students in the equivalent of considerable postgraduate work in a classic liberal arts education. Robert Merton summarized this absurdity in his famous dictum, "People may be unfitted by being fit to an unfit fitness."[17] The main problem in choosing "good bureaucrats" is the lack of consensus about what characteristcs such a person is expected to possess.

Of course, ambiguity in standards of competence is related to the ambiguity in what we mean by a bureaucrat. As we have stated, anyone who works for a large organization is, by definition, a bureaucrat. But we clearly expect more creativity from some members of large organizations than others. Generalized performance standards for public employees often fail to take account of the variation in expectations associated with different bureaucratic roles.

---

[17] Robert K. Merton, *Social Theory and Social Structure* (Glencoe, IL: The Free Press of Glencoe, 1957), p. 198.

There is also an absence of widely accepted standards of efficiency in the performance of bureaucratic roles. Efficiency is difficult to measure, of course, given the ambiguity about what bureaucracy is supposed to do. This absence of standards of efficiency and effective performance in turn contributes to the confusion about criteria for recruitment. In other words, what characteristics are we trying to uncover when we administer a civil service entrance exam?

The absence of manifest standards of efficiency tends to encourage a rigid reliance on comprehensive, impersonal rules as standards of behavior. These rules—the disposition to "go by the book"—become a substitute for pragmatic standards of performance, standards that have not been consensually discerned.

Bureaucratic Recruitment

Recruitment refers to the process of selecting members. We are here concerned with the standards of recruitment, the consequences of standards for bureaucratic personnel and behavior, and the cultural and other sources for the variation in standards.

Recruitment in Classic Administrative Systems

As we have suggested, an organization that possesses most of the characteristics comprising Weber's idealized prototype is referred to as a classic administrative system. The classic or Weberian model is of greater relevance throughout the Western industrialized world than it is in the non-Western or developing societies, or even in the Soviet Union. Among the Western industrialized nations, France and Germany are widely identified as possessing the most "classic" public administrative systems.[18] The fact that two systems are manifestly more "classic" than others demonstrates that bureaucracy is not an organizational form that remains unchanged despite the context in which it appears. We suggest that cultural considerations constitute the major contextual factors accounting for this variation in the form that bureaucracy takes in any given nation. The particular pattern of organizational behavior and interaction found in the administrative sector of a system will, to a large extent, be a function of that system's political culture.

The classic or Weberian mode of recruitment reflects the ambivalent French attitude toward authority discussed in Chapter 3. The French conception of authority, it will be recalled, includes the seemingly contradictory imperatives of egalitarian individualism (from the Revolution and the republican heritage) and a

---

[18] For example, Perrell Heady, *Public Administration: A Comparative Perspective* (Englewood Cliffs: Prentice Hall, 1966), p. 41 ff.

need to submit to strong, centralized leadership (from the heritage of the prerevolutionary monarchy).

Recruitment in the French system is based on the criterion of merit. Merit is measured by competitive examination, especially in the elite or policymaking levels of the civil service (*le grand corps de l'état*—less than one percent of the entire body).[19] An examination affords the trappings of egalitarianism in that anyone can take the examination without regard to birth or status. Moreover, in evaluating the results of the examinations, only performance criteria are considered; ascriptive criteria such as birth or social status are not taken into account.

The examinations, however, are very rigorous written and oral tests of the skills that can only be acquired by years of intense liberal education. These examinations require well-developed capacities to present ideas in both written and oral form. The skills needed to pass these exams are by and large confined to those few who have survived the selection and elimination procedures of each stage of the French educational system and made it through one of *les grandes écoles* ("the chief schools"—equivalent to graduate school), especially the *École Nationale d'Administration*.

The French educational system quickly separates the offspring of the bourgeoisie from those of the working class and peasantry with a tracking system that sends the former into a classic university preparatory curriculum and the latter into a terminal vocational program. The skills required for entry into the classic secondary schools or *lycees* are those skills of verbal and symbolic manipulation and abstract thinking that educated and professional parents begin imparting to their offspring in formative preschool years. There is very little interclass mobility through the educational system. That is, very few of the pupils at the lycees come from working or peasant class origins.

Upon completion of seven years study at the lycee, pupils present themselves for another competitive examination, the *baccalauréat,* which again emphasizes skills of classic education—verbal skills, mastery of Latin and Greek, knowledge of Greek, Roman, and European history, mathematical skills, knowledge of philosophy, etc. The failure rate here is quite high–usually 35–40 percent.[20] (In recent decades, several reorganizations of the baccalauréat have allowed students to present a wider range of subject areas for this examination. However, the rigor of this exam still effectively filters out most working-class pupils.)

Passage of the baccalauréat entitles one to admission to one of the universities. However, to enter the higher civil service (*le grand corps*), it is virtually necessary

---

[19] Lowell Noonan, *France: The Politics of Continuity and Change* (New York: Holt, Rinehart and Winston, 1970), p. 381.

[20] Margaret S. Archer, "Education," *France Today,* J. E. Flower, ed. (New York: Barnes and Noble, 1975), Second Ed., p. 102.

that one has graduated from the *École Nationale d'Administration,* although some technical specialists reach the grand corps by graduating from the *École Polytechnique,* another grand école. Admission to the grand écoles is by another rigorous competitive examination. Possession of the baccalauréat is far from sufficient.

Thus, the higher civil servants in France are among the best-educated people in the nation. Moreover, the educational process not only selects but also socializes candidates into certain orientations. The classic education, which is abstract, formalistic, and legalistic, inculcates these orientations in its most successful products. These orientations closely parallel the formalism, legalism, and impersonality that characterizes classic bureaucracies.

In Germany, candidates for the higher civil service must also take a rigorous competitive examination after a university education and years of intense, specialized training. Here, education up to the specialized training tends to be legal training, reflecting the legalistic aspect of the German culture.

Recruitment to the lower posts tends to be administered by the agency concerned on the *land* level and done on the basis of credentials instead of examinations.[21]

Recruitment by competitive means can formally satisfy the imperatives of egalitarianism in that any individual is legally free to compete on the successive tests. Birth and socioeconomic status are not officially considered to be criteria influencing the selection process. However, the selection procedures clearly limit recruitment to those with an upper- or middle-class background. The acquisition of the verbal skills and the capacity to manipulate abstract symbols are primarily inculcated in early formative years by parents who themselves possess those skills. Morever, in order to survive the rigorous competitive selection process described above, one must value the requisite skills and the career rewards these skills render possible in order to expend the great time and effort necessary for the acquisition of these skills. These values tend to be acquired from parents. Thus, the offspring of working-class families, whatever the genetics involved, rarely acquire the requisite intellectual tools and motivation necessary for survival in the rigorous selection process of French and German education.

The result is that the higher civil service of France and Germany "has the character of a semi-closed caste."[22] Entrants to the higher civil service in both systems are almost exclusively from an upper- or upper-middle-class background. A substantial proportion has a father who himself had a civil service career,[23]

---

[21] Brian Chapman, *The Profession of Government* (London: Allen and Unwin Ltd., 1959), pp. 77 and 83.

[22] Heady, *op. cit.,* p. 43.

[23] Robert Putnam, "The Political Attitudes of Senior Civil Servants in Western Europe: A Preliminary Report," paper delivered to the American Political Science Association, Washington, September 5–9, 1972, Table 2, p. 12. In Germany, 92 percent of senior civil servants came from fathers

although the parent generally had a lower level post than the son.[24] This situation exists in spite of the fact that in France "the elite's ideology stressed open recruitment."[25] As John Armstrong points out, French apologists for their system stress the fact that only about one quarter of the grand corps men had fathers in that role, overlooking the negligible proportion of grand corps members who come from working-class backgrounds.[26] With respect to parentage, the critical factor for entry into the highest class of the civil service in any industrial system seems to be whether or not the father had a nonmanual occupation—was he of the bourgeoisie.

Thus, recruitment to the elite of the so-called classic administrative systems can be argued to comply with the norms of one interpretation of egalitarianism in that no one acquires a right to a specific post from one's parents and performance standards do comprise the formal and direct qualifications for the job. However, the lack of upward class mobility by virtue of a civil service career in these systems indicates that the capacities and motivations to meet the performance standards are largely acquired from one's parents, whether genetically or through postnatal socialization.

Serious questions may be raised as to whether performance standards are reliable predictors of performance in the administrative job itself. It is certainly arguable, as was hinted earlier, that the high intellectual capacities one must possess to survive the competitive elimination procedures required for these elite posts are dysfunctional for concentration, motivation, and efficiency in a highly routinized role. This would be especially true if academic success entailed the development of a creative impulse and intellectual curiosity. However, the French educational system, according to Crozier, is highly centralized, impersonal, and rigid.[27] In this case, years in the educational system could contribute to the inculcation of dispositions suited to bureaucratic roles.

---

[24] The term *son* is used deliberately instead of a sexually neutral term. European and British bureaucracies have been overwhelmingly "sexist" or male dominated at the higher levels.

[25] John Armstrong, *The European Administrative Elite* (Princeton: Princeton University Press, 1973), pp. 84–85.

[26] *Ibid.*, p. 85.

[27] Crozier, *op. cit.*, p. 239.

---

with nonmanual occupations. About two-thirds had fathers with a civil service occupation. According to Alfred Diamant, "Tradition and Innovation in French Administration," *Comparative Political Studies,* Vol. I, No. 2, July, 1968 pp. 251–274, 41 percent of the grand corps in 1953–1963 had fathers who were civil servants, and less than 10 percent had fathers who were in the following occupational categories: "working," "agriculturalist," and "industrial and commercial employee," while 84 percent had fathers who were civil servants, professionals, heads of industrial enterprises, or commercial and industrial managers.

Recruitment in Less Classic Public Administrations

A university education is generally either a formal or an informal requirement for entry into the higher civil service in most Continental countries. In Austria, for instance, a university education is in fact a legal prerequisite for entry into the highest category of the civil service. Candidates for the highest class of the Italian civil service must have attained either a university degree or the highest rank in the second highest class. Similarly, competitive examinations to the higher posts in the civil service of the Scandinavian democracies render a college education virtually indispensable for entry into those posts. In Great Britain, the highest class of civil servants is recruited on the basis of university degrees plus elaborate written and oral examinations designed to attract the nation's intellectual elite. These European democracies all resemble the classic model with respect to the rigor of the education preparation expected of aspirants to the highest permanent positions.

Australia, with its egalitarian culture, has strived to be an exception to this pattern. Until the 1930s, entry into Australia's administrative class was restricted to promotion from within the bureaucracy. But it was recently found that well over half of the senior civil servants in Australia now possess university degrees.[28] Australia's egalitarianism is manifested quite differently in this regard than France's probably because Australia's egalitarianism is not tempered with a competing authoritarian tradition as in the French case.

The kind of education stressed in the background of British higher civil servants might be best characterized as the humanities. This preference reflects the British cultural preference for the generalist (or Renaissance man) as opposed to the technically trained specialist. Thus, the British higher civil service is less able to take advantage of the bureaucratic principle of specialization and division of labor. British civil servants are less able to perform their roles effectively as regulators or, in the case of public ownership, operators of technically advanced industries. In short, there is a serious question whether the British preference for the generalist is viable in a mature industrial society.[29] Such a preference would surely conflict with John Kenneth Galbraith's and Daniel Bell's vision of a postindustrial society dominated by a scientific elite or technocracy based on the monopoly by the elite of esoteric yet essential knowledge.[30] This monopoly of essential knowledge

---

[28] Samuel Krislov, *Representative Bureaucracy* (Englewood Cliffs: Prentice Hall, 1974), p. 49.

[29] For this criticism of this British cultural trait, see James Cristolph, "Consensus and Cleavage in British Political Ideology," *American Political Science Review,* Vol. LIX, No. 3, September 1965, p. 641. Perhaps the best-known and most vociferous critique along this line may be found in Brian Chapman, *British Government Observed* (London: Allen and Unwin, 1963).

[30] Daniel Bell, *The Coming of Post Industrial Society* (New York: Basic Books, 1973), and John K. Galbraith, *The New Industrial State* (New York: Mentor, 1971), constitute two of the best-known exercises in "futurology"—the prognostication of the essential characteristics of the just-emerging phenomenon of the mature industrial society.

by professionally tenured individuals raises serious question about their potential accountability to anyone.

Virtually all of the higher civil servants in the Netherlands are university trained. Yet, unlike the classic model with its norm of political neutrality, political affiliations are openly considered as well in making appointments. Thus, an effort is made to achieve political balance rather than adopt the pretense of political neutrality. This balance is rendered vital by the segmented cleavages that characterize the Netherlands's society (see Chapter 4).

Austria, another society characterized by cleavages, also takes political considerations into account in recruiting for its civil service. A proportional balance between the two subcultures or *lager* (discussed in Chapter 4) is sought in staffing the civil service. Thus, the high minimum requirement of university education in these two segmented societies constitutes a necessary but not sufficient criterion for entry into their respective higher civil services. Additionally, one must meet criteria of correct political affiliation. The policy of proportionality in the Austrian civil service is known as *proporz*. The idiosyncratic name for the Austrian policy and the considerable attention devoted to it in the academic literature conveys the impression that the Austrian policy is unique.

Another society where affiliation to a subculture constitutes a criterion for administrative recruitment is Belgium. An effort is made to achieve a representational balance between Walloons and the Flemish. Canada also attempts to maintain a balance between the French- and English-speaking subcultures in staffing the various agencies. The pattern is that rationalized merit criteria of recruitment are abandoned or seriously qualified in a segmented society.

Modifications of classic merit standards of recruitment are decried by adherents of the standards. The choice is posed as one of adhering to criteria of ability and merit or the criterion of politics. (There is usually a pejorative connotation to the term *politics*.) However, we doubt that there are any objectively testable and widely agreed criteria that are more relevant for a higher civil servant than political and social allegiances. We have attempted to stress that political neutrality is not possible for higher civil servants in a mature industrial society. The advanced state of technology of such societies necessarily allows specialists and technocrats wide discretion in making allocative decisions. The allocative nature of these decisions renders them political.

The political content of administrative decisions is particularly salient in a culturally segmented society, where the symbolic content of otherwise routine administrative decisions further extends the domain of the political into what otherwise would be administrative routine. For example, decisions about curriculum content in schools or about the language with which public business is conducted assume high emotional significance in societies in which "cultural defense" is a salient issue. Thus, it is not surprising that in Canada and Belgium the "merit system" is qualified by considerations of balancing the representation of the major subcultures and language groupings in those nations. Because the bureaucracy makes decisions on matters considered vital to those concerned with cultural defense, it is hard to see how it would be politically possible to do otherwise.

What do we find with respect to the classic merit standards of recruitment in the Soviet Union? In view of the involvement and control of the CPSU, significant deviation might be expected. It would appear that although the Soviet Union, like many Western nations, modifies the classic model, much of Weber's pattern applies. The modifications include such factors as correct political affiliation and some degree of accommodation of ethnic subcultures, modifications found in democracies with segmented societies.

Due to the nature of the Soviet ideology and political culture, loyalty becomes an important aspect of merit. Individuals seldom gain important posts without membership in, or at least loyalty to, the party. The symbol and heart of this process is the *nomenklatura*, a list of key positions to which appointment cannot be made without approval by the appropriate party body. Hough, in his study of local decision making, describes the *nomenklatura* as including posts in the party as well as in the society, education, ideology, construction and municipal services, and administrative industrial positions such as directors and chief engineers.[31] This network of jobs ranges from central to local levels and gives the party control over all important appointments to the bureaucracy.

The Soviet Union is another example of the segmented societies described above in which some effort is made to accommodate cultural and ethnic diversity. Given the degree of diversity present in a society containing over 100 ethnic groups, some effort in this direction is almost inevitable in spite of the eventual goals of integration and assimilation. Administrative, judicial, and other agencies function procedurally in local languages in heavily non-Russian areas. In terms of recruitment, it appears that while in the non-Russian units many offices are held by leaders native to the area, certain vital ones are reserved for members of the dominant Russian group.[32] One study found that certain types of ethnic solidarity, particularly among Armenians, were of great importance on an informal level.[33]

In spite of these departures from the classic pattern, the Soviet experience has much in common with other systems. Discussing the Soviet bureaucracy in the context of Weber, Hough refers to the party *apparat*—the military, industrial managers, agricultural experts, and police—as officials who "increasingly have

---

[31] Hough, *op. cit.*, pp. 151–154.
[32] On this point of ethnic background, see George Fischer, *The Soviet System and Modern Society* (New York: Atherton, 1968), pp. 72–91.
[33] John A. Armstrong, "Sources of Administrative Behavior: Some Soviet and Western European Comparisons," *American Political Science Review*, Vol. LIX, No. 3, September 1965, p. 650.

had orderly, 'Weberian' career patterns."[34] That is, significant officials are college graduates with specialized education appropriate for the position, promotion seems to be based primarily on performance, demotion is seldom more than one level down, etc. Hough also points out that although party membership is required for key positions, officials with higher educations are often admitted to the party only after they have proved themselves by job performance. In a separate study, Armstrong found that, particularly in industrial production, departures from hierarchical principles were similar to those in other Western European countries. He also found that the importance of "the old school tie" rule (persisting associations among former classmates) applied to the Soviet Union to a degree comparable to Western Europe in general.[35]

The Paradox of Modern Bureaucracy

It appears that we have a paradoxical situation. The imperatives of a mature industrial society demand increased reliance on technical competence for the higher civil service. But we have seen that these same imperatives increase the political salience of bureaucratic decisions. This progressive blurring of the distinction between politics and administration renders the political composition of the bureaucracy increasingly salient. This increased salience of the political characteristics of higher civil servants tends to transcend the merit criteria (measured on competitive examinations) that have been held by classicists in the Weberian tradition to be a hallmark of the civil service of a modern industrial state. Thus, the very force that supposedly increases the importance of the "objective" achievement criteria (what a person can do) for recruitment to the higher civil service in a mature industrial state at the same time increases the salience of ascriptive criteria (who a person is) in such states. Ascriptive criteria of recruitment, once postulated as distinguishing characteristics of non-Western political systems, now appear as unavoidable concomitants of mature industrialized systems. Moreover, in the mature industrialized systems, the very essence of the advanced state of technology brings political criteria of recruitment to the fore by introducing bureaucracy into the political process and vice versa.

The Structure of Administration

We have already pointed to an internal contradiction in the Weberian ideal type of bureaucracy—namely, the criteria of hierarchy and specialization and division of labor. Hierarchy, generally defined as the superordination and subordination of offices or roles (a chain of command), implies that there is someone at the top of

---
[34] Jerry Hough, "The Bureaucratic Model and the Nature of the Soviet System," *Journal of Comparative Administration,* Vol. 5, No. 2, August 1973, pp. 138–144.
[35] Armstrong, *op. cit.,* p. 650.

the organization chart who has control of those under him. The occupant of each office or role assumes responsibility for the behavior of subordinates. In this way, he can coordinate the activities of the various roles in the organization.

Specialization, on the other hand, entails the autonomy of each role. The specialist presumably possesses knowledge and skills not available to the occupants of the other roles. This breaks down the chain of responsibility and control. The supervisor cannot really control things he cannot understand. As Crozier states this principle, the centralization of decision making in the French bureaucracy breaks down because those who formally must make the decisions must "rely entirely on information supplied by their subordinates."[36] This is in part inherent in the nature of centralization. Those making the decisions are removed from the consequences of those decisions; hence, the feedback process breaks down.

This reliance on subordinates is also a function of the fact that subordinates have an interest in keeping their information and skills esoteric. In a sense, it is a way for nominal subordinates to tender themselves indispensable, enabling them to retain bargaining power with their superiors. This tendency of higher civil servants to bargain with each other and with the politically sensitive parts of the government to which they are in theory accountable is a manifestation of the pervasiveness of power relationships in large organizations. The quest for power in human relationships remains pervasive despite the theoretical impersonalization of roles in large organizations.

Centralization versus Decentralization

It follows from the foregoing that it is not entirely clear whether one should expect classic administrative systems (those that strive to resemble the Weberian construct) to be centralized or decentralized. As a matter of fact, of the two systems most frequently classified as classic, France is highly centralized while Germany is decentralized. Public bureaucracies tend to be centralized or decentralized as a function of the society in which they exist. Decentralization is most apparent in federal systems or in fragmented systems such as Belgium and the Netherlands. These systems lack centralized recruitment mechanisms (that is, the equivalent of a national civil service commission), and formal decisions are delegated further down the line of the organization chart. This can be seen in the great degree of centralization in the American civil service with its plethora of "independent agencies" and the actual autonomy of those formally in "the chain of command." (The unassailable fiefdom of the late director of the Federal Bureau of Investigation, J. Edgar Hoover, was a celebrated example of the latter phenomenon. Hoover's now-famous unauthorized collection of data on prominent members of the American political elite is but one of the more blatant examples of

---

[36] Michel Crozier, *The Stalled Society* (New York: Viking Press, 1973), p. 81.

the widespread efforts by higher civil servants to acquire information and other resources esoteric to themselves as a bargaining tool, as discussed above.) Even where a centralized personnel center does exist in fragmented countries (as in the Netherlands), the number of exemptions to its domain and the discretion of individual agencies to ignore it renders the Dutch recruitment in fact decentralized. In France, administrative decision making has been highly centralized since Napoleon's restructuring of the French public service. It used to be said that the French minister of education knew what page of *Virgil* all schoolchildren of a certain grade in France were reciting at any given moment.[37] While this rigidity has softened somewhat, essential curriculum and personnel decisions for the nation's schools are still concentrated in Paris. The French educational system is merely one manifestation of the centralization of most aspects of French life. This centralization removes authority from its subordinates.

The remoteness of policymaking authority from the action levels of bureaucracy and the actual application of policy helps reconcile the conflicting French orientations toward authority discussed in Chapter 3. (Earlier in this chapter, we discussed how these orientations toward authority are reflected in the classic mode of competitive, performance-oriented recruitment emphasized by the French higher civil service.) Recall that the French, from the tradition of the *ancien regime* (prerevolutionary monarchy), feel a need for a strong, centralized authority almost as an inexorable part of French sovereignty. Sovereign authority is regarded as essential for a stable nation-state. The concept of sovereignty originated with the Frenchman, Jean Bodin. Rousseau was greatly concerned with an undivided and nondistorted sovereign in *The Social Contract* (discussed in Chapter 4).

At the same time, the French fear direct, face-to-face authority relationships. In Chapter 3 we related this to the egalitarian traditions of the revolution. Centralized authority is strong, undivided, yet remote. In a manner of speaking, bureaucratic centralization thus allows the French to have their cake and also to eat it.

Centralization can be discouraging to all but those near the apex of the bureaucratic pyramid—the older civil servants who have attained the higher positions through the inexorable process of accumulating seniority. Younger men, entering the service at the lower levels, are given little outlet for enthusiasm and creativity. This kind of centralization also characterizes the Italian higher civil service.

The Soviet Union is highly centralized in comparison with other European systems because of the scope of the effort to direct virtually all aspects of economic and social life. The overall economy is centrally planned, and there is virtually no private sector of industry. Enterprises that would normally be under private control in other countries become in the Soviet Union part of the governmental

---

[37] Cited in Crozier, *The Bureaucratic Phenomenon, op. cit.,* p. 239.

hierarchy. All of this is in spite of some of the admitted problems, such as internal communication, which a huge bureaucracy involves. Yet, within the context of centralized planning there have been varying emphases. The Khrushchev period brought some decentralization in the late 1950s, followed in the early 1960s by recentralization. Khrushchev's successors have continued the recentralization and returned to earlier centralized patterns. Economic reforms may have given plant managers some discretion in meeting their production goals, but the goals and priorities are still centrally determined.

By contrast, the Swedish system is highly decentralized. Policy directives are issued by over 50 independent boards and agencies. There seems to be a fair amount of decentralization in the Federal Republic of Germany because of the federal nature of the system. Most civil servants in that system are employed at the *land* or municipal levels. Unlike the situation of provincial officials in France, *land* employees are not subject to any national chain of accountability.

Decentralization thus raises serious questions with regard to the accountability of each agency for giving effect to national policy directives. Given the reality of bureaucratic discretion in interpreting and carrying out policy directives, decentralization would also seem to be dysfunctional for criteria of consistency and coherence in giving effect to policy. The autonomy of numerous agencies in a large bureaucracy is bound to result in considerable overlap and repetition of function. Moreover, the agencies often pursue purposes that are in conflict with those of other agencies. Finally, the absence of overall direction and coherence in the national bureaucracy results in a lack of consistency or uniformity in the application of national law and policy.

Thus, neither a centralized nor a decentralized national bureaucracy can provide a satisfactory solution to the basic dilemma. The dilemma is how does one design an organization to be rationally efficient in its task of carrying out policy while at the same time being accountable and politically sensitive in the almost incompatible task of policy formulation.

The problem is that the role of bureaucracy has changed or at least expanded spontaneously in response to the needs of an advancing state of technology. But the structure of bureaucracy has never been systematically redesigned to cope with these unplanned new roles. It is not clear that bureaucracy could be so redesigned. Therein lies the crux of one of the basic problems of mature industrial societies.

Administrative Classes

Throughout this chapter we have been using the term *higher civil service*. This implies some classification system distinguishing higher from lower. Some of the nations under consideration have formally specified a classification system, while others leave the distinction between higher and lower civil servants implicit and

Administrative Patterns

vague. The nations specifying four general classes of civil servants are Britain, France, West Germany, Italy, Austria, and Belgium.[38] (Sweden and Holland, by contrast, have specific titles for specific jobs but no general classes.)

In Britain, the classes are called the administrative, the executive, the clerical, and the messengerial. In Germany, the corresponding names are *hoherer Dienst, gehobener Dienst, mitterer Dienst,* and *einfacher Dienst.* In Italy, the titles are *carriere direttive, carriere concette, carriere esecutive,* and *carriere del personale ausilario.* France simply entitles classes of civil servants *A, B, C,* and *D.* It is unnecessary to go further to make the point that the four classes are variously labeled from one country to another. Despite this variation in nomenclature, the role and duties of each of the four classes remain constant through the several nations that so divide their civil service. For convenience, we use the British terminology, although we are referring to all the nations unless otherwise stated.

The administrative class is the highest class of *permanent* civil servants (in the sense that their jobs are not contingent on the electoral fortunes of any given government). Above them stands the minister (often a member of the cabinet) and, in Britain, a parliamentary secretary—both political appointees. Also, in Britain there is one permanent civil servant to coordinate the administration of each ministry, the permanent undersecretary. With the exception of its foreign office, Italian ministries lack a single coordinating civil servant; more coordinating responsibilities are placed on the ministers.

Formally and theoretically, it is the task of the minister and other politically appointed supervisors to ensure that the civil service carries out the decisions of the politically accountable government. In practice, it is widely recognized that seniority and the presumed expertise of the permanent civil servants render them relatively impervious to direction by their nominal political superiors. Yet, it is precisely that direction of permanent civil servants by politically appointed ministers that provides the crucial and most vulnerable link in the chain of accountability in industrial societies. Societies must rely on this link to ensure that those who take official action with widespread social consequences will perceive a necessity to be able to justify their action to the society.

Given the increased political role of the bureaucracy, questions must be raised about the accountability not only of the political sectors of government but of the administrative sectors as well. The pertinence of such questions in putatively democratic societies is obvious. Even in the Soviet Union, questions may be raised about the responsiveness of the massive bureaucracy to the policy directives of the party.

---

[38] Chapman, *op. cit.,* p. 76.

Representative Bureaucracy

The effort to make bureaucracy accountable leads to the effort to make bureaucracy responsive to society or to political direction. The effort to make bureaucracy responsive leads to an effort to make it representative. The term *representation* is ambiguous as discussed in the previous chapter. It can refer either to responsiveness of political output by the elite to the demands of the governed, to concern on the part of the elite for the interests of the government as they perceive it (the British concept of virtual representation), or simply to the social and political background and affiliation of elite personnel (which we call sociological representation). The latter concept has dominated much of the literature on representative bureaucracy.[39]

Underlying this concept of sociological representation is the often unstated assumption that only individuals who formally belong to certain groups or who matured as members of the groups can be trusted to guard and promote the interests of the groups. This concept implies that there is a very close relationship between the sociological characteristics of people (or bureaucrats) and their psychological characteristics (the values they have and on which they are disposed to act). Thus, there is a tendency for French Canadians to prefer to be governed by their own kind. Apparently, they assume that only people who actually have their ethnic or religious affiliations (sociological properties) are capable of having empathy for French Canadian values and interests and acting to protect them (psychological property).

This assumption can be seen manifested in current "New Left" politics in the United States in the demands that each major decision-making structure contain a percentage of minority group members roughly proportional to that minority's percentage of the total society. The *proporz* system in Austria and the corresponding attempts to achieve cultural proportionality in the bureaucracies of other culturally segmented societies (Canada, Belgium, and the Netherlands) are manifestations of the concept of representative bureaucracy in the sociological sense. Each subculture concerned with issues of cultural defense assumes that vital interests are safe only in the hands of its own.

Once these assumptions are granted, the practical consequences of their logic present enormous difficulties; the number of groups who perceive that they have interests to protect is certainly enormous if not close to infinite. Clearly, for example, the French Canadians are not Canada's only minority that may conceivably generate political demands. Neither are the Flemish in Belgium (who perceive themselves a discriminated minority despite the fact that they outnumber

---

[39] A notable example is Frederick C. Mosher, *Democracy and the Public Service* (New York: Oxford University Press, 1968). Compare J. Donald Kingsly, *Representative Bureaucracy* (Yellow Springs, OH: Antioch Press, 1964).

the Walloons) that country's only conceivably politically conscious group. It seems equally questionable to assume that the problem of American minorities will or should always be confined to blacks, Chicanos, Indians, and women. The rising issue of women's liberation in the United States and elsewhere has already expanded the number of salient criteria of representation beyond ethnicity. There is no logical reason for assuming that expansion will stop there.

Furthermore, there is no hard evidence supporting a one-to-one relationship between social background, ethnicity, or previous sociopolitical affiliations (sociological characteristics) of a member of the elite and his or her values and behavior in office. On the contrary, the higher civil service in Britain seems to generate an esprit de corps that effectively socializes the few upwardly mobile recruits from the middle and lower classes into an acceptance of elite values and orientations.[40] Of course, upwardly mobile recruits to the British administrative class are few in number. It is hard to tell if large numbers of middle- and lower-class recruits to the British higher civil service may result in a great heterogeneity of values and opinions in that institution.

As Kenneth Meier points out, the claim that bureaucracy as a whole must be representative of its society's population overlooks the fact that decisions are not made by bureaucracy as a whole.[41] Instead, they are made by individual agencies. However, we are raising questions about the widespread attempt to apply standards of proportionality to individual agencies.

If, as we suggest may be true, responsiveness to public need and demand does not require sociological representativeness, we should be relieved. The data presented by Meier's study are not encouraging to those who see representativeness as imperative.

Meier's most important—and not surprising—finding is that representation becomes distinctly more distorted as one moves toward the higher classes. Meier found that in England the administrative class had the greatest distortion with respect to sociological representation, the executive class was second, and so forth. But the highest or least representative administrative class is most likely to become involved in policymaking.

Comparison data between Britain, Italy, and Denmark show that the British civil service is clearly the most representative of the three, Denmark second, and Italy a distant third.[42] This seems to suggest a positive relationship between

---

[40] Richard Rose, *Politics in England* (Boston: Little Brown, 1964), p. 96. For a summary of some literature implying that adult socialization takes place, see Kenneth J. Meier, "Representative Bureaucracy: An Empirical Analysis," *American Political Science Review*, Vol. LXIX, No. 3, June 1975, p. 529.

[41] Meier, *op. cit.*

[42] *Ibid.*, p. 536.

representativeness and commonly used indicators of social development. Possibly in the more developed systems there exists a wider distribution of the skills that constitute minimum qualifications for the higher civil service.

This minimal skill level constitutes the major impediment to representative bureaucracy in the sociological sense. Krislov suggests that the skill levels required for the higher civil service are greater than the average skill levels found in society as a whole.[43] While we are not sure what skill levels are necessary for government service, in practice middle- and upper-class characteristics are generally required of the highest class of civil servants. Accordingly, the higher civil service will remain a nearly exclusive province of these classes until the current conception of what constitutes merit is changed.

The problems of representative bureaucracy are in part the problems generated by the attempt to make any institution a microcosm of society as a whole. The first problem is the selection of salient criteria to be represented. Should bureaucracy mirror society with respect to race? Socioeconomic status? Ethnicity? Religion? Clearly, the number of possible criteria is staggering if not infinite. Moreover, it may be difficult to defend the selection of some criteria as deserving of representation and the concomitant omission of others.

Second, representation in the sociological sense entails the selection of bureaucrats on the basis of some group affiliation rather than on the basis of their characteristics as individuals. For a group to make up a percentage of the elite proportionate to that group's percentage of society, it becomes necessary to recruit individuals on the basis of their group membership. In some cases, the group affiliation (race, ethnicity, language group, or whatever) will have to override whatever measures of individual qualifications are used to select people for the job. This tendency runs counter to a major trend in Western philosophical tradition—namely, that group affiliations ought not to be relevant to the distribution of values and that people ought to be judged as individuals.

Third, the effort to place people in the higher civil service on other bases than performance or merit criteria means that candidates who would have been chosen on the basis of these criteria will be supplanted. After all, the number of available positions in the civil service (or any other institution) is finite. To say that a person is "qualified" when hired on some quota basis does not solve the problem. Clearly, the pool of individuals surpassing minimum standards is not an undifferentiated mass. Qualified is not an either/or proposition but a more-or-less proposition. To say that you hire the best qualified member of some sought-after group is different from saying you hire the best qualified individual.

On the other side of the coin, without some attempt to impose quotas, it is doubtful whether certain types of individuals would ever get into responsible posi-

[43] Krislov, *op. cit.*, p. 49.

tions in the public service. The attempt to set aside certain positions in the postwar Indian Civil Service for untouchables and other depressed castes is a case in point. Despite the admittedly murky relationship between group characteristics and behavior, it is likely that such a relationship exists to a significant degree in a rigid caste system like that of India. The relationship seems more problematic in a society like Great Britain with its tradition of noblesse oblige.

It is not sufficient to say that there is no evidence of a relationship between sociological representativeness and psychological or behavioral representativeness. The fact that such a relationship is widely *perceived* as existing places a political imperative on the achievement of sociological representation. In other words, if placing a given percentage of French Canadians in certain places in the Canadian civil service convinces the French Canadian population that the civil service is attuned to their interests, an important political function will have been fulfilled, irrespective of whether French Canadian bureaucrats actually behave any differently than their non-French counterparts.

The French Canadian demands extend to the equal status of French as an official language in all bureaucratic dealings. The insistence that all public servants be bilingual not only would place an additional difficult requirement on the recruitment of public servants, but also would seem to open the door to similar claims by a number of other ethnic minorities in Canada.[44]

Thus, the political role of the bureaucracy gives rise to a concern for the representativeness of that bureaucracy. This concern is greatest in societies with self-conscious minorities who perceive that they are discriminated against by the dominant culture or groups. Segmented societies where ethnic, linguistic, cultural, or geographic divisions coincide and reinforce each other are especially likely to generate these minorities. Minorities generate demands for sociological representation in the bureaucracy to the extent that they perceive the bureaucracy as an important decision-making structure. We have discussed demands for sociological representation and the consequent attempt to achieve proportionality in Austria, Belgium, Canada, and the Netherlands despite the paucity of evidence that sociological representation automatically produces pyschological and behavioral representation.

Representation in the Italian bureaucracy is badly skewed toward overrepresentation of Southern Italians. The evidence reviewed in Chapter 3 suggests that there is in Italy a widespread feeling that public officials are hopelessly corrupt and selfish. This leads to a withdrawal from caring about governmental institutions. Thus, the disproportionality is more readily tolerated. A demand for proportionality, after all, assumes that its achievement will improve the performance of the institution.

---

[44] *Ibid.*, p. 95.

In the final analysis, however, the sociological makeup of the bureaucracy is not crucial for its effect on society; the psychological orientations of the bureaucrats are.

Bureaucratic Values and Behavior

The values and behavior of the bureaucrats, not structural patterns of the bureaucracy, most directly determine the impact of bureaucracy on a society. It is therefore appropriate that we conclude this chapter with a consideration of these important variables.

There is, however, more information on the structural patterns of modern bureaucracy than there is on the values and behavior of bureaucrats. This is because the latter kind of micro-level information can only be obtained through expensive and difficult survey and interview methods.

The concern with representative bureaucracy discussed above reflects a corollary concern that bureaucrats in their political roles behave responsively to the demands and interests of their clientele. To the extent that bureaucrats act in an administrative role, the imperatives of democratic theory demand that bureaucrats behave responsively to the politicians who ostensibly set the policies limiting bureaucratic discretion. The probability that bureaucrats will behave in this way is a function of the values that they possess.

In other words, we assume that bureaucrats with a greater tolerance for politics (that is, the resolution of differing interests and differing perspectives on what constitutes wise public policy by bargaining and compromise) are more likely to be responsive both to inputs from the society in which they operate and to the political sectors whose bidding they are normally supposed to do. On the other hand, bureaucrats may actually believe in their theoretical political neutrality. They may believe that they are objectively using their expertise to give effect to policy rather than to make it. Robert Putnam has referred to such people as "classical bureaucrats,"[45] who have little tolerance for or patience with politics. They regard politics as divisive and chaotic as opposed to the rationalized and impersonal order of the bureaucratic process. That is, to the extent that the myth of the seperation of politics and administration is believed, bureaucrats are likely to regard political input as an illegitimate intrusion on the rationalized work of experts. Bureaucrats in the classic tradition assume that there is one proper and rational conception of the public interest; therefore, political conflicts constitute unwarranted factionalism. Almost by definition, classic bureaucrats are less supportive of democratic values than political bureaucrats. After all, democracy entails political conflict (pluralism, not monism) and the toleration of opposition.

---

[45] Putnam, *op. cit.*

Unfortunately, data on the cross-national variation in the possession of these attitudes are largely confined to Putnam's study covering samples of senior civil servants and "promising" younger civil servants in three nations: Britain, Italy, and the Federal Republic of Germany. The interviews consisted of a six-item "tolerance for politics" scale, a "support for political liberty" index, and an index of elitist (as opposed to egalitarian) attitudes.

Across all three nations, classic bureaucrats (high scorers on the first scale) are significantly more likely to support the elite and significantly less likely to support democratic values than are political bureaucrats. There was also a system level or between-system variation in the Putnam data. Italian bureaucrats were considerably more likely than British or German bureaucrats to be classic; that is, Italian bureaucrats were more likely than the others to show a low tolerance for politics, a weak support for civil liberty, and a stronger belief in elitism. This reinforces our earlier speculations about the democratic character of the British political culture. More importantly, these data give some support for our earlier speculations about the gradual growth of democratic values in the West German political culture. Putnam explains his discouraging set of data about the Italian bureaucracy in a hopeful fashion. Pointing out that the Italian bureaucrats were, on the average, much older than their counterparts in the other two nations, he notes that younger people in all three nations are significantly less likely to be classic bureaucrats than older people. This relationship between youth and less classic values is the basis for Putnam's optimism. Ninety-five percent of Italy's senior civil servants began their service under Mussolini's fascism. As we have pointed out, bureaucracies are designed to be unresponsive to changes in political ideals such as occurred with the overthrow of Mussolini in 1943. Yet, the very pervasiveness of the Italian "gerontocracy" should paradoxically bring about an almost complete turnover in personnel in the senior civil service as all of these older men reach the mandatory retirement age within 10 years.

The sympathy for political (and hence democratic) values by West German bureaucrats is as surprising as it is encouraging in the light of some haphazard data and much conventional wisdom identifying German bureaucrats as the epitome of classicism in the sense that term is used here. Here again, the less classic attitudes appear to be an attribute of the younger members of Putnam's sample.

It is unfortunate that data on this important question of the values of senior civil servants are not more widely available. There is, however, some basis for speculation about the other nations under consideration. Political values seem to be prevalent among a nation's senior civil servants to the extent that these values have acquired a legitimacy in that nation's culture. This would be logically expected. After all, civil servants are human beings who, like anyone else, are socialized by the culture in which they are raised. Politics, as we saw in Chapter 3, never acquired much legitimacy in the Italian culture. This finding is suggested by Almond and Verba's data on alienation in the Italian culture and by Banfield's controversial findings of "amoral familism" in a Southern Italian village.[46] The newly acquired tolerance for politics among the West German bureaucratic elite is a reflection of the recent development of these traits in German society. The early evolution of viable representative institutions in England could only have occurred in a milieu of these cultural traits—traits whose nature and probable causes were extensively discussed in Chapter 3.

We found a similar acceptance of the legitimacy of political bargaining in the Scandinavian democracies, perhaps somewhat less so in Norway than in Sweden and Denmark. While 79 percent of the Italian civil servants, according to one study, "resent the interference of politicians," the figures for Germany and Sweden are 47 percent and 37 percent, respectively, confirming our expectations with regard to this variable in these three systems.[47] The legitimacy of politics in this sense should logically be less pronounced to varying degrees in segmented societies such as Norway, the Netherlands, Austria, Canada, and Belgium. Accordingly, we might expect to find classic attitudes among the bureaucrats of such nations to a relatively greater extent than other nations such as Great Britain. However, Samuel Eldersveld has found that civil servants in the Netherlands are, compared with other systems, relatively tolerant of politics. For example, only 17 percent of the Dutch civil servants resent the interference of politicians.[48] However, this same study finds Dutch civil servants distinctly less political in this sense than Dutch members of parliament. For example, 68 percent of the Dutch civil servants "recognize that 'political factors' are as important or more important than 'technical factors' in policymaking," while 87 percent of the Dutch MPs agree with that proposition. While 69 percent of Eldersveld's sample of civil servants agreed that "social conflicts are not necessarily functional to progress," only 48 percent of his MPs so agreed.[49] In the unfortunate absence of data (to our knowledge) on this matter, we might expect that civil servants generally would be less tolerant of politics than MPs or members of cabinets. This is important in view of the political role of such civil servants.

Kurt Steiner finds (without presenting any hard data to support his findings) that Austrian civil servants take "an aloof and defensive attitude" toward political input.[50] It therefore seems difficult to generalize about the presence or absence of political as opposed to classic orientations among civil servants. By this same rea-

---

[46] Edward Banfield, *The Moral Basis of a Backward Society* (New York: The Free Press, 1956), especially Chap. 5.
[47] Samuel J. Eldersveld, "Political Elite Linkages in the Dutch Consociational System," paper delivered to the American Political Science Association, Chicago, 1974, p. 4.
[48] *Ibid.*
[49] *Ibid.*, p. 10.
[50] Kurt Steiner, *Politics in Austria* (Boston: Little Brown, 1972), p. 388.

soning, we would expect to find classic attitudes relatively pronounced among the senior civil servants in France. The impressions of one of the most respected observers of that bureaucracy, Alfred Diamant, seem in accord with this expectation.[51]

The question of bureaucratic behavior has not been ignored with respect to the Soviet Union. Some authors, such as Alfred Meyer, have argued that a communist state is a single bureaucratic system extended over an entire society and that a communist system can thus be understood best by comparing it with complex modern bureaucratic organizations anywhere.[52] A number of observers agree that the Soviet bureaucracy is more than just a collection of clerks who are the tools of policymakers, but they disagree on just what it is. One views it in fairly positive terms as composed of technocrats who act on the basis of rational, Weber-like criteria and who constitute a check on the power of an arbitrary dictator.[53] Others agree that the bureaucracy is powerful, but describe it as more self-serving, conservative, and even stagnant than rational and somewhat progressive technocracy.

Although Trotsky thought of the takeover of the bureaucrats as occurring shortly after the revolution, others take the ouster of Khrushchev in 1964 as the symbol of the "victory of the clerks." In other words, that event was the triumph of a group of more conservative procedure- and rule-oriented officials over the more "political" Khrushchev. This image of the *apparat* as rigid, conservative, colorless, apathetic, and lacking in incentive is widespread. In recent years, however, it has been challenged, especially with respect to the administration of Soviet industry. Several studies of the industrial and party areas question the description of rigidity, conservativism, and inflexibility and suggest instead a different direction.[54] Industrial directors and managers, education officials, and party secretaries all emerge as something other than passive and inflexible clerks.

It must be acknowledged that most studies have dealt with the industrial bureaucracy and that, as Armstrong suggested, other groups may behave differently. But as Hough suggests, for several reasons the industrial bureaucracy seems to be the key one. Technocratic specialists seem to be gaining in influence in industrial societies, and in the Soviet Union they seem to be the group from which the top leadership is recruited.

What, then, are the implications of the bureaucratic model for communist systems? Hough asserts that prevailing Western models of bureaucracy are more

---

[51] Alfred Diamant, "Tradition and Innovation in French Administration," *op. cit.,* p. 266.

[52] Alfred G. Meyer, "The Comparative Study of Communist Political Systems," *Slavic Review,* Vol. XXVI, No. 1, March 1967, p. 5.

[53] Barrington Moore, *Political Power and Social Theory* (Cambridge: Harvard University Press, 1958), pp. 19–20.

[54] For some discussion of such studies see Hough, "The Bureaucratic Model and the Nature of the Soviet System," *op. cit.,* pp. 156–158.

relevant for Soviet studies than we have recognized. Advocating a drastic departure from the dominant "directed-society"paradigm, he suggests that the Soviet system is developing several of the characteristics of pluralism. In place of the old framework, he offers the concept of "institutional pluralism."[55] In this new framework, change must be accomplished incrementally through existing structures and channels and by "establishment" leaders. Bureaucratic officials are seen in more of a broker role, as representing many different interests, and as using a style of bargaining and accommodation. These ideas are advanced tentatively, and it is not necessary that they be accepted or rejected immediately. What is important is the suggestion that we might be able to apply the dominant bureaucratic model and search for the directions in which it might lead us.

The importance of the predominance of democratic as opposed to classic values among bureaucrats should now be self-evident. In mature industrial societies, the bureaucratic elite constitute a significant portion of major policymaking roles. As Thomas Dye and Harmon Zeigler have suggested with respect to American democracy, the possession of democratic values by the elite of a system is a critical factor in the preservation of the values.[56]

If the tentative optimism of Putnam that political values (as opposed to classic bureaucratic values) are on the increase among the European bureaucratic elite proves correct, the fact of the progressive devolution of the policy formulation function to the bureaucratic sector need not be fraught with pejorative entailments for democratic values, as otherwise would be the case. After all, the tolerance and legitimacy of the attempts of various interests to influence the policymaking process most clearly delineate an open society. The preservation or spread of such values in a mature industrial society constitutes the core concern of this volume.

---

[55] *Ibid.*, pp. 162–164.
[56] Thomas Dye and L. Harmon Zeigler, *The Irony of Democracy* (North Scituate, MA: Duxbury Press, 1975), pp. 147–156, 454–458.

Chapter 7

Political Parties

In Chapter 4 we learned that individual societies are comprised of complex groupings of individuals into social roles. Each social role generates a perception of its own interests. Social groups, said David Truman, consist of interacting individuals with shared orientations.[1] The perceived interests arising out of shared orientations give rise in turn to demands on society or other groups. Thus, industrial societies contain a large complex of perceived interests or demands, which often conflict with each other.

The idea of democracy includes the expectation that social policies will be more responsive to the interests and demands of the society insofar as they can be known than would an authoritarian government. A major thesis of David Easton's "system analysis"[2] of politics is that the policy decisions (outputs) of a government must in a sense counterbalance the stress and pressure created by demands (inputs). In general terms, this can be accomplished by three means or some combination thereof: the demands can be satisfied by giving what is asked (for example, respond to the American anti-Vietnam war protest by

---

[1] David Truman, *The Governmental Process* (New York: Alfred A. Knopf, 1965), pp. 23-24. This book is Truman's classic statement of a qualified version of "group theory," the notion that public policy is simply the product of the interaction of social groups. This idea is discussed in Chapter 8.

[2] David Easton, *A Systems Analysis of Political Life* (New York: John Wiley & Sons, 1965).

immediately ending the American involvement there), by symbolically satisfying demands (announcing a "secret plan to end the war" and continuing the fighting), or by repression (arresting the war protestors). Democratic governments may be expected to place more emphasis on the first two alternatives; authoritarian systems may be expected to emphasize the last two alternatives.

In order for democratic governments to respond to demands and perceived interests in society, structures must exist to mobilize and articulate the demands and interests and then make the decision makers aware of them. Parties and organized interest groups are therefore expected in a democracy to perform the function of transmitting demands and interests to the political decision makers. One aspect of this function involves the mobilization of those interests that remain latent. Public opinion and demands with respect to public policy are seldom generated spontaneously among the masses. Demands are generally mobilized by the elite or leaders of opinion. Mobilization here refers to the process of organizing the individuals sharing a common orientation and articulating the demands arising out of that shared orientation. Consumers had until recent years exemplified a nonmobilized and hence latent interest in the Western world.

A second aspect of this function of party and interest-group systems involves playing the role of spokesperson for the various active interests in the national decision-making process. The focus of this transmission function is on the inputs, in Easton's terminology, instead of on policies or outputs. By this conception of their functions, party and interest-group systems are successful to the extent that they accurately mirror the distribution of opinions and interests in society. By this conception, it is not the function of party and interest-group systems to ensure a correspondence of policy or outputs to the distribution of public opinions or shifts therein.

A third view of the functions of party systems extends their responsibility to the conversion of the transmitted demands into responsive public policies.[3] This conceptualization is limited to party systems rather than interest groups. It implies a differentiation between the function of the party system and the function of interest-group systems. The function of the latter is confined to our first and second conceptualizations, the mobilization of interests and the representation of these interests in the political decision-making process. Party systems, on the other hand, can serve to filter demands and interests and to aggregate them at a higher level of generality. In doing so, party systems encourage or effect the necessary compromises among the many shades of opinion and formulate a more manageable number of policy alternatives. These alternatives will, if the party formulat-

---

[3] See Gabriel Almond and G. Bingham Powell, *Comparative Politics: A Developmental Approach* (Boston: Little Brown, 1966), pp. 11–12, for a discussion of the conversion function. See also pp. 201–203 for a discussion of responsiveness as a necessary capacity of a modern political system.

ing them is to attain electoral success, correspond as closely as possible to what is common among the demands of the numerically dominant segments of the population. In this way, party systems can act to convert demands into responsive policies. The function of the party system in this third view is not to represent demands on the input side, but to filter and aggregate demands so as to convert them into responsive public policies on the output side.

Typologies of Party Systems

In democracies, party systems tend to perform various combinations of the functions mentioned above. The emphasis on the first two functions on the one hand or the third function on the other is a product of the type of party system. The type of party system is a product of various factors such as the country's history, culture, etc. A country's electoral system may also affect the type of party system found in the nation, an issue discussed below.

Authoritarian versus Competitive Party Systems

Authoritarian party systems stand distinct from competitive party systems in that only the dominant party is allowed to function. The remainder of our categories will focus on competitive party systems whereby more than one party can legitimately compete at more or less regular elections.

As Huntington and Moore have pointed out, strong one-party systems as developed in the last century or so are the primary form of modern authoritarian politics.[4] While there are some obvious distinctions between one-party systems and the democratic ones discussed below, there are also some interesting questions as to possible similarities. In fact, a good deal of attention has been directed recently to the extent to which parties such as the CPSU perform functions similar to or different from those in complex societies.

The most conspicuous feature is, of course, the fact that only the dominant party is allowed to exist officially. We must recall at this point the privileged position communist ideology gives to the party on the premise that it alone understands the "true" needs and interests of society. Given this concept of "truth," it is logical that competitive political processes and parties are unacceptable. A responsible government is not defined in terms of the responsive and spokesperson roles discussed above. On the contrary, political processes and structures are designed to resist spontaneous, special-interest claims that might interfere with the directions and decisions of the "vanguard" elite.

The next question becomes that of whether the functioning of a single party is

---

[4] Samuel Huntington and Clement Moore, eds., *Authoritarian Politics in Modern Society* (New York: Basic Books, 1970), p. 509.

necessarily different from that of two- or multiparty systems. A basic disparity is often simply assumed to exist between democratic and authoritarian (totalitarian) types. Others observe that while the two may appear similar on the surface, they are in fact fundamentally different due to such things as the differing concepts of followers and leaders.[5]

In recent years there has been more examination of the traditional assumption that such single parties are *sui generis* or at the least fundamentally different. Although no one suggests that they are even close to the same in their operation as democratic parties, a number of observers of the Soviet Union have pointed to what they feel are similarities.

The "functional" approach has led some people to the position that many of the same functions are performed, but in a manner or by institutions that differ from the democratic. Michael Gehlen is one proponent of this argument.[6] He suggests that the role of programmatic social movement parties such as the CPSU is basically an integrative one. That is, these parties are concerned with such matters as political recruitment, socialization, and mobilization. However, the manner in which these are accomplished may seem unfamiliar to us and we may thus be tempted to conclude that they are not being done.

Elections are a good illustration of the manner in which the one-party arrangement operates. In the Western democracies, we often think of elections in terms of leadership selection as providing a direct link between the general public and its officials. Because communist countries do not hold competitive elections, we think of them as being unrepresentative. However, their process (which is actually more like a caucus than an election) may provide more explicit representation of particular interests than an elective one because it may very well select representatives from various societal interests.

What we are suggesting is that a one-party system performs a number of the functions of any modern political system. The mechanisms may be unfamiliar to us with our perspective of Western processes and institutions. Thus, interest aggregation may be accomplished as part of the recruitment process. Elections are not a farce if seen more in terms of socialization than recruitment.

In a very thought-provoking comparison of certain aspects of British and Soviet politics, Jerome Gilison approaches the subject a slightly different way.[7] He feels the two systems have much in common in terms of the political functions of parties. Both provide a link between masses and leaders, provide a framework for

---

[5] Sigmund Neumann, "Toward a Comparative Study of Political Parties," *Modern Political Parties* (Chicago: Chicago University Press, 1956), p. 398.

[6] Michael P. Gehlen, *The Communist Part of the Soviet Union: A Functional Analysis* (Bloomington: Indiana University Press, 1969); see especially Chap. 1.

[7] Jerome M. Gilison, *British and Soviet Politics* (Baltimore: The Johns Hopkins University Press, 1972).

the emergence of a leadership team, and mobilize public opinion. The fundamental difference is that although the CPSU does in this political sense everything that British parties do, it does much more by assuming additional social and economic roles that British parties do not. He is referring, of course, to the claim of the CPSU to legitimately infiltrate social groups and to guide and supervise all social and economic activities of the society.

To complete the circle of this discussion of one-party systems, it is precisely this claim with regard to economic and social activities that causes many to maintain that such parties are fundamentally and basically different from democratic types. Yet, as we will point out below, many democratic parties (such as Catholic parties) attempt an "inclusive" penetration of other aspects of the lives of their potential supporters.

The Two-Party System and Its Variants

The classic model of democracy, derived (at times erroneously) from the experience of Great Britain in recent centuries and the United States, involves a two-party system, where two parties alternate in possession of the office of the chief executive. The advantage of this kind of system is that a potentially cohesive majority is automatically provided. The indispensable role of parties in formulating cohesive voting blocs in a legislature is discussed under the topic of party cohesion below.

Policies are made in a democracy with the consent of majorities, and governments in parliamentary democracies continue to govern only with the consent of a majority of the lower house of their legislature. Therefore, cohesive majorities are a very important factor in stable, effective democracies.

The importance of a two-party system seems to lie in its ability to provide a stable, cohesive majority in control of the government. This result is also produced by those systems characterized by the alternation of two stable, cohesive political forces even if they are not, strictly speaking, two-party systems. For example, in Australia competition is between the Labour Party on one hand and a stable, permanent coalition of the Liberal Party and a distinctly smaller Country Party on the other. The Country Party is too far to the right ideologically to conceivably support any government dominated by the left-oriented Labour Party. The Liberal Party cannot control a government without the support of the Country Party. Hence, the Liberal and Country Parties operate as one to provide a cohesive political force to compete with the Labour Party for control of the government.

All democratic nations actually have more than two parties. There are more than two parties in Great Britain, where the industrial revolution generated the rise of the Labour Party replacing the Liberal Party. The latter, however, has remained on the scene, generating a significant number of votes (up to 11.2 percent in 1964) and from 6 to 12 seats since the Second World War. Irish, Scottish, and Welsh nationalist parties have received a rising amount of support in recent years. The question is whether the lesser parties can control enough electoral support to deny the winner a majority of seats in the legislature (or, in the case of the United States and France—the two presidential systems under consideration—the majority of votes needed to choose a president). When the cooperation of more than two autonomous parties is required to maintain a government in office, the probability of instability is increased. Autonomous parties are likely to disagree on some issue somewhere along the line. Although support of the government by individual legislators can be coerced within a party (see the discussion of party discipline below), this support cannot be coerced among parties. Thus, coalition governments face a higher probability of breaking up at some point short of the next scheduled election than do majority governments. This probability would seem to increase in close correlation with the number of parties required to compromise the governing coalition.

Much of Europe seems to be moving perceptibly in the direction of the two-party model in the sense we have discussed it—the alternation of two political forces. However, this generalization, like most generalizations, begs and overlooks numerous qualifications. Although the trend is to fewer parties, the party with a plurality of seats seldom gets a majority of seats. The most notable exception to this—and the most notable example of transformation of a highly fragmented party system to a two-party system—seems to be Austria. There the Socialist Party and the People's Party have alternated control of the government with some regularity, contrasting with the highly fragmented party system of that nation's prewar period.

The Federal Republic of Germany also exemplifies a significant reduction in the number of parties to the point where two parties dominate the political scene: the Christian Democratic Union (CDU), with its Bavarian branch, the Christian Social Union (CSU); and the Social Democratic Party (SPD).[8] A third party, the Free Democratic Party, has retained enough electoral support to prevent either of the two major parties from gaining a majority of seats. Thus, while the Free Democrats are not strong enough themselves to come close to forming a government whichever of the big two parties does form a government needs their support. In this way, Free Democrats are able to play a balance-of-power role and exercise an influence on output out of proportion to their strength. A fourth party, the National Democratic Party (NDP), with a right-wing, militaristic and nationalist orientation, has remained on the fringes of respectability. It has had

---

[8] F. R. Alleman, "Germany's Emerging Two Party System," *New Leader,* Vol. 41, August 4 and August 11, 1958, p. 18.

difficulty getting the minimum national vote (five percent) to be eligible to win any seats. None of this appears to have adversely affected the stability of West German cabinets.

Canada also approaches the two-party model. Only two parties, the Liberal Party and the Progressive Conservatives, appear to possess a reasonable prospect of providing a Canadian prime minister. Two other parties with a distinct regional base do acquire significant electoral support, however. The New Democratic Party (NDP)—formerly known as the Cooperative Commonwealth Federation (CCF)—has strength primarily in the wheat-belt provinces of Saskatchewan and parts of Manitoba and is a party of the left. This phenomenon of a social democratic party with a primarily agrarian base is unique among contemporary democracies.[9] The Social Credit party is also based in the wheat belt, in this case, Alberta. The Social Credit Party has become increasingly a party of the right through the years, although it grew out of the same 1929 depression conditions in the so-called Prairie Provinces that produced the old CCF. While each of these parties will place 10–30 members in the Canadian House of Commons (out of a total of 265), a majority has frequently, although not invariably, been attained by one of the two major parties.

Dominant Multiparty Systems

The alternative to the two-party model in competitive party systems is a multiparty system. Like the two-party concept, it is not entirely clear exactly what multiparty systems are. The above discussion makes it clear that three or more parties do not necessarily preclude one party from obtaining a majority of seats in the lower house of the legislature. This has frequently been the case in the Scandinavian democracies. In both Norway and Sweden, a single party has dominated the government until recently almost without interruption since the Great Depression. More often than not the governing party has had a majority of seats in the legislature and has remained free from coalition entanglements or has been so close to a majority that the weaker coalition party was considerably weaker than the dominant party.

The Scandinavian experience suggests a third type: the dominant multiparty system where one party in a governing coalition is overwhelmingly stronger than its partner or partners. This is a very different thing from a coalition between a number of parties of relatively equal strength. In the former case, the weaker partners, unable to bargain effectively with the dominant party, are less likely to threaten the stability of the coalition. After all, it is generally impossible to form a government without the dominant party. The minor party has nowhere else to go but out of power. Because the Labour Party in Norway and the Social Democratic

---
[9] Seymour Lipset, *Agrarian Socialism* (Berkeley: University of California Press, 1950).

Party in Sweden have retained a majority or near majority of seats for the period of their dominance, it does not matter how fragmented the opposition may be. Insofar as cabinet stability is concerned, the key issue is the cohesiveness of the government, not of the opposition.[10]

In a way, Belgium and Italy may be argued to fit this pattern. In both of these nations it has rarely been feasible to form a government not dominated by Catholic parties—the Christian Democrats (DC) in Italy and the Christian Social Party (PSC) in Belgium. The Italian DCs generally control about 40 percent of the votes and seats in the legislature; their nearest rivals, the communists (PCI), control around 25 percent. The DC thus cannot be ousted from the power, but it is not as dominant as the aforementioned Scandinavian parties. Likewise, Italy has not enjoyed the cabinet stability of Norway and Sweden. Italy endured 36 governments between the Second World War and 1974. A switch in Italian governments has meant a reconstituting of the junior coalition partners with the same DCs as prime minister. For example, when Mariano Rumor (DC) formed a center-left coalition on March 15, 1973, he replaced himself and formed his fifth goverment. This continuity in the leadership of the cabinet provides a certain coherence and stability to the Italian decision-making process. This is the converse of the situation that prevailed in France during the Fourth Republic when revolving-door changes in the premier were counterbalanced by great continuity in the occupancy of other cabinet and ministerial posts.

The Federal Republic of Germany was dominatd for approximately two decades after World War II by the CDU/CSU. This dominant party system then gave way to an interregnum of "grand coalition" between the two largest parties, and this in turn gave way to an SPD government. The prospects for a classic alternation between two major parties now appears brighter than ever.

The situation in Belgium is also not one of clear domination. A Socialist-Liberal coalition was replaced by a Christian Social Party (PSC)–Liberal Party—Party of Liberty and Progress (PLP) since 1961—coalition in 1958. Several PSC men served as premier until Edmund Leburton of the French-speaking wing of the Socialist Party was able to form a government comprised of a three-party coalition in early 1973. This cabinet lasted only until early 1974 when M. Tindemans of the Flemish wing of the PSC formed a coalition government with the PLP. It can be said that the PSC has been dominant much of the time since the Second World War in that the PSC leader has almost always held the post of prime minister. But this has given way to two socialist-led governments, and the PSC appears less dominant than the other dominant party systems mentioned.

Belgium has experienced considerably more cabinet instability than Sweden and

---

[10] This is close to the fourth proposition in the concluding remarks of Michael Taylor and V. M. Herman, "Party Systems and Government Stability," *American Political Science Review*, Vol. LXV, No. 1, March 1971, p. 37.

Britain, but far less than Italy. The Belgium premier has changed nine times from 1958 to 1974. The average life of a government in that period was therefore just under two years. (The average life of an Italian government has been less than a year—36 governments in 29 years.) In the 16 years in Belgium, governments have fallen on five separate occasions due to the breakup of a coalition (the resignation of a coalition partner). This has not happened at all since the war in Britain or Sweden, although governments have asked for the dissolution of their legislatures and new elections at some point before they were legally forced to do so.

Not only has a certain amount of cabinet instability become evident in Belgium in recent decades, but the once-vaunted stability of the party system itself is no longer as axiomatic as Belgian scholar Val Lorwin found it. Two parties favoring regional autonomy for their respective subcultural constituents began acquiring significant representation in the 1960s. The FDF, an extremely anti-Flemish union, and the *Volksunie,* the Flemish National People's Union, each gained over 11 percent of the vote in the 1971 general election. This development, emanating from the cultural linguistic crisis discussed in Chapter 4, means that Belgium can no longer be considered the stable three-party system it had been for the previous eight decades. Whether the resolution of the cultural-linguistic issue by the confederation of the nation, discussed in Chapter 4, has been accomplished and whether this resolution will result in the disappearance of these two parties of cultural defense remains to be seen.

It seems clear that a dominant party system is clearly different from the classic, fragmented multiparty system. The logical reasons why multiparty systems were said to be more likely to break down than two-party systems do not apply with anything like the same force to dominant or hegemonic multiparty systems. The claim of Alan Arian and Samuel Barnes that the dominant party system is *sui generis* instead of a modification or an impure version of the multiparty system is persuasive.[11] However, their claim that dominant party systems are "remarkably stable"[12] appears belied by Barnes's own case in Italy.

The issue of cabinet stability is a tricky one that requires careful definition, as implied above. The identity of the Italian premiers has not changed with notable frequency, despite their frequent resignations. Generally the same DC leader forms the next government. Clearly, such a situation will have less impact on policy than if a different party took over the government.

---

[11] Alan Arian and Samuel Barnes, "The Dominant Party System: A Neglected Model of Democratic Stability," *The Journal of Politics,* Vol. 36, No. 3, August 1974, pp. 592–614. The authors claim the dominant party system is sui generis (in a class by itself) at p. 592. Compare Joseph LaPalombara and Myron Weiner, eds., *Political Parties and Political Development* (Princeton: Princeton University Press, 1966). These authors, in their introduction (pp. 3–42), develop the term *hegemonic party system* (p. 35), which means one party maintains a hegemony of power. This term can be used interchangeably with dominant party system.

[12] Arian and Barnes, *op. cit.,* p. 600.

The most obvious differences between the Italian party system and the other more stable dominant party systems appears to be the psychological distance between parties—the extent to which partisan feelings are intense or to which one's opponents are accepted as legitimate. This partisanship or psychological distance between parties has appeared to be greater in Italy than in the other dominant party systems mentioned. The DC has not been able to respond to overtures from the communists and coalesce with them to govern the country.

The Netherlands had also been noted for cabinet stability in recent decades with a multiparty system. It was not possible to form a government without including the Catholic People's Party (KPP). The Dutch situation is in flux now due to a marked proliferation of parties since 1967. The KPP has not been dominant in the sense of regularly providing the nation's prime minister and has been losing electoral support to newer parties such as Democrats '66.

The reason for the apparent exceptions to the expectations that dominant party systems will be stable is that dominance is a matter of degree. To the extent that the dominant party relies on coalition partners to govern and to the extent that coalition partners approach the dominant party in strength, a degree of cabinet instability (due to the losses of a parliamentary majority or the unscheduled resignations of heads of government) is likely to appear.

The Fragmented Multiparty System

Since the demise of the Fourth French Republic, a classic multiparty system has been absent from the European picture. During the Fourth Republic, no single party could command more than about a quarter of the seats. Furthermore, the strongest party was the French Communist Party—an antisystem party effectively excluded from the government. Consequently, coalitions were formed by a number of parties of relatively equal strengths. No single party in these French governments possessed sufficient strength to exercise coercive pressure on the other parties in coalitions. Persuasion alone did not prove sufficient to hold several autonomous parties in line over a range of the kind of divisive issues that have plagued France. It is therefore not surprising that French cabinets fell with almost ludicrous frequency.

Similar situations occurred in prewar Germany (the Weimar Republic), Austria, and Italy. Cabinets consisted of several parties, no one of which approached dominance. Fifteen parties were represented in the German Reichstag from 1928 to 1932. Under such a situation, no coherent policies were able to be imposed to deal with the real problems of those systems. Any policy was bound to harm the perceived interests of some essential party in those multifaceted cabinets. The offended part of the cabinet would than proceed to bring down the government. F. A. Hermans has suggested that this failure of democratic governments to govern was a major cause in their being replaced by authoritarian systems that could govern.[13] For the sake of convenience, we refer to the systems in which governments are made up of numerous parties of relatively equal strength as fragmented multiparty systems to distinguish them from the Swedish pattern. The logic behind the assertion that fragmented multiparty systems are more likely to produce cabinet instability seems unassailable.

The question is then raised as to why any nation would adopt such a system. Hermans's simplistic answer that fragmented multiparty systems are the outgrowths of electoral systems is considered below.

Party System Types, Accountability, and Responsiveness

Two-party systems, despite their advantage in producing cohesive parlimentary majorities, are assailed on the grounds of the distortions they produce in their representative function.[14] It should be obvious that given free reign, interests, opinions, and coalitions do not naturally bifurcate into neat dichotomous factions. To force the spectrum of opinions and interests into a dichotomous grouping inevitably distorts them through forced compromises at best.

At worst, the two-party system fails to represent significant blocs of opinion in the decision-making process. Unrepresented blocs of opinion, when excluded from the electoral process, are likely to become alienated from the system. Who, for example, represents nonsocialist, liberal opinion in Great Britain if the Labour Party is more or less democratic socialist (a big "if") and the Conservative Party is, as its name implies, philosophically conservative? Who represents sentiment for radical structural change, whether by socialists or French Canadian separatists, in Canada?

Further distortions occur when very small shifts in public opinion can produce a complete change in government and policy, giving the few in the center—those who normally fluctuate in such a system—an influence far out of proportion to their actual numbers. Because elections are won by winning the uncommitted center, the committed of the left and right polar positions may be largely ignored by the major parties.

The interpretation focuses on the input side of the democratic process. For those who oppose the two-party system on such grounds, the proper function of a democratic party system is to present as close to a mirror "image of the feelings of the nation" as possible.[15] The question of whether the output—the public policies—reflects public opinion or shifts therein is neatly avoided.

---

[13] F. A. Hermans, *Europe Under Democracy or Anarchy* (South Bend: University of Notre Dame Press, 1940). Hermans went so far as to suggest that fragmented party systems were the proximate cause of the rise of fascism in Europe. This proposition as a simplistic causal statement has been largely rejected by serious scholars.

[14] For example, Enid Lakeman and James Lambert, *Voting Democracies* (London: Farber and Farber Ltd., 1955).

[15] *Ibid.*, p. 149.

A highly fragmented party will provide channels for the articulation of more shades of opinion. Accordingly, the perpetuation of finer distinctions in interests, demands, and opinions is tacitly encouraged. In this sense, a fragmented party system is more representative of public opinion.

The composition of this kind of coalition is determined by bargaining among party leaders after the elections. Governments must represent a majority of the legislature, and elections in a fragmented multiparty system do not delineate these majorities. Therefore, the electoral process has little impact on either the composition of the government coalition or the policies emanating from it.

This phenomenon thus involves the insulation of governments and policies from the impact of public preferences and demands. This situation was exacerbated in France during the Fourth Republic by the fact that governments could fail without the dissolution of the legislature, necessitating new elections. Accordingly, numerous governments fell and were reconstituted without reference to the electoral process. If elections are the principal vehicle for governmental accountability to the citizen and for citizen impact on public policy, the French party system, however representative it might be, was hardly "democratic" with regard to output (policy, etc.).

A two-party system greatly distorts the distribution of opinions on the input side, but exaggerates the responsiveness of the composition of the elite and public policy to shifts in public opinion on the output side. In Great Britain, the winner of an election rarely exceeds 50 percent of the vote by much, even when it wins a majority of seats. In fact, no party has garnered as much as 50 percent of the vote since the Second World War. The largest victory margin in the period was in 1945 when Labour's percentage exceeded the Tory percentage by 8.5 percent. Thus, a swing of no more than 10 percent and normally less than 5 percent will completely replace one elite party with another, its opponents. The replacement of one major party in virtually complete control of the government (see the discussion of party government below) by another major party presumably will be followed by some significant shifts in public policy. Moreover, it is reasonable to suppose that there will be some correspondence between the direction and the substance of policy shifts in public opinion. Thus, the British model of a two-party system may be defended in that it produces output in a far more responsive manner than party systems necessitating the formation of governments by postelection bargaining. In fact, the responsiveness of the British model to shifts in public opinion may be characterized as an an exaggerated response.

Dominant party systems of the Scandinavian type may be argued to combine representativeness and responsiveness. Their multiparty character renders them more representative than the British model. In addition to the Labour Party, Norway has a Liberal Party, an Agrarian Party, a Christian People's Party, a Conservative Party, and a Socialist People's Party (now known as the Left

Socialists). Labour and the Left Socialists basically compromise the Norwegian left (we are ignoring the communists, who have been without parliamentary seats). Voters who oppose the growing bourgeois orientation of the Labour Party have a parliamentary alternative to the left of Labour. The right opposition is comprised of four distinct parties. But, as noted above, the dominance of Labour has generated great cabinet stability.

Similarly, Sweden has combined a cohesive government by a Social Democratic Party with either a majorty or an overwhelming dominant plurality of seats in the Riksdag (lower house of the legislature) with a fragmented opposition that permits the representation of a variety of interests and opinions. The nonsocialist opposition is compromised by a Moderate (formerly Conservative) Party, a Center (formerly Farmer) Party, and a Liberal Party.

At first glance such a system may seem to combine the best of both worlds: government by a cohesive majority and direct representation of a wide spectrum of interest through the party system. There is, however, another function attributed to party systems in democracies, that of structuring the accountability of the elite to the masses. The accountability of the elite is structured by the presence of an effective, organized opposition that could conceivably replace any elite that transcends its bounds of discretion. When the opposition is so fragmented that it cannot mobilize its strength to unseat the government short of a major crisis, the elite's bounds of discretion extend to the crisis. The standards of performance that a government must meet to retain its power through competitive elections will be higher to the extent that the opposition is actually a believable threat.

Accordingly, in such situations as we find in Norway and Sweden, the very qualities of the oppositions that render them representative—their fragmentation—have also rendered them until recently an ineffective threat in challenging their respective dominant parties. It is therefore not surprising that both systems have been hegemonic. The Labour Party maintained a hegemony of power in Norway from 1935, except for a 28-day interlude in 1963, until 1965. The Social Democratic Party of Sweden has been in power since 1932. Although these systems foster more accountability than systems that do not tolerate opposition, they clearly provide less accountability than systems in which the opposition is more than a long-shot threat to replace the government. In the situation of Norway and Sweden, the governments of these countries have had wide leeway in deciding among policy alternatives and considerable room for generating unpopular socioeconomic consequences of their policy making, free from the expectation that they would be replaced.

It must be cautioned that accountability is present in these nations. Recent developments have in fact shown that the dominant parties are vulnerable. At this writing, Swedish Prime Minister Palme has been hanging on with a minority government since the Social Democrats suffered a significant electoral setback in late 1973. The Party lost seven seats in the September 1973 election and fell to a total of 156 seats in a 350-seat Riksdag. Together with their parliamentary allies, the communists, the left-wing coalition totals 175 seats, which puts them in an exact tie with the nonsocialist bloc (Center, Moderate, and Liberal). Apparently, the seemingly insoluble problems of inflation and unemployment that plague all industrial societies can make any incumbency vulnerable—even the 41-year (at this writing) reign of the Swedish Democrats. At the time of the 1973 elections, Swedish inflation had climed to 6 percent and unemployment to 3 percent, both high figures for that nation.

In Norway, the vulnerability of the previously hegemonic Labour Party has been even more pronounced. In September 1965 a four-party coalition of Conservatives, Liberals, Christian Peoples' Party, and the Agrarian Center Party gained 80 seats in the lower house of the Norwegian legislature (*Storting*), while Labour retained only 68 and Socialist Labour (often its left-wing coalition partner) retained only 2. Thus ended 30 years of consecutive Labour rule. The nonsocialist coalition was narrowly reaffirmed in the 1964 elections, and this government lasted until 1971. At that point Premier Per Borten of the Center Party resigned over a scandal emanating from agrarian-based opposition to Norway's prospective participation in the European Economic Community. Labour's Trygve Bralteli formed a minority government lasting only till 1972. In the 1973 elections, the coalition of Labour and Socialist People's and Communist Parties won a one-seat majority over the nonsocialist coalition, although the Labour Party itself lost 12 seats to a total of 62 in a 155-seat Storting. This can hardly be considered a decisive mandate.

It appears that incumbency is an increasingly vulnerable position. It is difficult to find any party in the noncommunist world maintaining what would be called a hegemony of power. Hegemonic parties maintained long-term control over their governments in open societies by maintaining a degree of public satisfaction with consequences of how they had governed. This satisfaction would have to be higher than needed to maintain an authoritarian party in power, such as the Communist Party in the Soviet Union. Clearly, more dissatisfaction is needed to catalyze a revolution than is needed to provoke a vote for a legitimate organized opposition party. Our previous suggestion was that the increasingly insoluble problems of the industrial world have resulted in these societies perpetually dissatisfied with the performance of the existing elite. The position of previously dominant parties is everywhere increasingly insecure.

The previously predictable dominance of the religious parties in the Netherlands can similarly no longer be assumed. In 1973 the head of the Labour Party formed a five-party center-left coalition. The Catholic People's Party and the Protestant Anti-Revolutionary Party held a distinct minority of cabinet posts. A new party, Democrats '66, appealing largely to the urban youth of a leftist orientation, has been a significant force in that nation's politics since they won 7 seats out of 135 in the lower house of their legislature (*Tweed Kamer*). By 1973 the three previously autonomous religious (confessional) parties were planning a merger in a Christian Democratic Union to try to maintain their declining influence.

The situation in the Netherlands has almost been the converse of Norway and Sweden. In the Netherlands, the labor-based party, previously excluded from the government for two decades, recently acquired control of the government and the confessional parties lost their monopoly of power. In Norway and Sweden, the labor-based parties maintained a near-monopoly of political power for three decades until their grip was broken by antilabor forces. What the two situations have in common is the ending of a clear, inpenetrable dominance by any one party.

Toward a New Typology of Party Systems

The foregoing data suggest that a classification based on the number of parties—the criterion that has received the widest attention in the literature—is of limited utility. The utility of any classification depends on its ability to make distinctions that contribute to explanation. For example, multiparty systems should behave more like each other than like a two-party system with respect to some important outcome (such as cabinet stability). We note, however that several multiparty systems have resulted in great cabinet stability, some in moderate cabinet stability, and some in great instability. In short, some multiparty systems (such as in the Federal Republic of Germany or Sweden) resemble the British party system in some respects more than they resemble other multiparty systems (such as that of Weimar Germany or the Fourth French Republic). For this reasoning, a classification based solely on the number of parties does not appear to be useful. For the same reason, the dominant category suggested by Barnes and Arian, while adding a useful variable, is not in itself a totally satisfactory category. We need to account for the differences among such systems (for instance, Italy and Sweden).

Party system types are both a function of the number of parties and the pattern of competition among them, the two variables being, of course, related to each other. The most important aspect of the pattern of competition is the strength (percent of seats) of the largest party. Perhaps rather than two- and multiparty systems, it might make more sense to speak of fragmented and aggregative party systems. The latter term refers to those systems in which the major parties bring together (aggregate) a larger number of diverse interests under one party label. The major party or parties in question aim for breadth of support rather than strength of commitment. The term *aggregative* avoids the necessity of having to rationalize systems such as those in Australia, West Germany, and Canada under the two-party rubric because they behave more like the British and the American systems than the systems of the Third and Fourth Republics.

Fragmented refers to those party systems in which compromises and alliances are made among legislators after the elections. In these systems, the homogeneity of each party's clientele is preserved by the absence of extensive bargaining and compromise within each party's structure. Parties in such systems transmit demands from society to the political decision-making processes with relatively little screening, consolidation, or distortion. Consequently, the decision-making process frequently must deal with demands that have greater variety and that are often more extreme (or out of the system's political "mainstream") than would be the case with aggregative party systems. Clearly, *aggregative* and *fragmented* are relative terms that are best conceptualized as poles of a continuum. A second dimension of the fragmentation-aggregation variable is the size of percentage of legislative seats held by the largest party. This dimension distinguishes Scandinavian multiparty systems from those of Third and Fourth Republic France.

A second variable is the distinction between those systems in which control of the government alternates from one party or political force to another at more or less frequent intervals and those systems in which one party or political force controls the decision-making process for a long time. Let us, in the words of La Palombara and Weiner, call the former a *turnover system* and the latter a *hegemonic system*. Because *frequent* and *long time* are relative terms instead of precisely dichotomized alternatives, we are speaking here also of a continuum. By *turnover,* we mean a situation in which control of the chief executive passes from one party label to a political opponent. Thus, Italy, with frequent cabinet resignations, would still be relatively hegemonic because cabinets are usually reconstituted under the same Christian Democratic leader or his Christian Democratic successor. The DC has maintained long-term dominance, but the relatively fragmented nature of Italy's party system distinguishes it from the hegemonic Swedish system. The dominance of the DC provides a continuity absent in systems like Weimar Germany or the Fourth French Republic, but the greater fragmentation of the party contributes to frequent cabinet resignations.

The party systems under consideration may be schematically placed with respect to these two variables. The two variables are placed as intersecting axes. The positioning of a party system with respect to either axis is in principle quantifiable. The criterion for the aggregative-fragmented axis should combine the number of parties winning seats in the lower house of that nation's legislature with the size of the largest party. Clearly, a nation like Sweden in which one party wins a majority of votes and seats against three other parties is different from a system with four parties of relatively equal strength and no party winning over 25 percent of the votes and seats. The criterion for the turnover-hegemonic distinction is the number of times the premiership or prime minister is transferred from one party label to another. The turnover-hegemonic distinction provides a useful weighting to the total number of cabinets as total index of cabinet stability.

This mode of classifying party systems suggests both similarities and distinctions not apparent under previously used classifications. The fact that Australia, Canada, and West Germany are closer to Great Britain than to Weimar Germany or the Fourth French Republic makes intuitive sense to us. So do the aforementioned similarities (hegonomy) and distinctions (fragmentation) between Sweden and Italy. We suggest that the apparently obvious cases of the two-party–multiparty stability proposition can be subsumed under an aggregative-stability proposition.

Parties And Electoral Systems

Even abandoning a simple two-party–multiparty dichotomy, the number of parties clearly remains one relevant variable for our typology. For a period of time in the 1940s, a vigorous debate flourished over whether the electoral system of a nation was a direct causal determinant of the fragmentation of the party system.

The electoral system refers here to the rules by which people are elected to the legislature. For purposes of simplicity, electoral systems may be grouped in a dichotomous typology: proportional systems and single-member district systems with a plurality vote (hereafter called plurality systems). The plurality systems are now by and large confined to the Anglo-American democracies (including the older Commonwealth). The Federal Republic of Germany elects its Bundestag by a combination of plurality and modified proportional systems.

Single-Member District Plurality Systems

The name of this system is descriptive of its operation. The nation is divided into finite legislative districts (as opposed to electing people "at large"—by the entire national electorate). Each district sends one and only one representative to the legislature, hence the name *single-member district system*. That representative is the one with the most votes (a plurality) irrespective of whether that plurality is a majority. If five candidates were running and divided the vote on a basis of 28, 24, 18, 16, and 14 percent, the candidate with only 28 percent would get a seat and all others would stay home. This system makes no distinction between the second-strongest and fifth-strongest candidates; they each get nothing. A party must win a district to get any representation at all. The result is that while the second-strongest party will win some districts due to an uneven distribution of opinion, the third-strongest may come in second here and there but will rarely win districts. Fourth-strongest and below will almost never win.

In these systems, doctrinally pure parties of fixed-minority clientele are permanently excluded from power. In order to avoid frustration, the pressure to expand the appeal of parties in order to win districts is enormous. the pressure on parties in these systems to coalesce, compromise, and become doctrinally diffuse should be readily apparent. It is to be expected that plurality electoral systems will be associated with fewer parties.[16]

Proportional Systems

Proportional representation is a generic term given to a variety of specific electoral systems. The thrust of "pure proportionality" is that the percentage of seats in the legislature that a party is allotted should equal that party's percentage of the national vote. This "ideal" type of proportional system presumes the nation as a whole as a constituency because the national distribution of seats is the standard of proportionality.

In actuality, European election systems distort the principle of proportionality by dividing the respective nations into election districts. In order to allocate seats proportionally, districts are multimembered. That is, each district sends several representatives to the legislature on the basis of some principle of allocation. The seats are allocated on the basis of a party's vote in that district. A typical system was the list voting system used in France's Fourth Republic. Each party would put up lists of candidates in each district. If, for instance, a district was assigned six seats and a party received about one-third of the vote in that district, the first two names on that party's list would go to the legislature. Generally, a direct apportionment of so few seats was impossible with such neat precision. One could not award a party fractions of a seat. Seats were therefore allocated on a system of highest average number of votes (D'Hondt system). The party with the most votes got the first seat in a district. Then that party's vote was divided by two and compared to everyone else's raw vote. The highest total after this calculation got the second seat. If the same party still had the highest total after its votes were divided by two, it got the second seat and for the third seat its vote was divided by three. This procedure was followed until all seats were allocated.

Proportional systems are clearly advantageous to parties whose prospective clientele is fixed at something less than a plurality. A smaller fraction of the vote will still net a party some parliamentary seats and possibly a post in the cabinet.

Plurality systems not only underrepresent minor parties, but there is also a psychology of wasted votes that tends to make the actual votes for such parties less

---

[16] Maurice Duverger, *Political Parties*, Barbara and Robert North, trans. (New York: Wiley Science Editions, 1963), p. 217, elevates this relationship to a "true sociological law." This near-classic book consists mainly of a comparative attempt to typologize western parties along numerous structural variables. It is a necessary point for serious students of such parties. See also his *L'influence des systemes electoraux sur la vie politique* (with F. Goguel, J. Cardat, G. de Loys, S. Mastellone, A. Soulier, A. Vlaches) (Paris: Armand Colin, 1950), for a more forceful statement that electoral arrangements have a causal impact on the type of party system.

than it otherwise would be. Knowing the third party cannot win, its sympathizers may choose to have some impact on the election outcome by voting for the lesser evil among the major parties. Something like this process has been working against the Liberal Party in Great Britain where that party's seats are disproportionally low in relation to its votes and the party's vote is smaller than the number of its avowed sympathizers would lead one to expect.

Smaller parties with fixed clientele and principled appeal can and do attain some success in plurality systems. Most noteworthy may be the case of the rising strength of the Scottish and Welsh Nationalist Parties in Britain. These parties concentrate their strength in a few constituencies. The problem of the Liberals is accentuated by the fact that their strength is spread relatively evenly over the nation. Actually, the effect of the plurality system may be to exert pressure for a reduction in the number of parties in any given constituency, but this is not the same as saying it causes a two-party system nationally. When pressures for minority representation become intense, a series of localized two-party systems with the identity of the major parties differing from place to place may result. *Le Parti Ralliement des Creéditiste* (commonly called the *Creditistes*) in Québec, the Scottish National Party, the American Dixiecrats, the Canadian New Democratic Party, and the Canadian Social Credit Party are all examples of minor parties gaining localized electoral success despite a plurality electoral system.

The majority system, used in both the Third and Fifth French Republics, does not precisely fit either of the two electoral systems mentioned so far. Like the plurality system, it is based on single-member districts, thus removing the opportunity for a proportional allocation of seats. Because the winner must receive a majority, runoff elections are the rule. Several parties other than the one with a plurality but no majority may decide to coalesce between the first and runoff elections and obtain the required majority. This bargaining opportunity results in far greater representation for small parties than the plurality system. The majority system can thus be argued to have a proportional effect.

In the Federal Republic of Germany, a mixture of the proportional and plurality systems is used to choose the Bundestag. Half are elected by the British method of single-member districts with plurality vote and half by a proportional arrangement. The German concern about small, extreme parties resulted in the proviso that any party must win three single-member constituencies and obtain five percent of the national vote to benefit from proportionality.

Electoral Systems and Party Systems

Despite the logical connection, it is a dubious proposition that electoral systems have had a direct causal impact on the number of parties. The viability of a two-party system requires a cultural disposition to bargain, compromise, and aggregate differences of interest and principle into broad, diffuse coalitions. Lacking these cultural properties, it is doubtful whether any electoral system could force a lasting two-party alignment. By the same token, it is doubtful whether proportional systems directly cause a proliferation in the number of parties in the absence of an already fragmented political culture. To say that the proportional system generates a greater opportunity for small parties to function is far from saying the electoral system creates small parties. A proportional system is designed to generate a party system that mirrors the distribution of opinion in a society; hence, it will result in a fragmented party system only in a fragmented society.

Denmark, for example, did not experience any increase in the number of parties when it switched to a proportional system in 1920. The case of Denmark is perhaps most instructive because it was the only Continental nation to employ a British-style plurality system prior to its adoption of proportional representation. Other nations used two-ballot majority systems or some form of multimember constituencies. This kind of electoral systems, it will be recalled, does not discriminate against small parties as much as the single-member district plurality system. Denmark had four parties under the plurality system. While the number of parties has increased somewhat in recent legislatures (the legislature in 1974 included Social Democrats, Socialist People's Radical Liberals, Moderate Liberals, Agrarian, Conservative, Center Democrats, Progress Party and Christian Party), this increase was not apparent upon the adoption of proportional representation. The Progress Party and Christian Party are new in 1974. Proportional representation may have facilitated some of the growth and development of some of these parties or it may have impeded the decline of others, but proportional representation was hardly the direct cause of the proliferation of parties. The time lag between the adoption of proportional representation and the recent proliferation is simply too great for such a causal inference.

Similarly, Belgium has maintained a stable three-party system from the adoption of proportional representation until very recently when the linguistic subcultural issue described in Chapter 4 generated two parties of cultural defense (*Volksunie* and FDF) and Flemish and Walloon wings of the three major parties. Thus, with the brief exception of the *Christus Rex* (Christ the King) Party, an antisemetic, anti-Marxist party of the 1930s,[17] Belgium maintained a stable three-party system from 1900 until the 1970s despite proportional representation.

Even if we accept the proposition that proportional representation facilitates the process of small parties gaining parliamentary representation, the question remains, why opt for proportional representation? In each of the European democracies under consideration, a multiparty system was in existence at the time proportional representation was adopted. Proportional representation should

---

[17] Val Lorwin, "Belgium: Religion, Class and Language in National Politics," *Political Oppositions in Western Democracies,* Robert Dahl ed. (New Haven: Yale University Press, 1966), p. 163.

Political Parties

therefore be viewed as a reflection of the degree of social fragmentation or the degree of irreconcilability between social divisions.

Conversely, a tendency toward a dichotomized style in political conflict in Great Britain far antedates the adoption of a pluralist electoral system.[18] Divisions such as Lancester versus York, Cavalier versus Roundhead, king versus parliament bifurcating political conflict in Britain clearly antedated mass suffrage let alone any particular electoral system. The election system followed the two-party system; hence, the former can hardly be argued to have caused the latter. Published demands that Britain switch to some form of proportional representation have been based on expressed dissatisfaction with the underrepresentation of the British Liberal Party, an existing political force.[19] It is probable that other adaptations of proportional representation in Europe were a reflection of the distribution of public opinions, interests, and ideologies rather than a cause of fragmented distribution. In short, an electoral system reflects the degree of aggregation or fragmentation of society; it does not cause aggregation or fragmentation.

Party Program, Ideology, and Base of Electoral Support

The distinction between ideologism and pragmatism was discussed in Chapter 3. The aggregation of social divisions is facilitated by a pragmatic orientation involving the framing of differences in terms of interests rather than symbols or principles.

This dichotomization of ideologism and pragmatism is related to the distinction between parties of expediency and programmatic parties or parties of principle. The raison d'être of the former is the maximization of votes and achievement of the widest possible appeal. The content and specificity of the platform and promises of parties will be pragmatically adjusted to that goal.

Parties of program or principle, on the other hand, exist to achieve certain substantive goals. These goals, whether the overthrow of the system or the passage of certain legislation, are the reasons why parties enter the political arena. They do not seek power, in other words, for its own sake. Instead, they are willing to sacrifice breadth of support to maintain purity of program or principle.

Party program, principles, and ideology are not quite interchangeable terms. Programs consist of a coherent and specific set of legislative proposals (such as nationalization of specified industries, a set of deflationary monetary measures, etc.), which may be derived from a set of principles (free enterprise, etc.). When these principles attain a coherency, comprehensiveness, and state of being closed—

---

[18] Leslie Lipson, "The Two Party System in British Politics," *The American Political Science Review*, Vol XLVII, No. 2, June 1953.

[19] For example, Lakeman and Lambert, *op. cit.*; J. F. S. Ross, *Elections and Electors* (London: Eyre and Spottiswoode, 1955).

of a *weltanschauung* (roughly, world view)—they constitute an ideology (for example, Marxism, laissez faire, Social Darwinism, etc.). A closed-thought system, it will be recalled, is not subject to influence by information external to the system.

It must be emphasized that the labels "party of principle" or "programmatic party" on one hand and "party of expediency" on the other constitute polar extremes or Weberian "ideal types."[20] Their relation to the actual parties we are discussing is to represent tendencies. Parties are more or less expediential or programmatic in relation to specified either parties; no party is purely ideological or purely expediential. Thus, one might argue that many European socialist parties, based as they are on a mass movement with a perception of being a subordinate class, are more goal oriented than their conservative opponents. Yet all of these parties have sought to broaden their support at the expense of their principles. Even the Italian communists make overtures to the Italian Christian Democrats.

No party can be totally without a principled base. Principles serve to relate citizens to an array of possible policy alternatives more extensive than they can consider and more complex than they can comprehend. Principles thus serve the function of relieving the citizen of the impossible burden of considering all alternatives of public policy on purely rational grounds. The cost of acquiring the information to do so would be prohibitive. Anthony Downs thus suggests that ideologies (in our terms, principles) may be considered as "cost-saving devices."[21] Paradoxically, because the return for making a rational decision on each vote without the intervening simplification of choices by party principles would not equal the information cost needed to be rational, it may be rational to be irrational. In short, it may be rational to vote on the basis of simplifying principles.

The distinction between expediential and programmatic parties is based on the goals of the party. The former type seeks power at whatever cost in principle. The latter seeks the enactment of legislation. A third alternative type of goal suggests itself—the destruction of the system itself. One may argue that revolutionary parties are not parties in the traditional sense in that they do not fulfill precisely the same set of functions performed by other democratic parties. The labeling of a party as revolutionary as opposed to democratic is also sometimes a function of the subjective judgment of the observer. Because an avowed opposition to the democratic process often condemns a party to electoral impotence, many parties heretofore regarded as more or less revolutionary, especially European Marxist

---

[20] Peter Merkl has suggested that one is more likely to label a party's position as pragmatic when one agrees with that position or, conversely, as ideological if one disagrees with it. Peter Merkl, *Modern Comparative Politics* (New York: Holt, Rinehart and Winston, 1970), p. 275.

[21] Anthony Downs, *An Economic Theory of Democracy* (New York: Harper & Row, 1957), pp. 98–99.

parties, have been attempting to disclaim revolutionary intentions. The Italian Communist Party has been most notable in this regard. They even disavowed the Russian invasion of Czechoslovakia to establish their autonomy from the Soviet Union.

Catchall Parties and Social Democracy

Otto Kirkheimer has postulated the progressive transformation of European parties from principled parties to expediential parties with the widest possible appeal. He calls expediential parties "catchall parties."[22] That is, the older programmatic parties are increasingly compromising the purity and internal consistency of what they putatively stand for in exchange for the search for a wider and more varied clientele. Consequently, what they stand for increasingly takes on the properties of vagueness and abstraction. American parties have always leaned in this direction. It is difficult to say with any precision for what the American Democratic Party stands combining as it does within its ranks the political spectrum from the likes of James Eastland (senator from Mississippi), George Wallace, George McGovern, and Edward Kennedy. Similarly, the British Labour Party has never had much concern with orthodox socialist doctrine. Never a Marxist party, even its Fabian Socialists (a brand of democratic socialism) have been a small and only moderately influential portion of its following.

It may be useful to note at this point that socialism is not the same as Stalinist communism. The former term connotes government ownership of the major (but not all) means of production, distribution, and exchange. It is an economic variable. Democracy, it will be recalled, entails a political system involving regular competitive elections as a means of choosing between the elite and some structural limitations on the discretion of an incumbent elite—that is, some system of checks and balances. There is no logical reason why a government so chosen and so accountable cannot own the major means of production, distribution, and exchange.

Stalinism, on the other hand, entails a set of political charactertics as well as economic ones. Zbigniew Brzezinski, a noted Kremlinologist, once referred to the system as an "oriental despotism." He was referring to the nearly total absence of accountability or restraints on the political elite. This is a separate issue from who owns the means of production. It might be useful to recall that in Nazi Germany, hardly a democratic or open system, the major means of production were in private hands and run for profit (for example, Krupp Industries). Private ownership of means of production run for profit does not guarantee a set of democratic political institutions. The point is that democratic socialism is not only a

---

[22] Otto Kirkheimer, "The Transformation of the Western European Party Systems," in LaPalombara and Weiner, *op. cit.*, pp. 117–200.

logical possibility; numerous major European parties have claimed to advocate it.[23]

Perhaps the clearest example of Kirkheimer's postulated trend, the transformation of what was formerly a party of principle or program into a catchall party, may be the Social Democratic Party of Germany (SPD). The original Marxist Party in Europe, the SPD in 1959 adopted a program that any capitalist would be able to live with. The program asserts that only "liberal methods" can secure economic growth and full employment. Such methods are spelled out as follows: ". . . free choice of consumer goods, free choice of employment, free competition and free initiative on the part of employers are the essential foundations of a liberal economic policy. When it exceeds a certain degree, immediate interference by the state in the economy . . . does away the economic freedom."[24] Such words, from what was originally Marx's own party, constitute an about-face that is astonishing. Going on to say government must sponsor competition between producers and guarantee autonomy of employer and employee groups in collective bargaining, the party avows a faith in the impersonal forces of supply and demand that nearly resurrects the ghost of Adam Smith (the guru of laissez faire price economics).

The reasons for this abandonment of old, fundamental principles lie primarily in electoral strategy and the frustration born of interminable exclusion from power. In a highly fragmented party system such as existed during the Weimar Republic, the SPD could expect to play an influential role in cabinet formation and policymaking. In the aggregated party system that evolved after the Second World War, however, a third of the votes and seats fell short of the plurality necessary for participation in Bonn governments. Consequently, the SPD found itself in seemingly permanent opposition (and importance), while the CDU's Conrad Adenauer and his successor Ludwig Erhardt established an apparent hegemony on the chancellorship from 1949–1965. Despite the mobilizing impact on the party faithful of such symbols as Marxist rhetoric and the singing of the "Internationale" (a rallying song for international Marxism), it was obvious by the 1950s that the party would have to appeal to a wider clientele including many repelled by Marxist symbols.

Throughout its history, the SPD has manifested a schizophrenic ambivalence between eschatological and utopian ideology and the imperatives of political problem solving. Because the former derives from a totally untested view of the future, presuming the absence of actual problems, it generates no solution for these problems. After all, who knows how a classless or syndicalized society would

---

[23] The theoretical foundations of democratic socialism have to a large extent been associated with the name of Eduard Bernstein. See Peter Gay, *The Dilemma of Democratic Socialism: Eduard Bernstein's Challenge to Marx* (New York: Collier Books, 1962).

[24] "Social Democratic Party of Germany," *Basic Program of the Social Democratic Party of Germany,* Adopted at the Bad Godesburg Congress (Bonn, 1959), p. 10.

really work and what the vision of such a society would tell us about how to deal with inflation and unemployment? Thus, Karl Mannheim can speak of "the chiliastic mentality" referring to the conception of the total transformation of society issuing in an unspecified millenium.[25] The process of transformation, "the revolution," becomes an end in itself rather than a means of improving the lot of the workers. The revolution is the ultimate end; little thought is given to the precise structure of the postrevolutionary order. Thus, eschatological ideologism involves a confusion of ends and means.

The irrelevance of eschatological ideologies such as pure Marxism became acutely apparent whenever the SPD found itself faced with the actual or potential responsibility of governing the country. Thus, in the late nineteenth century, the SPD sensing an opportunity to acquire power within the confines of the existing system, allowed the reformist wing of the party under Ferdinand Lassalle to prevail. This resulted in the reformist Gotha program of 1875, much to the dismay of Karl Marx himself.[26] The repressive antisocialist policies of Bismarck rendered the radical revolutionary ideologies more appealing, resulting in what Carl Schorske calls the Erfurt Synthesis of 1891.[27] This was a platform divided into two parts: a statement of ultimate objectives involving the overthrow of the capitalist order and a statement of immediate aims that could be attained prior to this overthrow, aims involving the amelioration of the working and living conditions of German workers. Marx recognized that these improvements would weaken the revolutionary fervor of the workers, and he thus opposed them. But the original impetus behind the revolutionary ideology was that it was ostensibly the only or best means of improving the lot of the workers. Now this amelioration is opposed as detracting from the revolution. The revolution, once a means or of instrumental value, was transformed by Marx and his followers into an end or ultimate value.

The dilemma of the SPD with its conflicting ideological imperatives came to a head when the party found itself governing the nation at the time of the outbreak of the First World War. Nationalism and the logic of socialist internationalism were antithetical concepts; a minority was loyal to the latter, but the party elite opted for the former. At this point, the SPD slogan "to this system, no man and no penny" was easily displaced by the slogan "in the hour of danger we will not leave the fatherland in the lurch."[28] Accordingly, the party's two most visible unrepentant Marxian purists, Karl Liebknecht and Rosa Luxemburg, were assassinated at the behest of the now-patriotic SPD leadership. Their "crime" was

---

[25] Karl Mannheim, *Ideology and Utopia* (New York: Harcourt Brace and World Harvest Books, 1936), pp. 224–225.
[26] Karl Marx, *Critique of the Gotha Program* (New York: International Publishers, 1935), p. 14.
[27] Karl Schorske, *German Social Democracy, 1905–1917: The Development of the Great Schism* (New York: Wiley Science Editions, 1955).
[28] *Ibid.*, p. 285.

that they led the "Sparticist" uprising of January 1919, an abortive attempt to bring about a proletarian revolution against the now-right-wing SPD provisional government.

The irrelevance of Marxist revolutionary ideology, given its utopian and millenarian character, to the processing of issues in any industrial society is undoubtedly a major consideration in its abandonment, either explicity—or, in the case of the CPSU, tacitly—by those parties faced with or aspiring to the responsibility of governing—that is, of processing real issues. Thus, parties with an ostensibly Marxist base tend to ignore the logical entailments of classic Marxism when governing a country or seriously engaging in the electoral process for both tactical and theoretical considerations. The tactical consideration is that the ideology places an intolerable upper limit on party support for increasingly aggregated party systems. The theoretical consideration is that the ideology does not generate answers to major questions with which these parties must deal.

Kirkheimer also pinpoints the Austrian Socialist Party along with the SPD as epitomizing this process of deideologization.[29] Rodney Steifbold reports that Austrian campaigns are still conducted in terms of extreme and intense partisan rhetoric evoking such recriminatory ideological symbols as "clerical facism" or "a communist-socialist popular front."[30] The pragmatism of the top elite and low-intensity partisanship of the Austrian masses appear to be contrasted with the direct opposite of these traits on the part of the party activists who conduct campaigns. Austrian campaigns are conducted to mobilize latent support of each party in its respective layer (subculture). An uncommitted floating vote is very small in this segmented system; hence, the logic of the British and American models is not applicable. In a classic model of the logic of democratic party and voting behavior, Anthony Downs postulated that because both parties in a two-party system compete for the same uncommitted center, rationality demands convergence and moderation of their programs and ideologies.[31] Such a center is not found in Austria with its bifurcated, segmented society. Downs recognizes that in such a bipolar situation, extremism becomes rational.[32] It appears that the appeal of the Austrian parties is limited to their respective layers; they can hardly be held up as the epitome of parties transformed from ideological to "catchall."

Besides the SPD, perhaps Kirkheimer's most defensible example of a party system so transformed is the French. The Fifth Republic with the enormous

---

[29] Kirkheimer, *op. cit.,* p. 187.

[30] Rodney Stiefbold, "Consociational Democracy and Segmented Pluralism in Austria: Problems of Political Stability and Change," *Politics in Europe,* Martin O. Heisler ed. (New York: David McKay, 1974), pp. 143–144.

[31] Anthony Downs, *op. cit.,* pp. 116–119. Downs, however, assumes a unimodal distribution of opinion.

[32] *Ibid.,* p. 120.

appeal of Gaullism has seen the development of a hegemonic and partially aggregated party system in contrast to the fragmented system of the Third and Fourth Republics. The value of the prize of control of the presidency may have contributed to the rationality of a broader, less ideological appeal. The Gaullist Party, the UNR (National Republican Union), perhaps most typifies this broad aggregative appeal among French parties. In any event, French electoral competition increasingly has come to take on a dichotomous character of Gaullists versus anti-Gaullists.

The anti-Gaullists, however, consist of several left-oriented parties that have not as easily shed their ideological views.[33] This is particularly true of the French socialists, who "reject social democracy as a compromise with the bourgeoisie."[34] This relatively rigid Marxist position is even implicit in the former name of the party, French Section of the Workers' International (SFIO). (The French SFIO has in recent years merged into a federation of the left. This federation is dominated by the former SFIO (now simply the Socialists) and includes other parties, such as the Unified Socialist Party (PSU), that are even more doctrinaire socialists.) Contrast this with the Social Democrats in Sweden, Denmark, Germany, and Switzerland or with the Labour Party in Britain, Australia, New Zealand, Norway, and the Netherlands. Both names eschew implications of overt affiliation with the Marxist "workers' international."

The term *Labour Party* is especially free from the taint of revolutionary socialism. It connotes the parliamentary representation of the trade union movement. The trade union movement relies on the tactic of collective bargaining, which is generally within a private enterprise system. It does not work as well when the employer is the state (especially when the state is the monolithic entity found in the Soviet Union).

Thus, the Australian Labour Party has always been more of a trade union than a socialist party. Its first platforms at the turn of the century omitted any reference to socialism, collectivism, or nationalism. From 1903 to 1947 its platform was dichotomized into a "fighting platform"—the immediate, serious, programmatic goals on which a given election was fought—and a "general platform"—a long range of philosophic goals including partial nationalization of major means of production, reminiscent of the aforementioned Erfurt Synthesis of the SPD. For a party seeking to aggregate a national majority, the image of socialist objectives, even one that had only an expressive function instead of a statement of serious legislative intent, worked to the electoral detriment of the party. For example, Labour leader Ron Chifley's plan to nationalize the banks and provide free

---

[33] Frank Wilson, "The Persistence of Ideologism on the French Democratic Left," *Politics in Western European Democracies: Patterns and Problems,* Gary Byrne and Kenneth Pederson, eds. (New York: John Wiley & Sons, 1971), pp. 217–232.
[34] *Ibid.,* 226.

medicine to those in need in 1947 was successfully used by the Liberal Party leader Robert Menzies in the 1949 campaign against the ALP. Menzies argued, "In 1946 you could reasonably vote for Labour supposing that it was a party of reform and not of socialization. In 1949 it was clear that a Labour vote is a vote for the socialist objective."[35]

The point is that socialism as an explicit and relatively coherent doctrine—even the democratic, revisionist variety—has never had wide enough support in the democratic West to provide a viable principal basis for a party seeking to aggregate enough support to acquire a majority of seats in the national legislature.

Parties of the democratic left can be found throughout Europe. In addition to the aforementioned names, some are simply called Socialist Party (Austria, Belgium, Italy). While Kirkheimer wrote of deideologization as a process, these parties have (with the exception of Austria, Germany, Italy, and France) always been relatively free from doctrinal rigidity. The situation in Italy is somewhat confusing. A pragmatic, nondoctrinaire wing of the Italian Socialist Party split off under the leadership of Giuseppe Saragat under the name of Social Democrats in 1947. In 1966 the party was reunited with Pietro Nenni's PSI when Nenni broke off his close association with the Italian communists. However, the right split off a year later as the Unitary Socialist Party (PSV), while the old left retained the name Socialist (PSI).

In sum, with the exception of the Social Democratic Party of Germany, those parties of the left that emphasized doctrine and principle (the Austrian Socialists, the Italian Socialists, the French SFIO) by and large still do so, while those parties of the left that have broader, more pragmatic policies (the British, Australian, Norwegian, and Dutch Labour Parties; the Swedish, Swiss, and Danish Social Democrats; the Belgian Socialists) appear to have always eschewed an espousal of Marxist or even explicit socialist principles as their primary appeal. It is hard to find much support for Kirkheimer's thesis of deideologization as a *process* here.

Further, a trend may be discerned for a reassertion of such principles of the doctrinaire left in the increasing proliferation of left-wing defections from the ideologically amorphous or bourgeoisie-oriented social democratic, labor, or socialist parties. After the Nenni and Saragat socialists were reunited in Italy, a group of left-wing socialists bolted to form the Socialist Party of Proletarian Unity (PSIUP). A Socialist Labour Party has gained some strength to the left of the Norwegian Labour Party. In the Netherlands, Democrats '66, a party entering the Tweed Kamer (lower house) first in 1967 and appealing to young, urban, counterculture types, and the Democratic Socialists of 1970 have cut into the sup-

---

[35] George Healy, *A.L.P.: The Story of the Labour Party* (Brisbane, Australia: Jacaranda Press, 1955), p. 184.

port of the traditional parties. (To a large extent, the support of these new parties appears to have come from the three major confessional or religious parties.) Denmark's Socialist Peoples' Party has grown up on the left of the Social Democrats in that country, obtaining 17 of 175 seats in the 1971 Folkting. The French PSU also exemplifies this trend.

This trend may be interpreted in either of two ways. On one hand, it may be read as a caveat and qualification to the Kirkheimer thesis of the progressive deideologization and aggregation of the European party systems. On the other hand, it may be read as a reaction to the increasing "bourgeoisification" of traditional left-wing parties. That is, the traditional left-wing parties have moved so far toward the center that their previous supporters on the left edges of the democratic left-right continuum can no longer support the traditional left. This rise of doctrinaire parties of the left may be read as a reaction to and thus confirmation of the process Kirkheimer was describing. Similarly, the Eugene McCarthy and George McGovern movements in the United States may be viewed as suggesting limits to how far toward the center right a left-of-center catchall party may drift while keeping its left-wing support. A party may not totally ignore its principles or its image.

Christian Democracy

The center right in most industrial democracies is represented by parties with a confessional base; that is, the parties espouse the principles of a religion and direct their appeal to religious people. The parties have various names: the Christian Democratic Union of West Germany with its Bavarian ally, the Christian Social Union (CDU/CSU); the Italian Christian Democrats (DC); the People's Party of Austria (OVP, called Christian Socials before the Second World War); the Belgian Christian Social Party (PSC, formerly the Catholic Party); the Popular Republican Movement of France (MRP, defunct since September 1967); the Christian People's Party of Norway; a new Christian Party in Denmark; Luxembourg's Social Christian Party; and the Netherland's three confessional parties, the Catholic Party (KVP), and two orthodox Calvinist parties, the Christian Historical Union and the Anti-Revolutionary Party.

Most of the parties in this center-right religious pattern are of a type that is commonly called Christian democracy parties. They largely rely on a Roman Catholic base of electoral support. The exceptions are the Norwegian and Danish parties and the two Protestant parties in the Netherlands. These two parties, the Anti-Revolutionary Party and the Christian Historical Union, differ more organizationally than doctrinally. The former is a tightly organized party with a mass membership; the latter is more loosely organized. A dispute over tactics caused the defection of the Christian Historical Union from the Anti-Revolutionary Party in

1894. (The name of the latter party stems from the original purpose of the party opposition to the liberal, secular ideals of the French Revolution of 1789.) The Catholic base of the other parties has been deemphasized somewhat in recent years, affirming the Kirkheimer thesis to that extent. The deideologization varies somewhat from nation to nation. In some systems, such as West Germany, the party (CDU/CSU) has successfully appealed to some religious Protestants and many opponents of the SPD. There are limits to the appeal of any such party, however. The Christian Democratic parties could not appeal to a militantly secular clientele no matter how doctrinally amorphous they may become on a left-to-right spectrum.

Similarly, the prewar Catholic Party of Belgium changed its name in 1945 to the Christian Social Party (PSC), thereby severing its explicit ties to the church in an effort to broaden its appeal.

These parties are limited in their potential appeal by the strength of their adherence to Christian principles in conjunction with an increasing secularization of the masses in most industrial nations. In the long run, essentially two choices are open to these parties. On one hand, they can abandon the religious basis of their appeal and try to co-opt the center-right of any religious creed or lack thereof. In a situation characterized by an increasing aggregated and bifurcated political conflict, the logic of vote maximization will pressure a party to opt for this strategy. The CDU/CSU of West Germany, for instance, seems to be moving in this direction. Some data presented by Juan Linz from the early 1950s indicate that a minority of CDU working supporters attend church regularly.[36] In the data presented, however, more than two-thirds of the party's supporters were Catholic. The preference of Catholic women who attended church with some regularity for the CDU was especially strong in these and other data. Among Protestants, regular churchgoers are significantly more likely to vote CDU than those who attend church seldom or never. The religious element in the party's ideological view has an effect on voter preference. The effect, however, is probably to attract a number of working-class Catholics (and perhaps some religious Protestants) who would otherwise, on a socioeconomic basis, prefer the SPD rather than to alienate many secular voters who would prefer to vote against the SPD (that is, vote right on a class-interest basis).

Similarly, the PSC of Belgium continues to attract many Catholic votes on the basis of its confessional image. Many Catholics, especially in Flanders, continue to view it as the Catholic party. This appears to be a partially successful strategy of having one's cake and eating it at the same time. The party is able to retain its

[36] Juan Linz, "Cleavage and Consensus in West German Politics in the Early Fifties," *Party Systems and Voter Alignments,* Seymour Lipset and Stein Rokkan, eds. (New York: The Free Press, 1967), p. 292 (Table 6).

church-based image for its religiously Catholic clientele while changing its name to attract less religiously oriented people.

The Christian Democrat Party of Italy not only attracts many voters on the basis of its religious appeal, especially in the more religious southern half of the country; the DC further maintains explicit links to the Roman Catholic church. It relies on the mobilizing effects of the priesthood to turn out the DC vote, and it carefully adheres to a Vatican line with regard to Catholic social policy (such as the attempt to reinstate the ban on divorce). As Raphael Zariski cogently put it, "when religious considerations are at stake, the DC ceases to be a catchall party and becomes a party of principle."[37] In other matters, however, the DC has sought a broad clientele on the basis of ambiguous principles (or lack thereof). Former party secretary Aldo Moro inadvertently responded to a question on the DC emphasis on prudence by stating with more than a tiny grain of truth, "the DC emphasizes everything."[38] The DC appears to be catchall, but, as a result of the strength of the Vatican in Italy, the DC is less deconfessionalized than other Christian parties in Europe. Whether the confessional basis of such parties continues to be on balance advantageous seems to depend on the strength of long-term secularization trends in industrial and postindustrial societies.

The explicitness of the Catholic appeal of Christian Democratic parties has generally declined throughout Europe. Thus, the CDU/CSU cannot afford to write off at one fell swoop the many Protestant or partially secularized citizens of the Federal Republic of Germany.

The Austrian People's Party (OVP) has also become deconfessionalized since the Second World War, although, like the other parties of Christian Democracy, its appeal to militantly secular portions of the society is limited.

The case of the Dutch Catholic Party (KVP) clearly exemplifies the limits on the extent to which confessional parties can broaden their appeal. Faced with a declining appeal to a fixed clientele (especially in losing younger voters to the newer parties like Democrats '66), the KVP attempted to negotiate a merger with the nation's two Protestant parties, the Anti-Revolutionary Party and the Christian Historical Union. The ARP, however, perceived that the strength of the party lay in its ideological purity. By mobilizing the faithful, the ARP had succeeded in remaining an influential force in the nation's badly fragmented party system, and it therefore wanted to maintain the party's autonomous identity in a loose confessional confederation. The effort of the KVP to broaden its appeal and eschew its Catholic image is hampered by the fact that most of its activists and voters are Catholic. Thus, the party is caught in a kind of vicious circle. To

---

[37] Raphael Zariski, *Italy: The Politics of Uneven Development* (Hinsdale, IL: The Dryden Press, 1972), p. 173.
[38] *Ibid.*, p. 171.

broaden its appeal, the party must attract more Protestant support; however, to attract more Protestant support, the party must broaden its image."[39]

The Secular Right

Several conservative or center-right parties in Europe do not have a confessional base. Perhaps the most famous of these is the Union for New Republic (UNR) of France, the Gaullist Party. This party, a successor of the Fourth Republic's Rally of the French People (RPF) had as its basic raison d'être support on a personal level for General DeGaulle and his political aspirations. As such, it lacks a coherent ideology or set of programs; however, in following the policy predisposition of the general, it has definitely been right of center. The non-Gaullist conservative element in France, operating under the party label of National Federation of Independent Republicans (FRNI), has supported the Gaullists on most issues. Accordingly, a broader Gaullist federation was formed in 1968 to cover not only the UNR, but also FRNI candidates called the Union for the Defense of the Republic (UDR). The identity of the FRNI has not been lost, however, as indicated by the successful opposition of Valéry Giscard D'Estaing to the UDR candidate Jacques Chaban-Delmas in the 1974 French presidential elections. After eliminating Chaban-Delmas on the first ballot, Giscard was able to attract the Gaullist vote in the runoff and thereby defeat the candidate of the United Left Federation (FGDS), Francois Mitterand.

Of course, the British Conservative Party, sometimes referred to as the Tories, is also free from explicit church affiliation. The Tories, however, are more supportive of the established church and the idea of the religious basis of society than Labour.[40] The Tories also stand more or less for a number of other principles, but these principles are not formulated with great coherence, nor are they rigidly held. The differences between the philosophical bases of British parties may be characterized as differences in emphasis. The Tory stand on free enterprise, for example, may be translated as saying the Tories are not prepared to accept as much social welfare legislation or as much nationalization of industry as the Labourites advocate. Tories are less inclined to sympathy with the claims of organized labor (especially the Trade Union Congress) and more inclined to sympathy with the claims of British industry (especially the Federation of British Industries). Yet, since half their vote is from the working class, the British Conservatives have been forced to accept a managed economy to a much greater extent than, say, the American Republican Party seems prepared to do.

---

[39] Steven B. Wolinetz, "Electoral Change and Attempts to Build Catch-All Parties in the Netherlands," Paper presented to the Annual Meeting of the Canadian Political Science Association, Montreal, August, 1973, p. 8.

[40] Quentin Hogg (the former Lord Hailsham), *The Case for Conservatism* (Harmondsworth, England: Penguin Books, 1947), pp. 16–23.

The critical differences between the philosophical bases of British parties seems to us to lie in the area of attitude toward basic institutions and the nature of people. The Tories are more inclined to support established institutions (the church, the monarchy, the empire) than are Labourites. The Tories avow a belief in the natural inequality of man—a natural hierarchical order of society in contradistinction to Labour's greater emphasis on egalitarian values.[41] The Tories tend to accept an organic view of society, the idea that society is an essential reality that is more than the sum of the individuals comprimising it. The Tories feel that the value of the individual derives from his role in the organic society. The Labour view entails a priority for individual well-being over some abstract concept of the good of society.

It must be cautioned that neither party's ideological base is very explicit or coherent, as suggested by the British "ideology of pragmatism" discussed in Chapter 3. The self-image of the Tories is more explicitly expediential than that of Labour. Labour, as with most parties that originate as a social movement outside the legislature instead of a faction within the legislature,[42] has had more of a programmatic raison d'être than the Tories.[43] For example, legislative proposals of postwar Labour governments were geared to implementing a party program (platform) unprecedented in British politics.[44]

In Scandinavia, non-Christian conservative parties dominate the business-oriented and -supported right. This is probably due to the secular nature of Scandinavian society, which does not afford the social base for a flourishing Christian democracy. Norway, Sweden, and Denmark all have a conservative party.

By contrast, in those nations in which religion is a highly salient political force, the conservative party, if any, tends to be overshadowed by the party of Christian democracy. The Republican Party in Italy is an example of a conservative party in the shadow of Christian democracy.

The obvious exception is the success of the UNR/UDR in France overshadowing the waning MRP. This may perhaps be understood by the extent that DeGaulle himself supported and therefore implicitly represented Catholic values or interests. The FRNI has not been one of the stronger parties in either the Fourth or Fifth Republics despite the fact that their man, Giscard D'Estaing, is now president.

Canada is an interesting case in that the segment of the population to whom

---

[41] The justifications of rank and hierarchy have shifted from a theological or cosmological view (it is part of a divine plan) to a sociological view in which differential capacities must be translated into differences in function and role if society is to work efficiently. Thus, Tories feel they should govern because they are more fit to govern. See Samuel Beer, *British Politics in the Collectivist Age* (New York: Alfred A. Knopf, 1965), pp. 10–13.
[42] LaPalombara and Weiner, *op. cit.,* pp. 9–10.
[43] S. E. Finer, *Comparative Government* (New York: Basic Books, 1971), p. 165.
[44] Beer, *op. cit.,* p. 179.

religion is apparently most salient tends to support the party that is ostensibly more left of center, the Liberals, because the Liberals have supported political decentralization and provincial autonomy. Consequently, the Canadian Progressive Conservative Party (PC) does not generally rely on Canada's major religious segment for support. The PC is clearly a secular conservative party.

Parties of Classic Liberalism

If a trend exists for European parties to lose their principled base, this trend may be most explicitly apparent in the case of European liberal parties. We are here using *liberal* in the classic nineteenth-century sense of the term. Liberalism refers to an emphasis on the value of the individual relative to the value of institutions (including the institution of the state). It refers to a minimization of restraints on human choice. It may be thought of as stressing *freedom from,* not *freedom to.* It entails opposition to the perpetuation of aristocratic and other ascribed privileges. It seeks political equality and does not concern itself with social and economic equality. Specific policy entailments of nineteenth-century liberalism included manhood suffrage, anticlericalism and laissez-faire.

Most of the goals of nineteenth-century liberalism have been achieved in the West. Not only manhood suffrage, but universal adult suffrage is everywhere a reality. The increasing secularization of Western industrial society has contributed to a decline in the political role, influence, and prerequisites of the institutional church. The rise of first Keynesian, then welfare economics, is an indicator of the fact that laissez-faire has never been a viable economic theory for a complex industrial society. It has been recognized in Europe and the British Commonwealth more clearly and quickly that the market never has been self-regulating.[45] The assumptions of this kind of economic theory are manifestly untenable. Laissez-faire economic theory presumes demand to be a function of price, but demand is clearly not totally elastic. The assumption of people pursuing their rational economic self-interests postulates an absence of competing motivations and the information to act rationally. The concentration of economic resources to the point of negating market competition is an inevitable concomitant of the growth of technology. Laissez-faire was a nineteenth-century rationale for opposition to mercantilism—the older economic theory that the wealth of nations was a function the quality of gold and silver they possessed. It was an argument in favor of free trade. Although nations still strive for a favorable balance of trade, the principle of mercantilism is no longer adduced, and laissez-faire as an economic theory is considered manifestly atavistic.

---

[45] Karl Polyani, *The Great Transformation* (New York: Rinehart and Co., 1944), is a classic argument that the concept of the self-regulating market, a foundation of nineteenth-century civilization, has collapsed and that the recognition of this can be traced to poor law legislation well back into the nineteenth century beginning with Britain's Speenhamland Law of 1795.

Thus, liberalism, once one of the great political forces of Western democracies, has been left without a doctrine. The principled base of liberal parties has become atavistic. To the extent that liberal parties have continued to use the rhetoric of their old principles, such as anticlericalism in France, they have appeared as recriminatory—trying to fan the embers of dead controversies of the past. Liberal parties have abandoned these principles, and they have appeared superfluous—standing for nothing in particular. Although they often appear to direct their appeal to the widest possible audience, they appeal to very few because they represent no specific claims or interests.

Like Christian democracy, liberalism represents a philosophic pattern represented in most European democracies by parties bearing a variety of names. Unlike the Christian parties, European liberal parties have everywhere been sharply declining in political importance (as measured by parliamentary representation), especially since the Second World War. The name "Liberal Party" applies to representatives of this tradition in England, Australia, Sweden, Norway, Belgium, and Italy. The Dutch liberals are officially called People's Party for Freedom and Democracy (VVD); the Belgian Party is officially the Party of Liberty and Progress (PLP); the French party was called the Radical Socialist Party. The last name was misleading because it was neither radical nor socialist in the modern meanings of those terms. It was radical in that it uncompromisingly opposed the monarchy during the French Revolution of 1789. It was certainly not socialist because, as a free market party, the radicals have stood foresquare for the defense of property. In recent elections the radicals, with an independent electoral representation diminished to insignificance, have become largely absorbed in a federation of left-wing parties, Federation of the Democratic and Socialist Left (FGDS) with the old SFIO. The radicals stood for a rigid anticlericalism and a defense of French republicanism (as opposed to monarchal or fascist alternatives), issues that are increasingly less salient for contemporary France. The liberal tradition in West Germany is represented by the Free Democratic Party and in Switzerland by Radical Democrats.

Ironically, liberal parties have acquired a conservative image in recent decades. Their defense of property and laissez-faire lines them up with conservative or Christian democratic parties on domestic issues. The Belgian PLP has more explicitly aroused this conservative stance in disavowing its erstwhile anticlerical stance. The party has thus attracted some Catholic following, and in the 1965 election it gained some 28 seats and joined the government in 1966. Although the party lost some strength in the 1971 election, it was able to join a minority government with the Flemish wing of the PSC in 1974. It certainly continues to be a vital force in Belgian politics.

The Australian Liberal Party, partially filling a vacuum on the nation's right, has become a conservative force. The Swedish liberals are an exception to this trend in that they have abandoned their insistence on laissez-faire. They are mainly distinguished from the Social Democrats on the issue by the amount of social welfare legislation they favor.

Liberals have also participated in Norwegian anti-Labour coalition cabinets since 1965. The Free Democrats of West Germany had formerly allied with the CDU in opposition to the perceived socialist orientation of the SPD. The 1959 ideological about-face of the SPD, discussed above, opened new options for the Free Democrats, and they are presently in coalition with the governing SPD.

The options for liberals appear to be twofold. In a fragmented party system or with a vacuum on the right, they may attain a measure of political success (defined by participation in governments) by acquiring the image of a domestically conservative party (defined as opposition to state socialism or extension of social welfare policies). But they may be able to operate as a balance-of-power force exercising a parliamentary influence far out of proportion to their miniscule representation. Their amorphous ideological base ideally suits the kind of unprincipled hopscotching their balance-of-power role requires.

These roles are not mutually exclusive. The Belgian PLP, for instance, combines the two strategies, as does the German Free Democratic Party. The Liberal Party of Britain has tried to emphasize the balance-of-power strategy. Unfortunately, from their point of view, minority governments have been rare in Britain. The Swiss radicals, on the other hand, have become a party of business and the lower middle class. In a very fragmented party system faithfully reflected through a highly proportional electoral system, the Swiss radicals have maintained a major influence with something under a quarter of the votes.

In a few instances, parties of the liberal tradition have experienced a somewhat atavistic resurgence on the coattails of a charismatic leader—for example, Jean Jacques Servan-Schrieber, who gained a measure of personal political success in the early 1960s despite his leadership of the French radicals. Part of the recent measured success of the British Liberal Party may be due more to the personal attractiveness of its leader, Jeremy Thorpe, than to the attractiveness of the party itself. That could hardly be construed as a formula for long-range political success, however. The charismatic Bertrial Ohlin contributed to a measure of liberal success in Sweden from the 1940s to the 1960s.

Agrarian and Center Parties

The radical or liberal parties occupy the center or center right (sometimes the center left). To the extent that the parties are identified with the center right on one hand and the parties of the industrial proletariat identified as Marxist on the other, separate parties sometimes emerge on the center left. The clearest example of this is the Italian Republican Party (PRI), which differs from the Italian liberals in that the PRI is not committed to laissez-faire. The party has tended to be squeezed between the liberals on the right and the Social Democrats (the Saragat socialists) on the left; consequently, it has not had electoral success.

With their declining clientele, agrarian parties have attempted to change their image and appeal and move into this center-left spot. The declining clientele of agrarian parties is, of course, due to the diminishing percentage of the population engaged in agricultural pursuits as the process of industrialization proceeds. The former agrarian and now center parties of Norway and Sweden fit into this category. As with the former Catholic parties now striving for a catchall basis, changing the name of the party does not overnight change either a party's clientele or its policy preferences. The Norwegian Centre Party still relies on strong agrarian support, and its realization of the real limits of its appeal and corresponding concern for the interests of its agrarian clientele caused the Centre Party to bring down Norway's first nonsocialist coalition in 30 years. Premier Per Borten resigned in March 1971 after it was disclosed that he had tried to sabotage negotiations for Norway to join the European Economic Community. Borten and the Centre Party perceived that membership in the EEC would adversely affect agrarian interests in Norway. While the Swedish Centre Party attracts support from small business and white-collar workers, "... agrarian elements continue to provide the major source of Centre electoral strength."[46]

The Limited Validity of Kirkheimer's Thesis

It must be concluded that Kirkheimer's thesis of a process of deideologization and the rise of catchall parties is of limited applicability. Only three party systems have undergone a significant process of aggregation (that is, sharply decreased the number of parties): Austria, the Federal Republic of Germany, and France. The first two can only be said to have been aggregated when compared with their prewar days. Futhermore, although the Austrian party system has been aggregated to two major parties, the persistence of the *lager* mentality, referred to above, hardly qualifies the Austrian parties as ideologically bland. The Social Democratic Party of Germany is the prime example of a transformation to catchall status. Others mentioned by Kirkheimer, such as the Gaullist UNR, have been ideologically bland from their inception; thus, they can hardly have been transformed. Other European parties not mentioned by Kirkheimer have either failed to disavow their principled base or have been ideologically bland from the beginning.

It is worth recalling in this regard that the avowed desire of several confessional parties—the Belgian Christian Social Party or the Dutch Catholic Party, for instance—to eschew their image as Catholic parties has been rendered difficult by

---

[46] M. Donald Hancock, *Sweden: The Politics of Post-Industrial Change* (Hinsdale, IL: The Dryden Press, 1972), p. 122.

the fact that both the party activists and the party supporters are mostly Catholics. It is a kind of vicious circle whereby a more Protestant party is both a prerequisite and a consequence of attracting more Protestant (or secular) support. Again, it seems clear that a party cannot become a catchall simply by declaring itself to be so. Images of parties are acquired over long periods of time; accordingly, these images can only be transformed or shaken over time.

Ideology and Electoral Base

It thus appears that the coherence, rigidity, and content of a party's program or ideology are primarily affected by the party's basis of electoral support. The Catholic base of support in the Catholic parties renders it difficult for the parties to avoid supporting policies of salience to perceived Catholic interests. The Liberal Party of Canada, due to its support of political decentralization and provincial autonomy, attracted the support of French Canadian Catholics concerned with subcultural defense. As it came to rely on that support, the Liberal Party began to be pulled toward the right by the conservatively oriented French Canadians. It is not entirely clear whether the moderate, nonsocialist stance of social democratic parties attracted middle-class support or whether the middle-class support for the parties forced them to become or remain ideologically bland.

In this regard, Ronald Inglehardt notes a difference in value priority between a concern for economic security and what he calls "post-bourgeoisie values" (for example, civil liberties, dignity of the individual, etc.).[47] He further shows that younger respondents, raised in a situation of affluence, are more likely to take material needs (acquisitive values) for granted and give greater priority to post-bourgeoisie values. Inglehart projects from his data that the prevalence of post-bourgeoisie values is likely to increase. All of this is likely to affect seriously the basis of political partisanship. Throughout Europe, adherents of postbourgeoisie values prefer parties of the left (British Labour, the French FGDS, Democrats '66 in the Netherlands, PSIUP in Italy, etc.).[48] Either parties catering to this post-bourgeoisie clientele must emphasize a concern for these values and thus neglect the old socioeconomic concerns on which many of them were originally based, or, alternatively, if they still cater to their traditional older working-class clientele, they must become more conservative parties of defense of material well-being. Class-based voting should decline, and in those areas where traditional parties of the left have opted to cater to postbourgeoisie clientele, conservative parties should attract more working-class support.[49] Conservative parties, if they are to attract

---

[47] Ronald Inglehart, "The Silent Revolution in Europe: Intergenerational Change in Post-Industrial Societies," *The American Political Science Review,* Vol. LXV, No. 4, December, 1971, pp. 991–1017 at p. 993.

[48] *Ibid.,* pp. 1009–1011.

[49] *Ibid.,* pp. 992 and 1015.

working-class support, will have to devote some attention to acquisitive values. Thus, Christian democratic parties are under pressure to move from their strictly religious philosophical basis. To this extent, Christian democratic parties are given incentives to become somewhat more catchall than strictly church parties. (Perhaps the term should be catchmore instead of catchall.) All parties are clearly limited at some point in their potential appeal. Some voters are even beyond the potential reach of the notoriously bland major American parties. As long as there is some difference in center of gravity between parties, as long as parties advocate anything at all, however amorphous, certain interests and points of view are going to be alienated. Classifying parties as expediential or programmatic clearly involves a continuum. There are no pure types in the real world.

The ideological character of a party also appears to be in part a function of the culture in which that party operates. Parties tend to be ideologically amorphous to the extent that the culture in which they operate can be characterized as pragmatic. Even parties in relatively aggregated systems conduct their campaigns in terms of ideological partisan rhetoric in an ideological culture such as in France and Austria. The only clear example of transformation from party of principle to expediential party, the SPD, is found in the only culture that has been transformed from an ideological one to a relatively pragmatic one.[50]

It appears from the cases of France and Austria that a party system can become aggregated without becoming deideologized. The persistence of an ideological style in the campaigns of these nations has already been discussed, as has the bifurcation of political conflict in Austria. We have mentioned the federation of the French left, the FGDS. This is one of several more or less loose alliances that have emerged in the Gaullist era to combat the dominant strength of the Gaullists. The old center republican (MRP) and the French conservatives (CNIP) have more or less merged under a common banner, Democratic Center (CD). A number of left-oriented MRP refugees have formed a group called *Objectif '72,* which has not quite avowed the status of a party. The lack of coherence of these loose confederations, whose basic—if not sole—raison d'être seems to be opposition to the Gaullists, and the fact that more than one group remains suggest the continuing salience of an ideological style in France.

Antisystem Parties

Several European nations possess a significant ideological tradition that is difficult for most Anglo-Americans to comprehend: opposition to the existing political system. Here again, we are dealing with imprecise boundaries between those parties that are in opposition to the system and those that are not. On the right,

---

[50] Sidney Verba, "Germany: The Remaking of Political Culture," *Political Culture and Political Development,* Lucien Pye and Sidney Verba, eds. (Princeton: Princeton University Press, 1965), pp. 130–170.

for example, there is a highly nationalistic party in the Federal Republic of Germany called the National Democratic Party (not to be confused with Canada's New Democratic Party, which is on the left of the political spectrum). The German NDP has been characterized as neo-Nazi, a label that party leader Thadden disavows. However, most West Germans who are either ex-Nazi or consider themselves present Nazis support the party. Many party activists are former Nazis. The NDP received a disturbingly high percentage of support during the years of the Grand Coalition of the two major parties because the NDP inherited a virtual monopoly of opposition by default. Since the breakup of the Grand Coalition, the NDP has been unable to meet the five percent minimum vote requirement to secure parliamentary representation.

Similarly, the Italian Social Movement (MSI) has been labeled a neofascist party, although it denies any intention of setting up a fascist dictatorship. But Italians who were associated with or who espouse enthusiasm for Italy's Mussolini period tend to support this party, which continues to draw four to five percent of the Italian vote. Recent events have shown some of its members ready to seek attainment of political goals through violent means. Thus, although it advocates cooperation with other right-wing parties, its members lack democratic toleration for the political left.[51]

Although atavistically active well into the Fourth Republic, the French Monarchist Party has died out. However, the Italian Monarchist Party (PDIUM) continues to exist, although drawing less than two percent of the national vote. It is arguable whether advocating a restoration of the House of Savoy in place of a presidential head of state (meaning the monarch would assume the symbolic and ceremonial instead of the political role) constitutes "structural opposition" to the political system. The monarchists' position does not prevent them from seeking cooperation with parties of the center and moderate right.

As Robert Dahl points out, opposition to the system (he calls it "structural opposition") "is for all practical purposes a monopoly of the Communists. . . ."[52] The radical right is too small to be of significance anywhere in democratic Europe or the older Commonwealth. It is argued, however, that European communist parties are much more expediential in tactics and style than commonly assumed.

The two strongest European communist parties outside of the Soviet bloc are in Italy and France, in that order (as measured by the average percentage of national vote in postwar elections). The Italian communist party leader, Palmiro Togliatti, coined the phrase *polycentrism* to mean it is possible to have numerous centers of power in the communist world. This amounted to a declaration of autonomy for

---

[51] Zarisski, *op. cit.*, p. 180, takes this position arguing that it "is more than just another party of the Right."

[52] Robert Dahl, "Patterns of Opposition," *Political Oppositions in Western Democracies, op. cit.*, p. 343.

the PCI from Kremlin (or Peking) control. The PCI has been consciously engaged in the effort to play electoral politics, to appeal to sentiments and interest of patriotic Italians, and to assuage fears that PCI control of the Italian government would render Italy a sattelite of the Kremlin. Accordingly, the PCI has supported many Catholic legislative demands, such as a ban on divorce, and publicly censured the Soviet invasion of Czechoslovakia in 1968. This stance of quasi-respectability has enabled the PCI to remain as the second strongest party in the country, garnering about 27 percent of the vote in the 1968 general election.

The base of support of the PCI is clearly that of Italy's have-nots. Eighty-six percent of the PCI vote in the 1958 election came from industrial workers, tenant farmers, and agricultural workers.[53] The PCI draws only 13 percent of its voters from the lower-middle class, and its support from the higher strata in the socioeconomic hierarchy is virtually nil. It appears that the intense efforts of the PCI to attract Catholic and middle-class votes[54] has made little impact on those segments of the population. The fact that only about two-fifths of the industrial working class voted communist in 1958 and 48 percent of them voted either communist or socialist (PSI or PSDI) is undoubtedly because of the conflicting pull of the Catholicism of Italian workers.

At the present writing, the glaring failure of the dominant and hegemonic DC to cope with Italy's massive social and economic problems appears to be enhancing the legitimacy of the PCI as the only plausible alternative. It remains to be seen whether the United States pressure to regard any communist political success as a threat to NATO can impede this rapidly increasingly legitimacy of Italy's communist party. It seems that many Italians are able to overlook the party's name and do not regard it as antisystem, while the formulators of American foreign policy regard all communists as a threat.

The French Communist Party has also attained a degree of legitimacy, especially among the industrial class from whence it draws about 70 percent of its votes.[55] The Party had played a leading role in the Resistance of the Second World War and emerged with 26 percent of the vote in the first postwar elections. The party has gradually declined in total support to the point of winning 20 percent in the 1973 elections. In both France and Italy, many communist votes are votes of protest against the status quo, not votes for revolution or a Stalinist police state.[56] In general, however, the French communists have not gone nearly as far as the Italian communists in declaring their independence of the Moscow party line.

---

[53] Adopted from Table 15 in Mattei Dogan, "Political Cleavage and Social Stratification in France and Italy," Lipset and Rokkan, *op. cit.,* p. 158.
[54] Described in Norman Kogan, "Italian Communism, The Working Class and Organized Catholicism," *Journal of Politics,* Vol. 28, August 1960, pp. 531–555.
[55] From data taken from the 1956 election and reproduced in Dogan, *op. cit.,* p. 156.
[56] *Ibid.,* p. 177.

The invasion of Czechoslavakia in 1968 generated an internal split within the party between elements wanting to condemn it and old-line Stalinists wanting to support any Soviet move. The party has been trying to "de-Stalinize" its image somewhat since the death of the communist leader, Maurice Thorez, in 1964. Thorez, who had led the party since 1930, had ossified the party ideologically. The death of Thorez and the inevitable bureaucratization of the party (as with all strong Communist Parties) has resulted in an ideological incoherency for the party. Nevertheless, the party has been unable to penetrate to the churchgoing Catholic segments of the population and upper socioeconomic strata. The difference in the level of rural support for the Communist Parties in France and Italy is probably due to the greater salience of Catholicism to the French farmers. The Italian tenant farmers possess an anticlerical tradition going back to the resentment of large church land holdings. Communism and socialism have penetrated only that smaller proportion of French farmers who have acquired the anticlerical orientation of the French Revolution.

The legitimacy of the French communists is limited, however. Consequently, the party has suffered under the electoral system of the Fifth Republic. Success under the two-ballot majority system, it will be recalled, depends on the capacity to enter alliances between the general elections and the runoff. Other parties had been unwilling to coalesce with the communists, leaving that party underrepresented regardless of its relative strength on the first ballot. It should be noted that the communists, under the rigid Thorez, also eschewed such alliances. Although not underrepresented in the National Assembly under the Fourth Republic, the communists were similarly excluded from the process of coalition formation in the making of cabinets. The communists were able to join the federation of the left under Mitterand for the 1972 elections, but that alliance still fell short of increasing their number of seats in the Assembly and certainly did not deny control of the presidency to the Gaullists.[57]

Explanations as to why antisystem or extremist parties gain legitimacy and significant support in some democratic nations and not in others generally refer back to the now-classic Lipset hypothesis. Defining stable democracy as 25 consecutive years of the absence of any political movement opposed to the democratic rules of the game, Lipset finds that this index is correlated with indexes of economic well-being, urbanization, industrialization, and level of education.[58] Extremist parties are suggested as being more prevalent in areas with lower levels of economic prosperity, economic development, and literacy. *Prevalent* means, to Lipset, extremist parties that garner 20 percent or more of the national vote, but, in the democratic

---

[57] George Rice, "Electoral Prospects for Non-Ruling Communist Parties," *American Journal of Political Science,* Vol. XVII, No. 3, August 1973, p. 609.

[58] Seymour Lipset, *Political Man* (New York: Doubleday Anchor Books, 1963), pp. 30–32.

nations under consideration here, they have been prevalent in essentially three situations: Italy, Third and Fourth Republics in France, and prewar Germany and Austria. By Lipset's criteria, extremist parties are prevalent in the postwar period in France and Italy; however, right-wing extremism has faded to practically nil, and the Communist Party support has gradually declined from a postwar high of 27 percent in 1946 to 20 percent in the 1972 elections in the Fifth French Republic.

A basic research strategy for comparative analysis is to ask what these systems, different in many respects, have in common besides the object of explanation (presence of extremist parties). Several characteristics seem immediately apparent. First, France and Italy shared a situation of cabinet instability (the Fifth French Republic is not really an exception because an authoritarian presidential system ended the possibility of cabinet instability). Second, they shared an absence of economic well-being *relative to their neighbors* in the Western world. We assume here that it matters less to an Italian that he has a higher per capita income than the average citizen of Botswana than that he faces a much higher rate of inflation than is present in the rest of Europe.

What this seems to indicate is that significant support for extremist parties becomes more probable when the existing system is widely perceived as incapable of solving those problems that its subjects have come to expect government to solve. We suggest that the immobility of political institutions in any system where citizens have never experienced material well-being is not particularly likely to generate social and political movements in opposition to the system.

Thus, both the Nazi and Communist Parties during the Weimar period in Germany could plausibly claim that the parties and structures of liberal democracy had failed to provide the values that Germans had come to expect. Caught in the worst inflation in Western history and great socioeconomic uncertainity, socialized into believing in past national glory while perceiving governmental acceptance of national humiliation in the aftermath of the First World War, and seeing a parliamentary system unable to decide on anything in a situation of extreme party proliferation, German citizens were understandably attracted to the alternatives of the antidemocratic right and left.

Similarly, the French saw a system of revolving-door governments during the Third and Fourth Republics unable to cope with problems of economic stagnation and declining national status. The French have a term specifically referring to the concept of a stalemated political system, *immoblisme*. The world of *la petite bourgeoisie* (small shopkeeper, lower middle class) was in fact threatened by the coming of postindustrial society. It is understandable that the appeal of a romanticized past offered by the neofascist Poujadist movement attracted significant support from this group, as it did in the later years of the Fourth Republic. The French Communist Party has survived to a large extent as a protest party, implying that the French industrial worker had something to protest. In fact, the standard of living of French workers has not compared favorably with their counterparts in other industrial societies.

Rapid inflation and frequent governmental crises have been and continue to be characteristics of the Italian political system. At this writing, Italy has the worst inflation in the western world. Thirty-six cabinets since the Second World War is the worst record of cabinet stability by that measure in the Western world.

To sum up, parties whose essential philosophical base is perceived as in opposition to the liberal democratic system—that is, Communist Parties and parties of the extreme right—gain significant support (where the combined vote for the parties exceeds 20 percent of all votes cast) in those nations where liberal democracy is not working well. Indicators of not working well include cabinet instability, rapid inflation, or unemployment significantly greater than most other industrial democracies. Significant support for parties of the extreme left and right has been found in postwar industrial democracies only in Italy and France. Extremism also flourished in Weimar Germany and prewar Austria. The above conditions could have been found in all four systems. The decline of political extremism in France during the Fifth Republic is occurring under a government system that in its authoritarian "efficiency" and freedom from *immoblisme* may appear as more effective.

If our suggestion that the problems of postindustrial societies will be increasingly insoluble is valid, governments in postindustrial societies may come to be perceived as increasingly impotent. It is therefore possible that significant support for parties of the extreme left and right may not continue to be isolated in France (to a diminishing extent) and in Italy. Far from the decline of opposition of principle, such opposition could gain more widespread legitimacy.

Party Ideology in the Soviet Union

It is natural to think of countries such as the Soviet Union as being ideological because of the emphasis placed by the leadership on a blueprint or master plan. At least on one level the description is appropriate. These systems are characterized by an arrangement in which the leaders claim to understand and interpret an official "scientific" set of beliefs. Both the general population and members of the elite are expected to study and champion the prescribed ideology, and opposing ideas are simply not tolerated. Any student of the Soviet Union soon becomes familiar with the polemics, slogans, and standard phrases. Virtually all decisions and policies are discussed in terms of being in the "socialist" or "Leninist" path.

Within this context, we are concerned with the perennial and illusive question of the extent to which the party and its leaders are guided by and committed to ideological considerations on one hand or more pragmatic societal ones on the other. It is not, of course, a case of one or the other totally. Both factors are present in varying proportions in the decision-making process of any party or nation. But because parties such as the CPSU describe themselves as committed to implementing an ideological program, we are inclined often to take that as the way it is.

The following question is difficult to answer but must be posed: what is the impact of modern industrialization on these ideologically oriented systems? What happens when a revolutionary-based party committed to a future-oriented "scientific" ideology is faced with the task of governing a diverse, modern industrial society?

The process involved is one in which a revolutionary one-party system evolves into an established, postrevolutionary one.[59] The former is dynamic, charismatic, and disciplined. Max Weber, a German sociologist, coined the phrase "the routinization of charisma" to refer to this process of transferring the basis of legitimacy from charisma to rational, legal considerations.[60] The emphasis, through the use of coercion as well as propaganda and other mass-mobilization measures, is on the elimination of existing structures and the creation of a new society in accordance with a well-developed and highly systematic ideology. The party, often led by one person, plays the leading role in the destruction of the old order and the building of the new. Ideology is very important at this point. As the old is overthrown, ideology becomes the source of legitimacy for the party and its struggle by providing the vision of the future society to be attained, the path and methods to be used in achieving it, and a warning of the obstacles to be overcome along the way. In a society concerned with industrialization, ideology may be useful to legitimate the transfer of scarce resources from present consumption to capital accumulation. Thus, David Apter suggests that "consummatory values" would be more supportive of early stages of modernization than "instrumental" or pragmatic considerations.[61] At this revolutionary stage of the process, ideology is vital for purposes of legitimacy and mobilization.

Once the new order has taken over, the situation changes and ideology becomes less important. In this period the party is concerned with the consolidation of its position and the solution of day-to-day problems. Samuel Huntington suggests several points with respect to the role of ideology at this stage.[62] First, continued ideological commitment may actually become dysfunctional with respect to the

---

[59] For a more detailed analysis of this process, see Samuel Huntington, "Social and Institutional Dynamics of One Party Systems," in Huntington and Moore, *op. cit.,* pp. 3–47.
[60] Max Weber, *Essays in Sociology,* H. Gerth and C. Wright Mills, eds. (New York: Oxford University Press, n.d.), p. 54.
[61] David Apter, *The Politics of Modernization* (Chicago: University of Chicago Press, 1965), pp. 235–236 and *passim.*
[62] Huntington, *op. cit.,* p. 26.

consolidation of the party's position. Although it may gain its initial legitimacy from the ideology, the new regime will be judged increasingly on the basis of performance. As it attempts to build support and consensus for itself, the party is tempted to play down ideological aspects in order not to alienate those who might be inclined to support it for practical reasons. Further, ideology, as a *closed-thought* system, becomes dysfunctional for the information exchange required by a mature industrial society.

If there is a decrease in ideological emphasis and commitment, what is its significance? Huntington argues that the decline of ideology is an indication of stability and strength, not weakness. When a party feels a degree of support and consensus, it will not have to rely on ideology. In other words, a weak, unstable, threatened regime is more likely to carry on ideological campaigns than one that feels fairly secure in its position. This dynamic is clearly not limited to communist systems.

How does all of this work out in practice? At this point, some 60 years after the Russian revolution, it is almost routine to speak of the regime in terms such as *postrevolutionary, pragmatic,* and *bureaucratic.* Particularly since the mid-1960s, one can characterize the leadership this way. As illustrated by the 23d Party Congress in 1966 and the 24th Congress in 1971, there has been a turning from the utopian view and concern with the future (typical of the Khrushchev period) to a more sober and realistic concern with present problems.

One assessment of the postrevolutionary era in the Soviet Union describes the post-Khrushchev leadership as pragmatic men "agnostic" in everything but their commitment to national greatness and orderly procedure and who no longer believe in the possibility of transforming society in accordance with Marxist-Leninist ideology.[63] It appears more and more that this process of transforming society on the basis of a plan imposed from above by the party has ended and been replaced by a new dynamic. We will have more to say about the new phase later in connection with the subject of interest groups.

Ideology certainly does not disappear because of the changed circumstances, but it seems to play a changed role. Instead of being a dynamic, motivating force, it seems to be a standard against which to measure and prohibit "dangerous" ideas and a language with which to justify policy.

We are suggesting that although a party may start out as the champion of a revolutionary, dynamic, transforming, future-oriented ideology, as the party becomes established it is more and more committed to stability, bureaucracy, and its own well-being and power. When this evolutionary process takes place in a

---

[63] Richard Lowenthal, "The Soviet Union in the Post-Revolutionary Era: An Overview," *Soviet Politics Since Khrushchev,* Alexander Dallin and Thomas B. Larson, eds. (Englewood Cliffs: Prentice Hall, 1968), p. 1.

modern industrializing society with all of its economic and social forces, the leading and transforming role is made even more difficult.

Party Organization and Origin

Party organization and origin are discussed together to point out that they are related to each other. Both variables can in turn be related to the party-of-principle–party-of-expediency dichotomy considered in the preceding section.

The basic organizational variable may be dichotomized into cadre parties and mass parties. The criterion for the distinction is the formality of the connection of party members to the party. In the United States, when a person is a member of either the Republican or Democratic Party he or she is simply more likely to vote for that party's candidates for national office than the candidates of the opposition party, when and if he or she votes at all. In short, by *party member,* most Americans really mean *party supporter.* Between elections, participation in party activities is by and large limited to very small coteries of party activists or leaders (the "pols" or "pros," in the jargon of American journalists). This is called a cadre party, and the organizational form typifies most middle-class parties elsewhere in the democratic world.

A mass party is one in which the typical rank-and-file citizen who identifies as a member of the party performs formal acts of commitment beyond voting such as paying dues and attending meetings. Membership may be direct, indirect through membership in an affiliated organization, or some combination of the two.

Communist parties (and often fascist parties) also operate on the basis of formal, structured membership. But the proportion of the population of communist countries that holds membership in the party is quite small, approximately 10 percent of the adult population. Most other citizens are merely supporters of the party, as in the United States. Duverger calls this kind of restricted mass-membership party a "devotee" party, as if it were sui generis.[64]

The mass-cadre distinction is not rigid. While the British Labour Party is generally thought of as mass party and the British Conservative Party is thought of as a cadre party, both have large mass memberships. As we point out below, the difference between the organization of the two parties may lie more in the putative impact of rank-and-file members on party policy than in the size or breadth of membership. Although in American parties supporters overwhelmingly outnumber members and activists, in most parties the imbalance is not so extreme in one direction or the other.

There is, as we have suggested, a relationship between party program and party organization. Typically, programmatic parties are more likely to be mass

[64] Duverger, *op. cit.,* p. 63 ff.

parties than are expediential parties of the center. Socialists or working-class parties are thus able to finance themselves from their membership dues, an important consideration because the financial base available to business-oriented middle-class parties is not available to working-class parties.[65]

Exceptions to the generalization linking programmatic and mass membership parties seem to abound. As noted above, the British Conservative Party may be thought of as a mass membership party. It has about 2 million members in a nation of some 55 million. The Italian DC is a "highly articulated" branch type of party structure—that is, it possesses a highly organized mass-membership base.[66] In fact, Christian democratic parties in general have attempted to develop a complex and formal organization of their supporters outside of parliament.[67] Attempts to organize all aspects of the daily lives of supporters under the aegis of the party have often caused Catholic parties to be known as "parties of social integration."

Membership may be direct or indirect through an affiliated group. Most membership parties use a combination of direct and indirect membership. The British Labour Party, for example, has some directly affiliated members in its constituency associations. However, the majority of its members are indirectly associated through their membership in affiliated trade unions or socialist or cooperative societies. Members of affiliated unions are automatically enrolled in the party, and their dues are deducted from their paychecks unless they formally request otherwise in writing (a process known as "contract out"). Under this system, passive individuals become party members. A Conservative government in 1927 changed the system to "contract in," where the individual union member had to join the party actively in order to belong. Under this system, party membership dropped precipitously from 3.2 million to 2 million. A subsequent Labour government in 1946 reinstalled "contract out," and Labour Party climbed back to 4 million.[68] We must conclude that around half of the Labour Party membership is due to inertia—that tendency to take the option that requires no action. The present membership of the Labour Party is around 7 million, with about 6 million of this figure attributable to indirect trade union membership.[69]

A question is raised about the relationship between membership and voting behavior. Fragmentary evidence suggests that members are no more likely to sup-

---

[65] Duverger, *op. cit.*, p. 67.
[66] Raphael Zariski, "Intra-Party Conflict in a Dominant Party: The Experience of Christian Democracy," *Journal of Politics,* Vol. XXVII, February 1965, pp. 3–34 at pp. 4–5.
[67] Hans Daalder, "Parties, Elites and Political Developments in Western Europe," in LaPalombara and Weiner, *op. cit.*, p. 74.
[68] These figures are from Duverger, *op. cit.*, p. 78.
[69] Leon Epstein, *Political Parties in Western Democracies*, New York: Praeger, 1967), p. 113n.

port the party in the voting booth than nonmembers.⁷⁰ The primary purpose in party membership appears to be the financial base it affords the party. Party members may also provide campaign workers.

The pattern in Western industrial democracies is that mass-membership parties obtain the bulk of their members through affiliated groups. An exception to this is the British Conservative Party, which possesses the largest direct membership. A trade union base is the more typical pattern among mass parties. In some cases, however, the trade union connection is less formalized than the relationship between the British Labour Party and the TUC. The relationship between the West German SPD and its major trade union confederation, the DGB, is one case of a less formalized relationship.⁷¹ The relationship between the Swedish Social Democratic Party and its LO is another based primarily on overlap in leadership personnel.

Due to the communist domination of the major French trade union confederation (CGT), the French SFIO lacks the trade union base and even a large portion of the electoral support available to other social democratic parties. The smaller, noncommunist Work Force (FO) is closely tied to the SFIO, however. Similarly, the divisions in the Italian labor movement between the communist elements, the Catholic elements, and the noncommunist secular elements have deprived the Italian Social Democrats of a strong trade union base. After a split between the trade unions and the Socialist Party in Belgium over communist influence in the former in 1945, the two were reunited in 1950.

The pattern of indirect organization through affiliated groups also generally applies to European agrarian parties. The pressure from such affiliated organizations is one factor that makes it difficult for parties to eschew their explicitly agrarian orientation despite a pattern in their changing their name to center party to broaden their base of support. Norwegian Premier Per Borten's breakup of the nation's first non-Labour governing coalition in 30 years over an essentially agrarian issue was a case in point. It will be recalled that Borten was leader of the Centre (formerly Agrarian) Party, and the issue was Norwegian agriculture's objection to Norway's entry into the EEC.

There is some tendency for the pattern in party orgnization to center the variation around countries instead of around ideological party types, as conventional wisdom holds. That is, while it is true that parties of the left are somewhat more likely to be mass parties than parties of the right, we have noted numerous parties of the right that possess considerable mass membership. Moreover, mass-membership parties are more likely to be found in some countries than in others regardless of the ideological thrust of the parties in question. We know, for

---

⁷⁰ Robert McKenzie, *British Political Parties* (New York: Praeger, 1963), revised ed., p. 544.
⁷¹ Harvey Rothman, *European Society and Politics* (Indianapolis: Bobbs-Merrill, 1970), p. 405.

example, that the British parties all have a fairly sizable membership, while the French parties, with the exception of the MRP, the socialists, and the communists, do not.[72] Although parties of the left are almost invariably mass-membership parties, parties of the center and right tend to be cadre parties in some nations and mass-membership parties in others.

The Origin and Purpose of Parties

Typically, cadre parties originated as factions within the legislature before the advent of mass suffrage. These groups developed organizations to cope with the extension of the suffrage by mobilizing sufficient support in the electorate to maintain the group in power.[73] The raison d'etre of the party organization outside the legislature was the support of the party inside the legislature. There was never any thought of the legislative party being subject to the dictates of party structures outside the legislature.

In the late nineteenth and early twentieth centuries, social movements, especially those representing the growing and increasingly self-conscious industrial proletariat, began to seek parliamentary representation of their aims. These movements originated with a programmatic purpose, whether ideological—such as envisioning a total transformation of society—or pragmatic—representing the interests of some corporate sector of society. The parliamentary representatives of these movements were regarded as agents of the movement, subject to the direction of those structural manifestations of the movement in society and at least morally obligated to the advocacy and support of the programmatic aims of the movement.

Externally created programmatic parties were most clearly manifested in the parties of the industrial labor movement. While many of these parties were organized with ostensible Marxist aims, others were largely a creation of their nation's trade union movement. Thus, the SFIO antedated the French trade union federations. (There are three such federations in France: the communist-controlled *General Confederation of Workers* (CGT), the largest of the three; the Catholic-oriented *French Confederation of Christian Workers* (CFTC); and the anticommunist *Work Force* (FO).

In contrast, the first Labour MPs in Australia were so clearly considered an arm of the trade union movement that they were designated the Labour-in-Politics Movement. These early candidates, first in New South Wales and then on the federal level, were expected to pledge formally their support of the aims of industrial labor as determined by the trade union organization (for example, the Trades and Labour Council in New South Wales and later the Labour Electoral Leagues). This pledge has often been viewed by some independent-minded MPs

---

[72] Epstein, *op. cit.*, p. 121.
[73] *Ibid.*, p. 19.

and prime ministers as an unjustified restriction on their discretion and was something of an issue in the party's history. The point is that the pledge epitomized the way that an externally created party could conceive of its ministers as agents of the party.

The British Labour Party was, to a large extent, a creation of the British Trade Union Congress (TUC)—the major British trade union federation roughly equivalent to the American AFL-CIO. The norm that members of the legislature be independent of ties or loyalties to corporate interests in society has never been established to the same extent in Britain as in the United States. There is a long-established tradition of the "interested MP" who openly identifies himself as a spokesman for one such interest.[74] The idea was that the bias of one MP would be balanced by the biases of the other members. Because no one individual makes policy, the biases of individuals do not necessarily bias the policy output of the collective body. Thus, the Labour Representation Committee could avow in 1906: "landlords, employers, lawyers, brewers and financiers are there [in the House of Commons] in force. Why not Labour?"[75] Accordingly, the Labour Representation Committee undertook to sponsor candidates who would promote the interests of industrial workers. Similarly, many deputies in the West German Bundestag openly admit to direct association with and overt representation of organized interests. For instance, about one-third of the then-ruling COU deputies were directly affiliated with business organizations from 1953 to 1958.[76]

The Labour Representation Committee was a coalition of the TUC and the Fabian societies. The latter group preached socialist doctrine, but it advocated a nonrevolutionary, democratic variety, as one would expect from such middle-class intellectuals as George Bernard Shaw, Beatrice and Sidney Webb, Graham Wallace, and others who provided the driving force behind the society. Fabian socialism can even be distinguished from Eduard Bernstein's "revisionism" in that the latter purports to be a revision of Marxism and accepts class conflict as axiomatic. Fabian socialism does not. In short, while Bernstein attempted to modify Marxism, the Fabians rejected Marxism from the beginning. But, the Fabians undoubtedly had a major influence on Bernstein, the so-called father of democratic socialism, who became acquainted with the Fabians during a lengthy exile in England.[77] This intellectual component of the Labour Party has been much more of a force in the direction of a party of principle than the trade union component. This difference has contributed to something of an internal bifurcation through the years between the pragmatic party elite and the more principled leftist-oriented elements of the party, usually confined to the "back benches." (*Backbencher* is a

[74] Beer, *op. cit.*, pp. 112–173.
[75] Quoted from *ibid.*, p. 113.
[76] Lewis Edinger, *Politics in Germany* (Boston: Little Brown, 1968), p. 211.
[77] Gray, *op. cit.*, pp. 107–108.

term referring to those MPs who are not considered part of their party's leadership, such as being a member of either the cabinet or shadow cabinet. Ordinary MPs sit on benches above and behind the leadership of their respective parties; hence, the term *backbencher*. See the diagram of the layout of the House of Commons in Chapter 5.)

Representatives of both the trade unions and the Fabian societies are accorded certain guaranteed representation at the Annual Conference of the Labour Party. In theory, the Annual Conference determines the principles and programs on which the parliamentary Labour party and cabinet will stand. In practice, the Annual Conference cannot impose programs or principles on any Labour government or shadow cabinet that the leadership of the party does not itself espouse.

The British party system has been the subject of a considerable body of academic literature in which can be found a running disagreement as to whether the Labour Party's commitment to rank-and-file democracy and control of the parliamentary party (Labour MPs) by the party organization outside Parliament actually renders the parliamentary Labour Party less autonomous of that organization than their Conservative counterparts who espouse a philosophy of party elitism. Clearly, the Labour Party's ideological view emphasizes greater internal party democracy and control of the parliamentary party by the Annual Conference than their Conservative counterparts; indeed, Labour logically must do this from its origin, raison d'être, and its perception of MPs as agents of the movement.

As Winston Churchill once observed, the specter of Britain being governed by a cabinet that is accountable to a particular set of interests or one corporate sector of British society contravenes the logic of the British constitution. Constitutionally, the cabinet is accountable to the representatives of the whole nation in Commons: therefore, it cannot be accountable to the Annual Conference or the TUC.[78] A British government, for instance, must feel free to compromise the claims and interests of the TUC against those of the nation as a whole.

The logic of Churchill's assertions would apply more clearly to a Labour government in power than to one in opposition. Yet, once the party leadership develops the ability to control or function autonomously from the party rank and file, it is unlikely that it will stop doing so once the party is out of power. Possessors of power do not always require a rational excuse for its exercise. Thus, although the Labour Party leader is annually reelected by the Annual Conference, Labour leaders have run unopposed since 1922.

By contrast, the Conservatives chose their leaders until recently by an almost mystical process of consultation that was consciously informal. It was said that

---

[78] See the discussion of the "politics of power" (roughly, the governing function) and the "politics of support" (roughly, the programmatic function) and the point that the latter is constitutionally subordinate to the former in Andrew Gamble, *The Conservative Nation* (London: Routledge and Kegan Paul, 1974), p. 24, referred to in the notes of Chapter 5.

"you just looked around and there he was." However, after the confusion surrounding the accession of Sir Alec Douglas-Home to party leadership in 1963, the party decided to formalize its procedures of choosing a leader. Ted Heath was the first Conservative Party leader to be elected in 1965.

Thus, R. T. McKenzie, in his classic study of British parties, has concluded that the Labour party leaders are not as subject to rank-and-file control as the ideological view of the party seems to suggest.[79] Samuel Beer, on the other hand, implies that McKenzie has overstated the structural similiarity between the British parties. Beer infers more rank-and-file control in the Labour Party than does McKenzie.[80]

The classic generalization with regard to leader-follower relations in political parties (and in any large organization) is probably Italian sociologist Roberto Michels's "iron law of oligarchy."[81] Michels's thesis, derived from an early twentieth-century study of the Social Democratic Party of Germany, is that while parties tend to accept internal party democracy as the norm and even go through the motions of adhering to that norm in form, in practice the leadership of any large organization is inherently oligarchic. That is, any large organization is led by a relatively small number of individuals who, regardless of egalitarian principles, cannot be strictly accountable to the rank and file of that organization. Michels argues that the imperatives of efficiency, the raison d'être of large organizations, necessitate a highly developed specialization of roles and division of labor. Leadership is a specialized role to which accrues competence, esoteric knowledge, and interests not shared by the rank-and-file membership. The rank and file cannot control those activities of which they are ignorant. Thus, the organization, created as a means, becomes an end in itself—an entity whose purpose is the advancement of the ambitions of its leaders, not the amerlioration of the circumstances of its membership. Clearly, the leaders of most trade union confederations or proletariat-based parties have more in common culturally and intellectually with the management and professional sectors of the society than with the industrial workers they ostensibly represent.

While it was clearly naive to take the egalitarian protestations of left-wing parties at face value, Michels's "iron law" is, as the writings of Beer and McKenzie suggest, equally an oversimplification. The relationship between leaders and followers in both major British parties appears to be one of reciprocal influence. The leaders of both parties, on the one hand, are far more than clerical order-takers from their respective backbenchers. The British Conservatives have institutionalized this backbench influence with the formation of the 1922 Commit-

---

[79] McKenzie, *op. cit.*
[80] Beer, *op. cit.*, pp. 156-163, 371-373.
[81] Roberto Michels, *Political Parties,* Eden and Cedar Paul, trans. (New York: Dover Publications, 1959), especially Part 6, Chap. 2.

tee, an organization of backbenchers whose meetings are attended by party whips. Formed in 1922 in reaction to the high-handed disregard of backbench sentiment by Tory Prime Minister Stanley Baldwin, the committee is formally named the Conservative Private Members' Committee. While Labour Party leaders must meet with the parliamentary Labour Party and present and seek approval of their program, Tory leaders do not themselves attend meetings of the 1922 Committee. However, Tory whips are expected to keep party leadership informed of committee sentiments and decisions. Further, Tory leaders are expected to take account of committee sentiments and decisions in the formulation of their decisions and programs. This institutionalization of backbench influence on party leadership exists despite the vaunted autonomy of Tory Party leadership.

The point of disagreement between McKenzie and Beer is whether formal organizational differences result in differences in the actual autonomy of the party leaderships from their respective parliamentary colleagues. Our guess is that they do not.

The major contribution of McKenzie's book in our view is the suggestion that the distribution of power in a political party is not so much a function of the party's egalitarian or oligarchic principles as it is a function of the imperatives of the political structure in which the party operates.[82] The imperatives of cabinet government require greater centralization of power than Labour's egalitarian philosophy espouses. But the system also requires that the views of the backbenchers be taken into greater account than provided for by the elitist orientation of the Conservative Party. In McKenzie's analysis, constitutional structure is the major independent or causal variable, and the real distribution of power in British parties is a dependent variable. Beer would differ from this in that he would allow for some real causal impact of differences in party philosophy on the actual distribution of power in British parties.

Richard Rose suggests that a major oversimplification exists in McKenzie's analysis, an oversimplification that may be one source of the disagreement between McKenzie and Beer.[83] McKenzie relies on retention of office as virtually the sole index of the power and autonomy of the party leader. He neglects the impact of party rank and file or even of extraparliamentary organizations on party programs and policies.

Party Discipline and Party Cohesion

Related to the variable of the leader-follower relationship in parliamentary parties is the degree of party cohesion on legislative voting. This refers to the extent to

---

[82] McKenzie, *op. cit.,* p. 635 ff.
[83] Richard Rose, "Complexities of Party Leadership," *Parliamentary Affairs,* Vol. 16, No. 3, September 1963, pp. 257–273.

which members of a given party vote as a bloc on a legislative vote or, put otherwise, the extent to which knowledge of the position of party leaders on a given legislative issue enables one to predict the vote of other legislators of the same party label. Party cohesion is one of the imperatives of cabinet stability in parliamentary regimes.

Because governments (prime ministers and their cabinets) govern in parliamentary regimes at the sufferance of a majority of the lower house of the legislature, cabinet stability depends on the stability of that majority. Where individual legislators are left to make up their own minds as to how to vote on each given issue, the probability that a large enough number of individuals to form a majority of the legislature would spontaneously come to a meeting of minds over a wide range of issues is obviously remote. Consequently, a mechanism is needed to compel those individual legislators upon whom the government relies for support to continue to vote the government's position even if they may personally disagree with that position on one or more specific issues. This mechanism is party discipline.

Clearly, party discipline cannot be applied absolutely—that is, with the requirement that each legislator votes to support the party's position no matter what it is. If party discipline were applied that absolutely, legislative voting would become totally redundant, and an important mechanism of governmental accountability would be destroyed. Normally, the effect of party discipline is to broaden the bounds of discretion of the government within which they can still count on party support. The individual legislator will not choose to suffer the penalties of breaking party discipline for a minor disagreement with the party; however, a major conflict between the party position and the fundamental principles of the individual legislator would presumably result in a break in party discipline.

One mechanism of enforcing party discipline is ultimate control of the nominating process. That is, while constituency organizations may retain the right to nominate their candidates to represent that constituency in the national legislature, national party organizations may reserve the right to veto locally determined choices. Thus, unless the individual member of the legislature is acceptable to national party leadership, he or she loses the right to campaign under that party label. To the extent that a party system is relatively aggregated, one's probability of electoral success without the label of a major party becomes increasingly remote. In some countries, expulsion from a party would probably end a potential political career. In Great Britain, for example, Winston Churchill was the only modern politician to leave the ranks of a major party without descending into the ranks of political obscurity. (Churchill's career ran from being a Conservative to a Liberal to an independent and back to a Conservative. Churchill's personal charisma was, however, unique.)

The contrast in this regard between Britain and the older Commonwealth on one hand and the United States on the other is worth noting. In the United States there is very little formal structure in the way of national parties among the Democrats and Republicans. Final control of nominations is at the state and local levels. Thus, for example, American southern Democrats have been notorious for producing candidates that were highly persona non grata for the more liberal northern Democrats who dominated the presidential wing of the party. When President Franklin D. Roosevelt toured the South in 1934 in an effort to encourage the nomination of candidates more congenial to his social and political philosophy, he was soundly rebuffed in the results of the primary elections. Roosevelt was apparently viewed as an outsider meddling in state and local prerogatives. Thus, the Democratic party can contain men like Senators James Eastland of Mississippi and James Allen of Alabama who oppose and vote against every significant policy that recent Democratic presidents have espoused. This situation would not be possible in Great Britain where party discipline is perhaps most tightly maintained.

It has been pointed out that denial of constituency choice by the central party machinery is very rare, as is expulsion from the party. For these reasons, some prominent scholars have suggested that this is a poor explanation of party cohesion. Leon Epstein thinks the common acceptance by MPs of cohesion as part of the British rules of the game is the best explanation.[84] This kind of nonexplanation begs the question of why did rules of the game develop in some places and not in others. Epstein is saying that the British accept cohesion because the British accept cohesion.

It seems to us that the power to control nominations must be understood by individual MPs to impose some limits beyond which they may not blatantly go. This understanding would generally keep the MPs within limits, thereby rendering actual expulsion or veto of nomination unnecessary. In other words, the threat of expulsion or denial of nomination, not their actual use, has some impact on party cohesion.

A second factor pointed out by Epstein probably contributes to party cohesion. In cabinet democracies with strong cabinet control of the legislature, one must succeed to a cabinet post to have a significant political impact.[85] One cannot build a career based only on seniority in the legislature and without disregard to the feelings of the executive branch of the government, as can, say, a committee chairman in the United States Congress.

The biggest overall incentive for party discipline in parliamentary democracies is probably the perception on the part of individual MPs that only disciplined

---

[84] Epstein, *op. cit.*, p. 323.
[85] *Ibid.*, p. 322.

parties can play a significant role in the policymaking process and only members of the parties can play this kind of role. The logic of parliamentary democracy encourages internal party cohesion in government parties in two-party or aggregated-party systems and in aggregated opposition parties that are a potential alternative government.[86]

In Britain and the older Commonwealth nations, individual MPs are informed of their party's position on impending votes by a notice called a *whip*. The term is somewhat confusing because it also refers to the party official—a member of the legislature—who serves as a liaison between the parliamentary party leadership and the rank-and-file MPs. This whip is sometimes viewed as the person who is expected to "whip" the rank-and-file MPs into line. Due to the reciprocal flow of influence between party leadership and backbenchers, the former description of the whip's functions is more accurate.

The written whips are supposed to bring individual MPs into conformity with the party line. They are addressed to each individual MP in the party and list the agenda that is impending in the House of Commons together with the time when divisions (roll-call votes) are expected. They say something to the effect that, "Your attendance is [particularly] requested." These statements may be underlined from one to four times, and the number of underlinings indicates the urgency with which support of the party's position is demanded. It is extremely serious to violate a three-line whip; it is less serious to violate a one-line whip. The whips occasionally inform the MPs that there will be a "free vote"—that is, each MP is free to vote his or her conscience. These divisions, of course, are not considered confidence questions.

Where cabinet government and federalism are combined, as they are in Austria, Australia, Canada, and West Germany, potentially conflicting imperatives are generated. Thus, cabinet government generates the centralizing imperatives just discussed based on the need to insulate cabinets from the day-to-day shifting currents of legislative opinion and to give them the discretion inherent in the function of governing. Federalism, by contrast, should generate decentralizing imperatives. Federalism, after all, presumes that certain geographically defined subsystems have distinct sets of interests that must be represented in the national decision-making process. Federalism presumes that geographically defined diversities will be of such salience as to render their assimilation by the forces of national integration out of the question.

Thus, when the perceived interests generated by a geographically defined diversity conflict with the policy position of a disciplined party, the potential conflict between federalism and cabinet government becomes salient. The imperatives of federalism require the legislator to vote for the interest of the constituency he or

---

[86] *Ibid.*, p. 333.

she represents; the imperatives of cabinet government require that one vote according to the dictates of party leadership.[87]

The impact of federalism on such things as party discipline should be greater in a nation such as Canada, where the provincial boundaries reflect cultural or economic diversities, than in a nation such as Australia, where cultural and economic differences between states are not significant. This expectation is confirmed by study of these nations, although cohesion is so high in all British Commonwealth nations that differences among them with respect to party cohesion are minimized.[88] Cohesion is higher in Australia than in Canada; however, the only modern governments to fall in Canada have been due to the defections of coalition partners from a minority government, not to defections of majority party MPs from their government's position. Breaks in party cohesion in all parliamentary democracies tend to occur on those roll calls, when they do not threaten the capacity of the government party to maintain its parliamentary majority. Thus, the Christian Democrats of West Germany have experienced numerous breaks in party cohesion when they were a governing party but never enough to threaten the life of a government.[89]

One would expect some tendency for aggregated party systems to be more internally cohesive than fragmented party systems. The logic of parliamentary democracy involves the need to aggregate stable majorities in the lower house and to have an alternative force capable of aggregating an alternative government. Aggregated parties perform these functions more effectively than parties with a narrow electoral base. In fact, the clearest example of noncohesive parties among the systems we have discussed was found in the Fourth French Republic. This system, it will be recalled, also manifested a highly fragmented party system. The Fourth Republic was about the only system among the parliamentary democracies we have discussed where a high degree of party cohesion did not generally exist.

Although very high by American standards, the degree of cohesion does vary somewhat among these parliamentary democracies with a party's organization and its place in the ideological spectrum.[90] It tends to be stronger in mass, programmatic parties than in cadre parties of expediency. In other words, urban labor-based or socialist parties tend to be somewhat more cohesive than center-

---

[87] See Lawrence C. Mayer, "Federalism and Party Behavior in Australia and Canada," *Western Political Quarterly*, Vol. XXIII, No. 4, December 1970, pp. 795–807, for a discussion of the resolution of this conflict in those two countries based on electoral and legislative roll-call data.
[88] *Ibid.*
[89] George Rueckert, "Parliamentary Party Cohesion in the West German Bundestag," Doctoral dissertation, Department of Political Science, University of Wisconsin, 1962, cited in Epstein, *op. cit*, pp. 335–336.
[90] Hancock, *op. cit.*, pp. 109–110; Henry Valen and Daniel Katz, *Political Parties in Norway* (Oslo: Universitets fortage I, 1964), p. 225; Robert Bone, "The Dynamics of Dutch Politics," *Journal of Politics*, Vol. XXIV, No. 1, February 1962, pp. 23–40; Zariski, *op. cit.*, pp. 3–34.

right or Christian democratic parties. Communist parties tend to be the most cohesive of all.

How do the organizational criteria suggested above apply to the CPSU? It is a mass party in the sense of commitment of members to the party and the formal and serious nature of membership. It is not mass in terms of its total size or its accessibility to all who wish to join. Beginning with some 24,000 members in 1917 and growing to over 14 million at present, the CPSU has always consisted of a small portion of the total population. In recent years the proportion of party members to general population has remained about the same in both the Soviet Union and Eastern Europe: 5 percent of the total figure and 10 percent of the adult population. The party is intentionally maintained as a relatively small, elite organization, to which admission is by invitation only. Prospective members must submit a detailed life history and must have the recommendations of three party members who have been in the party themselves for at least five years, who have known the applicant for at least one year in both an occupational and social context, and who are willing to accept responsibility if the person does not work out as a good party member.

The statutes or rules of the party make it very clear that it is intended to be an organization of activists. Whereas Western democratic parties focus on elections, Communist parties see their task as a much larger one of providing leadership for the entire society. Members are expected to do all the things one would expect in a disciplined group, such as voting, paying dues, attending meetings, and generally working on behalf of the party. In addition, there are "vanguard" functions such as joining study groups, volunteering for civic responsibilities, and in general providing the example of model citizen and worker. The rules contain a lengthy list of the duties and responsibilities of members and provide for a one-year "candidate" or probationary period before full membership is granted. These matters are taken seriously, as indicated by the fact that General Secretary Brezhnev, in his report to the 24th Party Congress, noted that not all members were living up to their responsibilities and in effect called for the dropping of these people from the party's rolls.

Those willing to assume the activist role and responsibilities enjoy certain benefits not available to the general public. CPSU membership is advisable for anyone wishing a career in the professions or at the managerial level, is virtually a necessity for sensitive positions such as the military or internal security, and is a foregone conclusion for anyone planning a political career. On a more day-to-day practical basis, it may be the means of benefits such as travel opportunities, better housing (a commodity in short supply), vacations in subsidized facilities, and greater access to a variety of consumer goods and comforts.

There are a number of ways of approaching the subject of the matter in which the CPSU is organized. Formally, it parallels for the most part the structural divisions of the government of the Soviet Union. This dual, parallel, and overlapping arrangement of party and government bureaucracies is one of the confusing aspects of a communist system. The party bureaucracy, in addition to running the party, is the context in which major policy decisions are made for the Soviet Union. The decisions are then legitimated and implemented by means of the governmental structures. As of early 1974, Brezhnev is the top party official, while Kosygin and Podgorny occupy the two highest government positions.

On the government side of this dual structure (which was discussed in greater detail in Chapter 5), there are four basic levels: all-union, union republic, *oblast* or regional, and local (city or *raion*). *All-union* is simply the term applied to the central government in Moscow. The Soviet Union is federal in form and is divided into 15 union republics. The larger union republics are further subdivided into a number of units of which the most important is a regional or provincial one called the *oblast*. The final level is obtained by dividing the *oblasts* into rural (*raion*) and urban (city) districts. There are a number of other units along the way, but these four are the most common and basic.

The party's structure parallels that of the state and adds at the bottom of the hierarchy the primary party organization (PPO), which is the basic organizational unit. As the level at which rank-and-file members of the party meet and operate together, the PPO is organized on a functional or production principle. That is, whenever possible groups are formed among members of farms, factories, schools, military units, etc. When this is not possible, residence is the basis used. With approximately 80 percent of the 370,000 PPOs containing fewer than 50 members each,[91] these are small face-to-face meetings at which fairly tight discipline can be maintained and some degree of cohesion can be developed. This may be the only point where the ordinary member is active relative to the party structure because it is the only level at which general meetings of all members take place. All higher levels are composed of delegates from lower units. Subjects considered at PPO meetings include the admission of new members, supervision of the activities of farms, enterprises, and other such units, and the general task of improving attitudes, productivity, and awareness in accordance with current policy. Decisions of PPOs must be approved by the next highest level.

In larger PPOs and at all higher levels, the party consists of a three-stage structure. First, there is a conference or congress composed of a relatively large number of delegates; it meets infrequently. At the all-union level, the congress of the CPSU is attended by almost 5000 persons and meets every five years. Because of these factors of size and infrequency of meetings, this level "elects" a second and smaller group to act on its behalf. At the all-union level, this is the Central Committee, which has approximately 400 members. The committee in turn selects two

---

[91] Ellen Mickiewicz, *Handbook of Soviet Social Science Data* (New York: The Free Press, 1973), p. 169.

other groups that are responsible for the day-to-day operation of the party: the bureau and the secretariat. The bureau, which at the top level is called the Politburo (political bureau) and has approximately 20 members, is the most important executive policymaking body. The Secretariat, 10 members and their staff at the all-union level, is the administrative center of the party. Its power derives in large part from control over personnel matters within the party at all levels. The single most important position in the Soviet Union in recent years has been that of First or General Secretary of the CPSU. Both Nikita Khrushchev and Leonid Brezhnev used the position to consolidate power.

In theory, power flows from the PPO up the ladder to the all-union level and from the larger body (congress or conference) to the smaller bureau or secretariat. In practice, the opposite is true. The Secretariat and Politburo of the Central Committee of the CPSU are the most powerful organs, controlling the membership and activities of the larger bodies at the same level and of all lower bodies. The cardinal principle of party organization is the Leninist "democratic centralism." According to the "democratic" aspect of this concept, election of all party bodies is to be from lowest (PPO) to highest (all-union), and party bodies are to be accountable to their respective organizations. The "centralism" portion is that once a decision is reached there is to be strict subordination of the minority to the majority, and that decisions of higher party bodies are unconditionally binding on all lower ones. In practice, there is far more "centralism" than "democratic" because selection of party organs is really from highest to lowest. Along the lines of Michels' "iron law of oligarchy," the CPSU is dominated and controlled by a small group at the top. In the Soviet Union this group is known as the *apparat*.

Another method of describing a communist party is in terms of three layers, the top one of which is the apparat. These are the individuals who are full-time paid party officials whose primary responsibility is the operation of the party. *Apparatchiki* (men of the apparatus) are dispersed from top to bottom of the party hierarchy and in all probability constitute less than 0.02 percent of the total party membership.

The second, and to an extent the third, layer arises from the assertion that the CPSU is the nucleus of all social organizations. That being the case, a second group of party members are not party officials but have key leadership or supervisory positions in the society as a whole. Rigby concludes that party membership levels are highest in structures such as the police, judiciary, upper levels of the policymaking bureaucracy, and probably the communications media. The armed forces and administrative bureaucracy also have high concentrations at the "line" positions, but not so much at subordinate levels.[92] The objective of this, of course,

---

[92] T. H. Rigby, *Communist Party Membership in the U.S.S.R. 1917–1967* (Princeton: Princeton University Press, 1968), pp. 511–512.

is to assure as much as possible that these organizations are not operating at cross-purposes to the party. There is always the possibility of a conflict arising between party loyalty and identification with a functional group.

The final group is the overwhelming majority of party members. These are the people who are neither part of the leading cadre nor part of those who play an important role in the guidance and monitoring of social organizations on behalf of the party. They are workers, clerks, farmers, students, etc., who constitute the base of the organization and perform a variety of functions on a voluntary basis. Rigby speaks of a "leavening" of party members in various occupational and residential groupings to act as the party's "eyes, ears and mouthpiece" and as the example for the general population of exemplary conduct and attitudes.[93] The general membership also serves as a pool from which replacements can be recruited into the higher echelons of the elite. In the Khrushchev period, there was a strong emphasis on mobilizing a large number of unpaid nonprofessional party workers and correspondingly decreasing the number of paid officials. Khrushchev's successors have tended to reverse this "populism" and to reemphasize the role of the professional *apparatchiki*.

Conclusions

We have shown how parties either perform or fail to perform the functions of the transmission of demands from society to the political system and the filtering, aggregation, and interpretation of those demands into phenomena that are politically manageable. We have also shown how parties can be used to mobilize demands or otherwise control them. Parties perform the function of selecting and training the elite. They share this function with other social institutions, such as the agents of socialization (for example, the family, schools, etc.).

The functions that parties perform depend to a large extent on the dominant cultural properties of the system, with certain structures often acting as a kind of intervening variable between the society and the nature and performance of the party system. For example, we have seen that the distinction between a fragmented and an aggregated party system is to a large extent a function of a fragmented or aggregated culture. This cultural variable is often reflected in the degree of proportionality in the electoral system. Certain kinds of electoral systems logically seem to encourage more or less fragmentation in the party system, although electoral systems seem incapable of generating more or less fragmentation that runs counter to cultural imperatives.

We have noted that certain functions are performed by all of the party systems

---

[93] *Ibid.*

in industrial societies, while other functions appear to be confined to parties in democratic systems. Thus, we have a degree of convergence, but a finding of convergence must be qualified.

We have noted that parties share many functions with less explicitly political structures. We refer here to the groups and organized interests of society. We now turn to the patterns of these organizations and their role in the decision-making process.

Appendix to Chapter 7
Political Parties and Their Legislative Strength for the Nations Discussed to a Significant Extent

	Seats in Lower House as of 1974
Australia	
Country	20
Liberal	38
Australian Labour	67
Democratic Labour	0
Austria	
Freiheitliche Partei Osterreichs (Austrian Freedom Party)	10
Osterreichische Volkspartei (Austrian People's Party)	80
Sozialistische Partei Osterreichs (Austrian Socialist Party)	93
Kommunistische Partei Osterreichs (Communist Party)	0
Belgium	
Volksunie (United People's) [Flemish]	21
Front Democratique des Bruxellois Francophones (Democratic Front of Pro-French Brussellites)	24
Rassemblement Wallon (Walloon Assembly)	
Parti Pour Liberté et le Progres (Party of Liberty and Progress)	34
Parti Social Chretien (Social Christian Party)	67
Parti Socialiste Belge (Belgian Socialist Party)	61
Parti Communiste Belge (Belgian Communist Party)	5
Canada	
Social Credit	15
Ralliement des Creditiste (Social Credit-Quebec)	0
Progressive Conservative	107
Liberal	109
New Democratic	31

Appendix (Continued)

	Seats in Lower House as of 1974
Denmark	
Conservative	16
Christian People's	7
Liberal Democratic (Venstre)	22
Radical Liberal	20
Justice	5
Progress	28
Centre Democratic	14
Social Democratic	46
Socialist People's	11
Communist	6
France	
Union des Democrates pour la République (Union of Democrats for the Republic) [Gaullists]	185
Independent Republicans	54
Centre Democratie et Progres (Progress and Modern Democracy) [includes old MRP, the Popular Republican Movement]	21
Socialists } former Federation of the Left, incl. old	89
Left Radicals } SFIO	12
Communists	73
Others	15
Parti Socialiste Unifié (Unified Socialist Party and extreme left)	3
Federal Republic of Germany	
Nationaldemokratische Partei Deutschlands (National Democratic Party of Germany)	0
Christlich Soziale Union (Christian Social Union) Christlich Demokratische Union (Christian Democratic Union)	225
Freie Demokratische Partei (Free Democratic Party)	41
Sozialdemokratische Partei Deutschlands (Social Democratic Party of Germany)	230
Deutsche Kommunistische Partei (Communists)	0
Italy	
Movemento Sociale Italiano (Italian Social Movement) [fascist] Partito di Unito Monarchica (Monarchists)	56
Partito Liberale Italiano (Liberals)	20
Democrazia Cristiana (Christian Democrats)	267
Partito Republican Italiano (Republicans)	15
Partito Social Democratico Italiano (Social Democratic Party)	29

Appendix (Continued)

	Seats in Lower House as of 1974
Italy (Continued)	
Partito Socialista Italiano (Italian Socialist Party)	61
Partito Communista Italiano (Communists)	179
Sudtiroler Volkspartei (South Tyrolian People's Party)	3
The Netherlands	
Statkunig Gereformeerde Partij (State Reformed Party) [Calvinist]	3
Boeren Partij (Farmers' Party)	3
Anti-Revolutionaire Partij (Calvinist) (Anti-revolutionary Party)	14
Christelijk Historische Unie (Christian Historical Union)	7
Katholieke Volkspartij (Catholic People's Party)	27
Democraten '66 (Democrats '66)	6
Partij van den Arbeid (Labor Party)	43
Pacifistiche Socialistiche Partij (Socialist Pacifist Party)	2
Communistiche Partij (Communists)	7
Five others	10
Norway	
Höyre (Conservative)	29
Kristelig Folkparti (Christian People's Party)	20
Sentepartiet (Centre Party) [agrarian]	21
Venestre (Liberals)	1
Anti E.E.C. Venestre	2
Socialistisk Folkeparti (Socialist People's Party) } Socialist Electoral Alliance	16
Kommunistiske Parti (Communist Party)	
Anders Lange Parti	4
Sweden	
Moderata Samlingspartiet (Moderate Unity Party—formerly Conservative)	51
Centerpartiet (Center Party—formerly Agrarians)	90
Folkpartiet (People's Party—formerly Liberals)	34
Socialdemokratiska Arbetarepartiet (Social Democratic Party)	156
Vansterpartiet Kommunisterna (Left Party Communists)	19
United Kingdom	
Conservative (Tory)	330
Liberal	6
Labour	287
Scottish Nationals and others	7

Source. Britannica Book of the Year, 1974, pp. 552–554.

Chapter 8

Interest Groups

It was suggested in the preceding chapter that democratic theory has parties functioning as a link between those who make decisions about public policy (the elite) and those who are affected by the decisions. Parties are supposed to serve to render the elite more responsive to those they ostensibly govern. This general function within the political system is also performed by groups, albeit often in a somewhat different way.

Like parties, interest groups serve to mobilize latent and inarticulate demands in a society and to transmit the demands to the national decision-making process. In so doing, they filter and modify the demands to a volume and format that is manageable for the political process. It will be recalled that public opinions do not tend to formulate themselves spontaneously; interests and the demands emanating from them that are not mobilized tend to go unarticulated; that is, the interests tend to remain latent.

Interest groups, by filtering demands, perform a function of insulating the elite from the extremes of such demands, both qualitatively and quantitatively. Further, by performing this function of insulating the elite, groups give the elite freedom from the day-to-day pressures of public opinion. This freedom is inherent in the concept of elite discretion. Discretion, in turn, is inherent in the function of governing.

Groups may be created by the elite in order to mobilize support for the elite. This partially describes the purpose behind the creation of many groups in authoritarian regimes. These groups may also be found in democratic regimes. The groups organized under the aegis of the Catholic church in many Catholic countries constitute a case in point. The organizational life in both Austrian *lager* and in the several Netherlands subcultures also exemplify groups that function as much to mobilize the various facets of individuals' lives in support of and under the aegis of subcultural or partisan elite groups as to transmit demands to the elite. Women's groups, family groups, and youth groups are among the types found under church aegis in France and Italy. In Italy groups are under the umbrella organization, Catholic Action. In France, Catholic Action is a separate organization. The role of Catholic Action in Italy is to socialize its basically young adult membership for entry into the Christian Democratic Party. Catholic Action in France takes a more direct political role in support of conservative candidates.

Pluralism and Polyarchy

Robert Dahl and others have postulated a model of the democratic process that he called *polyarchy* and others have labeled *pluralism*.[1] The essence of the model is that the policymaking process, however centralized it may appear on paper, is in reality a highly decentralized process of bargaining among relatively autonomous groups. Frequently juxtaposed as an antithesis to elitist conceptualizations of the political process, polyarchy or pluralism is conceptually similar to the old Bently, Truman, and Latham paradigm popularly known as group theory.[2]

Group theory holds that public policy is merely the outcome of the interaction of all of the groups who make claims upon or express an interest in that particular issue. The extent to which groups will get their way is a function of the strength of the groups and the intensity of their participation. The intensity of their participation refers to the fraction of the group resources that the group chooses to allocate to the attainment of that particular goal in the face of other goals and finite resources. It is a sort of parallelogram of forces concept, as indicated in Figure 1.

The significance of group theory is that the role of government in the construction of public policy is minimized. In this theory, government does not make policy so much as act as an arbitrator in the bargaining process. This theory would require the revision of the democratic conceptualization of policy being made by representatives of a coherent majority and the authoritarian concep-

---

[1] Robert Dahl, *Modern Political Analysis* (Englewood Cliffs: Prentice Hall, 1963), p. 73 ff, and *Pluralist Democracy in the United States* (Chicago: Rand McNally, 1967).

[2] Arthur Bently, *The Process of Government* (Chicago: University of Chicago Press, 1908); Earl Latham, "The Groups Basis of Politics: Notes for a Theory," *Pressure Groups in American Politics*, H. R. Mahovd, ed. (New York: Charles Scribners, 1967), p. 21; David Truman, *The Governmental Process* (New York: Alfred A. Knopf, 1951).

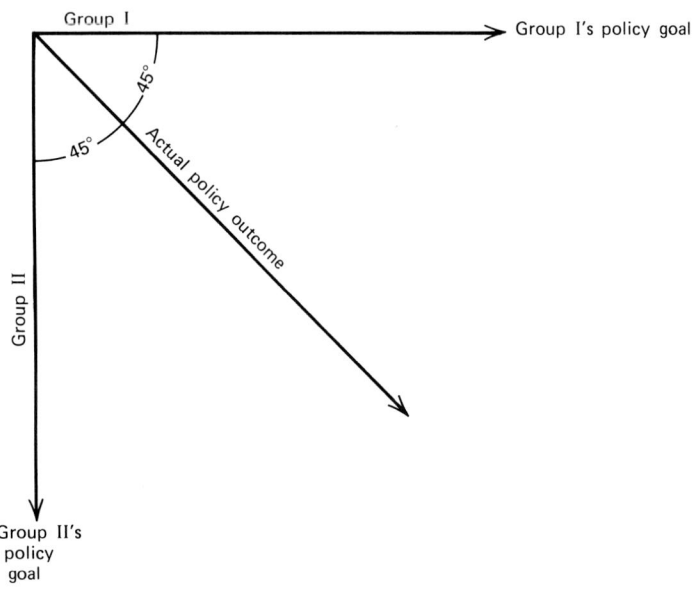

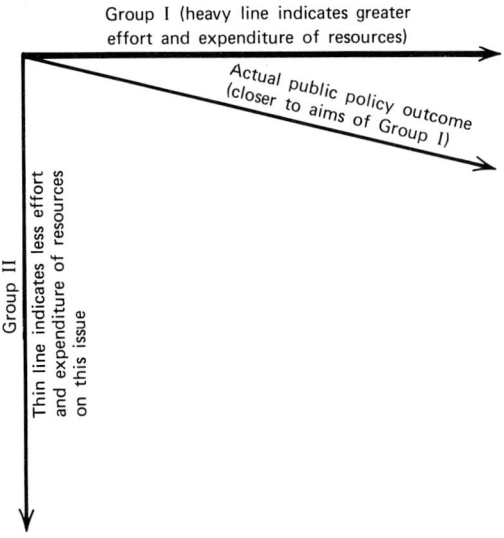

Figure 1.

tualization of policy being made by an autonomous and unresponsive elite. If public policy were actually merely the outcome of bargaining among the groups interested in a given policy issue, the importance of variations in the format of the government would be minimized. (Recall that this format refers to constitutional arrangements.) To the extent that public policy is the outcome of bargaining among organized groups, the actual policymaking process in the countries under consideration would become similar despite the differences among them with regard to explicitly political structures. This would be additional support for the convergence theme that underlies this book.

The consensus among most reputable scholars is that on one hand group theory contains more than a germ of truth in its critique of the most simplistic and extreme elite or establishment theories and in its recognition of the once-overlooked role of groups in the policymaking process. On the other hand, the consensus among these scholars is that group theory in its more extreme and naive form is far overstated.[3] Aside from the methodological difficulties of group theory (it is not a theory because it cannot generate testable propositions), it is substantively criticized as understating the role of government as just one more group interacting with others in the policymaking process. Surely, constitutionally designated structures, given their monopoly of legitimate coercive potential and their integrative functions, cannot be treated as just another group. To the extent that the variable of the political format has an independent impact on the policymaking process, our convergence thesis must be qualified (as surely it must). The differences between proponents of polyarchy and elite theory have never been demonstrably resolved. Our feeling is that groups and bargaining among them have a powerful impact on the policymaking process either explicitly or implicitly. However, the importance of the unique role of government itself or political format as a variable cannot be dismissed.

The polyarchy model overlooks latent interests. When the interests of organized groups conflict with latent interests, public policy tends to favor the former. For example, consumers have heretofore been one of the classic latent interests in the Western world. Accordingly, when the interests of the two conflict, public policy has favored producers over consumers.

To the extent that the pluralistic or polyarchy model is descriptive of reality, policymaking is highly decentralized. If, as Almond and others have suggested, the aggregative and integrative functions are indispensable for any society as a going concern,[4] the importance of parties and government to perform these functions

---

[3] One of the most lucid critiques is Harry Eckstein, "Group Theory and the Comparative Study of Pressure Groups," *Comparative Politics: A Reader,* Harry Eckstein and David Apter, eds. (New York: The Free Press, 1963), pp. 389-397.

[4] Gabriel Almond, "A Functional Approach to Comparative Politics," *The Politics of the Developing Areas,* G. Almond and J. Coleman, eds. (Princeton: Princeton University Press, 1960), pp. 12-13, 33-45.

becomes manifest. Extreme pluralism would result in a lack of coherent policymaking.

As Karl Deutsch has succinctly pointed out, "Groups with limited power usually find it easier to veto someone else's proposals than to push through any positive policy argument of their own."[5] Decentralized policymaking processes are frequently beset with an inability to act. Extreme pluralism can degenerate into a stalemate society.

The question remains of how governments can determine national or societal interests without the input from groups articulating particularistic demands. What is being raised here is the question of whether society is more than the sum of its parts and whether there exists a determinable national interest above and beyond the particular interests of that nation. If not, the task becomes one of mobilizing important latent interests to counterbalance the disproportionate impact of those already organized instead of decrying the divisive impact of "factions."

The Level of Organizational Life

The level of organizational life in a political system is to a large extent a function of whether such an "intermediate" level (between the individual and the government) of associational life is legitimate. The level of associational life refers to the extent to which individuals belong to formal associations instead of remaining as atomized individuals. It is regarded as axiomatic that individuals as such cannot have a significant impact on powerful modern governments. Individuals can only influence modern government and render it accountable to society through the intermediary structure of groups.

As discussed in Chapter 4, the legitimacy of organizational life in France has been diminished by the permeation of French society with the political philosophy of Jean Jacques Rousseau. This has resulted in the fact that in France the term *interest group* has had a pejorative connotation. Further impeding the level of organizational life in France is what Jesse Pitts has called "the cult of prowess."[6] It is an individualistic component in the French culture, a mechanism for symbolically asserting one's individual worth. It contributes to the fear of face-to-face power relations discussed in Chapter 3.

By contrast, the representation of particular interests has always been considered an entirely legitimate enterprise in Great Britain. The concept of the "interested MP" refers to the openness with which a member of the House of Commons avows sponsorship of the aims and claims of particular organizations in

---

[5] Karl Deutsch, *Politics and Government: How People Decide Their Fate* (Boston: Houghton Mifflin, 1974), p. 61.
[6] Jesse Pitts, "Continuity and Change in Bourgeoisie France," *In Search of France,* Stanley Hoffman, ed. (New York: Harper Torchbooks, 1963), pp. 235–304, especially p. 241.

British society.⁷ Many MPs make no secret of the fact that they either had or still maintain a formal connection with "special-interest" organizations.⁸ Even in the United States it is considered unethical for a member of Congress or the government to retain formal connections to any private interests or corporate sector of the economy. The British simply recognize that to divest oneself of an active office or stock portfolio in a private organization does not foreclose a natural predisposition to empathize with that organization's perspective on various issues.

Consequently, organizational activity is more covert in France than in Britain. Only France among the democratic nations we are considering is so pervaded by a philosophy that impedes organizational life. No other nation puts as much stress on individualism. (The closest, perhaps, is the United States. While special interests are deplored by Americans—beginning with *The Federalist Papers* Number 10—their inevitability is widely recognized. Although constraints are placed on the overtness of the interest connections of members of the government, lobbying is a quite legitimate and pervasive activity.)

In Italy, especially in the southern half of the peninsula, the "familism" pattern discussed in Chapter 2 also has a negative effect on the level of organizational life.⁹ This is not to imply, however, that interest groups do not have a powerful impact on the policymaking process in Italy. They clearly do. We are merely suggesting that a larger portion of the Italian population is not organized and that individuals belong to fewer organizations than is the case in, say, Anglo-American and Scandinavian democracies.

A system such as that found in the Soviet Union is the least tolerant of interest groups. As observed earlier, the ideological claim of the communist party to understand the "scientific" laws of social development rules out the activities of competing and spontaneous interests. A communist system does contain a large number of formal mass organizations for youth, workers, writers, and many other groups, but their purpose is to allow the elite to mobilize and direct society along the "correct" path. The level of organizational life is thus relatively high, but the groups are controlled, not autonomous. An intermediate level of autonomous groups representing particular interests would not be considered legitimate.

An important influence of interest groups, whether legitimate or not, appears to be an inevitable concomitant of an advanced state of technology (that is, in mature

---

[7] See the statement of Winston Churchill on the matter quoted in S. E. Finer, *Anonymous Empire: A Study of the Lobby in Great Britain* (London: The Pall Mall Press Ltd., 1958), pp. 40–41. Finer's work is a standard one on the topic.

[8] Finer reproduces a table naming the MPs, the organizations they represent, and the nature of the formal connection between them. See Table II in *Ibid.*, pp. 136–145.

[9] Joseph LaPalombara, *Interest Groups in Italian Politics* (Princeton: Princeton University Press, 1964), pp. 38–43. He speaks of the dominance of primary associations and how the traditional culture renders the formation of secondary associations difficult in that nation.

industrial and postindustrial societies) for two reasons. First, as already discussed, industrial and postindustrial societies are characterized by a knowledge explosion. The quantity and variety of information required to reach decisions and process issues for these societies have expanded geometrically. Western legislators, as we will see, tend to be generalists—often people with a legal background. Interest groups, by definition, focus on specific issues or particular sectors of society. Because they are more specialized than most politicians, interest groups are able to provide information on which most politicians have come to rely. The reliance of the Italian Ministry of Industry and Commerce on the technical reports provided by Confindustria (Italy's equivalent of the American National Association of Manufacturers or the Confederation of British Industries) was acknowledged to LaPalombara by an inspector general in that ministry.[10] Although aware that these reports are likely to be biased, the Italian officials feel obliged to overlook such bias because they lack alternative sources of information. This is apparently just a more pronounced example of a tendency discernible throughout the Western world—the reliance of political decision makers for information on the very corporate sectors of society they are supposed to regulate.

Second, an advanced state of technology facilitates the formation of secondary associations. This is true because a secondary association is one in which the members do not all come at some point into face-to-face contact. Therefore, associations require the development of communication grids permitting interaction that is not face to face. Despite culturally caused variations in the level of secondary associational life, associational activity will be significantly more well developed in industrial and postindustrial societies than in preindustrial or industrializing societies.

The Relationship Between Parties and Interest Groups

Although the articulation and aggregation of demand functions are shared by parties and groups, the degree to which party systems perform the aggregation function varies from system to system. There have been highly fragmented party systems in the Netherlands, Weimar Germany, and Third or Fourth Republic France and highly aggregated systems in Britain, the older Commonwealth, and the Bonn Republic. Almond emphasizes that articulation and aggregation of interests are necessary in any political system, but he fails to point out that they are, to a large extent, logically conflicting imperatives. That is, the aggregation process involves the filtering of demands and their restatement at a higher level of generality. This clearly distorts the actual configuration of demands in a society. The British Labour Party, for example, may try to articulate the interests of the working class in general and, in so doing, oppose the interests of a particular sec-

---

[10] *Ibid.*, pp. 281–283.

tor of the labor force. Accordingly, it was found that the 1974 demands of the coal miners would have an adverse impact on other sectors of British society or even on the British working class. Thus, aggregation involves a distortion of demands instead of their undiluted transmission. To the extent that demands are aggregated, the structure performing the aggregation function is not articulating the specific demands.

In those systems with aggregated party systems, a well-developed set of interest groups becomes necessary to articulate the demands of society at a greater degree of specificity. The specific trade unions in Great Britain speak for the specific demands of their members, thereby "freeing" the Labour Party to concern itself with the interests of British society as a whole or at least with a more generalized segment of that society. The fragmentation of the party systems of pre-Gaullist France, Weimer Germany, and, to a lesser extent, Italy may be in part reflective of a less well-developed associational life in those systems.

In continental Europe, the boundary between political parties and the interest groups that support them has tended to be less precise than in the United States. There is a logical basis for expecting this blurring of the distinction to be more pronounced in fragmented party systems than in aggregated ones. This follows from the proposition that the functions performed by parties are more similar to those performed by groups in the fragmented party systems than in the aggregated ones.

These generalizations describe reality only approximately, however. In the case of some highly aggregative labor-based parties such as the British Labour Party, this expectation of a clear distinction between party and group is simply untrue in a structural sense.[11] We have discussed how the TUC is a source of membership and financial support for the British Labour Party through the mechanism of "contract out." In France, the General Confederation of Labor (CGT) is closely associated with the Communist party, as was the Work Force (FO) with the old SFIO, as expected in a fragmented party system. But the tie between the Swedish LO and its aggregated Social Democratic Party, while not formalized, is in fact close with some of the same individuals occupying elite roles in both the LO and the party. It will be recalled that in principle externally created parties are thought of as instruments of the social movements that created them. Accordingly, continental labor-based parties tend to be closely tied to the trade union confederations of which they are supposed to be political agents.

Because the major concern of groups is to influence policy, not to control

---

[11] Maurice Duverger, *Political Parties*, Barbara and Robert North, trans. (New York: Wiley Science Editions, 1963). Duverger mistakenly attributes this property to the aggregated British Labour Party. The error lies in confusing formal structural arrangements with political realities. As discussed above, Robert McKenzie, *British Political Parties* (New York: St. Martin's Press, 1963), and Samuel Beer, *British Politics in the Collectivist Age* (New York: Alfred A. Knopf, 1965), effectively refute this gross oversimplification.

government, groups try to maintain a consistent access to authoritative decision-making processes regardless of who is in power.[12] This tactical consideration is taken into account with regard to group ties to particular political parties. If the connection becomes exclusive, the group loses much access when the group is out of power. This becomes an especially relevant consideration in hegemonic situations where one or more major sectors of the political spectrum is more or less permanently out of power.

In Sweden, for example, the employers association and federation of industries have not only eschewed close relations with their nominal parliamentary spokesmen, but have also sought close relations with the perpetually ruling Social Democratic Party through regularized consultative procedures such as Harpsund Democracy, the Research Council, and the Planning Board discussed below. The Social Democratic Party also receives the support of such groups as the Consumer Cooperative (KF).[13] This is not unexpected for a party receiving about half of the nation's votes.

When we speak of a close relationship between party and interest group, a question arises as to the direction of control and power flow. In other words, who is an agent of whom? In the case of labor and social democracy, the theoretical flow of power and control is upward from the group to the party, although in practice this is an oversimplification at best. In the case of Christian democracy, the theoretical flow of power is downward. Numerous Catholic groups exist under the ostensible aegis of the party. This, too, is an oversimplification in practice. The boundary between Italy's Catholic Action and the DC is blurred by the dependency of the latter on the electoral support of the former. Catholic Action not only delivers millions of Catholic votes to the DC, but has also strongly influenced, if not controlled, the party's nominations. According to LaPalombara, ex-Prime Minister Amitore Fanfani's major goal was to make the party more autonomous of that group.[14]

In the Netherlands, despite the fragmentation of the party system, interest groups are not instruments of the parties. In fact, they provide linkages across the boundaries of the subcultures. Thus, in a sense, Dutch groups perform an aggregation function that Dutch parties fail to perform.

Farmers' organizations may be closely tied to agrarian-based parties where these parties exist. The parties (now renamed center) are strongest in Norway and Sweden. The best example of close ties between a farmers' interest group and an agrarian party is probably that found in Norway.[15]

---

[12] David Truman, *The Governmental Process* (New York: Alfred A. Knopf, 1965), p. 264 ff, suggests access to power is the basic objective of interest groups.

[13] M. Donald Hancock, *Sweden: The Politics of Post-Industrial Change* (Hinsdale, IL: The Dryden Press, 1972), p. 154.

[14] LaPalombara, *op. cit.*, pp. 336–337.

[15] Harry Eckstein, *Division of Cohesion in Democracy: A Study of Norway* (Princeton: Princeton University Press, 1966), p. 151.

Group Tactics in Parliamentary Democracies

Harry Eckstein, in a classic discussion of the properties, strengths, and tactics of groups, made a self-evident proposition: "Pressure groups tend to adjust the form of their activities not so much to the formal (constitutional) structure of governments as to the distribution of effective power within a governmental apparatus."[16] In other words, pressure groups concentrate their activities on the structures where the actual decisions affecting their perceived interests are made.

In the following chapter, we note two major trends in the location of actual power in parliamentary democracies: first, the increasing predominance of the executive over the legislature in the formal process of policy formulation; second, the growing transfer of the function of the actual allocation of societal values from the political to the administrative sector. The most obvious entailment of these trends is the decline in the political importance of the individual member of the legislature. Under a system of party discipline such as exists in Great Britain, the discretion of the ordinary MP is virtually nil. As cabinet government replaces French-style assembly dominance, the scope of political choice afforded the legislature is significantly narrowed.

In the imperial presidency of Gaullist France, the importance of ordinary deputies fades into further insignificance. In that system, the legislature does not even provide the understood limits on executive discretion that it does in a highly centralized cabinet system such as Great Britain. Lobbying or otherwise trying to influence the individual legislator as interest groups do in the United States is therefore not likely to pay high dividends in the Anglo-American democracies or in Western Europe. Even if the legislator becomes convinced of a person's point of view, the legislator cannot exert much influence in the person's behalf.

In cases of executive dominance, the interest group is faced with the choice of trying to influence the political executive, an often inaccessible object of political influence, or of concentrating its efforts on the administrative sector. The latter alternative is most frequently pursued. In Italy, larger interest groups practically co-opt the ministry charged with regulating their sector of the economy. The extent to which Confindustria has dominated the Ministry of Industry and Commerce is one of the clearest examples of this.[17] Personal friendships between leaders of Confindustria and the leading bureaucrats in the ministry—plus reliance by those bureaucrats on information and other resources provided by Confindustria—have resulted in a situation in which the bureaucrats have come to see Confindustria as representative of that sector of the economy. Most prospective regulations affecting Italian heavy industry are not given effect without first granting Confindustria a strong input in their formulation. This clientele form of relationship, as labeled by LaPalombara, is possible where one group enjoys a virtual monopoly of representing a given sector of society. Where that sector—labor, for

---

[16] Harry Eckstein, *Pressure Group Politics* (Stanford: Stanford University Press, 1960), p. 16.
[17] LaPalombara, *op. cit.*, p. 266 ff.

example—is divided among several groups, as with Italy's Catholic, communist, and noncommunist, secular unions, no single group is able to achieve that kind of domination. On the other hand, Catholic Action, speaking for the Roman Catholic church in Italian politics, is said to possess the power to affect the course of bureaucratic careers significantly.[18] This group clearly is not forced to compete with other groups for the loyalty of its clientele.

Groups in Segmented Societies

Groups tend to be faced with competition in segmented societies. As pointed out earlier, where Catholicism is a dominant but not totally pervasive force in a society, organized labor will be divided among those who belong to Catholic unions, those who belong to secular unions, and those who belong to communist or socialist unions. The clearest example of this configuration of interest-group activity divided along subcultural lines is perhaps the situation found in the Netherlands. There each of the major corporate sectors of society divides itself into four major groups reflecting that society's four subcultural blocs: the Catholic, the orthodox Protestant, the nonsocialist secular, and the socialist. Thus, Catholic laborers tend to belong to a Catholic Union (NKV), the socialists belong to a socialist union (NVV), there is a Protestant union (CNV), and even the liberals have a small union (NVC). Similarly, there are three employers' associations: Catholic, Protestant, and liberal; there are three farmers' associations; and so forth.[19]

Austria is something of an exception to this tendency. Despite the *lager* division of Austrian society, discussed in Chapter 4, economic interest groups in Austria are organized along socioeconomic lines. Thus, labor is almost entirely under the aegis of the socialist *lager* and the SPO; business and agriculture are overwhelmingly in the camp of the OVP.[20] A few Austrian workers belong to the Catholic Workers' and Employers' League, which, as its name implies, is more reflective of potential conflicts of interests between Catholics and non-Catholics than between workers and employers.

Groups and the Policymaking Process

An increasingly prevalent pattern of interest-group impact on the bureaucratic sector is a conciliar type of activity. This involves the establishment of special advisory councils to deal with certain sectors of the economy. These councils are

---

[18] *Ibid.*, p. 331.
[19] Arend Lijphart, *The Politics of Accommodation: Pluralism and Democracy in the Netherlands* (Berkeley: University of California Press, 1968), pp. 36–40.
[20] Frederick Engleman, "Austria: The Pooling of Opposition," *Political Oppositions in Western Democracies*, Robert Dahl, ed., *op. cit.*, p. 267.

typically comprised of representatives of the various interests affected by policy in that area and members of the public administration sector who deal with policy. Economic policies are hammered out by a process of bargaining among the members of these councils and presented to the constitutionally designated lawmaking bodies (the cabinet or legislature) in the form of recommendations. Because these policy recommendations are supposed to reflect the functionally specific expertise of the members of the council, it is difficult for the generalists in the government to reject the recommendations or even to alter them significantly. In effect, significant economic policy is made by bureaucrats and interest groups.

Interest groups, instead of influencing government toward a favorable treatment of their clientele, often become in effect an agency of the government. Interests that become of such strength that government cannot disregard them may be co-opted by the government. This process of co-optation is one of the major ways in which the Soviet Union deals with articulated demands. Again, a similarity between the Soviet Union and the democratic nations in the industrial world may be discerned.

One of the most discussed such councils in the democratic world is the British National Economic and Development Council, known in characteristically British slang as "Neddy." Neddy is comprised of three cabinet ministers (the chancellor of the exchequer, the minister of labour, and the president of the board of trade), two chairmen of nationalized industries, six industrial executives, six trade union leaders, two "independents" (a Conservative banker and a Labourite economist were the first to fill these roles), and a director general.[21] Set up in response to a perceived need for increased economic planning (for example, setting production goals and allocating economic resources), Neddy is expected to produce detailed policy recommendations that cabinets find difficult to alter significantly, let alone reject. These policy recommendations are hammered out in a process of bargaining among the members of Neddy. Neddy thus provides a forum for bargaining among the major interests.

Neddy's conceptualization was influenced by the French *Commissariat Général du Plan* (roughly, General Planning Commissionership) that formulated several four-year plans contributing to France's rapid postwar economic growth. Committees of industrialists and trade unionists negotiated with bureaucrats, economists, and statisticians in the formulation of these plans.[22] The plans are not binding on private enterprise, but strong social pressures exist to take the prescriptions of the plans into account.

Economic policy hammered out by negotiation among governmental officials and representatives of major organized interests is institutionalized in Sweden by

---

[21] James Christoph, "The Birth of Neddy," *Cases in Comparative Politics* (Boston: Little Brown, 1965), p. 79.
[22] Lowell Norman, *France: The Politics of Continuity in Change*, (New York: Holt Rinehart and Winston, 1970), pp. 28–29.

two structures: royal commissions and the Planning Board. Royal commissions originally functioned in much the same role as American congressional investigative committees—to gather facts on specific issues on which the legislature could act. More recently, they have formulated recommendations on broader considerations of social and economic policy, recommendations "that often effectively bind the government to a given course of action."[23] The Planning Board is comprised of representatives of major Swedish interests and bureaucrats from the ministries of finance, trade, and commerce and transportation. The function of the Planning Board is to advise the government on long-term economic planning.

These interest groups also make up a Research Council coordinating fact gathering on specific economic and developmental problems. The Research Council and the Planning Board have supplanted a much-criticized process of formulating economic policy through regular, unofficial negotiations involving organization leaders and members of the government. These unofficial negotiations were known as "Harpsund Democracy" after the location of the meetings. The extra-parliamentary agreements were "subsequently 'rubber-stamped' by the Socialist majority,"[24] provoking much understandable criticism by the nonsocialist parties who rightly feared that they were being deprived of any impact on the decision-making process.

In the Netherlands, this kind of structure institutionalizing bargaining among relevant groups and hammering out policy proposals that the government is prone to accept may be found in the Labor Foundation. Created in 1945, it is composed of representatives of each of the three labor federations (secular, Catholic, and Protestant) and three major employer organizations (similarly organized). The cabinet, although not participating in the foundation, would be hard pressed to reject one of its policy recommendations supported, as such recommendations are, by both labor and management.

More closely paralleling Neddy is the Netherlands' Economic and Social Council created by the Industrial Organizations Act of 1950. Labor, management, and government are all represented in this body. The unions and employer organizations each nominate 15 members. Specific organizations nominate in proportion to their size. The 15 government representatives are chosen by the cabinet. This group can offer advice, both solicited and unsolicited, on any major domestic issue—advice that cabinets cannot practically reject.

Similar processes can be discerned in the United States. For example, the Business Council, made up of about 120 top industrial executives, provides "research and advisory services to more than a dozen departments and agencies, including the White House."[25]

[23] Hancock, *op. cit.*, p. 156. This discussion of Swedish interest groups relies heavily on information provided by Hancock.
[24] *Ibid.*, p. 162.
[25] *The Portland Oregonian*, October 31, 1966, p. 22.

In West Germany, workers are "directly represented in numerous governmental advisory bodies and supervisory councils."[26] Moreover, under the lengthy business-oriented Adenauer regime, business had direct, informal access to the chancellor. Labor, in addition, has acquired the formal right to participate in certain management decisions. This much-heralded policy of codetermination has had less impact than its proponents hoped because of lack of interest on the part of labor in such participation. Perhaps the habit of submission to authority mentioned in Chapter 3 impedes worker participation.[27]

It begins to appear that the formal institutionalization of a process of negotiation and bargaining among government and representatives of major corporate interests is an increasingly widespread pattern in industrial democracies. Further, negotiation and bargaining may increasingly be regarded as the source of major economic and social legislation in these countries. In short, structures that are not part of the government per se (that is, the legislature, cabinet, or bureaucracy) not only attempt to influence the policymaking process; the extragovernmental structures in fact directly participate in the policymaking process. Clearly, it is impossible to understand how policy is really made by confining attention to constitutionally designated structures.

Uncritical acceptance by the political processes of the recommendations in whose formulations interest groups participate directly is likely to be an increasingly inevitable fact of life in mature industrial societies. This is not a result of a nefarious design to subvert the public interest in the name of selfish special interests. Instead, it is a result of the extent to which policy is increasingly based on a large and complex body of knowledge that only specialized groups can provide. When groups play a role in the deliberative process that is roughly coequal with that of government, Dahl's polyarchy model and Bently's group process model are descriptive of reality.

Types of Interest Groups

Almond has offered a classification of interest groups that is useful for descriptive purposes.[28] As with Almond's other typologies, it is less useful for explanatory purposes because his criteria for which specific groups are included in a given category are too imprecise. Furthermore, the criteria that make one set of distinctions in his typology (organizational criteria) are not the same as those that make another set of distinctions (the purpose of the groups). Although it provides some

---

[26] Edinger, *op. cit.*, p. 226.
[27] Herbert Spiro, *The Politics of German Co-determination* (Cambridge: Harvard University Press, 1958).
[28] Gabriel Almond and G. Bingham Powell, *Comparative Politics: A Developmental Approach* (Boston: Little Brown, 1966), pp. 74–80; Almond, "A Functional Approach to Comparative Politics," *The Politics of the Developing Areas, op. cit.*, p. 33 ff.

preliminary order to the bewildering array of groups, Almond's classification lacks theoretical importance because it is not clear that groups in one of his categories are different from those in other categories except in those criteria that constitute his definitions.

For example, Almond distinguishes between "institutional" and "associational" groups. But it is not clear that institutional groups as a class engage in different tactics or have a different impact than associational groups. It will be suggested below that the tactics and impact of groups are a function of that society's culture, political format, etc. Despite all of this, we find the categories he sets up a useful tool for describing the otherwise bewildering array of interest groups.

Associational Interest Groups

When people use the term *interest group*, they usually have associational organizations in mind. Associational interest groups are those formally organized structures specifically designed to influence the political process for some corporate interest (such as labor, business, etc.). We think it is useful to distinguish between those groups whose purpose is to represent the perceived interest of some corporate sector of society and those groups specifically designed to influence the political process for some particular issue or cause. The former type of formally organized and explicit interest group tends to be an ongoing structure adjusting its aims to the perpetually shifting array of issues and circumstances. The latter type of group loses its reason for being as the issue in which it is particularly interested is resolved one way or the other. Accordingly, cause-oriented groups are discussed separately below.

Associational interest groups are pervasive in mature industrial societies because all such societies give rise to perceived differences in social and economic interests. Thus, patterns may be discerned in that in each society one generally finds some sort of organization purporting to represent industrial labor, one representing big business, one representing agriculture, etc.

The strength and effectiveness of the groups, however, vary with the legitimacy of group activity in that political system. As pointed out elsewhere in this chapter, strength is a function of a number of factors of which number of members is only one. Thus, there are about 80 million members of trade unions in the Soviet Union; about one out of every three citizens is a member. But these numbers are deceptive because Soviet trade unions, unlike their counterparts in more open societies, are not autonomous of the governing elite.

Among the democratic nations under consideration, trade unions and manufacturers' organizations tend to be the most powerful associational interest groups. A general confederation is the normal organizational form for these groups, and each of the nations has a federation or confederation of unions. In the United States, it is the AFL-CIO. The corresponding group in Great Britain is the Trade Union Congress (TUC), the Federation of Labor (LO) in Sweden, the General Confederation of Labor (CGT) in France, the Trade Union Federation (DGB) in Germany, and the General Confederation of Labor (CGIL) in Italy.

As pointed out above, groups tend to reflect the structure of the society in which they are located; therefore, trade union movements in segmented societies will be segmented along the same lines. The segmentation of the trade union movement in the Netherlands was shown above to parallel that society's four subcultural blocs. The Belgian trade union movement is similarly segmented into a Catholic Confederation of Christian Syndicates (CSC), a Socialist General Worker Federation of Belgium, and a Confederation of Liberal Trade Unions of Belgium (CGSLB). The Catholic federation is proportionately stronger than in any other Western nation.

In every nation with a strong Catholic population, there is a separate Catholic trade union federation. The appeal of this kind of federation to Catholic workers is enhanced when the main secular trade union federation is controlled by the communists, as is the case in both Italy and France. Some of these Catholic trade union federations appear to be as interested in mobilizing their members for the church as in representing their economic interests vis à vis employers. The French Confederation of Christian Workers (CFTC) exemplifies this problem to the point where most of their formerly affiliated unions have broken off and formed the French and Democratic Labor Federation (CFDT). The Catholic Union in Italy (the CISL) has become much more militant in recent years in making demands on employers. Thus, there may be a trend among Catholic labor federations to exhibit a greater concern for economic interests than for the souls of Catholic workers. If this is true, the federations should increasingly find ground for cooperative action with the secular confederations. Of course, this also depends on the extent and nature of the communist control of the unions.

There are large confederations to represent manufacturers and industrialists in the nations under consideration. The National Association of Manufacturers (NAM) is well known to most Americans. The Federation of British Industries (FBI) has recently changed its name to Confederation of British Industries (CBI) to avoid the obvious confusion over its initials. Confindustria of Italy has already been discussed at some length. The counterpart of these groups in West Germany is the Federation of German Industry (BDI). The close relationship between Confindustria and the Italian Ministry of Industry and Commerce is indicative of the particularly strong impact these groups have on the political process of their respective nations. While this impact may vary somewhat with the ideological nature of the party in power, the wealth and resources of the groups plus the obvious potential impact of each group on its nation's economy ensures that the groups have a large measure of impact regardless of who is in power. The bargaining between the Swedish Social Democratic Party and both the Swedish Federation of Industries and the Swedish Employers' Federation provides a case in point.

The major industrialist federations are supplemented by other federations of business-oriented organizations in nearly every country under consideration, such as the American Chambers of Commerce, the Swedish Employers' Federation, the Federation of German Employers' Associations, and the Belgian Federation of Nonindustrial Enterprises. The raison d'être of these groups is that probusiness interests extend beyond those of heavy industry.

Agricultural groups comprise another set of associational interest groups in many of the nations under consideration. Obviously, like agrarian parties, the numerical strength of the constituencies of these groups is declining with the progressive urbanization of the industrial world. Their remaining strength is concentrated in the more rural sections of their respective nations. For example, the Belgian Farmers' League (Boerenbond) derives much of its strength from the more bucolic Flemish part of Belgium.

Institutional Interest Groups: Churches

Institutional interest groups are those formally organized groups whose primary function is something besides the promotion of interests or making demands on the political process. They make demands from time to time and thus intermittently function as interest groups. Some of them exert pressures or make demands on the political process almost constantly, but that is still not their primary function.

Churches exemplify institutional interest groups. Associational interest groups are organized for the explicit purpose of promoting a set of interests, while the primary function of churches is administering to the religious needs of their flocks.

To an extent that varies from one nation to another, churches attempt to influence the political process, although that is clearly not their primary purpose. Among the nations we are considering the political impact of the church is most manifest In Italy and France in that order. A church's political impact will vary with the extent that the religion it represents does not conflict with competing organized faiths in that nation and to the extent that the culture of the nation is *not* secularized. In Italy, the church tries to influence the political both through affiliated groups, especially Catholic Action, and through direct intervention by the clergy. Because Catholic social doctrine has specific policy entailments (for example, legislation concerning abortion, contraception, or divorce), it is perhaps inevitable that the church has been heavily engaged in promoting its claims on the political process. For centuries, the church interpreted nearly all manifestations of liberalism as antithetical to its interests and accordingly was prone to oppose them. Thus, in France the church opposed the revolution and strongly supported the prosecution of Dreyfus.

The Dreyfus affair was a famous emotion-laden event that bequeathed a lasting legacy on the French political community. Dreyfus was a high-ranking Jewish French army officer prosecuted for treason and sent to Devil's Island at the conclusion of the Franco-Prussian War. The search for a scapegoat to assuage France's humiliating defeat in that war probably motivated the prosecution in the first place. A Jew in the upper echelons of the army provided the perfect scapegoat. The church, together with the forces of the right, supported the prosecution, while the forces of the left strongly supported Dreyfus' claim of innocence. Both sides pursued their case with missionary zeal, and the issue was framed in terms of basic values, not in terms of Dreyfus' guilt or innocence, a not unexpected development in such an ideological political culture. When Dreyfus was eventually exonerated, the church and the military were so thoroughly discredited that they were rendered politically impotent for decades.

The decentralization of organized Protestantism and its doctrinal stress on individualism has resulted in its playing a much smaller political role than organized Catholicism.

The Influence of the Military

Another major institutional interest group in the industrial world deserving of particular mention is the military. In the countries discussed in this book, the influence of the military is generally distinguished by how small it is in comparison with many so-called "Third World" countries in Africa, Asia, and Latin America. A strong political influence by the military has generally been confined to those nations with a large standing army. It will be recalled from Chapter 2 that this means societies with permeable borders that have had greater difficulty consolidating themselves as a sovereign nation. Thus, the military has played a major political role in only France and Germany, and its role in those countries was intermittent. It will be recalled, for example, that the influence of the French army went into eclipse after the Dreyfus affair.

The impact of the French army once again became strong after the Second World War. It played a major role in the collapse of the Fourth Republic and its replacement by the more authoritarian Fifth Republic. Concern over a conciliatory attitude toward Algerian nationalism by the French government was a prime motivating force for the French army at this time. The army continued to work for the maintenance of French colonial control over Algeria (partially through the Secret Army Organization, the OAS, culminating in the abortive military putsch of April 1961.)

Writing in 1963, Bernard Brown suggested a continuing influence of the army under the DeGaulle regime negating the popular hypothesis that the influence of the French army was due to the weakness of the Fourth Republic.[29] A later assessment by Maurice Duverger, however, is that the influence of the military has declined precipitously since then.[30] This decline does not necessarily disprove the conjectural relationship between the influence of the military and a standing army; however, the current eclipse of French military influence is at least in part a reaction to the excesses of military activity during the Algerian crisis. It is too early to determine if this eclipse is temporary. After all, there were four major conspiracies involving the military during the Algerian crisis, and the penalties suffered by the perpetrators of these acts served to deplete the French officer corps of its top leaders and most politically active individuals.

The German army in the Weimar Republic supported the early aspirations of Hitler's Nazi forces. In reaction to the Nazi period, the political role of the military has been carefully circumscribed in the Federal Republic of Germany since its inception.

Noninstitutional, Anomic, and Violent Expressions of Interest

Because one of the hallmarks of an industrial system is a high level of organizational life,[31] Almond's other two categories of nonassociational and anomic groups are less characteristic in industrial societies than they are in developing or non Western societies. Nonassociational interests refer to those ethnic, religious, status, or class groups that do not possess formal organization and act as a group intermittently. In short, they correspond to latent interests. Although major latent interests clearly have existed in industrial democracies (consumers, etc.), the tendency is for their increasing organization. It appears that the percentage of interests in industrial societies that are not organized has gradually but progressively diminished. The organization of consumerism in the United States is one manifestation of this. This tendency is most pronounced in those systems that already possess high levels of organizational life.

---

[29] Bernard Brown, "Pressure Politics in the Fifth Republic," *Journal of Politics*, Vol. 25, No. 3, August 1963, p. 522.

[30] Maurice Duverger, *Party Politics and Pressure Groups: A Comparative Introduction* (New York: Thomas Y. Crowell, 1972), p. 155.

[31] This relation between development and level of associational life has become almost axiomatic in the literature on development. See for instance, Norman Nie, G. Bingham Powell, and Kenneth Prewitt, "Social Structure and Political Participation: Developmental Relationships," *The American Political Science Review*, Vol. LXIII, Nos. 2 and 3, June and September 1969, pp. 361-378, 808-832; Daniel Lerner, *The Passing of Traditional Society* (New York: The Free Press, 1958), Chap. 2; and David McCrone and Charles Cnudde, "Toward a Communications Theory of Democratic Development: A Causal Model," *The American Political Science Review*, Vol. LXI, No. 1, March 1967, pp. 72-80.

Anomic groups are those that are more or less spontaneous, such as mobs. This kind of activity has become disturbingly more prevalent in industrial societies since about 1960. Anomic group behavior frequently involves political violence.

Although there is a fair amount of information suggesting that political violence is, in the aggregate, less frequent in mature industrial societies than in developing ones, events such as the urban and student riots in the United States in the 1960s, the events of May 1968 in France, and student riots in West Germany indicate that violent and anomic behavior has far from disappeared in the nations with which we are concerned.[32] This kind of behavior has been related to what Ted Gurr calls "structural facilitation."[33] This refers, among other things, to the existence of organizations whose purpose is to mobilize behavioral expressions of antisystem sentiment (such as Communist parties). Thus, organizational life can facilitate violence. The question that is begged is under what conditions are these organizations formed to mobilize violence. Feierabend, Feierabend, and Nesvold have produced a body of literature relating levels of violence to what they call "systemic frustration."[34] This term basically refers to the failure of the system to satisfy consciously perceived demands. To the extent that this hypothesis is valid, the existence of more legitimate institutional channels to influence the political process should make violent or anomic behavior less likely. Violence in industrial societies may reflect the mobilization of previously latent interests prior to the development of legitimate institutional channels to process the demands ensuing from the mobilized interests.[35] Thus, a fully developed or modernized society (in the sense of a fully developed and inclusive set of institutions for articulating, aggregating, and processing demands) may be expected to have a low level of violence, while a modernizing or developing society may have a higher level of violence.[36] Where the industrial societies considered in this volume have not developed structures for articulating, aggregating, and processing self-conscious interests, the

---

[32] For example, William Flanigan and Edwin Fogelman, "Patterns of Political Violence in Comparative Perspective," *Comparative Politics*, Vol. III, No. 1, October 1970, pp. 1–20, discusses the negative relationship between violence and development. Compare Douglas Hibbs, *Mass Political Violence: A Cross-National Causal Analysis* (New York: John Wiley & Sons, 1973), pp. 21–31.

[33] Ted R. Gurr, "A Causal Model of Civil State: A Comparative Analysis Using New Indices," *American Political Science Review*, Vol. LXII, No. 4, December 1968, pp. 1104–1124.

[34] For example, Ivu and Rosalind Feierabend, "Systemic Conditions of Political Aggression: An Application of the Frustration-Aggression Theory," *Anger, Violence, and Politics*, Feierabend, Feierabend, and Gurr, eds. (Englewood Cliffs: Prentice Hall, 1972), pp. 136–181. Feierabend, Feierabend, and Nesvold, "Social Change and Political Violence: Cross National Patterns," *Violence in America*, Hugh Graham and Ted Gurr, eds. (N.Y.: Praeger, 1969).

[35] This is essentially the thesis of Samuel Huntington, "Political Development and Political Decay," *World Politics*, Vol. XVII, No. 1, April 1965, pp. 386–430.

[36] Huntington makes the distinction between the effect of modernity and modernization on instability in his *Political Order in Changing Societies* (New Haven: Yale University Press, 1968), p. 41.

society is less than fully developed in Huntington's sense of the term, and a certain amount of violent or anomic behavior is not unexpected.

Issue- or Cause-Oriented Groups

We have been referring to groups that speak for corporate interests of society (employers, labor, industrialists, farmers, white-collar workers, etc.) or institutions (the churches, the military, etc.). These groups articulate the point of view of the interests they represent over a wide range of issues. Other groups are organized around a single issue or ideological position that may aggregate supporters from several corporate sectors of society. For example, the antimilitary or "ban the bomb" groups that sprang up in Britain in the early years of the Cold War attracted clientele from several socioeconomic, religious, and ethnic groups. (In practice, however, middle-class intellectuals tended to be predominant.) Similarly, groups formed to protest America's involvement in the Vietnamese War attracted support across socioeconomic, ethnic, and religious lines. The New Left functions in Western Europe as well as in the United States and has generated a number of cause-oriented groups both of the formal (associational) and anomic variety.

The parochial school issue in France generated good examples of groups organized around a single issue. The intensely felt question of public aid to parochial schools resulted in the formation of a promotional group on each side of the issue: the French League for Teaching that opposed such aid and the Secretariat of Studies for Liberty in Teaching that supported the Catholic position. The latter group was instrumental in the passage of the *Barangé* law of 1951 granting aid to Catholic schools and the Debré law of 1959.[37]

The most visible promotional groups in Scandinavian democracies are temperance organizations. They tend to recruit their clientele from among practicing Protestants. Hence, their clientele is restricted.

Refugee organizations had some strength in West Germany prior to the construction of the Berlin Wall. Although not restricted to a single issue like the promotional groups just discussed, they were confined to the concerns of refugees from East Germany. Thus, these refugee organizations proved to be as temporary as promotional groups when the flow of refugees ceased.

The Autonomy of Interest Groups

One of the variables stressed by Almond is the autonomy of interest groups.[38] That is, to what extent groups are separate from the state so as to be able to make

---

[37] Brown, *op. cit.*, pp. 518–519.
[38] Almond and Powell, *op. cit.*, p. 79.

claims upon it instead of being co-opted by the state to regulate and control their alleged clientele for the purposes of the state.

Clearly, a degree of co-optation exists in Western democracies, although it is generally on an informal level. A blatant example is the extent to which the American Farm Bureau Federation has been informally co-opted by the United States Department of Agriculture.[39] The "parentella" relationship between Italian groups and the dominant Christian Democratic Party discussed earlier clearly limits the freedom of these groups to make claims on the government. The Italian Confederation of Workers' Unions (the Catholic trade union confederation) exemplifies such a relationship with the ruling DC, as do other Catholic groups.[40] It may be argued that the relatively lower degree of autonomy among many Italian interest groups is an indication of a relatively lower degree of modernization compared to other industrial societies. If subsystem or group autonomy is a criterion of development or modernity, this would confine the concept of modernity to the Western democracies. We regard this as absurd.

We have suggested that in Western democracies one cannot say either that government agencies have co-opted and controlled groups in the strict sense or vice versa. Instead, in the various economic councils already described, such as Neddy, interests and government exist in a kind of symbiotic relationship. The relationship might be described as one of *reciprocal co-optation*. We have suggested that a reciprocal relationship between interest and government is an outgrowth of the technological imperatives of a mature industrial society. Accordingly, we should expect to find some form of this kind of relationship in the Soviet Union.

Representation of Interests in the Soviet Union
The study of groups in the Soviet Union is a fairly recent development. The idea that interest groups might play a significant role in communist politics was not really seriously considered until the 1960s. The concept of totalitarianism, with its emphasis on the unique and closed nature of the systems, combined with the atmosphere of the Cold War to produce a situation in which it was usually assumed almost automatically that the position of the party was monolithic and unchallenged. In one of the early refutations of this view, Gordon Skilling denied assertions that there was no mechanism for social forces to express themselves and that groups were mere formless clusters.[41] He maintained that there were political interest groups in David Truman's sense of the term in the Soviet Union and other communist systems. This meant groups that on the basis of shared attitudes make certain claims on other groups and especially the institutions of government.

[39] Truman, *op. cit.*, p. 92.
[40] LaPalombara, *op. cit.*, Chap. IX.
[41] H. Gordon Skilling, "Interest Groups and Communist Politics," *World Politics*, Vol. XVIII, No. 3, April 1966. p. 450.

Groups in this sense are not necessarily unified or formally organized. Their styles are appropriate to the system in which they function.

In the decade since Skilling called for reexamination of the question of groups and their relationship to the party in communist systems, many have attempted to do just that. In fact, even earlier, Brzezinski and Huntington had suggested a hierarchy ranging from "amorphous social forces" at the bottom to "policy groups" at the top with "specific interests" in between.[42] Since then the prevailing system has been described as incipient pluralism,[43] co-optation,[44] competition,[45] and polyarchism.[46] In the same period, there has been specific criticism of the application of these terms to the Soviet Union on the grounds that groups there are unstable, ephemeral, random, and incidental in their impact.[47]

Due to the nature of the Stalin period, virtually all groups in the Soviet Union came to be considered "transmission belts" (to use Stalin's term). That is, they were structures used by the regime to mobilize the citizenry and to transmit in a downward direction the directives of the elite. There was no intention to include an upward flow whereby the interests of the groups would be communicated to the leadership. In the post-Stalin period, the situation has changed somewhat. The Soviet Union does not have interest groups of the type found in most democratic party systems. At the very least there must be a process for conflict resolution among competing groups within the elite. There are indications, however, that the situation involves more group consciousness and activity than that.

It was stated earlier that the influence of interest groups seems to be an inevitable concomitant of technology and that the style of the groups is influenced by the culture in which they operate. This seems to be applicable to the Soviet Union. The question of the political generalist versus the managerial specialist is more difficult in a system that does not recognize as legitimate the expression of specfic interests. But the increasing complexity of a modern industrial society has caused the party to have to adapt in order to deal with new forces. Beginning as a revolutionary elite directing the transformation of society from above, the CPSU now finds itself in a different position.

Few people question the fact that the party is still dominant and is the arena in

---

[42] Zbigniew Brzezinski and Samuel Huntington, *Political Power: USA/USSR* (New York: The Viking Press, 1964), p. 195.

[43] Leonard Schapiro, *The Communist Party of the Soviet Union* (London: Eyre and Spottiswoode, 1970), p. 628.

[44] See Frederick J. Fleron, Jr., "Toward a Reconceptualization of Political Change in the Soviet Union: The Political Leadership System," *Comparative Politics,* Vol. I, No. 2, January 1969, pp. 228–244; and Gehlen, *op. cit.,* Chapter 1.

[45] Milton C. Lodge, *Soviet Elite Attitudes Since Stalin* (Columbus, OH: Charles E. Merrill Publishing Co., 1969), p. 115.

[46] *Ibid.* See also Skilling, *op. cit.,* p. 449.

[47] Andrew C. Janos, "Group Politics in Communist Society: A Second Look at the Pluralistic Model," Huntington and Moore, *op. cit.,* p. 443.

which decision making occurs. The point is that changes are taking place, and the party is having to react to the spontaneous developments of the industrial and postrevolutionary period. This role has been described as one of keeping the evolution of society within acceptable bounds and acting as an arbiter among various institutional groups within the bureaucratic elite.[48] Another analysis of the post-Khrushchev period deals with a contradiction between the positions of two groups within the party as to the manner in which they should respond to the new social, economic and political problems of the industrial society. The analysis sees the result of the disagreement as forfeiture of leadership and limping along, not as leadership.[49]

The most crucial aspect of these social developments is that of technology. The emergence of a technical managerial group creates problems in any system, but especially the one-party type. If the party is to retain its position, it must gain access to new knowledge and techniques. One possibility would be to retrain the elite so that it acquires the skills among its present members. The difficulties in such a plan are obvious when the party is dominated largely by professional politicians, many of whom have spent virtually their entire careers in the *apparat* (the party "machine" or hierarchy). Because it is unacceptable to let the technocrats develop as separate groups and then deal with them, the most likely course is to bring those already possessing this expertise into contact with the policymaking process, a method that has come to be known as co-optation.[50]

A number of implications are associated with this co-optation process. If it works well for the party, two objectives will have been accomplished: the necessary expertise will be acquired and the specialists will be absorbed into the dominant elite. It is also possible that this new group, possibly more dynamic and innovative and not socialized within the elite, will thus come into conflict with more conservative elements of the *apparat*.[51] Some conflict is almost inevitable, and it is up to the top leadership to control it.

However it is managed, the process illustrates the fact that in a relatively closed system such as that of the Soviet Union one cannot examine properly the question of interests without considering the subject of recruitment. As leaders or potential leaders of particular interests are recruited or co-opted into the party, there may be a representation of particular interests. If the party is successful in this effort, it will reduce the chances of opposition to the party and create a situation wherein conflicting interests can be resolved within the party. If it is not successful, it will have to deal with outside forces.

---

[48] Lowenthal, *op. cit.*, p. 4.
[49] Wolfgang Leonard, "Politics and Ideology in the Post-Khrushchev Era," Dallin and Larson, *op. cit.*, p. 69.
[50] See footnote 44 above.
[51] Huntington and Moore, *op. cit.*, p. 35.

The question of groups is broader than just the influence of technology. The role specialization that accompanies any modern society facilitates the development of a number of subgroups often known as policy groups or specialized elite. Although there is often some overlap in the use of the terms, *policy groups* usually refers to the state bureaucracy, the military, agricultural, and industrial managers, and the police apparatus. These groups, along with the technocrats, are usually seen by the party as more or less loyal; as a consequence, their influence in the policymaking process is seen as legitimate as long as they acknowledge the perogative of the party to have the last word. Within these limits their role might be seen as advocating certain (often conflicting) policies and actions. They are not outside pressure groups, but their degree of organization may make it possible for them to influence *from within* certain decisions in accordance with their particular interests.

A study of the influences involved in the Educational Reform Act of 1958 offered several observations as to the prospects for interest groups.[52] First, the more technical the issue, the more influential a specialized group can be. Second, the more power that is diffused, the more access points there will be. From the perspective of the groups, collective leadership with a larger number of powerful leaders is preferable to one-person rule. Finally, the groups are more likely to become involved when there are disputes at the top level. Underlying all of these considerations is the fact that the role specialization found in more complex societies necessitates high occupational stability. This seems to mean that groups become a more important reference point and are not as subject to arbitrary actions or punishment for expressing their views. The overall conclusion of the study was that under some circumstances, groups can influence policy formulation.

In a somewhat similar case-study type of approach, Gehlen chose the military as an example in an attempt to test the usefulness of the group approach. At the conclusion of his effort, he suggested that instead of thinking of the CPSU as the dominant group among many, we might perhaps view it as a composite of various functional groups that perform separate but overlapping roles.[53]

Specialized elite or *specific interest groups* are terms that probably most nearly approximate the normal usage of the expression *interest groups*. In the Soviet Union, they are mostly institutional groups, including churches, economic managers, and various sectors of the intelligentsia such as scientific, literary, artistic, and legal. Although they are not recognized as interest groups in the insti-

---

[52] Joel J. Schwartz and William R. Keech, "Group Influence and the Policy Process in the Soviet Union," *American Political Science Review,* Vol. LXII, No. 3, September 1968, pp. 840–851.

[53] Michael P. Gehlen, "Group Theory and the Study of Soviet Politics," *The Soviet Political Process,* Sidney I. Ploss, ed. (Waltham, MA: Ginn and Co., 1971), pp. 35–54.

tutional sense, some research on their operation suggests that they attempt with some success to influence policy. In addition to the Educational Reform Act mentioned above, there are indications of influence with regard to legal reform and military and economic policy.[54] As mentioned earlier, one factor in this influence is the communication grid possessed by those sectors of the intelligentsia that have formal associations, conferences, institutes, newspapers, and journals. Skilling feels that the specialized elite have been able to express their views and exert an influence on decisions, and that the intelligentsia "have thus emerged as one of the main pressure groups affecting public policy."[55]

In an effort to examine further the position of the specialized elite, Milton Lodge employed the technique of content analysis of certain journals of the party and of the economic, legal, military, and literary elite.[56] Acknowledging that his data did not permit the measurement of actual elite influence, Lodge assumed a positive correlation between articulated attitudes and actual behavior and sought to ascertain the attitudes. Addressing first the question of whether the elite qualify sociologically as a group, he answers with a qualified affirmative. That is, as revealed in the journals, the attitudes of the elite indicate at least a tendency toward group consciousness and a set of commonly held values sufficiently distinct from those of the *apparatchiki*. Lodge concludes that in the period under study there was a steady progression in specialist elite attitudes from the "transmission-belt" relationship, through Truman's categories of potential and active interest group, and toward a polyarchal system as described by Dahl.[57]

Although they are not as important as policy or elite groups, brief consideration must be given to latent interests and the possible demand by popular groups for greater participation. These "amorphous social forces,"[58] which probably belong in the anomic category, include workers, students, peasants, and similar elements. There are a number of instances, not so much in the Soviet Union as in countries such as Poland and Hungary, in which their influence has been felt. Even Janos, who refuses to accept descriptions such as "polyarchy" and "incipient pluralism," agrees that in some of these Eastern European countries, groups have emerged from time to time to challenge policies and even to control a particular situation.[59] We are reminded in particular of uprisings of workers that have resulted in changes in policy or even leadership.

---

[54] See such studies as Harold Berman, "The Struggle of Soviet Jurists Against a Return to Stalinist Terror," *Slavic Review*, Vol. XII, June 1963, pp. 314–320; Matthew P. Gallagher, "Military Manpower: A Case Study," *Problems of Communism*, Vol. XIII, No. 3, May–June 1964, pp. 53–62.
[55] Skilling, *op. cit.*, p. 446.
[56] For details of the research method employed see Lodge, *op. cit.*, Introduction and Appendices.
[57] *Ibid.*, Chapter 8.
[58] Brzezinski and Huntington, *op. cit.*, p. 195.
[59] Jonas, *op. cit.*, pp. 442–443.

There has also been something of a trend in Eastern European communist countries to institutionalize greater popular participation through electoral competition. The significance is limited by the fact that it is intraparty competition, but in limited instances voters are being given some choice among individuals. It is necessary, however, to remember Janos's warning that the continued existence of such forces is always precarious. The short-lived liberalization in Czechoslovakia is a case in point.

It is difficult to summarize what all this means as to the impact of interest groups in one-party communist systems. What does seem clear, at least, is that we are no longer dealing with a closed, monolithic party controlling a society totally without regard for any other interests. Although the party is still the context in which decision making takes place, other interests are involved. For several reasons, including the imperatives of modernization and technology, the party has become more of an arbiter, mediator, broker, or composite of functional interests. Because of the nature of the system—one party with relatively few points of access—we should not expect to see overt, legitimate pressure groups in the mold of Western democracies. It is much more likely that the process of interest representation will be carried on more covertly or informally through co-optation or *apparat*-specialist elite relationships.

Conclusions: Patterns and Variations in the Policymaking Process

Despite the strong criticisms of functionalism as explanatory theory,[60] we have used an implicit functional orientation to examine groups and parties. Specifically, we have implicitly assumed the universality of the functions of interest articulation (the transmission of demands from society to political decision makers) and interest aggregation (the consolidating, filtering, and reformulation of demands in manageable terms). The discussion of the ways that parties and groups share these roles adds a dimension to the description of these structures.

Parties and groups are the principal structures performing the articulation and aggregation functions in industrial societies. Individuals as such have little impact on the industrialized political process. Yet, all societies, democratic or not, make some attempt to justify their actions in terms of the interest of the governed, take account of the perceived demands of the masses, and mobilize the support of the masses for whatever the government sees fit to do. The difference in this regard between democratic and authoritarian systems is one of emphasis on either adjusting government policy to social demands or mobilizing public support for government policies.

---

[60] Lawrence Mayer, *Comparative Political Inquiry* (Homewood: Dorsey Press, 1972), Chap. 8. The use of functionalism for descriptive purpose is duly noted here.

All industrial societies must resolve conflicts emanating from the inevitable differences in interests in societies. Industrial societies differ with respect to the structures and processes employed in conflict resolution. One difference is whether corporate interests are resolved between parties or within them. In fragmented party systems, conflict resolution occurs between parties. In aggregated party systems, by definition, some conflict resolution occurs within parties. As long as there is a competitive party system, some conflict between parties presumably remains. In the Soviet Union, all legitimate conflict resolution occurs within the framework of the party.

When conflict resolution occurs within a party, some structures must exist to mobilize and articulate the several potentially conflicting interests aggregated within the party. Groups perform this function. Thus, the group functions become more imperative in aggregated party systems. It is therefore not surprising that we found a lower legitimacy and level of group activity in nations with fragmented party systems (for example, France and Weimar Germany).

We have also discerned great similarities in the structures and processes for conflict resolution in industrial societies. The major similarity is the extent to which policy is the outgrowth of institutionalized bargaining among conflicting interests. The generic nature of this process raises profound questions as to whether the differences between parties in either fragmented or aggregated party systems are important.

In aggregated party systems, the ideology and program of the parties tend to converge because all parties are competing for the same majority. Some differences in the center of gravity or overall orientation of the parties remain. Do these differences between parties entail specific differences in the resolution of issues? In other words, does it matter very much which parties are in power for who gets how much of what? If, for example, the Swedish Social Democratic party was reduced to the status of an arbitrator in the bargaining process known as Harpsund Democracy and business interests were given equal consideration with labor interests, it is fair to inquire as to what significance the ideological and organizational differences between the Social Democrats and right-wing parties have for policy outcomes. To what extent are parties merely an arbitrator in that bargaining process between interests and bureaucrats and to what extent are they somewhat autonomous policy initiators?

We have also seen that parties in industrial democracies are becoming increasingly aggregative, while the nature of a technologically advanced society demands increasing specialization—specialization that generates specific interests demanding articulation. This would seem to generate conflicting imperatives for the party systems of mature industrial societies.

At the same time, the authoritarian Soviet Union lacks the structure for the representation of specific corporate interests in its mature industrial order.

Contrary to the Marxian dream, the Bolshevik Revolution has failed to usher in an era of the disappearance of economically based conflict.

Neither in the structures constitutionally designated for the policymaking process nor in the party systems of industrial societies has provision been made for input and bargaining by the corporate interests generated by any technologically advanced society. Thus, groups perform this function by default, even when neither their existence nor their function is authorized or accepted as legitimate by their respective constitutions or cultures.

It is therefore in the nature of mature industrial societies that an increasing amount of the actual policymaking process occurs in ways not designated by constitutions and autonomously from political structures designated by constitutions for this purpose. We have shown that a process of institutionalized bargaining occurs among representatives of corporate interests in society (for instance, labor and industry) and relevant bureaucrats. This process is a pattern found in industrial societies irrespective of dominant ideology, culture, or constitutional format.

Therefore, to understand how and why policy is actually made in mature industrial societies, we must understand the growing and inescapable role of the public bureaucracy and the increasing bureaucratization of society described in Chapter 6. Furthermore, we must understand the bargaining process among representatives of corporate interests and the public bureaucracy.

This is not to suggest that the constitutionally designated structures are without impact. We have shown how these structures, in setting the arena in which the bargaining process takes place, affect the tactics of groups. For example, we have seen that the centralization of the formulation of legislation as such in the cabinet and the decline in the influence of Parliament exemplifies a structural constraint on interest-group tactics in Britain and, to a greater or lesser extent, in other parliamentary democracies. We have seen that the growing dominance of the French presidency has had a similar effect on group tactics in France.

We have also seen that in those nations where the principle of the accountability of decision makers is culturally and hence constitutionally enshrined, the role of interest groups in the policymaking process has been more legitimate and more overt.

It may be suggested that the more open constitutional systems of the industrial democracies reflect a cultural disposition to resolve issues by bargaining and to regard differences in interests as legitimate. The process of bargaining that we have suggested is to some extent inevitable in all industrial societies is more overt, more legitimate, and more institutionalized in democratic societies than in authoritarian ones. (Structures such as Neddy and Harpsund Democracy illustrate this.) Moreover, the elite of more open systems probably feel obliged to compromise to a greater extent than the elite of authoritarian systems.

Thus, we can say that we have shown important similarities in the process by which issues are actually resolved and decisions actually made in industrial societies regardless of ideology, culture, or constitutional format. But this convergence must be qualified by the impact of those variables on the extent of the compromises made and on the legitimacy, overtness, and institutionalization of the bargaining process that to a greater or lesser extent characterizes the actual decision-making process of all mature industrial societies.

Part III

Policy Outcomes and Convergence Theory

Introduction to Part III

In the preceding section, we discerned some patterns in the policymaking processes among industrial societies. We suggested that procedural patterns emanate from the imperatives of the state of technology characteristic of industrial societies.

But it is obvious that the societies under consideration vary with respect to the values and ideologies that shape their cultures. Clearly, accountability is a greater value in a society pervaded by the ideology of liberal democracy than it would in a society shaped by Stalinism.

We have seen that differences in values result in some variations in the actual policymaking process despite the imperatives of the state of technology. Thus, the state of technology and the variations in value systems are conflicting imperatives, the former encouraging patterns or convergence and the latter encouraging variations among systems.

The unanswered question is how these conflicting imperatives affect the politics themselves—the outcomes of the processes discussed in Part II.

In this section, we examine this question with respect to two important policy areas: economics and welfare policies. These policy areas are related in that they both generate allocative issues—who gets how much of what and with what justification. We expect that these will be among the most salient issue areas in mature industrial societies in the years to come.

Chapter 9

Economic Policy and Social Welfare

Throughout this book, we have suggested that in mature industrial societies the state of technology generates certain imperatives that transcend the institutional or ideological variations among the societies. We have suggested that certain kinds of processes go on and that certain structural patterns emerge in all or most of the societies despite differences among them with respect to constitutional format. Institutionalized consultations among bureaucrats and interest groups in the formulation of much domestic policy in the industrialized world exemplify the kind of emerging structural patterns of which we speak. The process of co-opting the leadership of self-conscious interests into the elite is another process that can be found to some extent throughout the industrialized world. The growing political role of the administrative sector and the increasing insulation of heads of government from strict accountability are additional trends in industrial societies—trends that further distinguish political reality from the legalities of constitutional format.

We have found patterns of qualified convergence among mature industrial nations. By using the term *qualified convergence,* we are hedging against any implication that remaining differences between

Western democracies and the European communist nations or, for that matter, among nations within these two blocs are no longer significant. On the contrary, we have found that liberal democratic values such as the accountability of decision makers and legitimacy or tolerance of opposition are found and practiced to varying degrees among mature industrial societies. Moreover, we believe that the differences between the Western and Soviet nations with respect to these values are greater than the differences among nations within these groups. Pointing out and delineating hitherto ignored or underemphasized patterns of convergence does not entail the implication that significant differences among the nations are disappearing.

We have been concerned with patterns in structure and process but have not yet discussed the policies emanating from them. It seems reasonable to suspect that the imperatives of technology and the patterns in structures and processes have imposed patterns on policy as well. We will argue that these patterns, or trends, are in fact discernible in mature industrial nations, especially in the realm of economic policy.

The Triumph of the Market System in the West

The commercial revolution signaled a dramatic increase in the importance of private property and the concomitant decline of feudalism. This process occurred to varying degrees in various sections of the Western world, and scholars disagree in setting the precise century of its occurrence; however, the process had more or less permeated what is now western and northern Europe by the sixteenth century.[1] Feudalism was never strongly entrenched in what is now Great Britain and had virtually disappeared from the Western world before the development of the older Commonwealth. This commercial revolution did not take root in Russia at all; consequently, capitalist interests and ideologies never became entrenched in the system to resist and impede the adoption of collectivist economic policies.

Feudalism was not compatible with the new commercial economy beyond a certain point.[2] The new economy was based on money, which broadened the scope of commercial activity. The political atomization of the feudal period impeded this broadening of trade and commerce. In the thirteenth and fourteenth centuries, for example, there were some 60 toll stations along the Rhine River and some 35

---

[1] The current most celebrated treatment of the origins of capitalism in Europe is Immanuel Wallerstein, *The Modern World System* (New York: Academic Press, 1974). See pp. 18, 37, etc., for citations of varying interpretations of when the feudal economy broke down and why. A maverick economist, Clarence Ayres, in a provocative interpretation of various aspects of capitalism, says the capitalists were "in the saddle" by the sixteenth century. *The Divine Right of Capital* (Boston: Houghton Mifflin, 1946), p. 10.

[2] Wallerstein, *op. cit.*, pp. 20–21.

along the Elbe.[3] The manorial system that accompanied feudalism involved fixed incomes for the landed aristocracy in the face of a steadily increasing need for working capital. Probably also hastening the demise of feudalism was the fact that the commercial and subsequent industrial revolutions provided the masses with alternatives to a serf or peasant existence.

In any event, the triumph of the commercial, entrepreneurial middle classes or bourgeoisie only briefly preceded the construction of the theory of the self-regulating market. *Entrepreneur* refers to a person who owns and manages a risk-taking enterprise, investing capital and attempting to best competition through creative innovation. *Bourgeoisie* is used by Marxists to refer to the economic middle class. Clearly, it encompasses those who own and invest capital, but the scope of the term becomes quite vague when the question of such groups as white-collar salaried clerks is raised.

Market Theory and the Defense of Bourgeoisie Interests

In the theory of the self-regulating market, prices are determined not by any person or structure, but by the impersonal forces of the interaction of supply and demand. Market theory holds that if the economy remains unregulated and everyone pursues rational economic self-interest, the market will clear (no surpluses or shortages of goods), and the needs of society will be fulfilled. Selfishness thereby is held to have desirable social consequences. Thus, low wages were a way of indicating that a form of labor was not needed by society. Poor people can command good wages simply by fulfilling social needs.

This theory was never more than a logical construct; it never accurately described the reality of any time or place. For reasons that we presently suggest, it never could so describe reality. The idea of the self-regulating market was to a large extent created as a more or less systematic critique of mercantilism and, in some cases, of the surviving remnants of feudal institutions.

The work of Adam Smith is a classic case in point.[4] Mercantilism was the idea that the wealth of nations was measured by the quantity of gold and silver in their possession. Therefore, nations should try to export more than they import. This entailed the erection of tariffs to discourage imports and to encourage domestic production. Smith and his followers argued for free trade whereby each nation would produce only that which it could produce most efficiently and import the rest. In short, he wanted international free trade, which is not the goal of many modern businesses who use free-market arguments to get the government off their backs.

[3] Robert Heilbroner, *The Making of Economic Society* (Englewood Cliffs: Prentice Hall, 1972), fourth edition, p. 59.
[4] Adam Smith, *The Wealth of Nations* (first published in 1776) (New York: Modern Library, 1937).

Thus, the idea of the self-regulating market was essentially a bourgeois argument used selectively to promote bourgeois interests. (This is not to deny, of course, that many of the proponents of the theory sincerely believed in its validity.) A major appeal of Adam Smith's theory is that it is a coherent, logical system whose assumptions or axioms render its conclusions inevitable. Nevertheless,

> ... his system can best be understood in terms of what he was reacting against. ... Smith's system of thought took its shape from his intense reaction against the elaborate apparatus of controls which the surviving feudal and mercantilist institutions were imposing on the individual.[5]

In a capitalist system, capital begets capital. The business middle class, having acquired a competitive advantage with the possession of the newly important capital, had an interest in being free to exploit that advantage. Laissez-faire, the dictum that government ought not to regulate the economy, served those interests.

In any event, social policies, even those policies logically antithetical to the idea of the self-regulating market, continued to be justified in terms of classic economic theory—at least until the 1930s and in some places to the present day. Britain and Sweden, widely identified as epitomes of the welfare state, were no exceptions to this.[6] According to Hugh Helco, policymakers in these nations assumed that unemployment resulted from keeping wages artificially too high.[7] Further, he reports that the "one persistent theme" in the history of the poor law "was an effort to discriminate between the deserving and undeserving poor."[8] The logical remedy entailed by the assumption that high wages are the cause of unemployment, that of subsistence-level wages, would obviously benefit employers.

In his classic treatise, Karl Polyani correctly suggested that the British Speenhamland Law of 1795, a landmark poor law that in effect guaranteed a minimum income (albeit a very low one), antedated the market system by preventing the treatment of labor as a commodity.[9] The Poor Law Amendment of 1834 substituted a "workhouse" plan that deprived anyone of aid if he was deemed capable of work. This forced the able-bodied poor to accept employment with wages at or below the subsistence level in lieu of starvation, thus creating the cheap labor market that the industrial revolution required. Accordingly, this Poor Law Amendment may be taken as "the starting point of modern capitalism."[10]

The triumph of capitalism never generated a consistent policy of the complete

---

[5] Ibid, "Introduction" by Max Lerner, p. ix.
[6] Hugh Helco, *Modern Social Politics in Britain and Sweden* (New Haven: Yale University Press, 1974), p. 66.
[7] Ibid., pp. 66–67.
[8] Ibid., p. 87.
[9] Karl Polyani, *The Great Transformation* (New York: Rinehart and Company, 1944), p. 80.
[10] Ibid.

separation of the political and economic sectors of society as the philosophy of *laissez-faire* entailed. As Immanuel Wallerstein says, "Quite the contrary! Capitalism is based on the constant absorption of economic loss by political entities while economic gain is distributed to 'private' hands."[11] In other words, the bourgeoisie (meaning hereafter those who make money by investment instead of by labor) expect the state to eliminate the element of risk from their capital ventures while allowing them the full benefit of their profits if successful. They want to have their cake and also to eat it. The point is that the bourgeoisie selectively used market theory when it supported their interest and ignored it when it did not.

Until well into the twentieth century (approximately the 1930s), the economic triumph of the bourgeoisie coincided with the political domination of those same middle classes throughout Europe. The political machinery of the state was used to support the economic interests of the middle class or bourgeoisie. *Laissez-faire* meant that the state should not impede commercial enterprises undertaken by the bourgeoisie; it never meant that the state should not abet and support these enterprises. Smith used market theory to support an argument for free trade on a worldwide basis; however, business entrepreneurs who used the theory to attack government at the same time grew to expect government to erect barriers to protect them from foreign competition.

Market Theory and Technological Progress

It has been argued by some of capitalism's supporters that the market system was a major factor promoting the rapid technological progress that we now call the industrial revolution. The key figure in this scenario is the entrepreneur. This figure in a purely competitive market would over the long run retrieve the value of his capital investment, including the value of his labor. It is therefore a misconception to regard the return for one's labor as profit. After all, one could get that in wages without the risk that accompanies investment. If the entrepreneurs' incomes fell below this level, some of them would presumably cease independent production or move to more lucrative enterprises; thus, the supply of that product would be decreased. Market theory accordingly suggests that at this lower level of production, buyers would bid up the price of these now scarce goods to the level of long-term market price. If the entrepreneur's income were higher, the field would attract more producers and less efficient production, thereby increasing the supply and driving the price back down.

From a purely economic point of view, however, working for the market value of one's labor does not justify the risks involved in this entrepreneurial role. The

---

[11] Wallerstein, *op. cit.*, p. 348.

entrepreneur's incentive must consist of the opportunity for return above and beyond the market value of the total investment. This goal can be realized through the creation of a monopolistic situation in which prices can be *set* by the producer, not left to the impersonal forces of the market. This monopoly can be created by innovation. That is, the entrepreneur can undo his competition either by building a better mousetrap or by building the same mousetrap more efficiently. In this way, the competition entailed in the system of the self-regulating market is held to provide incentive for technological innovation, innovation that has supposedly provided such an enormous social dividend for Western society over the past 200 years. Of course, the competitive system generates innovation by providing the incentive for its own destruction; that is, entrepreneurial success entails the breakdown of the pure competition axiomatic to the system. In this sense, Marx appears to have been right when he predicted that capitalism carries the seeds of its own destruction. (The entire argument for the self-destructive tendencies of capitalism is more complex than this. We touch on other aspects of it below.)

Problems in Market Theory
The triumph of the market system in the West quickly generated attacks on the system. These attacks were precipitated by two types of problems. The first involved the practical consequences of the free hand that the economic policy granted to business enterprises. The social dislocations of the period of unregulated capitalism generated social and political pressures for remedial action.

The second type of problem involved serious questions about the theory itself. No matter how powerful its internal coherence and deductive logic may be, any theory is only as valid as the axioms or assumptions on which it is based. To the extent that the axioms of a theory describe reality imperfectly, the predictions derived from the theory will not be realized. It is useful, therefore, to examine those axioms or assumptions.

Questionable Assumptions of Market Theory
The most basic assumption of market theory is that of the economic person. That is, market theory assumes that people are motivated solely by the pursuit of their rational economic self-interests. Taken apart, this statement claims first of all that economic considerations dominate all other motivations. Clearly, human motivation is more complex than this. People bypass lucrative opportunities for employment, for instance, to live in another area, because they do not like the work, etc.

Moreover, to pursue one's economic self-interests, one must have the information and understanding necessary to identify those interests. Being rational is not, as often supposed, the crux of the problem. Rationality is always relative to one's perception of reality and to one's goals. Market theory assumes people of a single motivation have an accurate perception of reality and are accordingly aware of their actual self-interests.

For instance, free-market advocates assume that demand is "elastic,"—that is, it is a function of price. The American strategy for conserving oil in 1975 was to allow the price to rise significantly. But if some use of the item is a necessity and alternatives are not readily available, demand may not be a function of price. If the price of fuel goes up and alternative means of transportation are unavailable, people must still drive automobiles to a certain extent. Moreover, much of the discretionary driving (vacations and other pleasure trips) is done by the economically better off who can afford to absorb the additional costs. Thorstein Veblen's classic concept of "conspicuous consumption," published in 1899,[12] implied that wealthy people spend money ostentatiously, not for material value received, but to prove that they can afford to spend it. Noneconomic motivations come into play here. Instead of being a function of price, demand, as Galbraith has shown, is largely created by modern marketing techniques (advertising).[13] Testimony to the effectiveness of advertising in creating demand is the enormous amount of money spent on it. Surely, businesses would not invest that kind of capital in something unless they were confident of its effectiveness. Given the size of the investment required in an advanced state of technology, the risks in relying on spontaneous demand would be prohibitive.

In addition to problems in the theory itself, glaring inconsistencies between theory and practice make the free-market justification more difficult to support. As already pointed out, the business community did not want complete *laissez-faire*. They wanted government support of business enterprise through tariffs, tax "incentives," etc., while individuals were allowed to fail. Although the logical inconsistency of welfare-state security for larger businesses and *laissez-faire* for individuals did not readily penetrate mass consciousness, this inconsistency did penetrate and help alienate intellectuals from the system. As Schumpeter has pointed out, intellectuals are opinion leaders who prepare a climate of opinion in which modification of the economic system becomes not only possible but almost necessary.[14]

---

[12] Thorstein Veblen, *The Theory of the Leisure Class* (New York: Modern Library, 1934), especially Chap. IV.
[13] John Kenneth Galbraith, *The New Industrial State* (New York: Mentor Books, 1971), second edition, especially p. 48 ff.
[14] Joseph Schumpeter, *Capitalism, Socialism and Democracy* (New York: Harper Torchbooks, 1950), third edition, pp. 145-155.

Practical or Social Problems with the Self-Regulating Market

The most forceful imperative for the abandonment of strict market theory for policy formulation was not so much philosophical as social. Market theory regards human labor as a commodity whose price must be determined by the impersonal forces of supply and demand. Yet, despite whatever long-term social benefits may or may not ensue from allowing subsistence wages or less for any given segment of the labor force, the human costs become increasingly difficult to accept. It should be recalled that an important aspect of the classic liberalism that provided an important philosophical support for market theory is the exaltation of the individual. Given the importance of the individual, it was difficult to consign so many of the less successful of them to the status of human flotsam in the name of some higher social purpose.

The social dislocations of the early, unregulated industrial revolution were real, and, by today's standards, human misery was severe. As the factory system became established, exceedingly long hours, subsistence (and below) wages, widespread unemployment, hazardous working conditions lacking even basic safety precautions, widespread child labor, and the use of women at heavy labor became commonplace. Even children under the age of five worked such long hours that they rarely if ever saw the light of day. Mangling of limbs in the whirring blades of the early spinning machines was not only commonplace (although avoidable); the injured were immediately cast loose to starve without compensation. The slums in which the industrial labor force was compelled to live were exceedingly dirty and squalid even in comparison to modern urban slums.

The passionate description of such conditions seems to occupy a central position in the first volume of Karl Marx's *Das Kapital*; it rivals his theoretical critique of the capitalist system.[15] The reality of the conditions described undoubtedly contributed to the passion of Marx's exhortations and to the receptivity of many humanists to his appeal. For example, he describes the tile- and brick-making industry as follows:

> Between May and September the work lasts from 5 in the morning until 8 in the evening and where the drying is done in the open air, it often lasts from 4 in the morning until 9 in the evening.... Both boys and girls of 6 and even 4 years of age are employed.... a young woman, 24 years of age, was in the habit of making 2000 tiles a day with the assistance of two little girls.... The girls carried daily 10 tons up the slippery sides of the clay pits from a depth of 30 feet....[16]

---

[15] Karl Marx, *Capital*, Samuel Moore and Edward Aveling, trans., Frederick Engles, ed. (New York: Modern Library, 1906), pp. 506–588.
[16] *Ibid*, p. 507.

In another place, Marx describes conditions in an iron foundry where a 12-year-old girl had worked daily "from 6 A.M. to 12 P.M. for a fortnight on end."[17]

These conditions attest to the absurdity of treating individuals as a commodity and of assuming that parties to a negotiation necessarily actually bargain instead of having one dictate terms to the other. Collective bargaining is an attempt to allow labor to bargain more effectively with management by rendering the parties more nearly equal in strength. Collective bargaining, however, preserves the bargaining principle crucial to market theory. Trade union movements, once they are granted the essential tool of collective bargaining, the right to bring their industry to a halt (that is, compulsory unionism combined with the right to strike), will use that power to dictate wage rates as surely as employers formerly dictated rates to them. The inability of the Wilson Labour Government in Britain, first in the late 1960s and then in the mid-1970s, to contain wage increases within manageable bounds constitutes a case in point. Even in the nationalized coal industry, union demands forced a wage increase that far exceeded increases in either productivity or the cost of living, thus placing grave inflationary pressures on that already troubled economy. In any event, it is clear that collective bargaining can mitigate some of the dislocations resulting from forcing isolated individuals to bargain with vastly more powerful producers. However, collective bargaining tends to generate serious economic dislocations of another sort—serious inflation with dictated wage settlements exceeding productivity.

Social dislocations such as those characterizing the early industrial revolution can be expected to be endured only when those who suffer believe their lot to be just or inevitable. This belief was part of the philosophy of Social Darwinism—the belief in the "survival of the fittest" in unregulated economic competition. This means that those who succeed in economic pursuits do so because they deserve their success on the basis of greater contributions to society, greater skill, superior initiative, and general strength of character. One of that philosophy's more articulate proponents, American industrialist Andrew Carnegie, said:

> We of the capitalist persuasion put trust in the individual man.... We demote him when his ability fails, and discard him if we find a serious flaw of character. In our system there is nothing, save his own shortcomings to prevent his rising to the top. We have, then, a method better than that of practical politics for selecting the leaders of a democracy. By a process of pitiless testing we discover who are the strong and who are the weak.... So we demand that the political state shall leave us alone.... We demand of the state protection of property. For this purpose we ask an adequate police, a sound banking system, a sound currency based on gold and court decisions to nullify social legislation confiscatory in character. We demand a tariff to protect us

---

[17] *Ibid,* p. 285.

against our foreign competitors. . . . When the state has fulfilled these, its proper functions, we ask it to leave us alone.[18]

What Carnegie is in effect saying is that government should protect business from risk and competition, then allow business to exploit the advantage thus bestowed. In other words, government should uphold those aspects of market theory advantageous to business and ignore those disadvantageous to business. This inconsistency makes obvious grist for the mills of the critics of these policies.

The dogged defenders of market theory point to the fantastic technological progress of the industrial revolution as evidence that the system "worked." Ignored are a variety of alternative explanations for the industrialization of the West. The perception that market theory contained both truth and moral superiority sustained governmental policies remarkably insensitive to the political well-being of the masses for ostensibly democratic systems.

The Political Basis of Market Economics

Part of this insensitivity was rendered possible not by ideological but by political considerations. The broadening of the suffrage extended only gradually beyond the propertied middle classes in the nineteenth century. It was not until the latter part of that century that even the male British working class got the vote. (The goal of manhood suffrage was substantially satisfied by the Representation of the People Act of 1884). In Belgium, manhood suffrage had to wait until 1894, a date that not coincidentally marks the entry of the socialists into the political arena.[19] The Austrian Social Democratic Party won its first plurality in 1911, after the grant of manhood suffrage by Emperor Franz Joseph in 1907. In Prussia the vote of the working class was limited in its impact by a three-class system of suffrage. Thus, the workers were counted as one third of the electorate, although they actually comprised a numerical majority. The Norwegian Labor Party gradually came into prominence after the introduction of manhood suffrage in 1898. Universal manhood suffrage was introduced in Sweden in the early years of the twentieth century and the Swedish Social Democratic Party did not come into power until 1932.

Policy based on the myth of the self-regulating market was sustained at least until the turn of the century and until considerably thereafter in some places by the fact that only those who had an interest in the maintenance of the myth were permitted access to the political arena. Subsequent to the establishment of universal suffrage, parties catering to a working-class clientele began to appear

---

[18] Quoted from Andrew Carnegie "The Gospel of Wealth," *Capitalism, Democracy and the Supreme Court* Wallace Mendelson (New York: Appleton Century Crofts, 1960), pp. 53–54.
[19] Val Lorwin, "Belgium, "Religion, Class, and Language In National Politics," *Political Oppositions in Western Democracies,* Robert Dahl, ed. (New Haven: Yale University Press, 1966), p. 157.

and to achieve political effectiveness. Although the programs of Social Democratic or Labor parties were generally ambivalent at best about such openly socialist tactics as the nationalization of the major means of production, at a minimum they constituted a frontal attack on free-market economics. The participation of these parties in the national decision-making process (meaning their inclusion in the cabinets in parliamentary regimes) by and large signaled an end to Social Darwinism as a basis for economic policy. Because the members of working-class parties were in fact the losers in market economics, the parties found it in their interest to advocate some measure of economic planning. That means that the government used its powers of command to regulate the allocation of resources, the volume of production, and the prices of commodities instead of leaving the outcomes to the impersonal forces of unregulated competition.

Among the nations we are considering, those nations where working-class parties are either politically weak or practically nonexistent are precisely those nations that have been slowest to abandon a free-market justification for essentially probusiness economic policies. In the United States and Canada, for reasons discussed in Chapter 5, a labor-based party never achieved majority status. Consequently, there was no effective institution for the mobilization of public opinion against market assumptions. The American Democratic Party and the Canadian Liberal Party rely on significant middle-class support; consequently, neither of these parties was as free to attack market economics as those continental parties aiming at a more restricted working-class clientele. *Laissez-faire* economics maintained a strong influence on the policies of both the United States and Canada until well into the Great Depression. Moreover, unlike much of the rest of the industrial world, these countries are still resistant to frontal attacks on the market system. At this writing, American President Gerald Ford's stated economic positions are almost classically in the Carnegie tradition.

What has happened is that capitalism developed an economic oligarchy with a vested interest in maintaining faith in market economics. The dominance of this oligarchy was only finally weakened by those with anithetical interests (that is, nonpropertied classes) when they had the countervailing power of political democracy.[20]

There is then an unquestionable correspondence between the substantial modification of market economics and the effectiveness of political parties whose major targeted clientele is the working class. The question is whether the breakdown of the theory rendered the triumph of these parties possible or whether their political triumph caused the modification of the theory. This is one of those chicken/egg questions that are impossible to answer definitively.

---

[20] This term was popularized by John Kenneth Galbraith in *The Affluent Society* (Boston: Houghton Mifflin, 1969), second edition, Chap. XI, and in *American Capitalism: The Concept of Countervailing Power* (Boston: Houghton Mifflin, 1956).

Earlier, however, we suggested some plausible explanations for the development of economic class consciousness, a consciousness that led to a frontal attack on the theory. For example, the belief that the individual could, with talent and individual effort, improve his lot in life was more plausible in North America than on the Continent because the existence of the frontier and the richness of natural resources in America did in fact present many more such outlets for individual initiatives. Thus, the social dislocations of the market, even in the Depression, were less severe in North America than in Europe. One of the most striking and rapid about-faces in economic orientation from free market to heavy state intervention in the economy occurred in Germany's Weimar Republic in the 1920s where, it will be recalled, the effects of the Depression were extreme.

Although the effectiveness of labor-based parties has encouraged an attack on market theory, Hugh Helco has shown that in England and Sweden specific social welfare policies are not the result of the outcome of elections.[21] Victorious left-wing governments have often reneged on their promises. Nevertheless, as the parties attained prominence, they helped mobilize a loss of faith in market theory among the masses. Thus, their success at least indirectly promoted more state intervention in the economy. In any event, because the modification of market-based economic policies occurred at varying times and to varying degrees among the several countries under consideration, this variation must be attributable to social and political factors. Clearly, the problems in the theory itself were constant from one country to another; hence, such problems could account for the aforementioned variation in the rate of the modification of market economics.

Stanley Rothman suggests that "the later a society begins the industrialization process, the more active the role of the state in the economy."[22] We may well ask why this should logically be expected, but an answer is not provided by Rothman. Second, major exceptions to this generalization, such as England, come quickly to mind. It may be that nations industrializing relatively late never had to overcome an entrenched belief in market economic theory, a faith that was increasingly inconsistent with the manifest realities of the twentieth-century world. Classic market theory was clearly more plausible in the earlier stages of the industrialization process before the imperatives of technology mandated the concentration of capital that transformed an entrepreneurial economy into a corporate economy. It would require the most flexible use of terms to refer to a multinational corporation as an entrepreneur.

It seems reasonable to conclude that the logical inconsistencies in the theory of the self-regulating market and the manifestly untenable assumptions of the theory rendered the theory as such vulnerable to attack. The triggering mechanism for this attack was the massive social dislocations of the early unregulated period of

---

[21] Helco, *op. cit.*, pp. 289–290.
[22] Stanley Rothman, *European Society and Politics* (Indianapolis: Bobbs Merrill, 1970), p. 743.

industrialization. This potential or latent discomfort was mobilized in the form of class consciousness by political parties and other organizations. The progressive modification of *laissez-faire* as a criterion of social policy seems to have varied with the political success of these organizations.

What role, then, has economic theory played in social policy? We are skeptical of the causal role suggested by Keynes when he said, "Practical men, who believe themselves to be quite exempt from intellectual influences, are usually the slaves of some defunct economist."[23] Theoretical considerations seem to be a tool for mobilizing support for the pursuit of interests.

Of course, the concept of the self-regulating market was by definition never legitimate in a self-proclaimed Marxist state such as the Soviet Union. The Soviets, upon seizure of power, instituted a rigorous command economy with the requisitioning of grain, the abolition of money, and an attempt to impose a high degree of egalitarianism. The naivete of this soon resulted in economic chaos. Hence, the early period 1917-1921 (called the period of War Communism) was replaced by the New Economic Policy or NEP. Some means of production reverted to private hands, and to some extent the market mechanism was used. This apparent retreat from Marxism and even from state socialism, however, proved to be a temporary aberration in the pattern of Soviet economic policy. NEP ended in 1928 and was replaced by the First Five-Year Plan. This plan entailed both rapid collectivization and industrialization. Rapid industrialization may be achieved by directing the resources of the system away from consumption and into capital. (Capital means resources used for further production.) For this reason, market mechanisms and popularly accountable governments are less appropriate for the goal of rapid industrialization than a command economy and an authoritarian government. David Apter has therefore suggested that a "mobilization system"—roughly, an authoritarian political format capable of directing resources into capital purposes by fiat—is more commonly found in the early stages of the modernization process.[24] This industrializing process in the Soviet Union, directing the resources of society from consumption to capital whatever the long-term benefits, cost 30-40 million lives in the short run from purges, mass starvation, etc.

The Growth of the Welfare State

The nineteenth century saw the increasing proliferation of legislation designed to ameliorate the poverty and human misery of the working classes. Early attitudes

---

[23] John Maynard Keynes, *The General Theory of Employment, Interest and Money* (New York: Harcourt Brace and Company, 1936), p. 383.

[24] David Apter, *The Politics of Modernization* (Chicago: University of Chicago Press, 1965), p. 40 and *passim*.

reflected the Social Darwinist position that poverty was a matter of just deserts—an inevitable consequence of the natural inequality among human beings with respect to talent and initiative. Early reforms were granted out of humanitarian concern for suffering have-nots—given out of the beneficence of the hearts of the haves, not as a matter of right. As such, early social legislation was perfectly consistent with Social Darwinism.

When political forces gained ascendence and denied that the existing level of material inequality was deserved, just, and socially beneficial, they produced a fundamental change in the rationale of social policy. Ameliorative legislation, previously viewed as a grant, was now regarded as a matter or right. That is, certain minimal standards of material well-being came to be regarded as the right of every human being irrespective of what the person did or did not do, not as something that must be earned. The legitimation of this concept that every human being has a right to a minimal standard and that the state has a moral obligation to provide it constitutes the essence of the welfare state.

The welfare state does *not* mean material equality. In the most advanced welfare states, such as the Scandinavian democracies, inequalities in the distribution of resources are significant. It is clearly one thing to say that every person shall have a right to a nutritious diet, adequate clothing, shelter, medical services, and the like. It is something else to decree equality in the possession of luxury and recreational goods. Thus, the abolition of abject poverty does *not* entail the abolition of significant material differences as incentives to creative effort.

The welfare state does *not* mean state socialism, defined as government ownership of the major means of production, distribution, and exchange. In Sweden, for example, most of these remain in nongovernmental hands. Britain, by contrast, has accompanied its welfare state with a fair amount of nationalization of major industries (coal, transportation, a television network, an airline company, health care, occasionally steel, etc.). Thus, the welfare state does not preclude state socialism either. A system of public guarantees of material well-being says nothing about who owns the major means of production, distribution, and exchange.

Patterns of Health Care Delivery

By the close of the Second World War, much of the industrialized world had come to the position that many social and material values are matters of right, not rewards for competitive success. For example, the industrialized world has been moving toward the position that individuals have a right to medical care when they need it, not just if they can pay for it. This right is provided either through state-run or state-guaranteed health insurance schemes or, in a few cases, through direct nationalization of the health care industry.

Comprehensive Medical Insurance and the Fee-for-Service System

One method of delivering health care as a matter of right is the provision or financial backing by the state of a system of comprehensive medical insurance. This is by far the most common alternative throughout the Western world, an alternative whose proposal has generated considerable controversy in the United States in recent years. American students can learn from the experience of European nations in this regard.

The difficulty with comprehensive medical insurance is the social costs involved when combined with a fee-for-service system of compensating physicians. This system means the physician's fee is a matter between the doctor and patient, presumably set by bargaining and the forces of supply and demand.

The persistence of fee-for-service medicine in the Western world is testimony to the strength of faith in market theory in the face of manifestly invalid assumptions. In the case of medical care, demand is not simply a function of price. A person seriously ill or injured is in a poor position to bargain over the price of treatment. Unless there is some mechanism to hold down physicians' fees, state-run systems of health insurance can get to be quite expensive. The tendency is for physicians to raise their fees because the entire burden does not fall directly on the patient. Moreover, numerous potential patients who under an ability-to-pay system would be excluded from the medical care system now receive care with comprehensive insurance, thus raising the total cost of medical care to society.

An attempt to remedy this is setting a fee scheduled by the state for insured medical care. Enforcement, however, may be a problem. For example, in the French system, which consists of government reimbursement of fees paid directly to the physician, doctors' fees rose steadily despite a state fee schedule during the early years of the plan. However, reform legislation in 1946 required that the physician inform both the patient and the local medical society of fees charged in excess of the schedule, and the medical society is obligated to provide alternatives at the scheduled rates.[25] In Australia, the National Health Service Act of 1953 provided commonwealth benefits for a portion of physicians' fees (up to 90 percent), but fees have been rising.[26] The Australian Medical Association's objections to state fee setting were supported by the pro-free-enterprise Liberal Menzies Government. The "Pensioner Medical Service" did, however, provide for a negotiated fee schedule.

The fee-for-service system of medical care has been substantially modified in Great Britain, Sweden, and the Netherlands, where medical personnel, on salary

---

[25] Walter Friedlander, *Individualism and Social Welfare* (New York: The Free Press of Glencoe, 1962), p. 178.

[26] T. H. Kewly, *Social Security in Australia* (Sidney: The University Press, 1965), pp. 365–366. The insurance is done through medical benefit organizations, an indirect structure that increases medical costs.

from the state, exist as an alternative to such personnel in private practice. As well as providing medical care to anyone in need regardless of the ability to pay, this places competitive pressures on the private-practice personnel to charge fees that do not significantly exceed the state fee schedules.

In Sweden, physicians may be state employees (district doctors), members of the medical staff of a hospital, or in private practice. A person may go to a physician in private practice and be reimbursed through a comprehensive state-run insurance scheme including office as well as hospital visits, travel to and from physicians' offices, medicines, sickness cash payments, and maternity benefits.[27] The insurance scheme is potentially protected against the abuses of excessive fees normally associated with insurance in a fee-for-service system because the state sets the fee schedule. The state will only reimburse the amount in the schedule. A doctor in private practice is free to charge more, and a patient is free to pay more; however, the state will *not* reimburse in excess of the schedule. Moreover, the existence of state-employed physicians whose fees must adhere to the schedule ensures that no one is denied medical care for economic reasons. It would seem difficult for private physicians seeking a large volume of business to ignore the fee schedule due to the availability of competition adhering to that schedule.

Thus, placing medical personnel on a state salary cannot only replace but can also complement state-administered systems of comprehensive health insurance, such as found in Canada, Denmark, Australia, and West Germany. In West Germany, an insurance refund is given to those who make no claims within a specified time period. This is supposed to provide a certain incentive against abuse.[28]

Socialized Medicine

The fee-for-service system allows the fee of the physician to be negotiated between doctor and patient. In reality, we have seen, the fee is set by the physician. Because the ability of the patient to pay is no longer a consideration under a system of comprehensive state insurance, physicians' fees have tended to rise markedly under these schemes.

By contrast, the systems of socialized medicine place physicians on a salary as employees of the state; therefore, they are unable to extract all that the market will bear from a patient. Accordingly, salaried doctors tend to make considerably less money than their fee-for-service counterparts. We should remember, however, that the income of salaried physicians is in each nation well above that of the average citizen.

---

[27] Albert Rosenthal, *The Social Programs of Sweden: A Search for Security in a Free Society* (Minneapolis: University of Minnesota Press, 1967), p. 38 ff.

[28] The Federal Minister of Labour and Social Affairs, *Survey of Social Security in the Federal Republic of Germany* (June 1970), pp. 132–133.

The National Health Service in Britain and its Swedish counterpart are criticized for destroying the doctor-patient relationship, causing delays in obtaining medical care, and encouraging malingering. But there is no evidence that individuals using any national health service are unable to any significant extent to obtain the services of the doctor of their choice. Nor are doctors forced to take patients they do not wish to treat. Undoubtedly, some malingering does occur; however, it also occurs in fee-for-service systems. The difference is that in fee-for-service systems, malingering is largely confined to wealthy hypochondriacs. The issue is whether medical care should be distributed on the basis of need or of ability to pay. In nationalized health care systems, the geographic distribution of physicians can be adjusted on the basis of need. By contrast, in fee-for-service systems, there is a strong tendency for doctors to concentrate in the urban, upper-middle-class areas where people and wealth are also concentrated. Meanwhile, there is normally a scarcity of medical personnel in poorer rural areas.

The system of medical care in the Soviet Union is formed around a network of polyclinics and is considered by many observers to be among the most effective in the world at giving basic medical services to the general population. Doctors, who are state employees, work together in these clinics to serve patients who are assigned to them with very little freedom of choice on either side. There are problems, such as the apparently shorter and less thorough training period and the fact that medications and facilities are not always the most modern ones. On the other hand, the Soviet Union is proud of the number of doctors (among the highest in the world in either absolute or relative terms) and of the fact that virtually everyone has access to a physician. Thus, while much of the freedom of choice is removed, the Soviet system seems to do well in its goal of providing basic medical services to virtually the entire population.

Without the comprehensive insurance schemes mentioned above, the fee-for-service medical system places the cost of medical care for any serious malady beyond the reach of even the middle classes. The prime example of this among industrial nations is the United States, where the costs of hospital rooms alone are frequently in excess of $100 a day. The result is that despite the finest system of medical technology in the world, the United States in 1972 was seventeenth among the nations of Europe, Britain, and the older Commonwealth with respect to infant mortality and twenty-second among the nations with regard to life expectancy.[29] A state-supported or state-run comprehensive medical insurance scheme

---

[29] Compiled from Tables I and II in *The Britannica Book of the Year, 1974,* p. 727. Our rankings differ from some other rankings because, lacking a clear criterion of which countries to exclude, we simply counted all the listed nations under "Europe," "North America," and "Oceania" (Australia and New Zealand). Compare Michael Parenti, *Democracy for the Few* (New York: St. Martin's Press, 1974), p. 9, who claims that the United States is fourteenth in infant mortality and nineteenth in life expectancy for men. The precise ranking is not important. It is indisputable that the United States, despite its superior medical technology, does relatively poorly on these criteria.

spreads these burdens more evenly throughout the society. When such a scheme is combined with an essentially unregulated fee-for-service system, the total social costs tend to be enormous.

Protecting the Unemployed

Much of the industrial world has taken action to protect workers from the hardships of being out of work. Unemployment insurance, compensation for workers injured on the job, and "workhouses" that were primitive public factories in which the poor could be set to "socially profitable employment" comprised the specific policies to protect the workers. In England, these workhouses soon degenerated into a criterion for distinguishing between the "deserving" and the "undeserving" poor.[30] The preoccupation of the British with unemployment insurance, together with their preoccupation with distinguishing between the deserving and undeserving poor, illustrates the hold of classic market economics on the formulators of social policy prior to the Second World War.[31] Because this hold seems to have weakened in much of Western Europe since the war, the notion of planning has come into vogue. Provisions of material well-being as a matter of right have spread throughout the industrial world and sharply distinguish the United States from much of the rest of that world.

Even Belgium, despite its individualistic culture and the importance of the Christian Socials in its postwar cabinets, has adopted an impressive system of social insurance. Belgium was one of the pioneers in the move to payments as a matter of right to families with certain social characteristics (as opposed to poor relief with its attendent social stigma and administrative burdens).[32]

The extremes of poverty have in fact been substantially reduced if not virtually eliminated in advanced welfare-state systems compared with its being tolerated in the United States. Unemployment in Scandinavia in the worst of times (such as the 1970s) has been kept under 3 or 4 percent, while in the United States it was permitted to rise to 8 or 9 percent. But low unemployment is not inconsistent with prosperity; Sweden's per capita income is the second highest in the world.

Planning

Planning is the process of directing the production of goods and the allocation of resources by structures of command instead of relying on the market mechanism and relegating such important outcomes to the chance interplay of impersonal

---

[30] Helco, *op. cit.*, pp. 52 and 87.
[31] *Ibid.*, p. 92.
[32] Guy Peters, "The Development of Social Policy in France, Sweden and the United Kingdom: 1850–1965," *Politics in Europe,* Martin O. Heisler, ed. (New York: David McKay, 1971), p. 263.

forces. The more likely result of the absence of planning is to relegate outcomes to such nonaccountable economic forces as big business and organized labor. Planning enthusiasts assume that market mechanisms are inoperable. Moreover, they assume that the various sectors of the economy and society are mutually interdependent; hence, the imperatives of rationality demand that these sectors be controlled and coordinated by a single decision-making structure.

National Plans in the Industrial World

The several Five-Year Plans of the Soviet Union are perhaps the most famous examples of central planning in the industrial world. In general, the Soviet Union has fallen short of the goals declared by its plans. This is probably inevitable because of the number of unpredictable factors (such as the effect of weather on crops) and the difficulty in assembling the information necessary for rationally directing anything as complex as a modern industrial economy. In the post-Khrushchev period, the goals set by the Soviet plans have been more moderate (or, perhaps, more realistic); yet, the society has still fallen short of its projected goals. Rationality, it must be recognized, is a matter of degree. Therefore, the failure of planning to predict output perfectly and to realize 100 percent of stated goals does not mean that planning is worthless. If, as we suggest, the market mechanism is not operable, the alternative to imperfect rationality is haphazardness in which the public interest is ignored in favor of private interests.

Planning is also important in France, as pointed out in the preceding chapter. The *Commissariat Général du Plan* was identified as the agency in charge of this process. Enforcement is carried out more by means of rewards and punishments or implicit threats than by governmental fiat as in the Soviet Union. The bulk of the French means of production, however, is still in private hands, as discussed below. The Netherlands constitutes another example of an economic system characterized by central planning since the establishment of the Central Planning Bureau in 1945.[33]

Both the French General Commissionership for Planning and its Soviet counterpart, *Gosplan*, have delegated some planning responsibilities to regional subsidiaries. Thus, each Soviet constituent republic has a *Gosplan* whose plans must be consistent with the broader objects of the national plan. The Soviets issue long-range plans (10–15 years) that are without much effect on the real world, five-year plans that produce some effects but whose goals are seldom realized, and one-year plans.

Soviet plans determine what "profits" should be obtained by each of the major enterprises. When income is in excess of what is called for by the plan, the Soviet

---

[33] *Planning and Development in the Netherlands* (The Netherlands: Netherlands University Foundation for International Cooperation: Royan Van Gorcum Ltd., 1971), pp. 69–90, 111–129.

enterprise may keep this excess. They call this a bonus. It becomes a measure of accountability for performance of the enterprise. This policy is known as Libermanism. This is not strictly "free enterprise" because the state provides funds for incomes below those called for in the plan. In short, the state removes the critical capitalist element of risk.

Modern capitalist and other noncommunist nations often bail out failing major industries with public funds. The British did this with one of their major privately owned industries, Rolls Royce, and the Americans did this with Lockheed Aircraft Corporation in the 1970s.

The British have produced several national plans. The National Plan of 1965 had the stated purpose of encouraging manufacturers to forego part of the domestic market in order for the nation to achieve a favorable balance of trade. In Britain, with its large dependence on imports, some central direction was needed to get individuals and organizations to act not in their private interests but in the interests of the social whole. This clearly illustrates those situations where private economic self-interests (for example, the profit motive) manifestly conflict with the interests of the social whole, situations that provide the raison d'être of the move toward planning.

Despite the ruling DC's hostility to socialism, planning has even been present in Italy. A Ten-Year Plan, drawn up in 1954, was designed to reduce the economic disparities between the northern and southern sections of the country discussed at length in Chapter 3.[34] This plan was also intended to promote the industrialization of the country. Unlike Germany, which had already been an advanced industrial order prior to the Second World War, preindustrial attitudes and structures had to be overcome to produce Italy's postwar "economic miracle." To point out that Italy has resorted to planning to encourage the large task of industrialization does not imply that Italy is in any sense an advanced welfare state. Abject poverty, especially in the south, is still a fact of Italian life.

Reasons for the Pervasiveness of Planning

Planning thus represents an alternative to reliance on market mechanisms that does not necessarily entail either socialism (public ownership of the major means of production, distribution, and exchange) or the welfare state (the guarantee by governmental authorities of minimal standards of material well-being as a matter of right). Governmental ownership is not as pervasive as commonly supposed. The welfare state is most advanced in Scandinavia, the Netherlands, Great Britain, and, of course, the Soviet Union. Compared with the United States, the welfare state is also well developed in France, Austria, and Belgium. Planning is pervasive

---

[34] George Lichtheim, *The New Europe: Today and Tomorrow* (New York: Praeger, 1963), p. 129.

throughout the industrial world outside of North America, but it occurs to different degrees in the various nations. For example, although the idea of the market is less sacrosanct in Austria than in the United States, "overall, Austria must be classified as a free market rather than a planned economy."[35] However, wage, price, and rent controls and production quotas in agriculture have appeared to be much more readily accepted in Austria than in the United States. When such controls have been consistently applied in the industrial world, they have been effective in controlling inflation without creating unemployment. They did not work in the United States in the 1970s because while wages were frozen, profits and prices were allowed to rise sharply.

Planning is pervasive because wages, prices, etc., are in fact set in an industrial society and not determined by impersonal forces of supply and demand. It is not necessary to consider the unanswerable and moot question of whether the market mechanism has ever operated as classic economic theory suggests that it should. The point is that it does not operate nor could it be made to operate that way at an advanced state of technology. This issue is whether prices, wages, and the like, will be set by private power sources (business, organized labor, etc.) or set by public authorities. Otherwise put, the question is not whether the economy shall be planned but who shall do the planning, for what goals, and for whose benefit. The only accountability of business to society would be through a market mechanism that is in fact inoperative. Government, on the other hand, may conceivably be rendered accountable to some extent. The difficulty with that hope is that planning for a complex industrial society involves highly technical information and expertise. Therefore, the planning function passes from the political and hence potentially accountable sectors of government to what Galbraith calls "the technostructure." Galbraith says, "the technical complexity, planning and associated scale of operations that took power from the capitalist entrepreneur and lodged it with the technostructure, removed it from the reach of social control."[36] It is suggested that the functions of planning are carried out by technocrats who, regardless of whether they are officially in the public or private sector, are actually accountable to no one but themselves.

Keynesian Economics: Trying to Save the Market

Keynesian economics offers a kind of compromise to those Western nations imbued with a faith in the theory of the market while faced with the practical reality that it does not work. Keynesian economics offers a rationale for governmental regulation and partial control of key elements of the economy, especially of

---
[35] Kurt Steiner, *Politics in Austria* (Boston: Little Brown, 1972), p. 86.
[36] Galbraith, *The New Industrial State, op. cit.*, p. 114.

the level of investment and hence of unemployment and inflation, without explicitly rejecting the concept of the market itself. Accordingly, many Western nations, even those with advanced welfare-state economies, have justified their policies to a great extent on Keynesian principles. Assar Lindbeck's analysis of Swedish economic policy exemplifies this kind of justification of welfare-state economics in terms of Keynesian countercyclical fiscal policy.[37]

The publication of Keynes's *General Theory of Employment, Interest and Money* constituted one of the more significant inroads into the dominance of the theory of the self-regulating market in the Western world.[38] The Great Depression had provided a more receptive audience for the suggestion that perhaps the market was not entirely self-regulating. The inflationary peaks and depressionary valleys of the business cycle had become too severe to accept them as the product of impersonal forces.

Keynesian policy assumes that once the level of investment has been controlled, market forces can then reassert themselves. For example, Keynesians must assume that the availability of capital at desirable rates will in fact cause people to avail themselves of that capital and invest it at risk despite an otherwise negative economic climate. In other words, they assume that the demand for money is simply a function of the price of money, and the price of money is simply a function of its supply.

Keynesian economic theory thus represents a kind of half-step away from market theory—an implicit recognition that the self-regulating market cannot be relied upon—without explicitly rejecting the theory. The Keynesian solution to the problem of unemployment is to pump money into the economy in excess of any increase in productivity, a policy that is by definition inflationary. The Keynesian solution to inflation is constricting the economy in such a way that it amounts to engineered unemployment. The Keynesians present society with a choice between equally unacceptable alternatives. Therefore, even those nations whose economists are still speaking in Keynesian terms have been moving toward a comprehensively planned economy in which they hope the vicious circle of unemployment and inflation can be broken.

Nationalization and State Socialism

Governmental ownership of the major means of production, distribution, and exchange is an obvious and direct mechanism for economic planning and governmental control of the economy. This is an increasingly pervasive policy, even

---

[37] Assar Lindbeck, *Swedish Economic Policy* (Berkeley: University of California Press, 1974), Chap. 5.
[38] Keynes, *op. cit.*

though it is a blatant repudiation of classic economic theory. It has been utilized to varying degrees in the industrial world—obviously, to the greatest extent in the Soviet Union. But even there, some small-scale private enterprise is allowed to exist. Recall that socialism involves governmental ownership of only the *major* means of production, distribution, and exchange. The social impact of the activities of smaller means of production is so slight that it is usually not worth the trouble for government to undertake the effort to run them.

Great Britain is perhaps the most frequently mentioned example of a significant amount of public ownership outside the Soviet-bloc nations. There such industries as transportation, coal, steel, the airlines, television, and medicine have been publicly owned. In some industries, such as the airlines, television, and medicine, privately owned enterprise is free to compete with government enterprises and, in fact, does so. Government corporations can serve as a standard setter to keep private enterprise socially responsible. The effectiveness of standards in keeping private enterprise socially accountable is open to question, however, because the public lacks the information to choose what is in its ultimate interests. Thus, the intellectually dull commercial television network is more popular than the often culturally and intellectually superior offerings on the state-run BBC.

Austria and France have undertaken substantial nationalization of industry since the Second World War. In addition, both systems operate a novel arrangement whereby the state owns a substantial proportion of the stock in a major corporation with the remainder of the stock in private hands. It is interesting that these countries far outstrip the Scandinavian nations with respect to government ownership, while Scandinavia has carried the guarantees of the welfare state much further. Thus, nationalization and welfare ought to be distinguished from each other. The Scandinavian experiments with nationalization mostly involve such industries as power (hydroelectricity in Sweden), transportation (railroads and airlines), mass media, and some production of important metals—especially in Norway. In addition, Sweden owns the alcoholic beverage and tobacco industries. There is less nationalization in Scandinavia than in Britain despite the hegemony of left-wing parties in Norway and Sweden.

The absence of nationalization does not imply a reliance on market forces. Postwar West Germany, under the dominant influence of the United States and reacting to the centralizing tendencies of National Socialism, self-consciously avowed a faith in the free-enterprise system. Nevertheless, a well-developed system of social welfare measures has significantly ameliorated the consequences of the lack of economic success for individuals. Furthermore, the allocation of resources to desired levels of investment has been indirectly engineered through tax incentives and subsidies.

We may therefore suspect that the West German "economic miracle" is not simply attributable to the wonders of the free market and private enterprise. The availability of resources (such as Marshall Plan aid, coal from Ruhr, etc.) and the presence of technologically trained personnel to run German industries effectively (Germany was one of the most technologically developed systems) are among the more likely factors to account for German economic prosperity. The availability of capital and resources also help explain the United States's economic well-being. It should be recalled that Sweden, with a highly developed system of socioeconomic security and control of private enterprise, has a per capita income second only to the United States; thus, the free-enterprise system could hardly be a prerequisite to a healthy economy.

Nationalization and Social Control

Nationalization has been far from a panacea for the economic problems of a mature industrial society. One of the main objectives of nationalization is to establish social control of the means of production. However, as we have already suggested, ownership does not necessarily mean control. This has been true in the major corporations in the private sectors of industrial societies. General Motors is not run by its stockholders. This is also true for nationalized industries. Ministers rarely have the time or the expertise to read the lengthy reports submitted by the boards of directors of nationalized industries. Parliamentary representatives are even less likely to have the capacity to control such boards.

For example, in the British nationalized industries, the appropriate ministers have the legal authority to issue directives to the boards of directors of the public corporations they ostensibly oversee. In practice, these boards have attained considerable autonomy. In the first six years of the operation of these nationalized industries, no direct orders were issued by the responsible ministers to their respective boards of directors,[39] but the ministers did maintain considerable influence over the boards with informal ties. It is interesting that the "autonomy of the board" was defended against "political interference" when the ministers first began to exercise control. This overlooks the reason for nationalizing the industries in the first place. Clearly, the intent was to render the management of these industries less autonomous and more responsible because it was assumed that the decisions of management had significant political consequences. Curiously, it was a Conservative minister who gave the first order (to the British Transportation Commission) and Labour leaders who staunchly defended the "autonomy of the board." Apparently, the myth of the political neutrality of business enterprise knows no political bounds.

An attempt was made to establish direct accountability of the British nationalized industries to the consumers through the establishment of Consumers'

---

[39] Eldon Johnson, "The Accountability of British Nationalized Industries," *The American Political Science Review*, Vol. XLVIII, No. 2, June 1954, pp. 366–385 at p. 369.

Councils.[40] These councils were appointed by the minister; therefore, consumers still had to rely on the wisdom and character of that minister to protect consumer interests. Many consumer complaints still tend to be addressed to MPs, indicating a lack of either faith in or awareness of the Consumers' Councils.

As the previous chapter suggests, problems of democratic accountability are inherent in any large organization whether that organization is formally located in the public or the private sector of the society.

Conclusion: The Rational Engineering of Social Welfare

In a seminal work, Robert Dahl and Charles Linblom have drawn into question the possibilities for rational calculation in the formulation of social policy.[41] Only the bare outlines of their work can be sketched here, an argument of the utmost importance for the more or less pervasive shift in industrial societies from economic policies based on the market principle to some form of command economy (comprised of techniques such as nationalization, planning, and the welfare state). The concept of a command economy is predicated on the feasibility of rational calculation in policy formulation. If Dahl and Lindblom are correct, people's capacity to control their own destinies is severely constricted, and socialist and welfare economic policies become exercises in futility.

The crux of their argument is based on the assumption that human mental capacity is too limited to comprehend the available alternatives of public policy, let alone to understand the possible consequences each alternative would have for one's goals. Most people are incapable of even ordering their values in terms of priorities. Obviously, one cannot rationally select policies—which are, after all, means—unless one has explicitly ordered goals or ends in terms of priorities. (If means become ends in and of themselves, this must also be made consciously explicit for rational calculation). The problem is not one of the lack of rationality per se; instead, it is more a problem of knowledge and information. Thus, in the face of the knowledge explosion of industrial society, people can absorb knowledge of an area only by becoming specialists. Paradoxically, specialization requires that people ignore other salient variables. This leads to outcomes of policy that are unforeseen.[42]

The alternative to idealized and unattainable rationality may be called incrementalism. This means proceeding by small steps. Because it is not possible to

---

[40] *Ibid.*, p. 380.
[41] Robert Dahl and Charles Lindblom, *Politics, Economics and Welfare* (New York: Harper Torchbooks, 1953), especially p. 57 ff. A more concise statement of the argument that classic rationality is not feasible in policy formulation may be found in Charles Lindblom, "The Science of Muddling Through," *Public Administration Review*, Vol. 29, No. 2, Spring 1959, pp. 79–88.
[42] Dahl and Lindblom, *op. cit.*, p. 63.

comprehend all policy choices nor is it possible to predict the outcomes of the choices that mark a radical departure from experience, incrementalists caution us to consider only small changes in the status quo. Because the alternative to rationality is a kind of trial and error, small changes in the status quo produce more predictable outcomes and, when the result is error, are more reversible. For example, because neither has been tried, we have no basis for predicting how or if a purely free-market system or a system of pure communism would work. However, within the modified Keynesian framework in which we operate, we have a basis for predicting the outcome of some measured increase or decrease in the availability of credit.

Incrementalism is essentially a Burkean position (see the discussion of the ideas of Edmund Burke in Chapter 2) in that the limits of rationality are emphasized, making it appear wise to rely a great deal on the institutions and systems that have evolved over time by the process of trial and error, a cumulative building of civilization.

The failure of the Soviets to anticipate the consequences of their radical policy of War Communism, including the abolition of money following the Bolshevik revolution and the need to revert to familiar ground in the NEP, constitutes a prime example of the limits of human rationality. This limit is a result of the inability to reformulate an entire economic system apart from experience because of the unanticipated consequences of untested choices. The problems of unanticipated consequences may also be seen in the cases of the nationalized industries in Britain and France—consequences such as the incompatibility between expertise and accountability.

Clearly, social policy in the industrial world has failed either to render economic power accountable to society or to engineer social and economic equality. We have pointed out in several parts of the book that the functional differentiation that appears as an inevitable concomitant of a complex industrial order also renders differences in economic well-being inevitable. Therefore, despite the explicit egalitarian ideology in the Soviet Union, significant inequalities do exist. The leaders, producers, and other elite groups are significantly better off than the masses. While the role of economic incentive has been overstated by free-market advocates, these incentives cannot be totally abandoned.

Although social policy has limits, it has not been the complete failure that its detractors imply. *Rationality* and *control* are relative terms. To say that economic plans or command economies have fallen short of their objectives is not to say that the plans have been without positive effect. With regard to the availability of health care, Sweden, Iceland, and Norway rank first, second, and third, respectively, in life expectancy, while the United States, despite its superior medical technology, ranks twenty-second, as noted above. Clearly, the welfare-state guarantees of the availability of medical care in Scandinavia have their effect on longevity. Abject poverty and significant levels of unemployment have been rare in the Scandinavian democracies. In 1965, for example, only 3.5 percent of the Swedish population received any form of public assistance despite its wide availability. In the mid-1970s during a worldwide recession, unemployment in Sweden remained under 4 percent, a high figure for that system, while the comparable figure for the United States was in excess of eight percent. The size of the overall "pie" to be divided in command economies has not been seriously diminished. The per capita income in Sweden is the second highest in the world.

Statistics on comparative prosperity between market and command economies tell us little about how either the market or command systems can encourage or impede prosperity. Economic prosperity is a function of many things, such as the availability of resources, climate, location, etc. If economic philosophy has a causal impact on the probability of material prosperity, it is hard to isolate that causal nexus in the complex maze of interacting variables. Clearly, planned or command economies do not preclude economic well-being, nor does any particular economic system guarantee well-being.

Chapter 10

Patterns and Themes in Industrial Politics

We have been discussing patterns of decisions and decision making in a body of nations that are called postindustrial or mature industrial societies. Although the term postindustrial has gained widespread popularity in the literature, we prefer to emphasize the concept of mature industrial societies.

The term *postindustrial* suggests that it applies to a society quite distinct from industrial society. One may view the change from what has been called the industrial world to the world "futurologists" are predicting as one of continuity. To conceptualize the postindustrial world as distinct from its industrial predecessor implies that there are threshold measures enabling one to decide without ambiguity whether a nation has moved into the new category. When we say mature industrial society, we imply that systems can be more or less mature and we do not impose an either/or choice on the matter. Further, because the concept of postindustrial society has been defined in terms of several criteria, the question arises of how to classify a system that is postindustrial by some criteria but not by others.

Daniel Bell has managed to specify the criteria of the postindustrial society as explicitly as anyone. He lists five: the majority of the labor force is engaged in services instead of production; the preeminence of a professional and technologically skilled class; the preeminence of theoretical knowledge; technological planning; and the growth of intellectual technology—tools for problem solving such as statistics, computers, and information-gathering systems.[1]

By the strict terms of that definition, only the United States has moved into the postindustrial age. Only in that system is a majority of the labor force in service industries, for example. But the movement of personnel into service industries is a fact throughout the Western industrialized world. It is apparent that nations at a later stage of industrialization do differ from nations in the earlier stages. The extent of functional differentiation throughout society increases with the knowledge explosion entailed by a higher state of technology. This is the critical characteristic of a mature as opposed to a newly industrialized society. However, this characteristic is best conceptualized as a matter of degree. There is no threshold at which one can precisely and unambiguously distinguish mature industrial societies from other industrial societies.

One theme of this book is that the structure of decision making—that is, the patterns of interaction by which decisions are actually made—is to a large extent a function of the state of technology in a society. When a system has an advanced state of technology, the critical allocative decisions (who gets how much of what) are made in characteristic kinds of processes by the occupants of identifiable kinds of roles. This is to some extent irrespective of other differences such as those in constitutional format, culture, and even historical experience.

We are not suggesting that these other variables are without impact. Cultural differences do seem to make a difference in decision-making structures and processes and seem in turn to be a function of historical experiences (Chapter 2). For example, nations whose format has evolved gradually over time and that accordingly acquired legitimacy prior to the generation of divisive substantive issues tend to be more pragmatic and more tolerant of political and social differences. This pragmatism and tolerance are both related to the maintenance of cabinet and constitutional stability. Stable systems have been more successful in processing issues in a responsive fashion.

It seems that the patterns we have found in industrial societies lend considerable credence to the work of Samuel Huntington on political development.[2] To oversimplify for the purposes of brevity, Huntington has suggested that developing

---

[1] Daniel Bell, *The Coming of Post Industrial Society* (New York: Basic Books, 1973), pp. 14–33.
[2] Samuel Huntington, "Political Development and Political Decay," *World Politics*, Vol. 17, No. 2, April 1965, pp. 386–430; *Political Order in a Changing Society* (New Haven: Yale University Press, 1968), especially p. 53 ff.

nations would do well to develop institutions capable of processing demands before mobilizing masses and increasing participation so as to generate demands. Generating demands before legitimating viable institutions and processes will add the divisiveness of socioeconomic issues (such as the distribution of material well-being) to the difficult question of the nature of the regime. Unless the institutions and processes acquire legitimacy before the substantive issues, the institutions cannot be utilized to resolve those substantive issues peacefully. Divisive issues can only be resolved in a peaceful and orderly fashion when the rules of the game become more important than the outcome of the issue.

Institutionalization prior to mobilization has also been an important factor in the industrial world in accounting for differences in the ability to process issues in an orderly manner. Thus, it seems that a critical factor in the success and effectiveness of a regime is its legitimacy. Legitimacy can be acquired in one of two ways. First, it can be acquired when a political format has existed for a time unhampered by the demands of divisive issues requiring resolution. Second, as in the case of the Soviet Union, legitimacy may be acquired through the support of a powerful ideology such as Marxism-Leninism. In the case of medieval Europe, the ideology was Catholicism.

Any attempt to establish a viable nation in today's world is beset with a dilemma—what may be called a "vicious circle of failure." Political formats can acquire legitimacy best through longevity, which can be achieved best in the absence of unsolved problems, whose existence would generate pressures on any new regime. The absence of unsolved problems requires either legitimate institutions to process divisive issues or a lack of mobilized demands. Newly consolidated regimes in the tenth to fifteenth centuries had the blessing of a relative lack of mobilized demands. The ideology of the Catholic Church, with its otherworldly orientation, provided a cushion of time during which these newly established formats could acquire legitimacy without having to meet high performance standards. A situation of relatively inert masses, either because mobilization has not yet occurred or because of a future-oriented ideology focusing attention on an unspecified better world to come, may be necessary to establish the legitimacy of a new political format. A situation of inert masses may be harder and harder to come by in today's state of media technology. It is simply too easy technologically to mobilize the masses for one cause or another.

The implications of the above analysis are pessimistic for the prospects for political order in many of the newer states of the world. Western Europe does not provide a very good model for these states because the successful states of Europe were consolidated and acquired legitimacy at a time when the masses were still relatively apathetic and uninvolved. This leaves the importance of a powerful, legitimating, future-oriented ideology and thus helps to explain some of the appeal of Marxism and the Soviet or Chinese models in the non-Western world.

The Convergence Theme

There are actually two distinct categories of political variables considered in this book. First, there is the formal level of the constitutional format. This is a variable in the sense that it is manifested in a variety of ways in the several nations. Second, there are the informal processes by which decisions are actually made. These processes include such things as the political role of the bureaucracy, the co-optation of interests, and the institutionalized bargaining processes that go on among these parties. These processes are an outgrowth of the need for specialization and expertise entailed by an advanced state of technology.

The variable of political format—the pattern of constitutionally designated structures and processes—appears to be a function of geographic factors, historical experiences, and a variety of cultural characteristics that have been specified in earlier chapters. These apparent causal factors are either part of the past or have such deep roots that they are not readily amenable to change. If this analysis is correct, the prospects for "constitutional engineering" on the level of constitutional format are also poor.

The second question concerns the extent to which such constitutional formats influence the processes by which decisions are actually made. If these processes are the product of the state of technology, we should note a convergence pattern at this level irrespective of constitutional format. We have, in fact, discerned patterns or similarities in the processes by which decisions are actually made, not only among Western industrial democracies but even between these democracies and the Soviet Union.

This convergence implies that there are patterns or similarities. That is, the systems have some things in common with respect to the processes by which decisions are made. A pattern does not imply an identity, however. Although these systems have an increasing number of processes and structures in common, important differences remain. Most important of these is the degree of discretion available to decision makers or, conversely, the accountability of the decision makers. These remaining differences are the result of deeply rooted values, attitudes, beliefs, and historical experiences that probably place an upper limit on the degree of convergence that is possible.

It is useful to distinguish process from substance. The former refers to how decisions are made and how decision makers are chosen. The latter refers to the decisions themselves. We have argued that there is a qualified convergence in the actual processes by which decisions are made to the extent that such processes are an outgrowth of the state of technology.

We have also discerned some convergence in the policy areas, especially in the areas of economic policy. These patterns include such things as the decline of market economics (where a faith in this theory existed in the first place), the pervasiveness of social welfare policies guaranteeing minimal standards of security and material well-being for individuals, and the drive to guarantee either symbolically or substantively greater material equality. The realities of the industrial order demand that command processes supplant a reliance on market forces irrespective of the philosophical support for market theory.

But important differences remain, especially in the policy areas. The extent to which the short-run individual well-being can be sacrificed to long-run social purposes depends on deeply rooted values that differ from society to society. Individualistic values—values that have been essentially Western phenomena—would probably preclude that engineered human sacrifice called for in policies such as the collectivization of agriculture in the Soviet Union. Such values had been weaker in Eastern Europe than Western Europe. This difference may have been a factor in rendering the Germans more susceptible than their Western European counterparts would have been to the triumph of Hegelian values of the superiority and essential reality of the social unit (the state) over the individuals who comprise it. These collective values in turn provided a more fertile ground for National Socialism. A reaction against the consequences of National Socialism is probably at least partly responsible for what appears to be a gradual value change in West Germany in the form of the rising importance of individualistic values noted in Chapter 3. Evidence for this value change may also be noted in West Germany's greater resistance to collectivist economics than most Western nations.

The idea of convergence, especially in terms of a possible coming together of the Soviet Union and Western countries, has interested scholars for some two decades. Works such as Rostow's *The Stages of Economic Growth*[3] and Brzezinski and Huntington's *Political Power USA/USSR*[4] took note of some of the questions we are asking about the role of industrialization and modernization. While the latter work concluded that convergence was not taking place, it also contained several points relevant to our theme. Included among these is the observation that the complexities of modern planning and scientific knowhow are pushing industrial states into a greater concentration of the decision-making process into fewer hands.[5] Jerome Gilison suggests that one of the factors stimulating a limited convergence of those two systems is the policy formulating process, "including the growth of bureaucratic norms and the oligarchic structural integration of leaders" related to organizational imperatives in the management of modern society.[6]

Both of the above sources seem to be saying that while there will not be any

---

[3] Walter W. Rostow, *The Stages of Economic Growth* (Cambridge: Cambridge University Press, 1971).

[4] Zbigniew Brzezinski and Samuel Huntington, *Political Power USA/USSR* (New York: Viking Press, 1965).

[5] *Ibid*, p. 433.

[6] Jerome Gilison, *British and Soviet Politics* (Baltimore: Johns Hopkins University Press, 1972), p. xiv.

total convergence of Soviet and Western systems, some kind of evolution or limited convergence is occurring in the processes of modern industrial nation-states. Perhaps the idea that systems are not converging but do possess certain similarities is best illustrated in the conclusion of a recent work on Soviet policy. Indicating that it is useless to try to show that Soviet policies are the result of industrialization, Osborn states: "Instead, there is every evidence that the ideas which the Soviet leadership has brought to bear had a specific history of their own. True, the practical measures which have resulted from these ideas often resemble the things that noncommunist governments have promoted also."[7] In using the term *qualified convergence,* we are suggesting that there are differences and similarities not only among the Soviet Union and Western systems, but among all modern industrial societies.

The differences we have noted among industrial nations appear to be attributable in large part to differences in values and other cultural factors, which have deep historical roots. Constitutional formats tend to reflect cultural attributes. This suggests a certain skepticism about the potential of constitutional engineering. Cultural factors are not necessarily unchangeable, but they are not readily engineered. The persistence of values such as the "work ethic" and the idea of the self-regulating market is a case in point. These values, appropriate to an earlier stage of industrialization, persist even though they are largely outdated and inappropriate considering the present state of technology.

Nevertheless, there are grounds for optimism. This book has chronicled a tale of the manner in which structures, processes, and policies have evolved in an adaptive fashion to changing social and especially technological imperatives. The very idea of qualified convergence illustrates this kind of adaptation. Political scientists believe that adaptable political systems have a better chance of survival than do nonadaptive ones. The unanswerable question is whether the rate of evolution of the structures, processes, and policies in industrial societies is adequate to cope with the imperatives of the problems societies must resolve.

---

[7] Robert J. Osborn, *Soviet Social Policies* (Homewood, Il: The Dorsey Press, 1970), p. 274.

Index of Authors and Names

Adorno, T. W., 76
Alford, Robert, 14n, 123, 124
Almond, Gabriel, 9n, 17, 58, 77, 79, 91n, 92, 102, 104, 105, 158, 248n, 315, 325
Amalrik, Andrei, 82
Amery, L. S., 196n
Apter, David, 14n, 291, 357
Arian, Alan, 255
Armstrong, John, 81, 229, 233

Bagehot, Walter, 71, 188
Banfield, Edward, 79, 102–103
Barber, Bernard, 110n
Barghoorn, Frederick, 82n, 221
Beck, Carl, 144n
Beer, Samuel, 128n, 279n, 299
Bell, Daniel, 95–96, 124n, 141, 230, 372
Bendix, Reinhard, 140n
Berman, Harold, 337n
Blackwell, Robert, 143n
Bodin, Jean, 29
Brezhnev, Leonid, 194, 306
Brinton, Crane, 5
Brown, Bernard, 330
Brown, Roger, 126n
Brzezinski, Zbigniew, 97n, 98, 221, 334, 376
Burke, Edmund, 52, 174
Bulter, D. E., 72

Cardozo, Benjamin, 89n
Carnegie, Andrew, 353
Churchill, Winston, 89n, 301
Churchward, L. G., 143n
Cohn, T. S., 76n
Cristoph, James, 88, 90
Crozier, Michel, 68n, 224, 234

Dahl, Robert, 286, 313, 369
Dahrendorf, Ralf, 141n
DeGaulle, Charles, 16, 114, 188
Deutsch, Karl, 77, 100, 316

Diamant, Alfred, 219, 229n, 245
Dicks, Henry, 80
Djilas, Milovan, 61, 129n, 130
Downs, Anthony, 268, 272
Dreyfus, Alfred, 47, 329
Duverger, Maurice, 264n, 293, 294, 319n, 330
Dye, Thomas, 69n

Easton, David, 9, 86n, 99, 247
Eckstein, Harry, 70, 77, 122, 160, 198, 315n, 320n, 321
Edinger, Lewis, 77
Ehrman, Henry, 140, 219
Eldersveld, Samuel, 244
Epstein, Leon, 294n, 302

Feierabend, Ivu and Rosalind, 331
Feldmesser, Robert, 129n
Festinger, Leon, 85n
Finer, S. E., 317n
Fleron, Frederic, 220, 334n
Florinsky, Michael, 35
Frey, Frederick, 66n
Fromm, Eric, 76n, 78

Galbraith, John Kenneth, 201, 230, 351, 365
Gehlen, Michael, 143n, 144, 250, 336
Geiger, H. Kent, 143n
Gilison, Jerome, 184, 186, 200, 250, 376
Gurr, Ted, 331
Gusfield, Joseph, 17

Hancock, M. Donald, 75, 91, 101n, 283n, 320n, 342n
Hazard, John, 160
Hegel, G. W. F., 46, 84
Heisler, Martin, 93, 116, 118
Helco, Hugh, 133, 137, 356
Hempel, Karl, 3n
Henry II, 89

379

Hitler, Adolf, 20
Hobbes, Thomas, 7n
Hoffman, Stanley, 69n
Hough, Jerry F. 221n, 232, 245
Huntington, Samuel, 97n, 98, 175, 221, 249, 291, 292, 331n, 334, 373, 376

Inglehart, Ronald, 284
Inkeles, Alex, 80, 129n, 130, 136

Janos, Andrew C., 334n, 337
Jennings, Ivor, 156n

Kalleberg, Arthur, 3n
Kaplan, Abraham, 3n
Kassof, Allen, 26, 81
Kautsky, John, 26n
Keynes, John Maynard, 357, 377
Khrushchev, Nikita, 194, 308
King, Anthony, 72
Kirkheimer, Otto, 269, 270, 272, 283
Kogan, Norman, 92, 97, 287n
Kornhauser, William, 16, 113n
Krislov, Samuel, 230n, 240
Kristol, Irving, 138n

LaPalombara, Joseph, 95–96, 103, 105, 255n, 317n
Laski, Harold, 18
Lenin, V. I., 180
Lenski, Gerhard, 129n, 130, 139
Lijphart, Arend, 75, 93, 102, 118, 121, 166, 322n
Lindblom, Charles, 369
Linz, Juan, 276
Lipset, Seymour, 14n, 54, 91, 95, 96, 288
Locke, John, 7n
Lodge, Milton, 113, 334n, 337
Lowenthal, Richard, 97n, 292
Lowie, Robert, 78n
Luther, Martin, 34, 37

McClelland, David, 38
McKenzie, R. T., 73n, 299, 300

Marx, Karl, 46, 94, 271, 352
Mayer, Lawrence, 3n, 22n, 304n
Meier, Kenneth, 239
Meyer, Alfred, 97n, 245
Michels, Robert, 19, 299
Mickiewicz, Ellen, 306n
Moore, Barrington, 40n, 82n, 98, 245n
Muller, Stephen, 120

Neumann, Sigmund, 250n
Nie, Norman, 17n
Noonan, Lowell, 70n
Nordlinger, Eric, 72n

Osborn, Robert J., 377

Parkin, Frank, 110n, 129
Parsons, Talcott, 138
Peters, Guy, 362n
Pitts, Jesse, 316
Polyani, Karl, 280n, 348
Popper, Karl, 46n
Putnam, Robert, 67n, 86n, 93, 228n, 242

Rawls, John, 137
Rigby, T. H., 307
Riggs, Fred, 23n, 218
Rokeach, Milton, 105
Rose, Richard, 72n, 300
Rousseau, Jean Jacques, 53, 114
Rush, Myron, 163

Schaffner, Bertram, 78n
Schapiro, Leonard, 334n
Schumpeter, Joseph, 38n, 216, 351
Schwartz, Joel J., 336n
Seton-Watson, Hugh, 61
Skilling, H. Gordon, 333, 337
Smith, Adam, 347
Spiro, Herbert, 25, 87n, 91, 94, 101n, 105, 157, 173
Stalin, Joseph, 194
Steifbold, Rodney, 93, 119, 272
Stout, Hiram, 126

Index of Authors and Names

Tawney, R. H., 38
Taylor, Frederick, 217
Toynbee, Arnold, 48
Truman, David, 247, 320n
Tucker, Robert, 26n

Verba, Sidney, 13n, 77, 79, 92, 99, 100n, 104, 105, 158, 285
Veblen, Thorstein, 351

Von Herberstein, Sigmund, 43n
Von Treitschke, Heinrich, 46

Wahl, Nicholas, 69n
Wallerstein, Immanuel, 346n, 349
Weber, Max, 38, 222, 291
Wilson, Frank, 94
Wilson, Harold, 73

Zariski, Raphael, 43n, 103, 277
Zeigler, Harmon, 69n

Subject Index

Achievement motivation, 38, 138
Administration theory, classical, 217, 218, 221
Aggregation of interests, 318, 328, 329
Aggregative party systems, 261–262, 319
Alienation, 113
Aristocracy (nobility):
 financial independence, 41–42, 50
 in House of Lords, Britain, 177–178
 Russian, 60
Australia:
 bureaucracy, 230
 continuity with past, 61
 Country Party, 251
 federalism, 22, 176
 Labour Party, 133, 251, 273
 Liberal Party, 251, 281
 National Health Service, 359
 religious cleavages, 133
 Senate, 176, 177
 social structure, 132
 trade unions, 133
Austria:
 bureaucracy and bureaucrats, 230, 231, 244
 interest groups, 322
 party system, pre-war, 56, 290
 People's Party, 252, 272, 277
 Segmented subcultures or lager, 119, 283, 313
 Socialist Party, 252
Authoritarian personality, 76

Belgium:
 cabinets or governments, 196, 198
 Christian Social Party, 254, 270, 283
 continuity and stability, 37, 56–57, 255, 266
 F.D.F., 255, 266
 Flemish and Walloons, 39, 57, 117, 120, 231
 Liberals, 92
 monarchy, 190
 Party of Liberty and Progress, 254, 281
 segmented society, 57, 111, 116, 117, 120, 125, 231
 Senate, 181
 social insurance, 362
 trade unions, 327
 Volksunie, 255, 266
Borders, insular or permeable, 11
Bourgeoise, 347
Bureaucracy, see Civil service

Cabinets, see Governments
Cabinet stability, 251, 255
Canada:
 cabinet stability, 169
 French Canadians, 238
 health insurance, 360
 history, 61
 Liberal Party, 145–146, 253, 279, 284
 New Democratic Party, 253, 265, 286
 Parti Ralliement des Creditiste, 145, 265
 Progressive Conservative, 253, 279
 regionalism, 131
 Senate, 61
 Social Credit Party, 253, 265
Catholics or Catholicism, 32–34, 53, 91–93, 110, 112, 132, 313, 320, 327
Civil law, 89
Civil service:
 accountability of, 217
 adaptability of, 237
 classical bureaucrats, 242–243
 political role of, 219, 237, 340
Class, socio-economic and class conflict, 98, 110–111, 123ff, 130, 132
Cleavages, cross cutting versus segmental, 13–14
Cognitive dissonance, 85
Commercial revolution, 346–347
Committees, legislative, 182–183
Common law, 88–90
Commonwealth British, 61
Conceptualization, 3, 4
Confidence question, 8, 166, 167, 169–172, 174, 202

Conservatism, 52-43
Consociational democracy, 93, 118, 145
Conspicuous consumption, 351
Contextual factors, 2, 10, 27-28, 65
Co-optation, 334, 335, 345

Darwinism, social, 142, 353
Democracy:
   accountability and, 153, 343
   bargaining and, 340-341
   defined, 19
   responsiveness, 247
   stable, 288
Denmark:
   Conservative Party, 279
   Folkting, 275
   health insurance, 360
   party system, 266
   Socialist People's Party, 272
   unicameral legislature, 182
Diffuse support, 59
Dissolution, power of, 170
Dreyfus Affair, 47, 329
Duma (Russian), 60

Education:
   British system, 71, 139, 230
   French system, 139, 227, 229
   Soviet system, 143
   United States system, 139
Egalitarianism:
   alienation and, 99
   attitudes toward authority and, 68
   bureaucracy and, 68, 228
   education and, 139-140, 227
   France, 69-70, 227
   mass society, 70
Elites, 19
Entrepreneur, 38, 347, 349

Fabian socialism, 297
Fascism, 53. *See also* Germany
Federalism, 22, 119, 124, 146, 176, 303-304, 346

Fragmented party system, 262, 356-357
France:
   alienation in, 101
   attitudes toward authority, 70, 235
   bureaucracy, 219, 224, 227, 229
   class conflict, 26
   constitutions, 157
   educational system, 139, 227, 229
   Fifth Republic, 157, 189-190, 288, 329-330
   Fourth Republic, 56, 70, 192, 193, 219
   general planning commission, 323, 363
   health service, 359
   individualism and organizational life, 316-317
   nation building, 42
   party system 273, 278, 279, 281, 286-287
   Third Republic, 55-56, 70, 192, 219
   trade unions, 295, 296, 327
   see also Dreyfus Affair
Frankurt Assembly of 1848, 43
Functional specificity:
   bureaucracy, 223, 230
   industrial society, 109, 150, 370
   inequality, 137

Germany:
   attitudes toward authority, 76-79
   Busic law, 159
   Bundestag, 188
   Bundesrat, 176
   bureaucracy and bureaucrats, 228, 243
   C.D.U./C.S.U., 135, 252, 254, 270, 276
   codetermination, 235
   confidence question, constructive vote of, 166
   economic system, 367
   Free Democrats, 252, 281
   health insuranc, 360
   ideologism, 94
   legitimacy, 58-59
   militarism, 45-46

Subject Index

National Democratic Party, 36, 158, 252, 286
national pride, 100
Nazis, 8, 20, 95, 134, 269
President of Republic, 193
S.P.D., 94
trade unions, 295
Weimar Republic, 58, 80, 134, 160, 166, 256, 289, 290
Governments (cabinets), 8, 194–197
Great Britain:
   attitude toward authority, 71–74
   cabinets, 167, 169, 194–195, 196, 198
   class conflicts, 125–128
   common law, 88–90, 155, 198
   Conservative (Tory) Party, 73, 74, 171, 257, 258, 278, 294, 295, 298
   constitution, 154ff
   crown power, 58, 89, 164
   education system, 71–73, 127–128, 139, 230
   egalitarianism and welfare, 138–139
   elites, 93
   enclosure movement, 40–41
   evolutionary development, 48–50
   House of Commons, 171, 173, 178, 179, 186–187
   House of Lords, 151, 178
   Labour Party, 73, 171, 257, 258, 269, 279, 294, 299–300, 318–319
   Liberal Party, 74, 265
   monarchy, 154–155, 197
   M.P. and interests, 317
   national consolidation, 43, 44, 45
   National Health Service, 361
   Nationalist (Scottish, Welsh, Irish) Parties, 252, 265
   Neddy, 323
   planning, economic, 364
   pragmatism, 88, 97, 198
   prime minister, 50, 155
   Privy Council, 50, 74, 179, 197–198
   question hour, 168
   regionalism, 131
   Standing Committees, 183
   trade Unions, 327. *See also* Labour movement
   see also Parliament
Groups, 113–114
Guyana (British Guiana), 155

Hegemonic system, 262
Hierarchy, 223, 233
Huguenots, 36

Industrial revolution, 352–354
Istitution, 108, 373–374
Integration, national, 11
Interests, conflict of, 7, 339
Ireland, Northern, 112, 118, 122
Italy:
   alienation, 100, 158, 244
   amoral familism, 103, 244, 317
   attitude toward authority, 79, 83
   bureaucracy and bureaucrats, 230, 241, 243
   cabinets, 195, 196
   catholicism and tolerance, 92
   Catholic Action, 320, 322
   Christian Democratic Party, 135, 254, 277, 294, 320
   Communist Party, 97, 286, 287
   Confindustria, 318, 321, 327
   constitutions, 158
   elites, 93
   extremism, 289
   Italian Social Movement, 286
   Monarchist Party, 286
   national unification, 42
   organizational life, 317
   partisanship, intensity of 104–105
   planning, economic, 364
   pluralism, degree of, 116–117
   President of Republic, 193
   Republican Party, 282
   Senate, 181
   Socialist Parties, 274
   Standing Committees, 183

Jews, 38, 47, 54

Keynesian economics, 18, 280

Labour movement:
  collective bargaining, 353
  France, 295, 296, 319
  Germany, 295
  Great Britain, 71, 294, 295, 297, 298, 319
  Netherlands, 121
  Sweden, 319
  trade union confederations, 326–327
Lager, see Austria
Laissez faire, 8, 18, 280, 349, 351, 355, 357
Latent interests, 330
Liberalism, 96, 136, 280
Luxemborg, 37

Manoralism, 39–40
Marxism-Leninism, 82, 86, 87, 96, 116, 137, 271, 272, 292, 374
Mass party, 293
Mercantilism, 280
Merit system, 223, 225, 227, 231–232
Militarism, 45–47
Mobilization, 248
Monarchies, 101–102

Nazi, see Germany
Netherlands:
  Anit-Revolutionary Party, 260, 277
  attitudes toward authority, 75
  bureaucracy and bureaucrats, 231, 244
  Catholicism, 39, 92, 94
  Catholic People's Party, 256, 260, 277, 283
  confidence questions, 166
  Democrats '66, 256, 260, 272, 277
  Democratic Socialists, 272
  Economic and Social Council, 324
  elections, 192
  First chamber, 181
  health insurance, 359
  interest groups, 320–322
  monarchy, 190, 192
  segmented society, 111, 121, 313
  Spanish Netherlands, 37, 56
  States General, 166
  support for system, 101
  Tweed Kamer, 166, 181
New Zealand, 61
Nobility, see Aristocracy
Norway;
  Agrarian (centre) Party, 258, 260, 283
  attitude toward authority, 70
  cabinets or government, 195–196
  Christian People's Party, 258, 260
  Conservative Party, 258, 260, 279
  government ownership, 367
  interest groups, 320
  Labor Foundation, 324
  Labor Party, 253, 258, 259, 260
  Liberal Party, 258, 260, 281
  monarch, 190
  segmented society, 122
  Socialists People's Party, 258–259
  Storting, 182, 260

Oligarchy, iron law of, 299
Open society, 11

Papacy, 32, 33, 34
Parliament, English;
  decline of, 340
  educational background, 72
  functions of, 173
  origins, 49–50, 172–173
  Standing Committees, 183
  see also Great Britain: House of Commons; House of Lords
Partisanship, intensity of, 104–105, 112, 119
Patriarchate, Eastern Church, 35
Peasants, 40–41, 52
Pluralism, 8, 54, 115, 313–316

Subject Index

Politburo, 10
Polycentrism, 85
Populism, 54
Post-Industrial Society, 236, 290, 318, 372–373
Public opinion, mobilization of, 248, 312

Question hours, 168–169

Race and racism, 131
Reformation, Protestant, 38
Regionalism, 130–132, 134, 135
Responsive capacity, 9
Revolution:
    French, 4–5, 43
    Glorious or Bloodless of 1688, 49
    Russian, 5, 60
Rights, civil or individual, 159
Role, defined, 6

Scientific inquiry, 96
Scotland, 127, 131
segmented society, 111, 115–123. *See also* individual country listings
Social contract, 164
Socialism, 358, 367, 368–369
Socialization, 146
Social mobility, 14, 72, 129, 136FF., 141–143
Sovereignty, 29–32
Soviet Union:
    attitudes toward authority, 80–82
    bureaucracy, 220, 232, 245
    class conflicts in, 129ff
    Communist Party, 161, 164, 180, 194, 250, 305–306
    constitution, 159–160
    elections in, 21
    executive structures, 193, 198
    Federalism, 22, 159, 176
    ideologism, 97, 290–292
    legislative committees, 183
    New Economic Policy, 357
    organizational life, 317, 313–338
    planning and Gosplan, 357, 363
    regionalism and ethnicity, 135
    Soviets, 180
    succession, 163
Specialization and division of labor, *see* Functional specificity
Stalinism, 269
Structure, 6, 108
Suffrage, adult male, 354
Survey research, 66
Sweden:
    attitudes toward authority, 75–76
    authoritarian monarchy, 43
    bureaucracy, 236
    Center Party, 259
    constitution, 154, 156, 159
    economic prosperity, 362
    egalitarianism and welfare, 138
    government ownership, 367
    Harpsund Democracy 319, 324, 329
    health care system, 360
    interest groups, 320
    Liberal Party, 259, 281
    Moderate Party, 259, 281
    national consolidation, 42
    Planning Board and Research Council, 319, 324
    pragmatism and secularism, 91
    Riksdag, 51, 154, 156, 183, 260
    Riksraad, 51
    Social Democratic Party, 253–254, 259
    support for system, 101
Switzerland, 116, 203, 281

Technocrats, 2, 96, 325
Terror, in totalitarian systems, 26
Totalitarianism, 16, 25
Trade unions, see Labour movement

United Kingdom, 89
United States;
    Business Council, 324

Congress, 175, 182, 183
electoral college, 156
health care, 359, 361
impeachment of presidents, 167, 171
national power, 165
parties, 269, 279, 293, 302
presidents of, 171, 172, 189

regionalism, 132
Supreme Court, 165

Violence, 55, 61, 331

Wales, 127, 131
Welfare state, defined, 358